THE OFFICIAL® PRICE GUIDE TO

STAR WARS

Memorabilia

Jeremy Beckett

House of Collectibles
New York   Toronto   London   Sydney   Auckland

CONTENTS

PREFACE

When I was five and a half years old I picked up my first piece of *Star Wars* history—a first edition novelization of George Lucas's *Star Wars*. I, like 99.9% of North America, had no idea that this book and thousands of other everyday items were going to be transformed by some magical process akin to the Midas touch. And just as I was unaware of the collectible nature of this science-fiction hit, nor was I aware that just over twenty-five years later I would be writing a collectibles guide on the very same movie.

When the offer came to write a *Star Wars* collecting guide I was filled with magnificent ideas, high expectations, and delusions of grandeur, and never once doubted that I could pull this off. And then the realization hit me—it was a Herculean undertaking for one person. Luckily for me *Star Wars* has not only led me to have a room full of colorful plastic toys, but it has also provided me with a multitude of highly educated, knowledgeable, and articulate friends and colleagues who stepped forward to help. Like little Dutch boys, they thrust forward their fingers and committed themselves to the task.

Initially this book was going to be the be-all and end-all of collecting books, but we soon realized that there were other resources more capable of providing this material. While this book is a price guide, its true purpose is to serve as a fully armed and operational walk-through to help the members of the *Star Wars* Generation recapture the collection they lost in their youth, and the latest *Star Wars* fans who have just bought their first action figure enter the hobby of *Star Wars* collecting.

AUTHORS' BIOGRAPHIES

Jeremy Beckett: A resident of the United Kingdom, Jeremy has been collecting *Star Wars* items since he first picked up George Lucas's original novelization of *A New Hope* back in 1976, and since then he has amassed a collection numbering in the thousands. Jeremy joined Rebelscum.com in 2001, and now manages their dedicated European *Star Wars* collecting sister site, as well as running his own retro computer *Star Wars* gaming Web site, The Emulator Strikes Back. When he has the opportunity he likes to spend as much time visiting *Star Wars* filming sites around the world, and has written a travel guide to the locations in Tunisia. He wrote the Introduction, Condition and Grading, Buying, Restoration, Prototypes, Accessories, and the Valuation and Selling chapters.

Dave Myatt: When he woke up on his birthday to discover a Darth Vader action figure waiting for him, there was no way Dave could have known this would start a lifelong fascination. That was the spring of 1978, and to this day, the original Kenner line serves as a very large point of interest for him. Having become a so-called public figure in 1996 with the creation of Jawa Force, the Internet's first comic book, Dave was able to springboard on to projects that he was passionate about, including being a staff writer for Rebelscum.com since late 2000. He has spent the last five years researching sculpt, mould, and factory variations in the vintage Kenner line, and is preparing a documentary about *Star Wars* for release in spring 2005. Dave authored the Vintage Toys chapter.

Anne Neumann: Anne has been an enthusiastic *Star Wars* fan since 1977. Since starting her collection in 1999, after renewed interest with Episode I, she has accumulated more than 6,000 items, including Topps trading cards. Being a database designer and developer, Anne decided it was more fun—and economical—to catalog data about *Star Wars* collectibles instead of acquiring them. Since joining Rebelscum.com in 2003 Anne has managed the Jedi Archives, a database of more than 37,000 collectibles worldwide. All her spare time is dedicated to adding and updating information in order to create the most comprehensive searchable database ever available. Anne wrote the Trading Cards chapter.

Jay Shephard: Like many boys of his era, having been raised on the original *Star Wars* films, Jay has long collected Kenner toys. Jay also had a growing comic book collection that includes the *Star Wars* comics. Since the reintroduction of *Star Wars* to popular culture in the early 1990s, nearly every toy, book, or comic that has to do with *Star Wars* mysteriously finds it way into his home. Jay lives outside Baltimore, Maryland, with his wife, their two sons, and his large *Star Wars* collection. When he's not working as a Web and database programmer, he is an administrator on the Jedi Journals comic section at Rebelscum.com and hosts local meetings of the DC Metro area *Star Wars* Collecting Club. Jay wrote the Comics chapter.

Shane Turgeon: Born in 1977—the year that started it all—Shane has literally been a *Star Wars* fan all his life. After growing up with the original line of toys, he began collecting in 1992 when chance turned his love for his childhood toys into a lifelong hobby. Since then, he has amassed a diverse collection of vintage toys, including prototypes, bootlegs, and foreign items, as well as packaged and loose items. Shane has been a contributing staff member at Rebelscum since 2002, and runs his own Tattoos and Toys Web site. He currently resides in Edmonton, Canada. Shane's contributions to this book include Preservation, Reproduction and Fake Items, Prototypes, and Bootlegs and Knock-Offs.

Joseph Yglesias: Joseph has been a *Star Wars* fan since he first saw *A New Hope* in the theater at the age of seven, in 1977. He began collecting at the age of nineteen. About 5 years after starting his collection he acquired some of his first bootleg figures at a toy show. They sparked an interest in acquiring and learning about these misfit toys and why they were made. This started his collection on the path to owning one of the most comprehensive assortments of unlicensed *Star Wars* memorabilia in the world. Outside of the collecting hobby, he owns and operates a pair of body piercing studios (Evolution Studios LLC) in Rhode Island. Joe co-wrote the Bootlegs and Knock-Offs chapters.

ACKNOWLEDGMENTS

First and foremost, I would like to thank Dave Myatt, Shane Turgeon, Anne Neumann, and Jay Shephard for being such excellent little Dutch boys. Philip Wise from Rebelscum (www.rebelscum.com) and TheForce.net (www.theforce.net) gets a huge pat on the back for helping me get the commission on this book. Many thanks also go the two ladies who made this possible: my wife, Rachel, who had many late nights in order that the book made the deadline, and Lindsey Glass at Random House for having the patience to deal with a first-time author.

Unless otherwise indicated, all images are from the collections of the contributors.

The author and the contributors would like to thank the following, without whose help this book would not have been possible:

Rob Amantea

Scott Bradley *(www.ncf.ca/~cn333/starwars.htm)*

Leslie Bush

Todd Chamberlain *(www.toychamber.com)*

Mike Chomyn *(www.womprat.com)*

Curtis Comeau *(www.eternalimages.ca)*

Dan Curto *(www.rebelscum.com)*

Jayna Derby *(www.cloudcity.com)*

Tom Derby *(www.cloudcity.com)*

Luis and Josefina Galvez

Chris Georgoulias *(www.toysrgus.com* & *www.12back.com)*

Guerra de Las Galaxias *(www.guerradelasgalaxias.com.mx)*

Tyler Ham *(www.hamstudios.com/starwars)*

Jeremy Hamley *(www.toygrader.com)*

Chris Holoka *(www.rebelscum.com)*

Peter Hubner

Mark Hurray *(www.rebelscum.com)*

Lois Javi *(www.loresdelsith.net)*

Maureen Kuppe *(www.rebelscum.com)*

Josh Ling

Gus Lopez *(www.toysrgus.com)*

Adam Lovera

Dustin Roberts *(www.rebelscum.com* & *www.r2d2central.com)*

Tim Roberts *(www.realstands.com)*

Ron Salvatore *(www.toysrgus.com)*

Joanie Stevenson

Vic Wertz

Andrew White *(www.thehairyfairy.dk)*

Part One
Star Wars: The History and the Hobby

1 AN INTRODUCTION TO *STAR WARS* COLLECTING

It's been over twenty-five years since the first *Star Wars* film was released, and in the intervening decades the phenomenon has grown to become the single largest grossing film franchise in history. During the late 1970s and early 1980s, *Star Wars* was as big a part of contemporary culture as the Cold War, which played a key role in the lives of many Generation Xers. Boys in particular were susceptible to the marketing spin played out in television ads and in toy stores, video arcades, restaurants, and department stores, though girls weren't left out of the picture with dolls, clothing, and bedding made especially for them. Even now, the very same boys and girls (twenty years older and tens of thousands of dollars richer) are still obsessed with the *Star Wars* universe.

Many of the Generation Xers who have achieved their goals of a house, a car, and a family are now looking back at their childhoods in the 1970s and 1980s. They are reminiscing about the friends they had, the schools they went to, the toys they played with, the clothes they wore, and the television shows they watched. They have a strong sense of nostalgia toward this period, and *Star Wars* plays an important part.

The *Star Wars* phenomenon doesn't stop there. With the revival of the *Star* Wars license in 1995, the return of the original trilogy to the big screen in 1997, and the beginning of the prequel trilogy movies in 1999, many new fans are emerging.

Star Wars fandom is now part of mainstream culture, with local collecting clubs springing up all over the place, most conference centers and meeting halls playing host to a collecting convention at least once a year, and nearly every fan who has access to the Internet bookmarking half a dozen *Star Wars* Web pages in his or her browser.

Why Collect *Star Wars* Merchandise?

What is it about *Star Wars* that makes it not only the largest box-office hit of all time, but also the single most successful merchandising boom in Hollywood's history? Certainly the initial

The author opening his first Star Wars *figures.*

success of merchandising in the 1970s and 1980s came from the overwhelming popularity of the movies at that time, but why is there such demand for goods from the vintage era as well as today's new products?

Perhaps it is as Philip Wise, the webmaster at Rebelscum.com, once said about *Star Wars,* "There has never been a movie that has had such a profound effect on so many people as this movie has. It is truly rare to find somebody, almost regardless of age, that isn't aware of it or doesn't care about it. And those that don't care don't matter to me anyhow."

One school of thought is that most collectors suffer from the "Peter Pan Syndrome": as children, we were filled with excitement and a yearning for adventure after we saw the movies, and each subsequent time we watched them that sense of wonder grew. Mix in the pleasure many of us felt when we played with our *Star Wars* toys, reenacting the escapes, battles, and cliff-hangers that we enjoyed so much, many people will find that they have a strong cup of nostalgia just waiting to be sipped. Now, twenty years later, most of us have grown up, moved on—bought a car, got married, settled into a new home, and saved some money—and are looking to spend our extra money on additional pleasures. For many, the answer is to resurrect their youth and buy the toys they had to throw out, sell, or give away when their parents decided they were too old to play with action figures. For others, who were caught up in the excitement of the *Star Wars* prequel trilogy, it is a sense of getting involved in a phenomenon that started decades ago and has encompassed hundreds of millions of people around the world.

There are many answers to this question. The reality is that it doesn't matter what drives you to collect—just as long as you enjoy it.

The History of *Star Wars* Collectibles

IN THE BEGINNING (1975–1977)

From the comics to novels and then onto the big screen, toys, clothing, television, bedding, and computer and video games, *Star Wars* has spanned the decades and spread across the face of popular culture more rapidly than any other phenomenon before or after.

The story of George Lucas's *Star Wars* is well chronicled, but the tale behind *Star Wars* collectibles is not so well known, and few people are aware of how far back the hobby spans.

It all began in the summer of 1975, when the University of Southern California (USC) film school graduate Charles Lippincott bumped into Gary Kurtz, then the producer for a fledgling science-fictional fantasy film. Lippincott already had considerable experience and a well-deserved reputation as an inventive movie publicist at MGM when he met with Kurtz, who told him about *The Star Wars* (as it was then called). Both Lucas and Lippincott had attended classes together at USC and Lucas had previously turned to Lippincott to pitch *THX 1138*, Lucas's first movie, to Warner Brothers, so they knew each other well. Within a few months, Lippincott had left his job at MGM and joined the Star Wars Corporation as vice president of advertising, publicity, promotion, and merchandising to promote *The Star Wars* in U.S. colleges and many counterculture magazines.

A chance meeting with Lucas later that year illustrated to Lippincott that the writer/director was already well on his way to becoming the *Star Wars* mogul we know him as today. In a highly animated discussion, Lucas outlined his ambitions to have a range of *Star Wars* toys, including several shots in the dark—such as Wookiee coffee cups, lightsaber blades, and windup robots—that would later make it to the mass market and be sold in several *Star Wars* stores (owned by Lucas) across the country.

At the same time, successful movie spin-offs, particularly in the science-fiction genre, were a thing of the past. The studios felt that merchandising was only useful in promoting a picture and would never become a major money maker. Many studios had had their fingers burned and most studio executives preferred the concept of tying in to a television series. For Lucas, this was a blessing in disguise, because one of his greatest fears was that if he would not have control over merchandising and if Twentieth Century Fox would allow manufacturers to overproduce licensed goods, the *Star Wars* name would be cheapened.

Lucas believed that control of his vision was more important than the money he could make. So to preserve certain rights, Lucas stuck to the terms of a gentleman's agreement that he and Alan Ladd Jr. (who was president of Fox at the time) had stamped out in 1973, despite his success with *American Graffiti*, which potentially gave Lucas more bargaining power. In return for 60 percent of net profits, Fox agreed to give Lucas control of merchandising, sequels, and the soundtrack rights. In effect, Lucas traded profits for control of the project.

To Fox, the loss of the "garbage" clauses was no sacrifice, and many staff members at the studio scoffed at Lucas's ambition of seeing comics, toys, and clothing emblazoned with *The Star Wars*. As history now tells us, Fox's short-term gain was a long-term loss.

Marvel Star Wars: *number one*

Now that the Star Wars Corporation had full studio backing, the movie returned to the control of Lucasfilm and the pace at the Egg Factory offices in Studio City, California, jumped up a notch or two. Lippincott's first mission was to sell the comic and novel rights before the movie's release to promote the movie in a cost-effective manner. Tom Pollock, the lawyer for Lucasfilm, wanted to tout the movie rights in the normal industry fashion—to the highest bidder—but Lippincott opposed the idea, saying that they should instead target key audiences through publishers who had proven track records in the science-fiction market.

Lippincott's first coup was landing an agreement with Marvel to produce the comic book adaptation. After an initial rejection from comic book legend Stan Lee, the founder of Marvel, Lippincott fought to get the *Star Wars* merchandising ball rolling and eventually won an agreement with Marvel that would see *Star Wars* produced by the world's leading comic book publisher. The final agreement was for a six-issue serialization to be released coinciding with the movie (three issues before and three after) and no royalties to be paid until after sales reached 100,000 copies, though Lee unwisely allowed Lucasfilm to renegotiate any further rights after the run was complete. By 1986, when Marvel stopped publishing *Star Wars* comic books, it had printed over 100 issues, making it one of their most successful titles ever.

During the summer of 1976, Lippincott turned to the underground market—the comic book and fan conventions that are now the movie industry's standard launch point to kick-start the promotion of a new film. At the San Diego Comic Convention, Lippincott talked to attendees and retailers about the toy and model market, all the while wearing his promotional cap with an early *Star Wars* logo on it. To raise awareness, Lucasfilm produced a number of convention exclusives, including badges, t-shirts, and posters (originally sold at $1 but now worth nearly $1,000), but there was little interest and most remained left behind at the convention. Shortly before the release of *Star Wars*, Lippincott also targeted college campuses and student radio shows with interviews and posters—a tactic that proved successful for the movie's opening-day figures.

First Del Rey novelization

The third step in promoting *Star Wars* to the public was the book rights (including the novelization and the making of a sequel title and the script), which Pollock sold, under strict instructions from Lucas and Lippincott, to Ballantine Books. The honor of adapting Lucas's tale into a novel was given to Alan Dean Foster, who also penned the first spin-off title (an area of *Star Wars* collecting that would later become known as the Expanded Universe)—*Splinter of the Mind's Eye*. Lippincott knew the advantage of having the novelization out in advance of the movie and pressed for an early release. Despite skepticism from Judy-Lynn Del Rey, the commissioning editor for Ballantine Books, 125,000 copies were sent out to bookstores across the country in December 1976, making it the first *Star Wars* mass-market collectible. By February 1977, they had all sold out even though Ballantine Books had not actively promoted the title in bookstores with displays or author signings, and despite huge sales figures Ballantine refused to reprint the novel until after *Star Wars* proved a success.

December 1976 saw the release of the first theatrical trailer and poster into U.S. movie theaters, and marked the next phase for Lucasfilm's merchandising plan. Lippincott and Marc Pevers, Fox's contracts attorney, began with a mailing sent to several hundred companies that they thought might be interested in a stake. Predictably, the response was limited and Lippincott's belief that he needed to find the right company became the need to find any company. Those companies that did respond only wanted to make generic products and add a *Star Wars* logo just to cash in, so Lippincott and Pevers took their portfolio to the February 1977 New York Toy Fair (an event that *Star Wars* is still part of today). Armed with a collection of art (a few stills from the set and a slide show) by production artist Ralph McQuarrie, they attempted to wow the big manufacturers.

The majors—Mattel, Fisher Price, Ideal, and Aurora—all believed that television was where successful spin-off merchandising lay and looked to *Battlestar Galactica*, *Six Million Dollar Man*, *Charlie's Angels*, *M*A*S*H*, and *Planet of the Apes* for commercial inspiration. Mattel, which was the biggest player on the block at the time, had experience with Fox and tie-in merchandise when it entered into a merchandising agreement on the 1967 *Doctor Doolittle*. The movie fell flat on its face and Mattel was left with $200 million worth of unsold merchandise. The failure of the movie and the associated merchandising lines was a turning point in Hollywood and the U.S. toy industry. Many people felt that *Doctor Doolittle* had killed off movie tie-ins for good. Knowing they had their work cut out for them, Lippincott and Pevers doggedly knocked on doors until Kenner Products, a small division of the General Mills Food Group, showed interest.

Kenner Products, which had been in the toy industry for nearly thirty years and had a solid track record in designing, producing, and marketing quality toys from scratch, was just what Lucasfilm was looking for and negotiations began immediately. Bernard Loomis, the head of Kenner Products, had already declared he was looking for the next hot toy and was willing to take a chance on Lucas's venture.

Loomis had already heard of *Star Wars* when Lippincott made his presentation and had already begun his own research into the movie. While he didn't expect to see *Star Wars* lasting long at movie theaters, he believed that it would make a successful transfer to television, so he negotiated for a higher royalty rate if *Star Wars* made it to the small screen and for worldwide rights to all toy-related merchandise. This was a tactic that worked well for both Kenner Products and Lucasfilm because while Kenner Products reaped the rewards of global dominance in the *Star Wars* market, it would also protect Lucasfilm from inferior goods being produced by manufacturers who just wanted to cash in on what was going to be a worldwide phenomenon.

As more information about *Star Wars* reached Kenner Products, the level of excitement in the design offices reached fever pitch. Even though Kenner Products' license was limited to the number of different products it could market, all kinds of ideas were being put forward. Initially, the main part of the line was going to be 12-inch dolls because Kenner Products already had experience and success with its *Six Million Dollar Man* line—but the realization that a five-foot-wide *Millennium Falcon* would be too large to play with and too costly to make (never mind purchase) crept up on the design team. Eventually, Loomis suggested $3^{3}/_{4}$ inches as the standard action figure size and from there the line was born. The smaller size meant less plastic was needed, which was a strong concern in the 1970s because of inflated oil prices, and costs were further reduced by abandoning moveable joints. Kenner Products designers frantically began producing art work, plans, and mock-ups and before long Lucasfilm (which had the final say on every product) began green-lighting the toy line.

While he was making considerable headway in promoting the film to the public and merchandising manufacturers, Lippincott still struggled to bring the executives at Twentieth Century Fox to terms with the picture. At one presentation to the studio, the reception *Star Wars* received was one of unconcealed boredom. The consensus was that *Star Wars* was lacking in star quality and science fiction could not win the war against America's current favorite at the box office: the disaster movie. In turn, theater owners were skeptical about committing their movie halls to showing a dud when Fox was heavily promoting several other major movies for 1977, including *The Towering Inferno* starring Steve McQueen.

In an attempt to prevent the picture from becoming a B movie, Fox brought the release date forward so that it wouldn't have to compete with the summer's blockbusters and then went so far as to coerce cinema owners to show *Star Wars* by threatening to hold back on its bigger pictures. Even then the release was limited and Fox only received 10 percent of the expected advances. *Star Wars* was set to open on May 25, 1977, at only thirty-three theaters across the United States.

To make matters worse, the movie's advertising campaign was cut back to the bone—there would be no billboards, television spots, posters, newspaper adverts, or magazine articles to help hype the show up. The little work that Lippincott had done by targeting the grassroots science-fiction fan base would have to go a long way to make the film a success.

Lucasfilm and Fox both agreed that *Star Wars* needed to open with a big bang, but there weren't any theaters on Hollywood Boulevard, the heart of Los Angeles's movie district, so the Avco General Cinema near the University of California, Los Angeles, medical campus in West Hollywood was booked. At the last minute, Mann's Chinese Theater had a free slot and agreed to show it for one month.

May 25, 1977, dawned on an unsuspecting movie industry, and no one was in for a bigger shock than Lucas, who spent the day opposite Mann's Chinese Theater unaware that all the huge crowds outside were lining up to see his movie. Fox was taken totally unaware and wasn't prepared for the demand for more prints of the movie. It had to increase production of 35 mm and 70 mm prints to keep up with the 50 to 100 theaters that were ordering it every week. By its peak in August, over 1,000 theaters in the United States and Canada were showing *Star Wars*.

THE GOLD RUSH (1977–1986)

By the end of the summer, *Star Wars* was an unequivocal hit and Fox was beginning to realize how much it had lost out when it relinquished control of the merchandising rights. Soon, Darth Vader was becoming a household name and the stars of the movie were being asked to do guest appearances on dozens of television shows. Likewise, Lucasfilm was being inundated with licensing requests from the sublime to the ridiculous, and all through this roller coaster Lucasfilm maintained its stance on quality over quantity and could now take a stronger position when negotiating licensing contracts.

When Lippincott met with Marvel's Stan Lee to renegotiate their comic deal, he learned that the company's presses were running at full capacity and had gone into three reprints for the first six issues of the *Star Wars* comic. Now, with sales far beyond the 100,000 issue mark, Marvel was faced with paying its overdue royalty fees and under the terms of the original agreement Lippincott was able to renegotiate a far better deal for Lucasfilm.

It wasn't only Marvel that profited from Lucas's good fortunes. Those investors who had decided to take a chance were all seeing returns far beyond what they expected, often recouping their original licensing fee in a few weeks after the release of the movie and going on to become multimillionaires before the long ride was over. As the paperback adaptation of the movie became a best seller, Del Rey was overcome with orders for the novelizations and several other tie-in books including *Star Wars* blueprints.

Kenner's Early Bird box front

With the explosion of the largest merchandising boom in Hollywood's history, Twentieth Century Fox wanted to tap into the market. In one instance, Lucas used his right to veto products he deemed inappropriate when he blocked a deal set up by Fox to license a range of jewelry.

This attitude strained relationships between Lucasfilm and Fox.

Back in Cincinnati, Kenner Products' development time on its action figure line stretched out past the release date for *Star Wars* and was only able to get out a few puzzles, a board game, and some paint-by-numbers sets. To break into the Canadian market, Kenner Products affiliated itself with Irwin Toys, a Canadian company that had long achieved commercial success in the domestic toy markets. Together, they formed Kenner Products (Canada) Ltd.

Meanwhile, consumers and retailers were clamoring for more toys, but Kenner Products wouldn't be able to get its action figure line out before Christmas, so Loomis took the unprecedented step of offering a gift certificate that could be redeemed for the first four figures. The gamble paid off, to an extent. When the toys came out in the spring of 1978, the line was an instant hit and Kenner Products entered the record books by selling over 42 million separate *Star Wars* items to the U.S. market in 1978 alone. Over half of this number was made up of the first twelve action figures released and by the time the line drew to a close the figure was over 250 million worldwide, including sales through Kenner Products (Canada) Ltd. and Lili-Ledy S.A. in Mexico.

Though Kenner Products undoubtedly made the largest impact on *Star Wars* merchandising, the market wasn't entirely toy-based. There were also over 200 licensees selling thousands of different products between 1976 and 1985 when the furor eventually died down.

Across the continent, licenses were being snapped up to produce every product imaginable to fill the public's need to identify themselves as fans by eating, sleeping, and wearing *Star Wars* (a practice that is still obvious today).

From the outset, food producers were keen to get in on the action, but Lucasfilm kept strict control to make sure that any *Star Wars* food-related products weren't junk food. Early entries into the bonanza included Topps, Burger Chef, Wonder Bread, Hershey, Kellogg, Libby, and Coca-Cola.

Since General Mills owned Kenner Products, it gained the license for *Star Wars*–related cereal premiums and throughout 1978 produced a range of boxes, posters, mobiles, and collector's cards to accompany the movie. Curiously, General Mills would only produce *Return of the Jedi* cereals in Canada and eventually lost its license when it sold off Kenner in 1984. Later, Lucas wouldn't allow the *Star Wars* brand on any artificially sweetened cereals as an attempt by to get a more nutritious breakfast for America's youth. Eventually, he relented and permitted Kellogg to market the infamous C-3PO cereal.

Topps Chewing Gum Inc., a bubble gum company that had realized it could sell even more gum by inserting trading cards, jumped on the band wagon and picked up a domestic and worldwide license to distribute trading cards (with or without gum) through its affiliates in Mexico (Labratories y Agencies Unidas S.A.) and Canada (O-Pee-Chee Ltd.).

It was perhaps Coca-Cola that had the most widespread impact in the food market. With its huge domestic and international presence, it was able to use its own marketing clout to get a multitude of tie-in products into a huge number of convenience stores and restaurant chains. These products included a range of plastic cups and glasses, collector's cards, a Frisbee, and a limited edition sonic-controlled toy that looked like a cross between R2-D2 and a can of Coke. One ingenious step was to provide outlets with different promotional items: while Burger King served Coke in glasses, the now extinct fast-food chain Koolee had a range of plastic cups, and 7-11 sold frozen Coke in large beakers. The marriage between Coca-Cola and Lucasfilm was one of great success and lasted more than half a decade.

One of the first companies to invest in a *Star Wars* license was Factors Inc. Eventually, it produced most of the *Star Wars* t-shirts, posters, badges, patches, and caps that fans proudly displayed to declare their allegiance to either the Rebel Alliance or the Empire. Harry Geissler, the owner of Factors, spent $100,000 on a license from Lucasfilm and within a month of the movie opening he had doubled his investment, and went on to bank $1 million by the end of 1978.

It was a similar story of success for Bibb Co., which held the license for *Star Wars* bedding (sheets, pillows cases, bedspreads, and blankets), towels (beach, hand, face, and bath), curtains, and sleeping bags for all three classic trilogy movies. Don Post Studios, which kept its license from 1977 to 1990, was to achieve a similar success with its range of rubber masks. It wasn't just manufacturers who were taking a gamble on *Star Wars*—Lucas was also willing to take a chance on manufacturers. When Ken Films approached Lucasfilm to release a home version of the movie, it was the failing Super-8 that was suggested as the format of choice. Taking into

Marvel Ewoks: *number one*

account that 8 mm was still the most common form of home viewing, Lucasfilm agreed and Ken Films packaged a few minutes worth of *Star Wars* and reaped the rewards.

By 1979, requests for licenses were flooding into the Lucasfilm offices, so Lucas could deflect pressure from Twentieth Century Fox to accept all licensing applications. To cope with the demand, five administrative assistants were hired to assist Lippincott, and a system to track messages was devised based on importance and went "Call back immediately," "Call when convenient," and "Why bother."

It was apparent that *Star Wars* wasn't going away, and the public happily accepted the deluge of clothing, shoes, watches, posters, kitchenware, party goods, food stuffs, restaurant promotions, newspaper articles, television interviews, jewelry, household items, bedding, costumes, and toys. What they didn't know was that Lucas would produce two sequels and keep the momentum going well into the 1980s.

THE END OF THE GOLDEN AGE (1985–1987)

In 1985, Lucas popped the *Star Wars* bubble when he announced that there would be no more movies in the series. Fans were amazed—they had been led to believe that there would be nine parts to the story and were now being told that the glory days were over. With waning interest, many license holders, like Topps, Bibbs, and Factors, had already ceased production of their goods, though Kenner Products and Marvel hung on to the end.

It began looking bad for the *Star Wars* franchise in 1985 when Australian businessman Rupert Murdoch bought Twentieth Century Fox, which allowed Lucas to cancel Fox's rights to distribution *Star Wars* and its sequels.

While attempts to rekindle interest in *Star Wars* through two *Ewoks* movies and *Ewoks/Droids*-inspired Saturday morning television cartoons and comics proved successful overseas, it was obvious that the appeal was fast losing steam. Though Kenner Products had permission for 250 vehicles, characters, and play sets and already had a number of nonmovie spin-offs in the pipeline, it eventually made the decision to end the *Star Wars* line with its Power of the Force selection, a final extension of its action figure range that revisited the three *Star Wars* movies to fill in gaps from previous ranges. As the year came to a close, it was clear that even this last flutter wouldn't pay off and Kenner Products made preparations to sell off its remaining *Star Wars* items to overseas clearance houses.

The last of the original pre–*A New Hope* license holders to go was Marvel, whose lackluster *Droids* and *Ewoks* comic books, aimed at young children, did nothing to stop the decay. In 1986, it published its last *Star Wars* title and turned its attention elsewhere.

Despite the obvious decline in popularity, West End Games Inc. acquired the license for role-playing and adventure board games set in the *Star Wars* galaxy in 1986. For nearly twelve years (the company went bankrupt in 1998), it allowed thousands of fans to take turns at being Wookiees, Imperials, bounty hunters, and Jedi Knights.

THE DARK YEARS (1987–1994)

Between 1987 and 1994, the *Star Wars* collecting scene was practically dead. The general consensus among fans and manufacturers was that the glory days were over and even Lucasfilm was a fading star. In these eight years, Lucasfilm only made eight feature-length movies, many of which were personal projects that Lucas had put off until he had completed the *Star Wars* trilogy. In 1992, Lucasfilm turned to television as its medium of choice and concentrated most of its efforts on *The Chronicles of Young Indiana Jones*, and Lucas made a successful return to his swashbuckling roots.

In these gap years, Lucasfilm consolidated its prop, costume, and model collection into the now-famous Lucasfilm archives and took them on a series of tours starting in 1984 at the World Science Fiction Convention in Los Angeles, where the archive was based.

In 1987, there was a brief flurry of interest in *Star Wars* when the tenth anniversary rolled around. In this year, the trilogy was rereleased to the public for the first time since 1983, and Disneyland in Anaheim, California, opened the doors to "Star Tours"—a four-minute interactive ride simulator based on aspects of the original *Star Wars* trilogy—and annexed to it was the world's first store dedicated to *Star Wars*. Also in this year the *Star Wars* tenth anniversary celebration was held in Los Angeles. Both of these events kick-started a miniboom that saw mugs, postcards, badges, t-shirts, pens, watches, and posters. Sadly, neither of these events was a true reflection of the licensing power *Star Wars* had commanded in the previous decade.

A second Star Tours ride was opened at Disney Tokyo in the summer of 1989 and a third at Walt Disney World, in Florida, in the winter of the same year. The fourth, and so far final, Star Tours ride was opened in Disneyland Paris in 1992. All four Star Tours attractions were popular with park visitors, proving that there was still at least some interest in *Star Wars*.

It wasn't until 1991 that *Star Wars* started to make a comeback. Bolstered by the successful release of the original trilogy on VHS in 1990, Lucasfilm began to look for partners to continue the *Star Wars* tradition.

The first few companies to show an interest were Dark Horse, an independent comic book company that had a considerable track record in innovative and groundbreaking stories and art; Bantam Books, which had introduced one of the most popular additions to the Expanded Universe—Grand Admiral Thrawn; and Topps, an old favorite. By the end of the year, *Star Wars* was back in force, with new storylines, art, characters, and settings. The amount of excitement shared by fans was immense and the fan base held its breath, hoping that there was more to come—especially toys.

After a brief licensing hiatus, Just Toys, a company that had produced a variety of junior sporting goods and foam shooting toys, picked up the license to make action figures. Between 1993 and 1994, it produced a range of 4-inch-tall flexible rubber *Star Wars* characters called Bend-ems. Lacking in accessories or articulation, fans and collectors were disappointed with the range and the toys were soon consigned to clearance bins.

A NEW BEGINNING (1994–1999)

In 1994, Lucas announced to the world that he was beginning work on a prequel to *Star Wars*, stating that it was because of the recent advances in computer generated special effects made by Lucasfilm's sister company, Industrial Light and Magic.

The announcement that more *Star Wars* movies were coming not only rekindled fans' hopes, but also lit a bonfire under the seats of plenty of potential licensees, who immediately began to clamor for rights to the franchise.

Later that year, Kenner Products (now owned by Hasbro Inc.) returned to the fold when it made its first tentative steps back into *Star Wars* with the release of the die-cast Action Masters line. It proved an immediate success and by Christmas of 1995, nearly twenty years after Kenner Products first launched its action figure range, new toys began to roll off the production lines. Wave after wave of detailed 3³/₄-inch and 12-inch characters followed, with vehicles, play sets, exclusives, mail-ins, and promotions being eagerly snapped up by the public.

It was like *Star Wars* had never been away, but this time around one thing was different: It wasn't children who wanted the merchandise, it was grown-ups. What the executives at Lucasfilm and Hasbro didn't realize was that they had much more than the latest hot toy on their hands, they had a way for adults to get in touch with their lost youth. The *Star Wars* generation now had the money to express their fandom—and spend they did.

Buoyed up by the wave of nostalgia spreading across the millions of twenty and thirty year olds, Twentieth Century Fox jumped in feet first and reacquired the video distribution rights to the trilogy. Lavishly repackaged and digitally remastered to meet the exacting standard of THX's certification, the VHS tapes sold over 22 million copies in the United States alone.

Despite the coming of a prequel trilogy, the first new official chapter to be added to the *Star Wars* storyline was not on celluloid, but as a multimedia crossover with Dark Horse, LucasArts, Hasbro Lucasfilm, and Bantam Books using comic books, novels, computer games, and toys. In 1996, the *Shadows of the Empire* bridged the gap between *The Empire Strikes Back* and *Return of the Jedi* and told the story of the Rebel Alliance's attempt to track Han Solo and rescue him from Boba Fett before he was delivered to Jabba the Hutt. This extension segued neatly into the third chapter of the original trilogy.

Decipher Inc. joined the growing number of license holders in 1996 and began to produce a customizable card game set in the *Star Wars* universe. It was an instant hit with gamers and fans alike, and even though Decipher lost its license in 1999, it still has a cult following today.

The return of *Star Wars* was a runaway success and rumors began to circulate that the original *Star Wars* trilogy would soon make its way back to the place it all began: the big screen. Fans didn't have to wait long, because in 1996 they were told that George Lucas would not only rerelease the original trilogy to mark the twentieth anniversary of *A New Hope*, but he would remaster, reedit, and reshoot scenes to depict Lucas's final vision of the original trilogy story. Most fans were ecstatic, but many were confused or even hostile toward the idea that the tale could be changed. The wait was a short one: *A New Hope: Special Edition* opened early in 1997, and instead of waiting three years between episodes, there was only a one-month delay before *The Empire Strikes Back: Special Edition* and another month for *Return of the Jedi: Special Edition* appeared.

To coincide with the rerelease of the remastered *Star Wars* trilogy and the tenth anniversary of Star Tours, Disney's MGM Studios in Florida held its first *Star Wars* Weekend, where *Star Wars* characters mingled with visitors to the park. The next year saw a similar event, and again in 2000, which marked the start of a series of annual affairs that got grander with each occurrence.

As toys continued to flow from Hasbro Lucasfilm and more licenses were sold to cover almost everything under the sun, fans began to look forward to the next trilogy of movies. While Lucasfilm was keeping details of the new toys, books, comics, and games close to its chest to protect the prequel trilogy, it was the Internet that had the biggest impact on the *Star Wars* community. Fan sites covering almost every aspect of the franchise were sprouting up all across the World Wide Web.

The late 1990s saw a stampede of fans creating their own Web pages to show off their collections, express their opinions about the special editions, and share news on the upcoming prequel trilogy. This revolution became the next stage of evolution for the hobby and rid the community of the fragmentation that it had suffered from for so many years—now *Star Wars* collecting was a truly global pastime.

THE PREQUEL ERA (1999–PRESENT)

If Lucasfilm had been through some peaks and troughs in the past, it was now about to enter a stage that would see it surfing on a wave of popularity that was unprecedented since the weeks following the original release of *A New Hope*. When it came to self-promotion, *Star Wars* was in a league of its own. Gone were the days when there was only a single trailer and the advertising campaign consisted of one man attending science-fiction conventions to drum up support. With millions and millions of dollars available and hungry investors ready to snap up a license at the first chance, television, theatrical, Internet, billboard, and press advertising was an unstoppable force.

Just like in the 1970s, Lucasfilm realized the potential of the convention-going public, but instead of taking itself to science-fiction get-togethers, it brought fans to the first official *Star Wars* fan club celebration. Held at a mothballed air force base in Colorado, thousands of fans flocked to the gathering, where they spent three rainy days enjoying props and models from the first prequel, previews to the new range of toys, trivia contests, and talks from those involved with the movies.

With the first prequel, *The Phantom Menace*, fast approaching, Lucasfilm's licensing department was in full swing as it dealt with thousands of requests for licenses. First at the door were Coca-Cola, McDonald's, and Pepsi, but it was Pepsi, whose international chain of restaurants included Kentucky Fried Chicken, Pizza Hut, Taco Bell, and Burger King, that eventually bought the rights for a reported $2 billion.

As always, the main focus of *Star Wars* collectors was on the toys. Hasbro Lucasfilm (now completely merged with Kenner Products and a number of other toy companies) received the rights to all games and toys derived from the three prequel movies. This time around, it wasn't going to get caught without the right product. Lucasfilm had given Hasbro Lucasfilm unprecedented access to its design and production departments so that everything from action figures, to games (board and electronic), to dolls and a huge variety of sundry items would be ready in time for the launch.

Unlike previous movie releases, Hasbro Lucasfilm organized its toy release to predate the release of the movie so that collectors would have a head start on those members of the public who would get swept along with the hype after the movie came out. It was Toys "R" Us that answered the call in the United States and Zellers in Canada. Together, they hosted a special early opening extravaganza across the continent, with some stores seeing lines stretching out of their parking lot.

Once the movie came out, there was even more merchandise to buy: Kellogg's cereals, Lays potato chips, computer games, food premium tie-ins, and competitions at Burger King, Taco Bell, Pizza Hut, and Kentucky Fried Chicken, plus an onslaught of products that had the public amazed and the *Star Wars* collecting community overwhelmed.

One of the biggest newcomers was LEGO, who in 1998 stepped outside the bounds of its own brand and acquired its first movie license. By the summer of 1999, it had released the first LEGO sets based on *The Phantom Menace*. Fans of the classic trilogy weren't to be kept waiting when LEGO released the first of its classic sets in time for Christmas 1999.

After the release of *The Phantom Menace*, the pace continued unabated, with Dark Horse, Del Rey, and LucasArts filling in more gaps in the *Star Wars* time line and taking great care to maintain continuity and to keep fans enthralled. The arrival of the second prequel movie in 2002 would have the largest following to date. A second spin-off story line came in 1999 with an invasion of aliens from outside the *Star Wars* galaxy. The New Jedi Order series would pose a number of questions about the nature of the force that would take nearly twenty novels to tell.

As before, Toys "R" Us held another Midnight Madness and fans and collectors blitzed the aisles to pick up the latest releases. However, the 2002 affair was markedly different from the previous event. It was easy to see that licensing was more restrained this time around. After the rush of excitement following *The Phantom Menace*, stock piles of unsold merchandise hung around for months. Lucasfilm had learned its lesson and returned to the old mantra of quality over quantity, allowing the collecting community to breathe a sigh of relief.

Just before the release of *Attack of the Clones*, Lucasfilm held another fan event. Celebration 2 was bigger and better, with over thirty stars of the original and prequel trilogies attending, a vast dealers area so collectors could keep their collections up to date, talks with guest stars hosted by Anthony Daniels, product displays from the major license holders, and a prop, costume, and model exhibit brought all the way from Skywalker Ranch and its own brand of merchandise.

As big a success as *The Phantom Menace* was, *Attack of the Clones* was greater and left audiences on the edge of their seats as galactic war broke out across the Republic. Hasbro Lucasfilm, Dark Horse, Del Rey, Cartoon Networks, and LucasArts, all under the watchful eye of Lucasfilm, neatly used their licenses to produce a range of toys, games, books, television cartoon series, and comics to carry the excitement on to Episode 3.

The big event of 2004 was the release of the classic trilogy on DVD. Even though Lucasfilm had already issued *The Phantom Menace* and *Attack of the Clones* on this format, fans were anxious to get their hands on the original trilogy. Hasbro Lucasfilm and Topps marked the occasion by traveling back in time and coming up with a range of toys and trading cards that harkened back to the vintage releases of so many years ago.

Now as the last installment draws closer, the collecting community can only guess at new plots and products that are to follow and wonder if *Star Wars* will ever truly end.

About This Book

The evidence of the collecting hobby's growing popularity is everywhere: Lucasfilm has a department dealing solely with the official Starwars.com Web site; the popular *Star Wars* movie news site TheForce.net is ranked with Microsoft.com and CNN.com; Rebelscum.com is one of the most visited *Star Wars* collecting sites in the world; and on any given day online auction sites such as eBay have tens of thousands of *Star Wars* items up for sale.

People all over the world have taken their childhood toys and turned them into an adult pastime. Adults who collect *Star Wars* items have moved from the underground to mainstream culture thanks to the popularity of celebrities who no longer eschew their "geeky" side. Every day, there are millions of fans looking for news on the latest movie, hunting for the hottest auctions, and communicating with fans about topics as diverse as "Will Chewbacca appear in Episode 3?" to "Which is more valuable: a brown-haired or a blond-haired Luke Skywalker?" (The answers are "yes" and "brown.")

Fortunately, this information is easy to come by, but because of the volume of information and the speed at which it is acquired, it is hard to keep track of what a collector needs or already has. Although nine out of ten collectors are computer literate and Internet savvy, they have to resort to the tried-and-true paper-based price guide to keep track of their collection. Speaking from personal experience, it can be frustrating to maintain a collection cataloged without any references.

The Official® Price Guide to Star Wars Memorabilia is the latest comprehensive reference guide to the core collectibles in this hobby. This book serves both newcomers to the pastime with articles introducing them to different aspects and facets of collecting *Star Wars* items and experienced collectors who want to keep up to date with prices and new items or want to expand their collections into new areas.

The book is divided into three sections: the first serves as an introduction to the hobby, the second is a product list and price guide of the most popular areas of collecting, and the appendices contain references such as reading lists and recommended Web sites for further information.

This book covers *Star Wars* collectibles from 1976 through to 2004, with additional information on upcoming Episode 3 items, and includes the mainstream items released in North America (Canada, Mexico, and the United States). The purpose of this book is to take the hobbyist through the entire collecting range: choosing what merchandise to collect, what to look for in an item and where and how to buy it, preserving the collection, restoring pieces, researching new items and areas, having the collection valued, and finally selling off extra or unwanted items to fuel the hobby further.

The Official® Price Guide to Star Wars Memorabilia is meant to be an up-to-date print guide that covers over twenty-five years of merchandise with today's collector in mind, and a definitive resource for the novice to expert collector. While previous guides have concentrated on itemizing every single *Star Wars* collectible, this guide focuses on the main items that collectors look for. Where other books have leaned in the direction of being a photo archive/coffee table book, this book makes the collector the center of attention. Finally, where earlier guides have taken it for granted that the collector has full knowledge of his or her chosen hobby, this book addresses the various aspects of the pursuit of *Star Wars* collectibles that the inexperienced should know.

Also provided is a price guide listing the going rates for the core collectibles sold on the retail and secondary markets, as well as on the Internet by dealers and at online auctions. Internet auction sites—such as eBay.com—have proved to be a great leveler. As an online marketplace, eBay has had a singularly impressive effect on the price and rarity of *Star Wars* collectibles by breaking down national and international boundaries, opening up new avenues of collecting, and bringing new and interesting items to the attention of the hobbyist. So exit the local market and enter a community where few collectibles can truly be called rare, and two things set the prices: knowledge and patience.

2 CONDITION AND GRADING

Each area of collecting has its own methods of grading items—whether it is stamps, comics, toys, posters, or coins. *Star Wars* collecting spans many such areas. This book will attempt to illustrate as many grading systems as possible with the most commonly accepted methodology.

There is only one hard-and-fast rule about grading the condition of a collectible—whether it is a MOMC 12-back Darth Vader with double-telescoping lightsaber or the latest Anakin Skywalker action figure you picked up at Toys "R" Us the day before yesterday—it is that condition is one of the most important factors (but not the only factor) in determining the value of an item.

It is important to recognize the difference in the terms "condition" and "grade." Condition is an assessment of the state of an item (whether it is loose, the packaging that it came in, or any accessories that are associated with the collectible), and grade is a rank that is used to indicate the condition. How you use these terms is also critical. While it is much easier and more convenient to say an item is C6, it is far more evocative to describe the item as "card is intact with no holes or cuts, but there is a small fold in the corner and the sides show edge wear."

What to Look For

No matter what aspect of the hobby you are interested in, when it comes to determining the condition of a collectible item, it pays to know what defects to look for:

Toys: The actual figure will be considered mint unless it has a defect that detracts from its overall eye appeal. Defects include paint wear, discoloration, overspray, fading, or dismemberment. If the carded figure comes with a collector coin, trading card, or other insert, it will be rated separately.

Blister/Windows: The condition of the blister/window will be used to determine the overall condition. Defects such as dents, scratches, fading, yellowing, clouding, sticker residue, tearing, cuts, lifting, soiling, rub marks, crushing, gluing, factory cut, and foreign items (ink mark, staple, etc.) are the types of defects that impact the final condition.

Packaging/Cardback: The packaging or cardback will be judged against creasing, bending, rolling, tearing, scuffing, scratching, lifting, print marks, loss of gloss, soiling, discoloring, edge wear, nicks, punctures, ink or foreign markings, peg hole punch, tape repair, focus, price sticker, sticker tear, sticker residue, water damage, bubbling, and attached foreign objects.

Paper Items: Collectibles such as trading and gaming cards, as well as posters and many party items, suffer from the same faults as packaging. As such, they are judged on creasing, folding, tearing, scuffing, fraying, discoloring, edge wear, ink or foreign markings, tape repair, punctures, and mounting residue.

Books

One of the oldest of areas of collecting in the world and the first mass-produced example of a *Star Wars* collectible, books are a key part to the hobby.

GRADE	CONDITION
As New (N)	Flawless, as in straight from the presses. It is technically feasible to keep a book As New if it is sealed immediately after printing.
Fine (F)	A virtually flawless example, with minor, tiny, and virtually unnoticeable flaws, such as a few tiny nicks to a dust jacket and as close to being a new book as possible.
Very Good (VG)	Implies that the book is still basically sound and collectible, but with visible, though not serious, flaws. It will typically have some fading and/or staining to the covers, and older books will exhibit shelf wear. A Very Good dust jacket will have some rubbing, some chipping, possibly even some tears or small pieces missing, but it should still be substantially bright, clean, and complete
Good	Considered below collector grade, and will have heavy fraying to the edges of the paper, strong shelf wear, and show yellowing. A Good dust jacket will show color loss, moderate tearing, and damage to the ink.
Fair (F) to Poor (P)	Used only to grade books that are so damaged through wear, tear, and abuse that there is no other term for them. Even these should still be complete and readable, although the pages may be browned and the covers detached.

This format can be used to describe the book itself. To describe the book and the dust jacket, use two grades such as F/VG (Fine/Very Good) to indicate a fine book in a good dust jacket.

Other grading terms associated with books are included in the list of terminology at the end of this chapter.

Toys

Toys are the most popular and complicated area of *Star Wars* collecting, so they deserve the most attention.

Packaged Toys

With packaged goods, there are more potential problems with damage to boxes, so packaging is graded less strictly than carded figures. Packaging grading does not reflect the condition of the items within the box (toy and insert) and does not require the packaging to be sealed.

TERM	DEFINITION
C10	This is the highest grade that is assigned to packaged items and will be absolutely flawless. The box will be free of creasing or edge wear. No soiling or fading has occurred and there are no print defects. This box doesn't exist.
C9	This is a high-condition box. Packages graded C9 or better are difficult to obtain and will have either minor wrinkling to the cardstock or some edge wear. There will be no tearing.
C8	Overall clean and displayable condition, but will have some minor to moderate problems. Problems may include those listed above or a small sticker tear and some creasing to the box, or wear to the edges or corners.
C7	Average wear to the box. Overall, there will be noticeable defects such as tears on the flap or heavy creasing, but the package will still display okay.
C6	Below average box. This condition is not recommended for display. It is mainly of use to collectors who want to have a box, but do not want to pay a premium for the packaging. This is considered a low condition.
C5	Box has major wear and tear and will not close. May have a missing flap or a large tear, with tape repairs.
C4	Box is extremely damaged and will not stay upright. Has heavy tape repair.
C3	There is less cardboard than tape, and product image and graphics are eradicated.
C2 and C1	The packaging is not discernable, as if it was run over by a bulldozer (C2) and then by a marching band (C1).

Other grading terms associated with packaged toys are included in the terminology section at the end of this chapter.

CARDED FIGURES

The key factor to grading carded figures is that it relates only to the status of the cardback and blister and in no way describes the item held within the blister. Many collectors incorrectly consider a bubbled item to be mint, but there are many influences that could affect the condition of the toy within the blister and as such should be graded separately from the cardback.

For the most part, collectors use two systems of grading: a quantitative system that starts at C1 and rises to C10 and a qualitative system that ranges from Very Poor to Mint. The most common of these is C1 through C10.

Though these classifications are most often used for determining the state of carded action figures, they can just as easily be employed for blistered toys such as the POTF Mini-rigs and the modern accessory packs.

GRADE	CONDITION
C10	A perfect example, even under a microscope with no stress marks, edge wear, or flaws of any kind. Does this exist?
C9	Card should look nice from a distance of one foot. Light stressing if any at all, no color breaks, and light to minimal edge wear.
C8	Card should look nice from a distance of two to three feet. Light to medium stresses, light color breaks, and light edge wear.
C7	Card may have medium stress marks, some color breaks, and medium to heavy edge wear.
C6	Overall card should be intact with no holes and not cut. Deep stressing, color breaks, and tears on picture, etc., are acceptable.
C5	Obvious tears, stresses, color breaks, card may have been cut or proof of purchase (POP) removed. Usually not more than two or three large flaws to qualify as a C5.
C4	Similar to C3 but with slightly less damage.
C3	Deep stresses, tears, punches, holes, many color breaks, card may have been cut, POP removed, etc.
C2 and C1	Basically, what the card would look like if run over once (C2) by a car and then stomped on by an elephant (C1). This grade is too heartbreaking to illustrate.

The use of a qualitative system was considerably more widespread in the early 1990s, but the recent trend has shifted to the previous grading method. This method of describing carded figures and toys equates roughly to the following:

Card Condition: C9

Card Condition: C8

Card Condition: C7

Card Condition: C6

Card Condition: C5

Card Condition: C4

GRADE	EQUIVALENT	CONDITION
Mint (M)	C10	Perfect in every aspect. Does this exist?
Near Mint (NM)	C8 to C9	From a distance of one foot light to medium stresses, and light edge wear will be visible.
Fine (F)	C6 to C7	At arms length card should only have medium edge wear but may have heavy stressing.
Good (G)	C4 to C5	Has tears, cuts (POP removed) and heavy fraying. No more than four defects to qualify.

Poor (P)	C2 to C3	Deep stressing and folding, card cut in multiple places, and no intact edges. Five or more flaws to qualify.
Very Poor (VP)	C1	No features on the card are discernable, and individual flaws can not be counted.

The biggest point of degradation occurs on the blister, and a number of terms have been devised to solely describe its condition:

TERM	DEFINITION
Yellow Bubble (YB)	A descriptive term for the condition of a blister bubble that is no longer clear. Also used is Slightly Yellow Bubble (SLB), but since this is subjective it is uncommon. The prefix "Y" can be added to a grading such as Y-NM or C8-Y.
Reformed	Some blister defects can be at least superficially corrected by reshaping the bubble gently by hand. This includes popping out small dents or reshaping dings. Many times, this reformation is quite evident in a whitening of the clear plastic.
Separation	Since blisters are affixed to card in some manner, there is a chance that they can become detached. Some blisters are detached (at least partially) from the card to remove the figure inside. Conversely, these figures can also be replaced at a later time.
Ding	Similar to a dent, but on a smaller scale. May or may not be accompanied by a whitening of the clear plastic.
Dent	An indentation or concave section of the clear plastic bubble not originally intended by the manufacturer. May or may not be accompanied by a whitening of the clear plastic.
Crack	In terms of a blister a crack is a noticeable fracture, crevice, split, or chip-like flaw in the plastic covering of the action figure but does not include the separation of the bubble from the card itself (though cracks may be present along the boundary of the separation).

Other grading terms associated with carded figures are included in the terminology section at the end of this chapter.

LOOSE ITEMS

Grading loose items is not the same as packaging because there are a whole new set of factors that can affect the condition of an item including cleanliness, tightness of joints, paint chipping/wear, and damage to extremities (noses and figures). It must be remembered that even though production flaws, such as faults in the injection process, bad paint jobs, and incorrect assembly, can affect the value, these inconsistencies should in no way reflect on the grading of an item.

Loose Figure: C6   Loose Figure: C5

Again, there are two ways to depict the condition of a loose item, whether it is an action figure, a play set, or a vehicle. As with carded figures the dual methodologies are quantitative
and qualitative, and as before it is the former that is currently the most commonly used:

GRADE	CONDITION
C10	In perfect condition, absolutely no paint loss or damage to plastic. Joints are extremely tight, figure will stand up unassisted in breezy conditions. Complete with perfect weapon/accessory. Does not exist.
C9	Joints are tight and figure can stay upright with arms extended, no scratches or paint loss, complete with weapon and accessory (may show slight wear). Considered to be the average grade of figures removed from the packaging immediately after purchase.
C8	Joints are tight and can stay upright with base, figure is clean, no scratches to plastic, light wear to paint around waist, no damage to fingers or nose, complete with weapon/accessory (may show creasing).
C7	Moderate wear to paint around waist, ankles, and shoulders, light paint wear to face and hands. Joints becoming floppy, weapon may have dam-age, accessories may have tears or bends, details may be soiled.
C6	Heavy wear to paint at points of articulation, moderate paint wear to nose, scratches and some gouging, joints are loose, no accessory, detailing clearly soiled. Some discoloration to plastic. Weapons/accessory missing.
C5	Fingers damaged, figure can not stand upright (tries to touch toes), ink and heavy soiling to large body areas. Heavy discoloration to plastic. Some limbs may be salvageable.

C4	Figure cannot hold accessory, face damaged, little paint left, extreme wear to plastic. No weapons/accessories.
C3	Severely damaged, limbs missing, no paint, hands and face chewed.
C2	Torso and several limbs still attached. No discernible paint.
C1	Chewed and spat out by a dog and then buried in a garden for twenty-five years.

As with carded figures, the qualitative method is currently not as popular as the C1 to C10 usage. However, it is still employed by some collectors.

GRADE	EQUIVALENT	CONDITION
Mint (M)	C10	In perfect condition, absolutely no paint loss or damage to plastic. Joints are extremely tight, figure will stand up unassisted in breezy conditions. Complete with perfect weapon/accessory. Does not exist.
Near Mint (NM)	C8 to C9	Joints are tight and figure can stay upright with arms extended, figure is clean, light scratches and some wear to paint around waist, no damage to fingers or nose, complete with weapon/accessory (may show creasing).
Fine (F)	C6 to C7	Light wear to paint around waist, ankles, shoulders, moderate paint wear to face and hands. Some plastic damage to hands, joints are loose, detailing clearly soiled. Some discoloration to plastic. Weapons/accessory damaged.
Good (G)	C4 to C5	Fingers severely damaged, figure cannot stand upright (tries to touch toes), face damaged, ink and heavy soiling to large body areas. No weapons/accessories.
Poor (P)	C2 to C3	Severely damaged, limbs missing. No discernible paint.
Very Poor (VP)	C1	Driven over by a truck, and then stomped on by a marching band

The clear advantage of using the qualitative method is that it can easily be combined to describe a carded figure. For example, POGC (Poor on Good Card) indicates that while the figure is in poor condition, the card is still good, or NMOFC (Near Mint on Fine Card) is a near mint figure on a fine card. However, because of the complexities of the scaling system, this method of grading was dropped.

Collecting Cards

Card collecting is one of the oldest of the "modern" hobbies, and when *Star Wars* became one of the subjects of the card publishing industry, the same grading system that was used to rate sports cards was used for Topps's addition to the *Star Wars* collecting hobby.

GRADE	CONDITION
Mint (M)	This is a flawless card, all corners are sharp, centering perfect, original color and gloss, and the photo has transferred in perfect focus. The card has no spots or gum stains.
Near Mint (NM)	On close inspection the card has one minor flaw, such as slight fraying at the corners, slightly off-centered, rough edges, or minor printing spots. It should still have its original color and gloss.
Excellent Mint (EM)	Has some minor flaws. It should have its original gloss but could have slight color or focus imperfections.
Very Good (VG)	The card may show obvious signs of handling, a minor crease, rounded corners with slight layering, some discoloration of the borders, and some loss of gloss.
Good (G), Fair (FR), and Poor (P)	These cards have had quite a bit of handling and wear. They have major creases, no gloss, and well-worn layered corners.

This grading system has also been extended to trading card (TCG) and collectible card (CCG) games. Because these cards are created to be constantly handled, they are printed on heavier cardstock and use more durable inks, so tend to rate higher than the typical collecting card.

Comics

As with trading cards, the grading system for *Star Wars* comics was adopted from longstanding comic book grading systems.

GRADE	CONDITION
Mint (M)	Absolutely perfect in every way. As soon as it is touched it drops to Near Mint. Mint is as an imaginary ideal that cannot be attained in the real world.
Near Mint (NM)	Almost perfect. On close inspection, one or two tiny imperfections may be found. This is the highest grade assigned to any item in a catalog.
Very Fine-Near Mint (VRNM)	An excellent copy with only minor imperfections such as a few tiny stress lines on the spine or a minor printing/binding defect.

Very Fine (VF)   Excellent copy with slight wear beginning to show. Still sharp, glossy, and clean.

Fine-Very Fine (FVF)   A glossy, clean copy with a number of small imperfections or slight wear such as tiny stress lines or slightly rounded corners.

Fine (F)   An above-average copy that shows less than average wear. Typical defects could include a small corner crease or some loss of cover gloss.

Very Good-Fine (VGF)   A slightly better than average copy with some imperfections that keep it out of the higher grades. Obviously handled but fairly well cared for; still basically a decent copy.

Very Good (VG)   A copy in average condition. Some wear is obvious but not damaged or soiled.

Good-Very Good (GVG)   A well-read copy with some significant defects such as tears, long creases, or writing, or perhaps several smaller but noticeable defects.

Good (G)   A worn copy with an accumulation of defects such as tears, creases, writing, pieces out of the cover, etc.

Fair-Good (FR-G), Fair (FR), Poor-Fair (P-FR), and Poor (P)   These grades all indicate a much-worn copy with many significant defects, such as tape, pieces missing, stains, or water damage, increasing in number and/or severity down the list. However, even comics graded Poor have complete stories, though parts of the cover or panels might be missing.

Posters

Collecting posters—both promotional movie pieces and decorative prints—is gaining popularity in the hobbyist community, and *Star Wars*–related movie posters are among the top ten highest movie memorabilia sellers on eBay.

Unfortunately, posters, unlike most other popular collecting areas such as toys, comics, and cards, have no standardized system universally embraced for terminology and the rating of condition. As such, the condition and grading guide presented here is only propositional.

GRADE	CONDITION
Mint (M)	An unused poster. As pristine as the day it was printed with little exception.
Near Mint (NM)	Basically unused or carefully used. Showing some signs of age or storage but no abuse of any kind. Clean folds (standard and not considered a flaw for posters pre-1980). Post-1980 posters are rolled and the same standards

apply. Linen-backed posters, with no restoration needed, fall into this category.

Very Fine (VF)	Minimal signs of wear and usage with usually no pinholes, fold damage, or paper loss. Image area is still bright and paper quality not brittle. Linen-backed posters usually fall in this category, as minor restoration to the fold lines and borders may be likely and evident to a discerning eye.
Fine (F)	Average used and aged condition showing signs of edge wear, pinholes, slight hairline tears, minor discoloration. Paper is not brittle. Image is still striking and linen-backed restoration more evident. Post-1980 rolled posters that have been folded.
Very Good (VG)	Below average, used, trimmed, or weathered condition showing paper loss, stains or soiling, larger pinholes, extra prominent folds, light ink or pen marks, tape on the back, and prominent border damage. In need of restoration.
Good (G)	Overly used, worn, or brittle, including large chunks of missing paper, dirt, dry mounted or laminated, water stains, scotch or masking tape, flaking, or discoloration.
Poor (P)	Unpresentable and in worse condition than anything above.

Professional Grading Services

While many other collecting hobbies (such as baseball cards, tin cars and robots, and coins) have many professional valuation services, *Star Wars* is such a multiproduct-spanning license that there is no one single company that can accurately grade every *Star Wars* item in existence.

However, for vintage and modern *Star Wars* toy collectors there is Action Figure Authority (AFA; www.toygrader.com), whose aim is to provide a grading service on action figures, play sets, and vehicles (plus associated and sundry $3^3/_4$-inch- and 12-inch-scale items). The purpose of AFA is not to ascertain a toy's worth but to provide a definitive scoring system that avoids prejudice and has backup nonanecdotal evidence to support the grade.

GRADE	CONDITION
Gold (AFA 90, 95, and 100)	The select few figures that receive these grades are among the highest quality in existence. A small percentage of figures submitted to AFA receive a Gold grade. The flaws are minor, subtle, and are sometimes hard to identify with the naked eye. The collector who is extremely condition sensitive will be satisfied with the condition of a Gold-level figure. To date, only two figures have received an AFA 100 grading. Equivalent to C9 to C10.
Silver (AFA 75, 80, and 85)	The Silver level consists of the grades 75, 80, and 85. The figures that receive these grades are in excellent condition. A figure graded an 85 will often be referred to as "case fresh" and

AFA Grade 80 Carded Figure (Image courtesy of Action Figure Authority)

AFA Grade 75 Carded Figure (Image courtesy of Action Figure Authority)

AFA Grade 40 Carded Figure (Image courtesy of Action Figure Authority)

should be close to Gold-level condition. The term "case fresh" is certainly justifiable as the average figure pulled from a sealed case will grade an 85 because of small flaws that occur when the figures are packaged or shipped in the case. The average figure pulled from a store shelf is usually an 80, which represents a nice specimen with minor flaws apparent on close inspection. The final Silver-level grade, a 75, represents an item with more minor flaws than the average Silver-level piece. An item grading 75 does have significant wear but does not have major flaws that would draw the eye to them at first glance. For most high-grade collectors, an 85 is satisfactory. For most discriminating collectors, an 80 is satisfactory. A 75 will be satisfactory to those who are not overly concerned with light stresses, small bubble imperfections, and other flaws that do not jump out at first glance. Therefore, the Silver-level grades do represent a much larger range than the Gold-level grades. Equivalent to C6 to C8.

Bronze (AFA <60, 60, and 70)   The Bronze level consists of the grades below 60, 60, and 70. The figures that receive these grades typically have damage ranging from simply noticeable on first glance to extremely significant. The card may have creases on the front and the blister may be crushed or cracked. The Bronze level covers a large range of figure conditions and the scope of the flaws range considerably. Condition for Bronze-level figures is determined by how many "major" flaws are present on the card and how severe each flaw is. Bronze-level figures may have major flaws such as a torn off POP or other large paper tears.

> Bronze-level figures may not be satisfactory to condition-sensitive collectors. Equivalent to C1 to C5.

The downside to using a professional toy grader is that a certain amount of the service's reputation becomes attached to the graded item. In a hobby that is already expensive, inflation because of a grading sticker can be detrimental—collectors may eschew certain aspects of the hobby purely because it is no longer affordable.

Terminology

The following are the most commonly used terms and acronyms for conditions and grading of *Star Wars* collectibles:

AFA   Action Figure Authority: A company that provides a grading and certification service on many *Star Wars* collectibles.

Card surface tear   Noticeable rip or tear of the paper, cardboard, print, or ink of the card surface. May occur on either the card front or back. Most commonly caused by the removal of a price tag or sticker. Other causes include removal of store stickers, antitheft devices, or special offer stickers.

Condition   The particular state of repair or ability to function of a collectible.

Corner curl   One of the most frequent flaws found with modern carded action figures. Since most of the cards are square or rectangular or have angular edges, corners can be easily curled up because of poor shipping, shelf wear, poor storage, or improper handling. Corners generally curl at approximately a 45-degree angle.

Crack (blister)   In terms of a blister, a crack is a noticeable fracture, crevice, split, or chip-like flaw in the plastic covering of the action figure but does not include the separation of the bubble from the card itself (though cracks may be present along the boundary of the separation).

Crack (card)   In terms of the card, a crack occurs when part of the print or ink is removed or damaged. Usually occurs because of a crease or fold, but may also occur spontaneously because of improper exposure to light or heat.

Crease   A severe curl or bend that leaves a permanent mark or crinkle on the print or ink. A crease can occur without completely cracking or removing the print or ink. Severe creases may allow portions of the underlying cardboard to show through.

Curl   A bend in the cardboard that doesn't damage the print or the ink.

Dent   An indentation or concave section of the clear plastic bubble not originally intended by the manufacturer. May or may not be accompanied by a whitening of the clear plastic.

Ding

Similar to a dent, but on a smaller scale. May or may not be accompanied by a whitening of the clear plastic.

Ex-lib

A former library copy. Ex-libs are generally considered not collectible, especially if the library markings are prominent and pervasive and if there is the usual pocket glued in the back.

Fraying

When cardboard fiber is pulled apart or stretched, individual fibers begin to show, giving a fuzzy impression to the cardboard (at the edges especially). Nonfrayed cardboard is usually tightly packed and firm.

Grade

A mark to indicate a level, step, or stage in a collectibles condition.

Hole

Any complete piercing or perforation of the card or bubble. Occasionally, some older items did not come with a hook or hole to hang the item on a peg or rack.

Laid-in

Something is lying loose in the front of the book such as book plate, postcard, or other premium.

Loose

An item that is no longer contained in any packaging.

MIB

Mint in Box: A packaged item that can be described as in brand new condition. Often, it also denotes that all cardboard inserts used to hold the item in place are included. By inference, this acronym is only describing the item and not the packaging itself, so an MIB toy could contain a perfect toy that comes in a damaged box.

MIMB

Mint in Mint Box: An expanded description of an MIB, where the packaging is being described as brand new.

Mint

In perfect condition as when first made.

MIP

Mint in Packaging: An alternative to Mint in Box and Mint on Card. This term is not commonly used because it is purposefully vague about the cardback or packaging.

MOC

Mint on Card: A carded item that is carded can be described thus if the packed toy is in brand new condition. By inference, it is only describing the item and not the cardback.

MOMC

Mint on Mint Card: An expanded description of MOC, where both the item within the blister and the card itself are being defined as in brand new condition.

NRFB

Never Removed from Box: An item that has been opened but kept in its packaging. It should not be taken as a literal example of the toy's condition because most items that have been opened have been removed from their packaging.

P
Punched: An action figure blister card that has not had the card from the hanging hole removed. Conversely, UP (unpunched) indicates a blister card that has not had its hole opened, but because punched cards are far more common than unpunched, this reference is never used.

Price clipped
The price—usually on the top right of the front inside flap of the dust jacket—has been cut off.

Reformed
Some blister defects can be at least superficially corrected by gently re-shaping the bubble by hand. This includes popping out small dents or reshaping dings. Many times, this reformation is evident in a whitening of the clear plastic.

Sealed
The box is still sealed with original tape if applicable. If the box was not originally sealed with tape, this term signifies that the box does not appear to have ever been opened or tampered with.

Separation
Since blisters are affixed to card in some manner, there is a chance that they can become detached. Some blisters are detached (at least partially) from the card to remove the figure inside. Conversely, these figures can also be replaced at a later time.

Staining
A permanent discoloration of the card or bubble because of contact with some foreign substance. Usually caused by a liquid of some type but may also be the result of contact with other materials (e.g., plastic, rubber, etc.). Separate from bubble or card yellowing, which may occur without contact with any foreign substances.

Sunning
The term used to describe the fading or browning of the spine, both of the book and jacket.

Tape repair
Occasionally, scotch tape (or other type of tape adhesive) is used to repair a card or reseal a bubble. Some types of tape may be removed without further damage. Some tapes themselves can damage the surface of the card or bubble, even if not removed.

Warping
A curving of packaging material caused by moisture.

YB
Yellow Bubble: A descriptive term for the condition of a blister bubble that is no longer clear. Also used is Slightly Yellow Bubble (SYB), but since this is subjective it is uncommon.

3 BUYING

The first step in starting a *Star Wars* collection is deciding what aspect of the hobby you are going to focus on. The range of merchandise is just too large to commit to collecting everything, and unless you are a millionaire several times over, it is an impossible feat to achieve. The only real answer is to collect what you like. Most *Star Wars* collectors want the Kenner and Hasbro action toys, while others go for bedding and other household goods, trading cards, point-of-sale displays, role-playing games, prop replicas, books and comics, food premiums, or prototypes. You can make your collection extremely specific or because of the volume of *Star Wars* collectibles you can mix and match themes and collecting orientations. For instance, you could only collect items made by Kenner Canada Products (*see* www.kenner-canada.ca) or concentrate on a particular character such as Boba Fett, Ewoks, or R2-D2 (*see* www.r2d2central.com).

Once you have determined what you are going to collect, you have to decide what condition you want your collection to be in. Many collectors start out by building up a selection of items to replace their long lost *Star Wars* toy horde from when they were young and start by collecting the toys that are in "played with" condition. This is a relatively cheap and easy way to begin and is a great starting point if you do not begin with an exhaustive knowledge of the hobby. The next evolutionary stage is to start improving the state of your collection by purchasing boxed and carded items, and from there going to packaged mint toys, and then finally on to mint toys in mint packaging. Many collectors then begin to branch out into other areas of merchandise like novels, source and reference books, preschool toys, props, magazines, autographs, foreign merchandise, and variations of items already in their collection.

Once you have chosen what areas of the hobby you are going to concentrate on, you need to research availability, price, popularity, and competition. Basic economics will tell you that if an item is widely available but there is little interest in it then prices will be low. With the huge proliferation of *Star Wars* goods in the early 1980s and again in 1999, when *The Phantom Men-*

ace was released, there were a plethora of companies jumping on the band wagon. Many of their products (like greeting cards, party goods such as napkins, paper plates, cups, and table clothes, and children's clothing) are available in such abundance that they are consistently low in value.

Don't, however, rely on the economics triangle to guide you in your collecting, because there are swings and shifts in the community that no one can predict. For instance, although Ewok collectibles generally have a poor following, there was a noticeable rise in *Return of the Jedi* and Kenner Preschool Ewoks toys in the late 1990s. The only reason that could explain the rise in activity was the twenty-fifth anniversary of *Return of the Jedi*. With the increased attention of the press and Internet sites on the sixth *Star Wars* film, there was a slight increase in Ewok popularity that in turn triggered a price rise. In a similar situation, the action figures and toys spawned from the spin-off *Droids* and *Ewoks* cartoon series have been rising in value since the mid-1990s, when you could get a full set for half the amount they cost today. The most likely reason is that, by now, many vintage collectors have completed their mainstream collections and are now starting to collect the toy lines that they previously ignored.

Understanding that the value of any single *Star Wars* item is equal to what someone is willing to pay for it, and not what the seller thinks it is worth, will take you a long way. I have not spent more than $30 on a *Star Wars* purchase in over a year, including an Ewok Village, a Canadian MIB Creature Cantina, a Sigma Tauntaun Tea Pot, and a *Return of the Jedi* book shelf. So, if you see an item that you need and think it is too expensive, then just move along and continue looking for a better deal. The ratio of collectibles to collectors is millions to one, which means that there is plenty of *Star Wars* merchandise to go around. Keep in mind that most collectors have many years of collecting ahead of them and have plenty of time to find that last elusive action figure or comic they need. Remembering these points will help you maintain a level head when you start buying, and will ultimately keep the cost of the hobby down.

Armed with this knowledge, you are now ready to begin shopping—but where do you go? There are a number of options to choose from, depending on your budget, time scale, and locality.

Retail Market

The first place most collectors, especially those interested in the modern toys and other collectibles, will go is the nearest retail outlet. The big box stores, such as Toys "R" Us, Wal-Mart, and Target, have long stocked *Star Wars* items in their toy, bathroom, clothing, household, and computer game aisles (many of which have special stock areas that are highly decorated and entertaining). The advantage of these large outlets is that they buy in bulk and their prices will be the least expensive. Competition between these retail rivals means that you can always check their ads and get them to price match.

The largest chains are also the first to be offered *Star Wars* items from the manufacturers and often buy such large numbers of goods that they order the entire production run of an item

TRU Times Square Star Wars Aisle

and get the exclusive distribution rights. Because such exclusives are more difficult to find, they are more highly sought after and command higher prices on the secondary market.

However, there is a disadvantage to shopping solely at chain stores: the short-packed items (such as the action figure, which is one to a case) can be impossible to find because the large chains prefer to order assortments (cases of toys with a range of action figures) instead of solid cases of the same figure. If the rarer item is in stock, it is often buried under unrelated toys.

Specialist Stores and Dealers

Nowadays, stores specializing in collectible merchandise are becoming increasingly hard to find. Often, they can be found in the yellow pages (or try www.yellowpages.com) under "collectibles," "toys," or "comics." In the past, vintage *Star Wars* collectibles were available in small stores known only to the collecting community. But with the dominance of eBay for vintage items and the chain retail outlets for modern toys, small shop owners are having a hard time making a profit, and many are closing. Luckily, the American comic industry is booming, so comic books stores aren't likely to go out of fashion any time soon.

Unfortunately, specialist stores and dealers tend to be more expensive than their larger retail competition and won't stock such large numbers of items, but they will have a more diverse range of *Star Wars* collectibles (including many pieces that retail outlets won't even consider) and the consumer will get a knowledgeable level of service as well.

E-tailers and Mail Order

To keep up with the market, many small specialist shops have closed their stores and moved their focus away from the brick-and-mortar aspect of retail. In the early to mid-1990s, fanzines and hobby magazines like *Toy Shop*, *Lee's*, *Toy Fare*, and *Tomart's* were full of advertisements listing a huge range of vintage and early modern toys. All you needed to expand your collection was a credit card, a telephone, and a mailing address. The late 1990s saw a shift in collecting from newspapers to the computer. When the Internet became widely available to the public, most retailers jumped from printed ads to their own Web sites. Early efforts were pretty basic and you still had to call up and pay for your purchases over the phone using a credit card.

Today though, online shopping has changed and the vast majority of collectors do all their shopping online, if not through eBay then through specialty e-tailers. Many of the large retail chains have realized the value in having a store that anyone with a computer and an Internet connection can reach, and have opened their own Web sites (visit www.walmart.com and www.target.com) with categories and searches that make finding *Star Wars* items easy. Others, like Borders Books (www.borders.com) and Toys "R" Us (www.toysrus.com), have teamed up with online giant Amazon.com to provide their online services. In addition, there are the well-known and respectable e-tailers such as The Earth (www.theearthtoymall.com), Cloud City Collectibles (www.cloudcity.com), which concentrates on vintage Kenner items, and Entertainment Earth (www.entertainmentearth.com), which has a wide range of modern collectibles including *Star Wars* toys.

Of course, buying off the Internet isn't the same as walking into your nearest toy aisle and finding the latest wave of figures, but it does have its advantages. Besides saving money on gas, not having to sift through hundreds of unrelated items, or only finding what you want on a bent card with a crushed bubble, online purchasing has credit card protection, gives you the ability to track your package online, and the items are well packed and won't arrive damaged. Many e-tailers have a policy whereby they will provide two grades of merchandise: regular or collector's grade. And finally, there is the added bonus that the larger specialized e-tailers have their finger on the pulse of the collecting community and know what hot items are coming up and can get product images and present them on their site well before they are announced by the manufacturers or other official *Star Wars* news sources. This allows the collector to preorder the item and not have to worry about missing the latest collectible.

Auctions

It cannot be stressed enough that the biggest revolution to affect *Star Wars* collecting was the arrival of online auction sites in the late 1990s. Though several competing companies tried to get a foothold in the market, it was eBay that won in the end.

EBay, the online auction house, is probably one of the most popular sites on the Internet, and to a *Star Wars* collector, it is certainly one of the most useful. Since its birth in 1995, eBay has effected great change in the collecting hobby and has the privilege of being the greatest leveler the community has ever seen. Where items were once rare, now everybody had access to them, creating a global marketplace where bargain hunters, the spare-no-expense buyer, the newcomer, and the elite could mingle and brush shoulders.

There was a time when *Star Wars* collectors had to rely on a friend willing to give away his or her childhood toys, mail-order catalogs, magazine ads, and the local not-too-honest toy dealer to build up their *Star Wars* collections.

It might be said that the early days of *Star Wars* collecting were far more enjoyable and needed more skill than today, but there is no doubt that the modern world of *Star Wars* collecting is easier, slicker, and more reliable. So exit the local market and enter eBay, the world's online marketplace and a place where few collectibles can truly be called rare, and two things set the prices: knowledge and patience.

Buying on eBay doesn't require a lot of advanced learning. With a few pointers, anyone with an idea of the basic workings of eBay can start building up a great *Star Wars* collection. The first thing to do is to spend a few days seeing how eBay works because it is not a "Going, going, gone!" auction but instead allows you to build up your bids over the duration of the auction. Unlike brick-and-mortar auction houses, eBay auctions can last over a week instead of the usual five to ten minutes of a traditional auction. To begin with, take your time and start slowly by bidding on some low-priced items. This way, you will learn the bidding process and, if you win, how to make your payment without risking too much money.

Once you are ready to start bidding on items that will fill your collection, you should remember that *Star Wars* collecting is not like it was back when the original toys were sold. Today, many buyers are people who are trying to make up for the fact that they did not save the old figures fifteen years ago and they believe that they are striking gold when they find new figures in the store. This has created a highly competitive edge to eBay bidding and leads people to scalping. It is likely that in another fifteen years there will be more *Star Wars* toys hidden in attics and garages than there will be displayed in living rooms and dens.

However, old *Star Wars* toys are usually worth something but often less than most people think. Price guides are available to give you an idea of market value, but the only real value is what someone is willing to pay for it. It doesn't matter if a seller has the most current price guide telling him that his Ewok Battle Wagon is worth $300; the price offered is the current market value.

It is important not to get distracted by the seller's opinion of the item, which could be clouded by his or her sense of nostalgia or need to sell it for as much as possible. No matter how many auctions you see with HTF, L@@K, and RARE included in the title, there are probably another dozen of them up on eBay. While pre-1995 *Star Wars* items are becoming harder to find, you have to factor in the fact that hundreds of thousands to millions of toys, books, posters, t-shirts, stickers, stationary sets, food items, and so on were made. It will be a long time before they become truly rare like a Penny Black stamp, a Stradivarius violin, a signed copy of *Sergeant Pepper's Lonely Hearts Club Band*, or a Gutenberg Bible. No matter how fervently the seller believes that he or she is selling the last existing Blue Snaggletooth in the world, he or she will never be able to retire to Boca Vista. It is definitely a buyer's market out there, and will be for a long time to come.

It is impossible to pass on every tip and trick to getting the most out of eBay—the space required just isn't available here, and there are many books on the market (ironically many of them are for sale on eBay)—so here are a few of the more important ones:

Watching items: use the Watch This Item option to keep an eye on something you are interested in. It is a good idea to select a couple of auctions for the same item and observe how the bidding progresses before deciding which auction you are going to get involved in.

Misspellings: keep an eye out for common words that are spelled incorrectly. Despite being showered by *Star Wars* through the media and merchandising for over twenty-five years, there are still people out there who can not spell "star wars." A favorite trick is to search "starwars" (with hyphen), "starwar," and "starwarz" or any derivation of the phrase. The first one always brings up results and the other two rarely, but sometimes you can find some dream auctions tucked away. It stands to reason that if some people can't spell "star wars" then specific terms like "X-Wing" and "Millennium Falcon" will really trip them up. Incidentally, the word "millennium" is one of the most misspelled words of 1999 so it's always a good idea to try "milenium," "milennium," "millenium," or "millanyum."

Wildcards: these are the best way to find obscure auctions, but they require a lot of work to get right and loads of trawling to find the really interesting auctions. Try searching for "yak*" and you'll get a thousand auctions with any word with the letters Y, A, and K in them. You'll have to refine your search slightly by telling eBay to exclude words like "yakuza," "yakima," and "yakutio" before finding all the auctions for Yakface figures.

Vague titles: these are another good way to find bargains. A recent search on eBay turned up an auction titled "Starwars 1977–1983 Toys," which is so vague that many collectors would pass right by. After inspecting the auction, it turned out that a Kenner 12-inch TESB boxed Boba Fett, a Palitoy 3³⁄₄-inch SW boxed X-Wing, a Palitoy 3³⁄₄-inch TESB boxed Snow Speeder, and a carded Tri-logo Lando Calrissian (General Pilot) were being auctioned as a package, and unsurprisingly it had no bids on it. The lesson to be learned is never ignore a badly worded auction title.

Wrong categories: these are a good place to look. While a GI Joe or Transformer fan might be up to speed on his or her own hobby, he or she might not know too much about *Star Wars* collecting. To many people, a plastic spaceship shaped like an X could just as likely transform into a truck as destroy a Death Star.

Save your favorite searches: did you know that your My eBay page has a page where you can save your search phrases? If you have devised a particular useful search string but it takes you ten minutes to type it all in, you might want to use this feature.

Researching past auction prices: by keeping an eye on price trends by searching through completed items in the Advanced Search page, a wise eBay shopper can build up a picture of what is good value and what is not. By applying this knowledge to current auctions, you can come up with some definite steals.

Using specific searches: if you are looking for carry cases, you could enter "star wars case" as your search string, but you will get other items that have the word "case" in their titles/descriptions, so try "star wars case -pillow" to avoid certain types of bedding.

Lack of seller's knowledge: if you are looking for a vintage Barada figure, you might search for "star wars vintage barada." It will list any title with all the matching words in it. What if a seller forgot to list the item with the words "star wars" in the title? Your search won't find it because it isn't an exact match. Simply searching for "vintage barada" will pull up every auction with the words "vintage" and "barada" in it, whether they have "star wars" in the title or not. Instead, try "vintage barada -(star, wars)." This search will give you a list of auctions that have "vintage" and "barada" and not "star wars" in their titles. Chances are fewer people will find this auction. Until now that is.

Getting advice: if you are unsure about the value of a piece, the claims (e.g., its condition and rarity) made by the seller, or any other point, ask a collector you trust to look at the auction. Of course, whoever you select to help you must be able to resist temptation and not bid against you.

And above all, have patience.

So, you have found the item of your dreams and are ready to make a bid, but your Jedi senses are on alert because something doesn't feel right, and no matter how long you stare at the page you can't see why no one else is bidding on it?

While this is pretty much common sense, there are many people who take risks on eBay just because they won't spend a few minutes checking out the facts. The most important thing about buying *Star Wars* toys is to do your research. The number of licenses given to manufacturers over the last three decades is colossal, so you'd be forgiven for not recognizing every single *Star Wars* item on eBay.

It is strongly advised to study past prices on similar sales and to watch current auction trends for at least a week before bidding on an item. You might also check out the item on reference sites such as 12-Back (www.12back.com), the *Star Wars* Collector's Archive (www.toysrgus.com), *Star Wars* Toy Resource Page (pages.map.com/starwars/), Yakface (www.yakface.com), Galactic Hunter (www.galactichunter.com), or Rebelscum (www.rebelscum.com). There are also plenty of good publications: anything by Steve Sansweet is a good place to start, as are Gus Lopez's many articles in *Tomart's Action Figure Digest*.

So, having found the auction and researched the item, it is now time to place a bid. Before you commit your money, review the item's description and look at any pictures closely. Is the product new or used? Like new is not new, almost new is not new, open box or open package is not new. Is it used? How used is it? A description such as "used to work like new" is not a good indication that the product is in top condition. How much time has the seller put into the auction—one line of text or a well-presented page? Does the description actually contain any useful information? Most eBuyers make it a rule not to touch an auction if it doesn't have any photographs.

Once you feel confident in the auction, decide how much you are willing to spend. Make a mental note that this is not the same as deciding how much the item is worth, because the two numbers may differ vastly. Once you have decided your top limit, stick to it like glue and don't be tempted to extend it.

When you set your ceiling, add a penny or two to the final value—many people use a simple and inexpensive method of raising their chances of winning by adding a few pennies to their bids. Many new bidders on eBay often place their maximum bids in rounded amounts such as $35.00. An experienced bidder would be one step ahead by bidding $35.02. Thus, if the pro is correct, then he or she would win the auction by a two-cent margin.

Bidding on the same item in several different auctions at the same time is not a good habit. Of course, you do actually need more than one Stormtrooper to build up your Imperial invasion force, but do you really want three sonic-controlled Land Speeders? For starters, you could end up winning more than one auction—and any bid you place is a binding contract. If you are honest, then you'll be stuck with duplicates (long term, this is good for trading; short term, this is bad for the bank account). If you are dishonest, you could try to duck out of the sale, but an experienced seller will know how to check up on your bid history to discover if you've already won the same thing elsewhere. Any excuse to field will fall on deaf ears.

If the price is quoted in a currency you don't understand, then you are likely on a different eBay site—ebay.ca uses the Canadian dollar while mercadolibre.com.mx (Mexican eBay) quotes in the peso. If you were to look at the same auction at your "local" eBay site (tip: copy the auction number from one eBay and paste it into the search tool of another eBay), you'll find that the currency has been converted for you.

A contentious way of bidding is by sniping—that is, placing a bid in the closing seconds of the auction to prevent counter bids. Sniping is a practice that infuriates many eBay buyers, but it is the only way of ensuring that you get what you want. If you get sniped, don't consider it stealing—it is just that the latest bidder is happy to pay more than you and is willing to risk it until the last few seconds of the auction. Sniping is becoming a more common practice on eBay nowadays, so it is worth learning the mechanics of the practice is case you want to bid yourself.

As we discussed, you will still go through the process of deciding what you think the item is worth and what your maximum bid is going to be. Instead of entering it as your bid—write it down on a piece of paper and stick it in your back pocket.

Now, click on the Watch This Item button to save the auction to you're my eBay page so you can keep an eye on it. It is also a good idea to set up some kind of alarm to remind you when the auction is closing so you'll be around to snipe. Most e-mail browsers have this facility in their calendars.

When the auction is about to close, you'll need to be already logged on to eBay, or else you could lose vital seconds during your bid as you frantically type in your details to fully submit your bid. You will also need a fast Internet connection since eBay page loads are pretty hefty and laden with graphics. A dial-up modem is too slow.

You should be prepared to make your final bid at least one minute before the end of the auction. Type in your maximum bid and submit it. If you succeed, then you have a strong chance of winning the item. If you do get outbid, then walk away. Getting caught up in a bidding war in the dying seconds of an auction will only cost you more money. After all, that's what setting your maximum bid is all about, right?

Because sniping is becoming more widespread, some software developers have realized that custom-made sniping programs would be a great tool to have. They are designed around Internet browsers that store your auction and maximum bid information and then submit your snipe automatically, thus increasing your success rate.

After you've won an auction, it's a good idea to print out the auction page so that you'll have a handy reference with all of the auction details. Keep this printout until you've received your merchandise and are satisfied with your purchase.

It is also a good idea to save any e-mails—keep an auctions folder in your e-mail software. You might use several subfolders to organize your auctions: For instance:

○ Bidding holds the auctions you are currently bidding on.

○ Ongoing has subfolders for each item you've won and or are in the middle of paying for or still waiting the arrival of.

○ Completed folder holds all the auction items that have arrived. When you have posted/received feedback, you can permanently archive the specific folder.

○ You should also keep a log of the transaction, including any communication you had with the seller, when you made payment, and when the seller sent the item. If you have any problems at a later date, you can use this log as an aid memoir.

Unless the auction specifically states what method or how much the postage will be, you do have the right to negotiate. Do not simply take the seller's word that the item will cost $XX to ship by airmail to you—ask him or her what service he or she will use and how much the fully packaged piece weighs. Nearly every postal and courier service has some kind of Web-based postal calculator. These are the exact same rates that post offices and couriers use when they charge the seller, so you can check this out. Allow for a slight margin of error because the seller is allowed to add a charge for the packing material.

If you are not happy with the service that the seller has opted for, then tell him or her. Maybe you can't afford or don't want your package sent via FedEx's twenty-four-hour delivery plan. All you need to do is let the seller know how you want it sent to you—most sellers are accommodating.

When the seller contacts you after you've won an auction, respond promptly. Reply with your full name and mailing address, and tell the seller precisely when your payment will go into the mail. Once you have settled on the cost of shipping and handling, you now have the final price, and the onus is on you to complete the payment for the item.

There are many ways to pay for your auction—but ultimately you can only use one that the seller is happy with, so check the auction's payment details first. With eBay's acquisition of the PayPal credit service (www.paypal.com) electronic payment of auctions has become considerably easier and safer. Credit card payment is secure and fast, and offers you protection and peace of mind from fraud. If your item doesn't turn up, all you need to do is contact your credit card or credit service and it will put a stop on payment. There is always the age-old method of sending cash to the seller, but you'd be doing so at your own risk. Some sellers will only take cash payment, but do insist that you send it as a registered letter so you know it has arrived with them. Personal checks and postal orders are also safe bets, and if you are buying internationally, you can use a Banker's Draft Check or an International Money Order in exactly the same way. Both are similar in that you buy a secure IOU that is equal to the value you paid for it. For costly items, you can use escrow. This is a service provided by eBay, whereby the seller sends the item to the buyer, and the buyer sends payment to a third party. The buyer is allowed to inspect the item for a defined period before either rejecting or accepting it.

Should you have a rare instance of needing to send a payment beyond the payment due date; e-mail the seller, explain the reason, indicate the date the payment will be made and how it will be made. What if you can't pay? Then you shouldn't have bid on the item. Trying to put off the seller indefinitely by citing that your cat had to go in for emergency surgery or asking for the item to be reserved for you until you have the cash is wishful thinking and nine out of ten times will result in negative feedback.

The seller should leave feedback as soon as you've made payment, but many commonly don't. Most often, he or she will leave feedback after you have received your win and posted your own feedback about the seller. It isn't really fair to do it this way, but most do, so don't expect anything immediately after you've sent your money.

Once your merchandise arrives, inspect it immediately and check it against the description on the auction page you printed. If it's what you expected, promptly get online and post positive feedback for the seller on eBay. If your purchase is not what you expected—don't be too hasty and leave negative feedback immediately. Instead, e-mail the seller and explain your problem. Clearly state what you think would be an effective remedy. Try to settle the problem at an early stage to avoid getting eBay involved.

Remember that your problem might not have been caused by anything the seller did—shipments get lost in the mail and merchandise can get damaged in transit. Angry e-mails directed at the seller won't accomplish anything.

Toy Shows and Conventions

Throughout the year, there are many local toy fairs and conventions run by show promoters who bring in local dealers to convention centers, meeting halls, hotel function rooms, and so on (often with a celebrity guest signing autographs). In the summer months, the convention circuit is the busiest. There are over a half-dozen national events, notably San Diego Comic Convention (www.comic-con.org), Gen Con (www.gencon.com), and Wizard World (www.wizardworld.com), all of which have high media profiles that attract star guests, A-list celebrities, and manufacturers like Hasbro that use the event to display forthcoming products to collectors. Toy shows and science-fiction conventions have a long history in the *Star Wars* collecting community—the first *Star Wars* collectibles were available at the 1976 San Diego Comic Convention—and it is still an excellent source for rare and hard-to-find collectibles.

Celebration II LEGO Display

Lucasfilm and the Official *Star Wars* Fan Club have also staged several fan conventions—the celebration events held in 1999, 2002, and 2005 were widely attended by fans of all ages and nationalities. Information about these events can be found on *Star Wars* Internet sites, in *Star Wars* comic books, on *Star Wars* collectibles sites like Rebelscum.com, and in specialty collectibles magazines.

As exciting as toy shows and conventions sound, their downside is that they are commonly held in metropolitan areas, so if you live far away from a large population center you will be forced to travel there and probably find accommodation. They also charge admission fees that can be expensive, particularly the big summer events.

Flea Markets and Garage Sales

Now that most people have caught on to the idea that one person's junk is another person's treasure, many people are turning to selling their old *Star Wars* toys directly to dealers or on eBay, instead of selling them for pennies at flea markets and garage sales. Those *Star Wars* toys that are sold at the smaller sales are often the dregs that couldn't be sold elsewhere, and are hardly worth the title of collectible. This is not to say that bargains don't happen, but they are rare. It is worth keeping your eyes open—just don't expect to find a Droids A-Wing in perfect condition for the price of a pack of bubblegum.

Collectors' Clubs

These fan-run organizations are incredibly helpful in keeping up to date with *Star Wars* collecting, because not only do they allow collectors to share news, they can also sell or trade duplicate items. In the past, collectors' clubs used to be at a local level, with groups of collectors from a city or a few towns getting together at a convenient location to catch up

OSWCC Summer Social
(Image courtesy of Ohio Star Wars *Collector's Club)*

and share news with each other. With the coming of the Internet, many clubs have spread across entire states and provinces, amalgamating smaller clubs along the way. The Internet has allowed collectors' clubs to have their own Web sites to promote themselves, forums to share news, and mailing lists to have detailed discussions about the hobby. Typically, they will have regional chapters that break up the club into smaller groups, which will have meetings once a month and a large annual gathering in the summer where the entire club meets.

Several such collecting clubs are the Ohio *Star Wars* Collectors Club (www.oswcc.com), Indy Knights (www.indyknights.com), Kentucky *Star Wars* Collectors Club (www.kswcc.com), DC Metro *Star Wars* Collecting (www.dcswcc.com), and Pennsylvania *Star Wars* Collecting Society (www.pswcc.com). Most states and major cities have their own clubs—if you can't find yours, check out TheForce.Net's own FanForce section (www.fanforce.net), which has extensive collectors' group listings and information on local events and get-togethers for the United States, Canada, and Mexico.

The Toy Run

One of the most enjoyable aspects of shopping for your *Star Wars* collection is the toy run, which is a shopping trip with preset locations purely to find new *Star Wars* items. This has been used by collectors for decades, and at its simplest form involves driving from one big box retail store, comic store, and specialty shop to another looking for the latest releases. The toy run can be used effectively when sharing information and traveling in groups, and is often the basis of small, local collecting clubs.

Toy runs typically occur early on the way to/from work, or on weekend mornings. A good tip is to be friendly toward the staff members who stock the toy aisle, and find out what the regular delivery times/days are so you can be one step ahead of the competition. Nowadays, they also include visiting *Star Wars* collecting news sites and forums like Rebelscum (www.rebelscum.com) and Galactic Hunter (www.galactichunter.com), as well as popular online sources like eBay and certain e-tailers.

Scalping

Scalping, the practice of buying toys at retail to sell at inflated prices, is one that affects the *Star Wars* collecting community and creates higher prices. The biggest problem in scalping is not that it inflates the cost of the hobby—but that it often takes available goods out of general circulation.

For example, going into a local Wal-Mart and buying five new figures for $5.99 to resell them at the local flea market for $10 each is scalping. These toys should have been available to anyone who walked off the street and into Wal-Mart. It is the same for a shopper who goes into Target and buys two of the same figure—one for himself and another to sell on eBay. Had this collector bought two figures to open one and to keep one sealed for later enjoyment, he would not be considered a scalper.

On the other hand, if a collector purchased the latest releases direct from a source in Asia before its general public release, this would not be considered scalping because it has not reduced the amount of toys available to the public. Nor is buying an extra figure for posterity and then deciding to sell it at a profit a few years later, because, most likely, by that time the figure will have been discontinued and not be available in general circulation.

Scalping is a given in the *Star Wars* collecting community, and some Web sites and collecting groups have taken action by encouraging readers to adopt a code of conduct. One of the more common ones is Rebelscum's "Collect to Collect" credo, which asks its members to:

- Buy only what you need and make sure others get one before you get many.

- Acquire pieces for your collection because you want them, not because you plan to profit from them.

- Help others achieve their collecting goals for the sake of the hobby, not profit.

- When you trade or sell available toys, do so at cost.

- When you trade or sell unavailable toys, do so keeping the golden rule in mind: you'll always win in the long run if you don't take advantage of people.

- Buy from scalpers as a last resort. They exist because people buy from them and do not make collecting toys easier. Scalping only promotes decay within the hobby.

- Understand it is more important for a kid to have the toys than you; help him or her out whenever possible. You're likely to get another chance at the toy, he or she may not.

At the end of the day, scalping is not an illegal activity, but in the long run it can only hurt the community and the hobby.

Terminology

The following are the most commonly used terms and acronyms in buying *Star Wars* collectibles:

Baggies   Action figures sealed in bags, typically from mail-away promotions.

Big box store   A large consumer retailer like Toys "R" Us, Wal-Mart, Target because it resembles a large packing carton.

Bin   A point-of-purchase display that consists of a cardboard box to hold the merchandise using a plastic tray, with an attractive header card to catch the attention of the consumer.

Blister   The plastic bubble that holds the toy to the cardback. (Also known as bubble.)

Bootleg   An unlicensed version of a preexisting, licensed product. Usually, a bootleg is a direct copy (albeit typically much shoddier in appearance) of its licensed counterpart. Unlike fakes or customs, bootlegs are made in factory environments to be sold in stores as *toys* and are not made specifically to mimic preexisting collectibles. Action figure toys are the most frequently bootlegged items.

Cardback   The cardboard packaging onto which a plastic blister containing the toy would be attached. Most often these are action figures, but a few Mini Rigs were produced on cardbacks instead of boxes.

CCG   Collectible Card Game: A turn-based card game where players have their own personal customized decks instead of playing from a common deck (*see also* Trading Card Game).

Custom   Refers to a homemade toy and is commonly an action figure, vehicle, or play set. Custom toys are made for the enjoyment of the individual and are not usually produced in larger quantities than one.

CW   Clone Wars: The toy line produced by Hasbro in 2003 and 2004 to span the gap between *Attack of the Clones* and Episode 3, and to tie in with the Expanded Universe Clone Wars spin-off series of books, computer games, comics, and television cartoons.

DT   Double-Telescoping Lightsaber: An early version of the 3³/₄-inch lightsaber accessory that had a double action of telescoping, meaning that there are two stages of extension. Not to be confused with the common single-telescoping lightsaber.

eBay   The largest online auction Web site in the world.

eBayer   Someone who buys/sells on eBay (also eBuyer—someone who buys on eBay).

Ep1

Episode 1: The packaging line produced by Hasbro in 1999 and 2000 to tie in with *The Phantom Menace*.

E-tailer

A retailer with an online store front.

FB

Flashback: The packaging toy line produced by Hasbro to bridge the gap between the Power of the Force 2 toy line and Ep1/*The Phantom Menace* toy line.

Hanger

A double-sided display card intended to be hung from the ceiling over a display area.

HC

Hardcover: A book bound in cloth, cardboard, or leather rather than paper.

Header card

Part of an in-store display system that could be hung from the ceiling or attached to the top of a shelf or to the back of a bin.

HTF

Hard to Find: An item that is elusive is considered hard to find. Not to be confused with rare.

Inserts

The cardboard (typically corrugated) inside a box that holds the toy in place. Can also include sticker sheets, instructions, and any catalogs or brochures placed inside the packaging.

Last 17

Refers to the final release of figures in Europe, all of which only appeared on the Tri-logo cardback. The term is often confused with Power of the Force, which, in the United States included only fourteen figures. Though counted as a POTF figure, the American assortment never included Yakface.

Loose

An item that is no longer contained in any packaging.

Mail-away

Items offered by companies as premiums through sending in redeemable proof of purchases.

Micro Collection

The packaging toy line of 1-inch-scale miniatures produced by Kenner between 1982 and 1983.

OSWCC

Ohio *Star Wars* Collecting Club: A fan-run collecting group organized to aid collectors in Ohio. It is one of many such clubs throughout North America.

OTC

Original Trilogy Collection: The packaging toy line produced by Hasbro in 2004 to coincide with the release of the Original Trilogy on DVD format.

P

Punched: An action figure blister card that has not had the card from the hanging hole removed. Conversely, UP (unpunched) indicates a blister card that has not had its hole opened, but because punched cards are far more common than unpunched, this reference is never used.

Packaging   The wrapping or container in which an item is presented for sale.

PB   Paperback: A book having a flexible paper binding.

POP   Point of Purchase: In-store displays that are intended to be positioned next to the product. Hangers, shelf talkers, and headers are all point-of-purchase displays.

POTF   Power of the Force: The packaging toy line produced by Kenner in 1985 that encompassed characters and vehicles from the original *Star Wars* trilogy.

POTF2   Power of the Force 2: The packaging toy line produced by Kenner/Hasbro between 1995 and 2000.

POTJ   Power of the Jedi: The packaging toy line produced by Hasbro between 2000 and 2002.

Proof of purchase A blue-and-white disc printed on vintage Kenner cardbacks that was used as part of mail-away offers. (Also known as POP but not to be confused with point of purchase.)

Rare   An item that is in short supply and difficult to get hold of is considered rare. This term can be subjective because one person's idea of rare may not match that of another person.

Rehash   An item that has been reissued with a minor modification to the item or packaging.

Reproduction Are items meant to look identical to one that has been produced under license. Typically, these are weapons and accessories (Double-Telescoping Lightsabers and blasters), blisters, dioramas, and cardbacks. Initially, they were meant to act as temporary replacements for missing parts, but nowadays they are used dishonestly to replace vintage parts and accessories. Also known as repro.

Rerelease   An item that has been reissued without any changes to it or its packaging.

Retro   Retrospective: Looking back at a certain style or collection of thoughts. In the case of *Star Wars* collecting, the retro period is considered to be the Original Trilogy years (1977-1985).

ROTJ   *Return of the Jedi*: The third movie in the original *Star Wars* trilogy. Also the packaging toy line made by Kenner between 1983 and 1984.

RRP   Recommended Retail Price: The maximum price at retail as recommended by the manufacturer.

Saga   The collector-coined term for the unified packaging toy line produced by Hasbro between 2002 and 2004.

Scalping The action of buying toys at retail prices to resell at a profit.

Shelf talker A strip of paper or plastic that would be fixed to the front lip of a display shelf to advertise and promote the product in question.

Sniping Placing a bid in the closing seconds of an auction to prevent counterbids.

SOTE Shadows of the Empire: An Expanded Universe story line that bridged *The Empire Strikes Back* and *Return of the Jedi*. It was accompanied by a number of books, computer games, comics, and toy lines.

ST Star Tours: An interactive Expanded Universe simulator ride based on aspects of the original *Star Wars* trilogy; found at several Disney parks worldwide. Also a packaging line produced by a number of manufacturers between 1987 and 2004.

SW *Star Wars*: The original and alternate title used to refer to *A New Hope*. Also the packaging toy line made by Kenner between 1978 and 1979.

TCG Trading Card Game: A turn-based card game where players have their own personal customized decks instead of playing from a common deck (*see also* Collectible Card Game).

TESB *The Empire Strikes Back*: The second movie in the original *Star Wars* trilogy. Also the packaging toy line produced by Kenner between 1980 and 1982.

Toy run A shopping trip solely dedicated to finding new *Star Wars* collectibles.

TPB Trade Paperback: A book that is typically of better production quality, larger size, and higher price than a mass-market edition and is intended for sale in bookstores. Specifically, it is a bound collection of comic books to encompass all or part of a story line.

TPM *The Phantom Menace*: The first movie of the prequel *Star Wars* trilogy.

Variation A running change to packaging or an item that makes it different from previously released versions of the same piece of merchandise.

4 VALUATION AND SELLING

There comes a time in every *Star Wars* collector's life when he or she has to sell some items from his or her collection. For a devoted collector, it can be a difficult period and if you find yourself in this situation, take solace in the fact that at one time or another most of us have been through the same ordeal, including the authors and contributors to this book.

Getting a Collection Priced

Getting certain individual items or your entire collection valued is still not an easy task, but there are resources that can make it less of a hardship. Having *Star Wars* collectibles assessed is hit or miss because the market fluctuates so rapidly and grading is so subjective. There is also the added factor that the monetary value of a piece may not match the nostalgic value the owner or evaluator has placed on the item, and this will heavily affect the valuation of the piece.

For collectors, there are a number of options to choose from, starting with the cheapest and working up to the most expensive:

Price guides: These should only be treated as an estimation of *Star Wars* collectible prices. Unless the collector is pricing a piece of memorabilia at the same time the price guide is compiled, the values printed in the book are not current. On the other hand, price guides are a useful tool in predicting long-term trends of collectibles. For instance, by using a price guide from each year between 1994 and 2004, a collector could see that the book value of a 12-back SW carded Han Solo (with large head) has risen by nearly 250 percent, but today's book price is still 150 percent higher than the current prices on eBay. The drawback is that each price guide is written by different authors who have different ideas on toy values.

Toy press: There are many monthly magazines, such as *Tomart's Action Figure Digest* and *ToyFare*, that have price guide listings. These tend to be more accurate than price guide books but less so than eBay, and because these magazines cover the most popular toys of the moment there is not enough space to cover every line in detail, so some are abridged.

Online auctions: A second option is using an online auction house such as eBay, which does give a true immediate value, and by using the Completed Listings search, which gives a short-term (three-month) price window. As with price guides, there are drawbacks—the depth of detail in the item's description and the quality of the photograph will strongly affect the number of bidders, as will the amount of publicity or promotion the auction gets. An item that is well presented and promoted through an online *Star Wars* collecting resource can expect up to a 200 percent increase in bidders, and this undoubtedly will affect the price.

Local collectible dealer: Many local collectible toy dealers have enough knowledge of their industry to offer a valuation service, particularly if you are a well-known customer at the shop. Though most dealers will expect something in return for their time, this is the cheapest third-party option. The drawback of asking a dealer to value a collection is that he or she may only have local knowledge of prices. For instance, vintage toys are more common in Cincinnati because of the city's connection with Kenner and in areas of Canada, where more numerous quantities of POTF Yakface action figures were released. There is also the danger that the dealer may only offer the price (wholesale) he or she is willing to pay.

Antique specialist: Some antique houses and auctioneers employ members of staff with specialist knowledge. This might be particularly useful if you are selling off a collection of *Star Wars* stamps or china figurines, but it will not prove an effective method of getting a collection valued if it is predominately made of twenty-year-old plastic action toys.

Professional toy appraiser: While many other collecting hobbies (such as baseball cards, tin cars and robots, and GI Joe dolls) have many professional toy valuation services, *Star Wars* is such a multiproduct-spanning license that there is no one single company that can accurately assess the value of every *Star Wars* item in existence. However, it may be possible to find a number of companies that could valuate the bulk of a collection.

Selling Fundamentals

It cannot be stressed enough that just because an item has the *Star Wars* logo on it does not mean that it is valuable. Nowadays, there are more people collecting *Star Wars*-licensed products than ever before, and a vast majority of them look to the value of vintage toys and believe that they can turn their modern collection into profit at a later date. With so many different goods for sale and millions of people hoarding toys, the prices of mainstream *Star Wars* collectibles are never going to be unreachable.

With the advent of eBay, the size of local and regional markets (essentially how far you were willing to drive on your toy run) has been reduced to mere drops in the global ocean of *Star Wars* collecting, and never more so has it been a buyer's market.

Whether a collector is selling an item to replace it with an improved version, or has to sell off a collection, there is little chance that a collector will be able to retire or send his or her children to college with the profits. Unless the bulk of a collection has not come from the big box retail stores, there is little chance that there will be anything unique enough to spark any real interest.

Before selling off any items or even an entire collection, a wise seller would break down the process into manageable chunks and start from there.

For beginners, decide what price you want for selling the item(s). What exactly is in your collection? Are you willing to break the collection up to be sold individually? Or will you sell it in lots? Is it the full market price you want or would you be happy with a quick sale at a discount? Will you be mailing the item(s) to the buyer?

Then you need to make an inventory of everything you are selling. For a large collection, this can be daunting, but when it comes to selling off one single lot there isn't a dealer on the planet who wouldn't balk at the thought of buying an uncatalogued collection.

Next, find out what each piece is—a seller who labels an item "Luke action figure" is not giving away as much information as "Luke with yellow hair action figure." Furthermore, identify the item. Find out who manufactured the item and the year it was made. For instance, there could be as many as a dozen different "Luke with yellow hair action figure" toys, but including "Hasbro" and "2002" in the description limits the search down to "Saga Luke Skywalker (Bespin Duel) action figure." Even with all this information, it would still make more sense to call the item "Saga Luke Skywalker (Bespin Duel)."

Deciding how you are going to sell the collection and how much you want to get back from the sale will pretty much dictate your options at this point. Selling huge lots on eBay is not unheard of, but buyers are hesitant to pay huge sums of cash on what is essentially a "sold unseen" transaction. If you are adamant about selling everything in one lot, then your best bet is to take it to a dealer and negotiate a sale. If, however, you want to get as much money back as possible, then eBay—whether you are selling a single piece, a small lot, or your entire collection—is the only place where you are going to get close to the true potential of the sale. Taking *Star Wars* items to a dealer and asking for full market value will only get you a quick refusal.

If you do take the mail-order or auction route, you will most likely be mailing your items to the buyer. Get your mailing supplies (envelopes, tape, wrapping paper, boxes, address labels, etc.), as well as a set of scales and postal rates ready in advance of the sale. It is frustrating to a buyer when he or she has to wait several weeks for an item to arrive because the seller wasn't prepared.

Where to Sell

These days, aside from eBay, there are only a few places that *Star Wars* collectibles can be sold. As outlined earlier, selling options are limited by the expected outcome.

RETAIL MARKET

Though a collector is not going to have any luck selling items to Toys "R" Us, Target, and Wal-Mart, he or she has a returns policy if he or she purchases anything, so a collector can return any recent purchases to the chain store from which it was bought.

▶ Specialist Stores and Dealers

A local science-fiction dealer or comic book store will be the most convenient way to off-load any unwanted *Star Wars* collectibles. It is wise to do a bit of research before approaching the store's buyer. Does the store have a good reputation? Does it have any *Star Wars* in stock? Has another collection been bought recently. All these are factors that could affect the final offer. Before packing the items and taking them to a dealer or store, prepare a list of the items that you want to sell and arrange a suitable time so that whoever is responsible for new stock is available. Make sure that the items are as presentable and in as good of a condition as possible. A bag of loose figures isn't going to interest anyone, but a box full of figures sorted into labeled ziplock bags and the correct weapons and accessories will. Last don't expect to leave with a lot of money in your hand. Dealers and specialty stores know the market and will only pay around 30 percent of the market value. They are not cash rich, so they might not be able to make the entire payment at once. On the other hand, they are often more generous if the seller is willing to accept store credit instead of cash.

E-TAILERS AND MAIL ORDER

Online stores or those that still advertise in the collecting press or that sell modern toys generally have people who supply them with the latest *Star Wars* collectibles straight off the boat from Asia. However, some of these outlets, such as The Earth (www.theearthtoymall.com) and Cloud City Collectibles (www.cloudcity.com), also stock older toys and do buy from private collectors to maintain their inventory. The first thing to do is find out who to contact (usually done through a contact form or a telephone number or e-mail address) and approach the outlet as you would a specialty store. Unless you happen to live in the same city as the e-tailer or mail-order stock list, you are going to be selling "sold unseen" goods. In my experience, getting 50 percent of the market value in return for credit is a good deal, so sellers shouldn't expect much back for cash.

AUCTIONS

Certainly the most popular way to sell *Star Wars* collectibles is through online auctions like eBay, where at any given moment there are nearly 50,000 *Star Wars* items up for sale—ranging from inexpensive Episode 1 trinkets to rare carded Kenner figures from 1978. The key to being a successful eBay seller is to put as much care and attention into the sale as you can.

First, research the item so you know what you are selling, and title the sale accordingly. Give a full written description to reduce any ambiguity and to cut down the number of e-mails from potential bidders. Many potential bidders will skip an auction if they feel they are not getting a clear description of the item, rather than contact the seller for more information.

When you compose your auction page, do it in a manner that makes the buyer feel comfortable. It is wise to avoid using JavaScript, Flash animation, or sound files to liven up the page.

Use the auction title space to carry as much information as possible. Since some buyers will search for "star wars" and others will use "SW," try to fit both in the title. When describing an item, be as unbiased as possible. Even though you might be selling the plush Ewok toy you cuddled in bed on a rainy night, this won't matter to another collector, who will want to know why the toy he or she has just bought is in such poor condition. Don't use terms like "HTF," "Rare," or "Mint" when an item is clearly a banged up Episode 1 Anakin Skywalker (Tatooine) figure.

The first thing a buyer will want to see is the product, so include a picture. Not all online auctions will allow sellers to put a large photo on the page, and not all buyers will be pleased about having to download a large image file. It is important that you learn how to use HTML to make a link to a larger, high-resolution picture (or better yet, use a thumbnail).

You can boost sales by showing off your item with a photograph. Since the condition of *Star Wars* collectibles is so important, it's crucial to provide your eBay auction buyers with an image of the item to allow the bidders to judge the condition for themselves. Many experienced eBay buyers will bypass an auction if it doesn't have a picture, and many auctions that have no pictures close without a sale or go for bargain prices. Be aware that there are a significant number of eBay sellers who surf eBay with the primary goal of snapping up poorly marketed items and then reselling them on eBay for a profit.

Make the description as clear as possible and do not waffle. If a buyer has to read 200 words about why the item is up for sale and the life history of the seller, chances are the buyer will move on to another auction. If there is any extra information that must be conveyed, be succinct—it is fine to tell buyers that the item will be sent by regular mail, but there is no need to tell them why.

Be up front about extra costs. If the cost of shipping and handling is known in advance, then include this in the auction. A buyer is more likely to make an impulse bid if all the necessary information is available.

When possible, give buyers a choice. Do not limit the number of payment methods to cash only because that will prevent all but the local *Star Wars* collector paying for the item. Offer as many shipping methods as possible and do not stick to just one courier firm. Just because there is a FedEx drop-off nearby, it should be considered that the buyer might prefer UPS instead.

Promote your item on eBay and to the *Star Wars* community. Make your item stand out by using eBay features such as bold or highlight or try putting a picture in the gallery. This adds a slight cost to the listing price, but it could catch the eye of a big spender. Many *Star Wars* collecting Web sites run occasional features on eBay auctions; for example, Rebelscum (www.rebelscum.com) has a daily column dedicated to highlighting interesting, unique, and unusual items for sale.

Finally, you might be able to sell more than one item at once. If you provided a clear and informative page on your item, the chances are high that a potential bidder will also look to see what other items you are selling. It is often convenient for a buyer to make more than one purchase from a single seller than to buy several items from multiple eBay sellers.

TOY SHOWS AND CONVENTIONS

The surefire way to make the most of your collection is to become a dealer yourself. In fact, many of today's biggest dealers are *Star Wars* collectors who began by selling off parts of their collection to upgrade their collection. If this becomes an appealing option, take the time to research prices, look at how other dealers sell their goods (boxed, bagged, and cased) and display their stock, and investigate where the best shows and conventions are held and how much a booth will cost. By having control over the costs and prices, and being aware of what the competition is stocking, a collector can make 100 percent of the current market price.

FLEA MARKETS AND GARAGE SALES

For many, selling at flea markets and garage sales is the first stepping stone to moving on to toy shows and eventually conventions. As with toy shows and conventions, research the various techniques that make for a successful booth. However, don't expect to make as much profit because customers won't have the level of interest in *Star Wars* that a convention crowd has, nor will they have the special knowledge necessary to understand what is available. To a member of the general public paying $10 for a brown lump of plastic might seem outrageous, but to a *Star Wars* collector $10 for a loose, complete C9 Wicket W. Warrick with staff and hood is a bargain!

COLLECTORS' CLUBS

Belonging to a collecting group is not only a good way to research prices and to find out what is currently riding high in the popularity stakes, but is also an educated market for the seller. Many collecting groups have a bring-and-buy aspect to their monthly meetings and annual get-togethers. Some even have guest dealers who bring in special items.

Terminology

The following are the most commonly used words and acronyms in valuing and selling *Star Wars* collectibles:

Baggies	Action figures sealed in bags, typically from mail-away promotions.
Blister	The plastic bubble that holds the toy to the cardback. (Also known as bubble.)
Cardback	The cardboard packaging onto which a plastic blister containing the toy would be attached. Most often, these are action figures, but a few Mini Rigs were produced on cardbacks instead of boxes.
CCG	Collectible Card Game: A turn-based card game where players have their own personal customized decks instead of playing from a common deck (*see also* Trading Card Game).

CW
Clone Wars: The toy line produced by Hasbro in 2003 and 2004 to span the gap between *Attack of the Clones* and Episode 3, and to tie in with the Expanded Universe Clone Wars spin-off series of books, computer games, comics, and television cartoons.

DT
Double-Telescoping Lightsaber: An early version of the $3^3/_4$-inch lightsaber accessory that had a double action of telescoping, meaning that there are two stages of extension. Not to be confused with the common single-telescoping lightsaber.

eBayer
Someone who buys/sells on eBay (also eBuyer—someone who buys on eBay).

Ep1
Episode 1: The packaging line produced by Hasbro in 1999 and 2000 to tie in with *The Phantom Menace*.

FB
Flashback: The packaging toy line produced by Hasbro to bridge the gap between the Power of the Force 2 toy line and Ep1/*The Phantom Menace* toy line.

Hanger
A double-sided display card intended to be hung from the ceiling over a display area.

HC
Hardcover: A book bound in cloth, cardboard, or leather rather than paper.

Header card
Part of an in-store display system that could be hung from the ceiling or attached to the top of a shelf or to the back of a bin.

HTF
Hard to Find: An item that is elusive is considered hard to find. Not to be confused with rare.

Inserts
The cardboard (typically corrugated) inside a box that holds the toy in place. Can also include sticker sheets, instructions, and any catalogs or brochures placed inside the packaging.

Last 17
Refers to the final release of figures in Europe, all of which only appeared on the Tri-logo cardback. The term is often confused with Power of the Force, which, in the United States only included fourteen figures. Though counted as a POTF figure, the American assortment never included Yakface.

Loose
An item that is no longer contained in any packaging.

Mail-away
Items offered by companies as premiums through sending in redeemable proof of purchases.

Micro Collection
The packaging toy line of 1-inch-scale miniatures produced by Kenner between 1982 and 1983.

OTC   Original Trilogy Collection: The packaging toy line produced by Hasbro in 2004 to coincide with the release of the Original Trilogy on DVD format.

P   Punched: An action figure blister card that has not had the card from the hanging hole removed. Conversely, UP (unpunched) indicates a blister card that has not had its hole opened, but because punched cards are far more common than unpunched, this reference is never used.

Packaging   The wrapping or container in which an item is presented for sale.

PB   Paperback: A book having a flexible paper binding.

Pegwarmer   An item that sits on the hanging pegs or shelves for a long duration of time because it is unpopular or overstocked.

POP   Point of Purchase: In-store displays that are intended to be positioned next to the product. Hangers, shelf talkers, and headers are all point-of-purchase displays.

POTF   Power of the Force: The packaging toy line produced by Kenner in 1985 that encompassed characters and vehicles from the original *Star Wars* trilogy.

POTF2   Power of the Force 2: The packaging toy line produced by Kenner/Hasbro between 1995 and 2000.

POTJ   Power of the Jedi: The packaging toy line produced by Hasbro between 2000 and 2002.

Rare   An item that is in short supply and difficult to get hold of is considered rare. This term can be subjective because one person's idea of rare may not match that of another person.

Rehash   An item that has been reissued with a minor modification to the item or packaging.

Reproduction Are items meant to look identical to one that has been produced under license. Typically, these are weapons and accessories (Double-Telescoping Lightsabers and blasters), blisters, dioramas, and cardbacks. Initially, they were meant to act as temporary replacements for missing parts, but nowadays they are used to dishonestly replace vintage parts and accessories. Also known as repro.

Rerelease   An item that has been reissued without any changes to it or its packaging.

ROTJ   *Return of the Jedi*: The third movie in the original *Star Wars* trilogy. Also the packaging toy line made by Kenner between 1983 and 1984.

Saga The collector-coined term for the unified packaging toy line produced by Hasbro between 2002 and 2004.

SOTE Shadows of the Empire: An Expanded Universe story line that bridged *The Empire Strikes Back* and *Return of the Jedi*. It was accompanied by a number of books, computer games, comics, and toy lines.

ST Star Tours: An interactive Expanded Universe simulator ride based on aspects of the original *Star Wars* trilogy; found at several Disney parks worldwide. Also a packaging line produced by a number of manufacturers between 1987 and 2004.

SW *Star Wars*: The original and alternate title used to refer to *A New Hope*. Also the packaging toy line made by Kenner between 1978 and 1979.

TCG Trading Card Game: A turn-based card game where players have their own personal customized decks instead of playing from a common deck (*see also* Collectible Card Game).

TESB *The Empire Strikes Back*: The second movie in the original *Star Wars* trilogy. Also the packaging toy line produced by Kenner between 1980 and 1982.

TPB Trade Paperback: A book that is typically of better production quality, larger size, and higher price than a mass-market edition and is intended for sale in bookstores. Specifically, it is a bound collection of comic books to encompass all or part of a story line.

TPM *The Phantom Menace*: The first movie of the prequel *Star Wars* trilogy.

5 RESTORATION

Just like Han Solo, every *Star Wars* collectible has a price on its head and how large that price is comes down to two factors: rarity and condition. Scarcity of an item is beyond the control of 99 percent of the collecting community, but its condition is not. Obviously, the better the condition a collectible is in the more value it will retain, so it is always a good idea to preserve your collectibles to keep them in the best condition possible.

Building up a *Star Wars* collection takes more than an education in toy history and more than an intimate knowledge of trading cards or knowing the ins and outs of collecting posters. A long-term collector must consider his or her *Star Wars* collectibles in the same way a museum curator would take care of a fine art collection. When it comes to making the most of your collection, it is a good idea to decide whether to be a restorer (by repairing any damage) or a conservator (preserve existing damage and prevent any more from occurring).

To many collectors, the existing condition of an item is the natural state of the collectible, and repairing any damage only detracts from the piece. Other collectors like to see their investments in as good a condition as possible, and if that means the addition of outside materials to an item to make it as pristine as possible, it is okay. In a way, it is like the old adage of owning a broom for twenty years, but despite changing the brushes five times and the handle eight times it is the same brush. Each collector has to decide whether he or she wants the broom he or she bought twenty years ago, or the broom to look as it did when it was first purchased.

Restoration and Value

Just as beauty is in the eye of the beholder, so is value. While removing price stickers, repairing blisters, and flattening warped packaging are acceptable means of improving the value of a *Star Wars* item, going too far, such as touching up chipped paint and recarding figures, can affect how original a piece is—and doing so without telling a prospective owner is fraudulent.

The key to restoring any *Star Wars* collectible is to make the work as subtle as possible and as sympathetic to the original item as you can. Of course, not all of us have the necessary expertise and materials to make a perfect repair, but there are a few techniques that can be employed for both vintage and modern collectibles.

Cleaning Toys

Years of being played with, and then having cobwebs and dust added to a toy does not make for an attractive piece.

Regular household dust mostly consists of dead skin cells and carpet lint, so unless a collection is hermetically sealed, keeping dust away is impossible. However, keeping a collection, particularly plastic toys, clean of dust is relatively easy through regular housekeeping. A feather or electrostatic duster will keep a collection dust-free. Once it is clean, wipe the surfaces down with a damp cloth and then apply a household polish to display surfaces. Be careful not to get the polish on any collectibles because the chemicals in the polish can damage plastics.

General grime from handling is just as easy to solve. In most cases, soaking an action figure in a bucket of lukewarm water, with a touch of dish soap, should suffice for getting rid of surface dirt. A light scrubbing with a toothbrush will get rid of any deeper soiling. Another technique is to leave the plastic item in a jar of water with a denture cleaning tablet. After the tablet has finished effervescing, wipe the figure down with a cloth and then rinse any cleaning residue away. The use of a dishwasher is not recommended because the heat of the water will damage the plastic, as will the caustic chemicals in dishwasher detergent.

Areas that have been excessively handled can contain oily and sugar-based layers passed on from young hands. In such a case, use a mild alcohol (such as isopropyl alcohol, which can be purchased at most pharmacies) to soften the dirt. Isopropyl alcohol can also be used to remove ink stains from most plastics, but if the plastic has had years to absorb the stain into the plastic, there is little chance that the deeper stain can be removed.

Any action figure with batteries or any kind of electronics in it should not be soaked: those figures should be only be cleaned on the surface. It is always wise to remove batteries to prevent damage from acid leaks. If this should occur, use a fine-grade sandpaper to lightly scour the surface. You can also use sandpaper to keep the metal contacts clean as well.

A frequent problem with vintage figures, especially Stormtroopers, is the yellowing of white plastic. There are two causes to this: cigarette smoke, which leaves a magnolia-colored patina on the plastic, and ultraviolet light in sunlight, which affects the molecular structure of the plastic. UV exposure is irreversible and because of the nature of the plastics used in the toy industry, yellowing with age is common.

Another common complaint from collectors is the smell that loose action figures can pick up, which is also often related to houses with smokers. To resolve this issue, place the smelly toys in a large plastic box with a lid and add a small bowl with a couple of tablespoons of baking soda. Leave with the box closed for a few days and the smells will have been absorbed by the baking soda.

Replacing Parts

Repairing damaged toys and action figures (whether they are $3^3/4$-inch or 12-inch scale) is cheap and simple. Since action figures, vehicles, and play sets are made in the same way today (and quite often using the exact same molds) as they were twenty-five years ago, restoration tips for old and new are the same.

The most common problem with toys is missing or damaged parts, such as weapons and accessories, or body parts (typically arms and faces). A surefire way to restore a lost or damaged weapon or accessory is to replace it. Many specialty stores (both in retail stores and online) have a small collection of replacement weapons, accessories, and small parts. One source that is particularly good for replacement vintage parts is The Earth (www.theearthtoymall.com). It sells a wide range of reasonably priced pieces. EBay is also another place to look, but vintage parts tend to be highly sought after and go for a premium. For the most part, modern replacement components are cheaper and easier to find. The best place to start looking is at Hasbro itself: it offers a free replacement service through its customer care number or Web site (www.hasbro.com). However, Hasbro only stocks current items and once a toy is retired excess parts are soon depleted. The next place to check is flea markets and then specialty and comic book stores, where broken toys often end up. Many collectors use eBay to sell redundant sections of their collections that might have just the part you need.

There are millions of *Star Wars* action figures in various states of repair in existence, so replacing missing body parts is often easier than replacing a missing play set or vehicle parts. Again, use flea markets, specialty stores, and eBay (and Hasbro if it is a modern item) to locate a suitable loose figure. Once the required limb is in your possession, use the boil-and-pop method of limb removal. For more detailed instructions on action figure transplants, visit the Forgotten Force Ultimate Resource Guide (www.ffurg,com).

Since original parts are often expensive, especially for vintage figures, many people turn to nonoriginal parts called reproductions. For many collectors, the inclusion of reproduction parts is a taboo, but for some collectors it is a necessary evil. (It is always a good idea to keep track of which parts are reproductions in case the item is going to be sold later.)

Decal Repair

Most *Star Wars* $3^3/4$-inch vehicles, as well as many other items, are decorated with decals but because of general wear and tear the stickers often get torn, dirtied, or fall off.

To clean a decal, wipe it with a damp swab or tissue, but be sure not to rub it too hard or get it too wet because this could ruin the decal. Once clean, pat it dry immediately. It is possible to remove decals, but soaking it in water is not the recommended method because this will ruin the paper it is printed on. Instead, use a mild cleaning alcohol (but not surgical spirits) or a water and vinegar mix to slowly dissolve the adhesive. Once the decal is free, dry it flat on a towel to dry any trapped moisture.

If the condition of the decal is beyond saving, the only options are to remove the decal and go without or to replace it. Leaving an item without a decal renders it incomplete, so most collectors will look to replace the damaged sticker. Some vintage specialist shops, such as The Earth, have small stocks of sticker sheets, but they are becoming rarer and more expensive with each passing day. The only other two alternatives are to buy another item with better stickers, or to use reproduction stickers. The reproduction stickers can generally be found on the Internet (e.g., www.erikstormtrooper.com and www.gadders.com).

Refurbishing Packaging

This is a more difficult step to make because repairing damage to packaging has a stronger impact on the originality of the item. Making alterations to the physical state of packaging is a last resort, and a collector who is faced with repairing damaged card stock should consider two things: is the repair essential and will the item be sold at a later date? In the eyes of the *Star Wars* collecting community, making such changes is acceptable to a point, as long as the item isn't being repaired to be sold as an original piece. Conventional wisdom says that if the piece is going to stay in the owner's collection, then any repairs made should be noted, fully described, and cataloged for future reference.

If it is a case of just making sure that the good condition of the card is going to last another few decades, the route of least impact is to make an insert of stiff, acid-free card to support the thinner packaging. Do not use corrugated cardboard because it has a higher acidity that will ultimately damage the card.

In most cases, tears are permanent and must not be seen as an invitation to fix the damage. At the end of the day, a tear should only mean one thing to a collector: Be careful when handling the box. Tears can be treated by adding tape, but this does not repair the rip, it just prevents it from extending any further. If adding tape is unavoidable, it should be done where it makes the least visual impact on the packaging, typically inside the box itself.

The greatest danger in adding tape to cardboard is that it will further add to the damage. Cellophane tape has a tendency to yellow and become brittle with age, which has the effect of staining the card and adding adhesive residue to the card. Staining can be removed using chemical bleaching agents, but since these can be harmful to organic substances (such as the cardboard and the user) they are not recommended. If a packaged item is worth the expense, it is advisable to use a professional toy or poster repairer. Removing tape residue, on the other hand, is a less risky prospect and can be done simply using several techniques that are outlined later in this chapter.

Another common packaging problem, especially vintage boxes that used thin cardstock and did not have the heavy, corrugated card that modern toys have today, is warping. Over the intervening years, most *Star Wars* collectibles have been stored in attics where moisture can get in, and compounded with heat rising from domestic boilers and appliances, most cardboard will warp. Fortunately, this is easy to remedy, and all it takes is a steam iron, several heavy books, and time. By using a small amount of steam, you can iron the card on a flat and solid surface to remove most of the warping. To ensure that the warp doesn't return, place a cloth over the cardboard surface (preferably on the plain/nonprinted side) and put four or five pounds of heavy books evenly across the cloth. Left for two weeks, the warp should be permanently removed from the card.

Card Revival

Carded action figures, while not as numerous as loose toys, form one of the biggest areas of the *Star Wars* collecting hobby. Unfortunately, a collecting *Star Wars* culture did not exist in the late 1970s and early 1980s, so most children didn't spare a thought for the cards their action figures came on. Thankfully, there are some easy techniques that can be employed to repair most of the common complaints of cardback collectors.

The main problem found in vintage cards is tearing and folding. Making repairs to tears using tape is not recommended because there are no hidden surfaces to cardbacks, and this will ruin the aesthetics of the card. Furthermore, tape that is removed from a card will only further damage the print. Folding is a problem that is more or less permanent and can only be partially treated. Just like warping (when moisture causes the cardback to curl), folding can be dealt with by using a light steam iron and then pressing for a week or two. Unfortunately, the damage to the print caused by the folding cannot be remedied.

Another issue with cardbacks is the adornment of price stickers. This is common on carded figures from the mid-1980s when retailers were trying to clear their *Star Wars* stocks and used large stickers to display clearance prices. Even though the adhesives used had low tensile strengths (in other words they peeled off easily), years of bonding and chemical decay has practically welded these decals onto vintage cards.

There are several methods of removing the stickers. Use a chemical release agent like Goo-Gone, made by Magic American (www.magicamerican.com). Mix the cleanser with some water and apply by dipping a Q-tip into the solution and dabbing it on to the sticker. Do not rub the paper while it is wet as this can cause the cardstock to tear. As the adhesive softens, use a fingernail or tweezers to pluck the edge of the sticker off the card and slowly peel it away. The same process can be performed with a hair dryer to soften the adhesive. If using a hair dryer, do not expose the card to long durations of heating, because this can warp the cardstock. Above all, be patient when using this method because it is the one most likely to cause tearing.

Dented or dinged blisters are another fault caused by neglect, and are all too common—even among modern carded figures. The first thing you need to know is that there is no method to totally remove a dent because an artifact will always remain, but there are ways to reduce the damage. One common technique is to take a piece of duct tape and roll it in on itself (sticky side out) and place the sticky side on the blister. Gently pull the tape away from the blister and draw the dent out. There are several other more extreme methods that are not necessarily any more effective in removing dents.

Other damages on card blisters are scuffs and scratches, and the only known trick to repairing these defects is to use some Tamiya Finishing Compound (www.tamiyausa.com). Dab some on a soft, dry polishing cloth that is lint free. Do not use paper towels because they are abrasive on soft plastics. Gently rub the cloth onto the blister in a circular motion to polish the surface.

Many vintage (and some modern) cards come with their proof of purchases (POP) removed because of mail-away promotions, but these can be restored using original parts (so no reproductions are necessary). First, scan or photocopy the card with the missing POP—if the original cardback has a messy hole, then trim the edges with a modeling knife first. Make a template from the copy by carefully cutting out the area where the POP is missing using a modeling knife. Lay this template over a cardback with an intact POP and trace the cut out area onto the complete cardback to mark out the POP hole. Use the modeling knife to cleanly cut out the POP to have an exact duplicate of the missing POP from the damaged card. Now lightly brush the edge of the POP with a thin coating of white glue and fix the POP into the hole, which will fit like a jigsaw piece. Wipe off any excess glue and allow to dry.

Clothing and Plush Maintenance

While clothing on action figures and plush dolls make up a small percentage of *Star Wars* collectibles, it is still an area that cannot be ignored.

In the case of the cloth items (particularly 12-inch toys), it is never safe to assume that the manufacturer made the clothing with treated material, so it is best to hand wash the fabric in tepid water with a mild detergent. This will prevent the colors from running and the material from shrinking. While denture tablets work well on plastics, it is not safe to use them on cloth. It is also important to rinse the wet item thoroughly to get rid of any detergents that can damage plastic later on. Never wring the cloth outfit either. Wringing can distort the material and damage the threads, which will cause the clothing to become ill fitting and reduce its lifespan. Instead, put the clothing between two folded towels and firmly press downward to squeeze any moisture out, just as if you were drying silk.

Plush items, and those with fur, are notoriously difficult to keep in good condition. To start with, wash the faux fur with a mild shampoo (baby shampoo works well) and warm water to soften up the strands. Be careful not to kneed the hair or rub vigorously, because this can uproot the strands from the "scalp" and create balding. Once the fur has been thoroughly washed, remove any tangles with a coarse comb, carefully picking out any knots. Comb it gently so as not to damage the nylon. To dry, pat the plush with a towel—don't rub or else your vintage Ewok could have a permanent bad hair day.

Another sore spot with plush items is that they can absorb household smells such as cooking and cigarette smoke. To rid your plush doll of odors, place it in a bag that contains an old sock full of cedar wood shavings and potpourri. The chips will absorb any smells and the potpourri will add a fragrance that will cover up any remaining aromas.

Repairing Posters and Trading Cards

Genuine *Star Wars* movie posters tend to be high-end collectibles and so should be treated by a professional. Check your local yellow pages or the Internet for suitably experienced poster restoration companies. These same firms can also return faded and worn trading cards to an almost mint condition, but while it is worth doing so with early baseball cards, Topps *Star Wars* trading cards have not yet reached the kinds of values that would warrant this type of specialist and costly treatment.

Terminology

The following are the most commonly used terms in repairing and restoring *Star Wars* collectibles:

Card surface tear Noticeable rip or tear of the paper, cardboard, print, or ink of the card surface. May occur on either the card front or back. Most commonly caused by the removal of a price tag or sticker. Other causes include removal of store stickers, antitheft devices, or special offer stickers.

Cardback The cardboard packaging onto which a plastic blister containing the toy would be attached. Most often, these are action figures, but a few Mini Rigs were produced on cardbacks instead of boxes.

Corner curl One of the most frequent flaws found with modern carded action figures. Since most of the cards are square or rectangular or have angular edges, corners can be easily curled up because of poor shipping, shelf wear, poor storage, or improper handling. Corners generally curl at approximately a 45-degree angle.

Crack (blister) In terms of a blister, a crack is a noticeable fracture, crevice, split, or chiplike flaw in the plastic covering of the action figure but does not include the separation of the bubble from the card itself (though cracks may be present along the boundary of the separation).

Crack (card) In terms of the card, a crack occurs when part of the print or ink is removed or damaged. Usually occurs because of a crease or fold, but may also occur spontaneously because of improper exposure to light or heat.

Crease A severe curl or bend that leaves a permanent mark or crinkle on the print or ink. A crease can occur without completely cracking or removing the print or ink. Severe creases may allow portions of the underlying cardboard to show through.

Curl A bend in the cardboard that doesn't damage the print or the ink.

Decal An adhesive paper or plastic sticker used to decorate an item.

Dent An indentation or concave section of the clear plastic bubble not originally intended by the manufacturer. May or may not be accompanied by a whitening of the clear plastic.

Ding Similar to a dent, but on a smaller scale. May or may not be accompanied by a whitening of the clear plastic.

Fraying When cardboard fiber is pulled apart or stretched, individual fibers begin to show, giving a fuzzy impression to the cardboard (at the edges especially). Nonfrayed cardboard is usually tightly packed and firm.

Inserts The cardboard (typically corrugated) inside a box that holds the toy in place. Can also include sticker sheets, instructions, and any catalogs or brochures placed inside the packaging.

Packaging The wrapping or container in which an item is presented for sale.

Proof of purchase A blue-and-white disc printed on vintage Kenner cardbacks that was used as part of mail-away offers. (Also known as POP but not to be confused with point of purchase.)

Reformed Some blister defects can be at least superficially corrected by gently re-shaping the bubble by hand. This includes popping out small dents or reshaping dings. Many times, this reformation is evident in a whitening of the clear plastic.

Reproduction Items that are meant to look identical to one that has been produced under license. Typically, these are weapons and accessories (Double-Telescoping Lightsabers and blasters), blisters, dioramas, and card-backs. Initially, they were meant to act as temporary replacements for missing parts, but nowadays they are used to dishonestly replace vin-tage parts and accessories. Also known as repro.

Separation Since blisters are affixed to card in some manner, there is a chance that they can become detached. Some blisters are detached (at least par-tially) from the card to remove the figure inside. Conversely, these fig-ures can also be replaced at a later time.

Staining A permanent discoloration of the card or bubble because of contact with some foreign substance. Usually caused by a liquid of some type but may also be the result of contact with other materials (e.g., plastic, rubber, etc.). Separate from bubble or card yellowing, which may occur without contact with any foreign substances.

Sticker sheet The sheet of adhesive paper on which decorative decals are printed.

Tape repair Occasionally, scotch tape (or other type of tape adhesive) is used to re-pair a card or reseal a bubble. Some types of tape may be removed with-out further damage. Some tapes themselves can damage the surface of the card or bubble, even if not removed.

Warping A curving of packaging material caused by moisture.

6 PRESERVATION

Most *Star Wars* collectors spend a considerable amount of time, energy, and money building their ideal collection. Displaying and preserving that collection are two topics that go hand in hand and can often be one of the most rewarding aspects of this hobby.

Of course, the first and foremost problem collectors run into is space—how much do they have and how can they use it effectively. Whether displaying their entire collection or just some individual pieces, collectors should always be aware of their surroundings and should make an effort to work within them as efficiently as possible. Few collectors can have an entire house dedicated to their *Star Wars* collection and many, in fact, are lucky to have just one room! This problem can be further compounded if the collector is either renting or sharing the living space. If renting, especially a small apartment, one can be seriously limited as to what kind of display that can be set up. However, it is possible, even in the most cramped conditions to set up a quality display—it's all about choosing the right kind of displays that best suit your lifestyle.

Low-End Furniture

A good display doesn't have to start with a bank account and unlimited finances, because there are many inexpensive and effective ways to display a collection without costly purchases.

Cardboard store display shelves can often be had for free when stores have finished with a particular promotion. These shelves may be a good way to organize items, but they aren't sturdy and the cardboard may contain high levels of acid that can be detrimental to a collection.

Thanks to Todd Chamberlain and Josh Ling, who made a presentation on this subject at Celebration II in 2002 and have allowed me to use their notes as the basis for much of the information given in this chapter.

Inexpensive used furniture can be found at thrift stores and garage sales. Even though it may be difficult to have a matching set of furniture this way, it's a great inexpensive way to set up your collection, especially if you're renting a small place. Old store fixtures can often be found when stores are going out of business. Usually, these fixtures can be had for a few dollars (or even free!) and when fixed up they can be made into attractive display units. Keep an eye on your local newspaper for bankruptcy auctions or find local commercial furniture liquidators who deal in store fixtures.

Purchasing "as-is" or floor model display units from stores that carry furniture is another way of getting sturdy, attractive furniture for a good price. They might need a little repair but often the quality of the furniture is still greater than the reduced price would suggest.

Midrange Furniture

Often, collectors want something more sturdy and attractive than second-hand furniture, and luckily the home improvement revolution has supplied plenty of options.

Plastic ventilated shelving, rubber-coated metal shelving, and Gorilla Racks (www.rapidrack. com) are popular, inexpensive ways to both store and display collectibles, but unfortunately they are not aesthetically pleasing.

Particle or pressboard shelving with laminate surfaces can be found at most major big box department stores, such as IKEA, Wal-Mart, Home Depot, and Target. These displays are both attractive and affordable, so it's possible to buy several to have a running theme. Chain stores that specialize in home furnishings offer a wide range of display cabinets and curio cupboards that are designed for displaying collections. The prices on these items can range from moderate to expensive.

Bespoke Displays

Custom display cases made to fit a specific room can be expensive to design and build, but there are few ways to better showcase a collection. Of course, it's best to own your own property before pursuing this avenue.

Designing and building a theme area for your collection is probably the most expensive and impressive way to display a collection. Again, it's best to own your own property when doing a set-up such as this and if this is something you're considering doing, be prepared to shell out hundreds of dollars. Still, nothing will beat displaying your collection in a room based on the interior of an Imperial Star Destroyer!

Preservation Enemies

When displaying your collection, you must also make sure that you're taking the proper steps to preserve it at the same time. Whether you collect toys, food premiums, props, posters, or any of the other numerous *Star Wars* collectibles, it's important that your collection stays in mint condition. Many outside influences we may take for granted can actually be detrimental to a collection, and collectors need to be aware of what these elements are and how to prevent them from irreversibly affecting their collection.

The basic enemies to any collection are heat, light, dust, moisture, cigarette smoke, and pests. Although most of these factors may seem impossible to control, there are specific guidelines collectors should follow that can help protect their collections from these external influences:

Temperature: Collections kept in hot conditions, such as an attic, are at greater risk of succumbing to plastic deterioration, discoloring, warping, and general breakdown. Ideally, the room that a collection is stored in should be between 60 and 70 degrees Fahrenheit and should have a relative humidity of about 50 percent.

Light: Both sunlight and certain types of artificial light can be damaging to collections. Exposure to these elements can cause severe fading and discoloration. The room should have as few windows as possible to avoid exposure to both heat and light. If windows are present in the room, it's best to either purchase UV-resistant windows or apply a UV-resistant filter and cover the windows with heavy dark curtains. Avoid using fluorescent lights to light your collection room, as these lights can be as damaging as sunlight. Using incandescent or low-wattage lights is best.

Dust: Like heat and light, prolonged exposure to dust will cause plastics and paper goods to deteriorate prematurely. Air filters on a home furnace or negative ion filters in a collection room can greatly reduce the amount of dust a collection is exposed to. If this is too costly an addition, then simply keeping your collection area dusted and swept or vacuumed is the only other effective way to control dust.

Moisture: Paper-based collectibles exposed to moisture, whether in large or small doses, will permanently become warped and discolored. Obviously, not storing a collection in a basement or noninsulated outside storage is a surefire way to avoid moisture damage, but some collectors may not have much of a choice. Dehumidifiers are the best way to combat air moisture and can be found at many home improvement centers. Failing that, using moisture traps made of pouches of silica gel (those small packets of translucent grains that often come packed with electrical goods) is a much cheaper solution, though these can only absorb a finite amount of moisture and will need regular replacement.

Cigarette smoke: This is possibly the easiest deteriorating effect to avoid and still, many collectors insist on smoking around their collections. Cigarette smoke can cause plastics to yellow and become brittle and leaves behind a distinct odor that is difficult to get rid of. Aside from not smoking near the collectibles, air purifiers are an inexpensive way to reduce the amount of smoke in the atmosphere. Many of these devices come with negative ion filters and air fresheners built into them.

Pests: Insects such as silverfish and rodents like mice or rats can make short work of any paper-based collection such as boxed or carded action figures and posters. Take immediate steps to remove these pests at their first appearance. Keeping your collection off the floor will help minimize exposure to pests and flooding. If your collection is kept in a basement, purchase a ball valve for the floor drainage pipe. Should the water in the drainage pipe start to rise, this valve will seal off the hole and prevent flooding.

While the general guidelines outlined here may help prevent some of the most basic forms of damage, there are, of course, specific steps collectors can take to protect particular items in their collection and at the same time display them in an eye-catching manner.

Safeguarding Action Toys

Vintage and modern action figures and toys are some of the most widely collected types of *Star Wars* memorabilia. Even in this particular genre, there are several subgenres that people focus on. As such, finding ways to protect and display all the different types of toys can be a serious undertaking.

The most convenient way to preserve loose items, such as action figures, play sets, and vehicles, is to avoid as many of the enemies of preservation as possible. Most collectors use Mylar bags for storage (which is what comic book collectors use) and cases made from acrylic to both display and preserve their items.

Preserving carded action figures, one of the most highly sought-after areas of *Star Wars* collecting, is an easy task. There are specific materials made for just this purpose. Mylar bags come in a variety of sizes, including ones large enough to hold most carded figures. Adding a backboard will further ensure the item's safety. Soft cases, such as those made by Protech (Star Cases) are inexpensive and specifically designed to house carded figures from both the vintage and modern eras. Hard plastic (acrylic) cases are also made to suitable sizes to protect carded figures. Toy Cases (www.toycases.com) sells a wide variety of acrylic cases for cardbacks.

Large boxed items such as $3^3/4$-inch vehicles (and some 12-inch-scale items) are more difficult to preserve. Many collectors rely on acrylic sheeting, which can be found in most major craft stores, and can be used to wrap up larger boxed toys, thereby protecting them from dust and moisture. However, acrylic is a plastic that can degrade with time and should not be considered a permanent means of protecting packaged collectibles. Though more commonly used for protecting carded action figures, acrylic cases can be employed to preserve large boxed items as well. Because acrylic is significantly stronger than cardboard, these cases can also be used to display items. Since they are costly, most collectors choose only to use them for prized possessions. One such company is Oscar's Cases (www.kennertoys.com/cases), which can make custom acrylic cases to almost any size. Shrink-wrapping is another effective method of protecting items from dust and moisture. There are, however, several downsides to shrink-wrapping machines. They can be expensive to purchase and many larger items simply may not fit. Even more important, the heat from the shrink-wrapping gun can cause damage to the item you're trying to protect.

Posters and Store Displays

Because of their sheer size, collecting, displaying, and storing posters and store displays can be a challenge for collectors, but there are several effective ways to manage these types of collections.

Cardboard items such as point of purchase store displays are best stored vertically and because many display pieces are made of acidic corrugated cardboard, they can contaminate items that come in contact with them. As such, a plastic sleeve should be used.

If possible, store posters flat and not rolled. An engineer's blueprint drawer case is a perfect but expensive solution and may be hard to come by. If a poster must be rolled, place it inside a protective sleeve and then inside a cardboard poster tube.

Do not dry mount posters or displays. Dry mounting fundamentally alters the original state of the piece, thus making it virtually worthless. Framing is the preferred choice.

Framing

Framing is an effective way to both display and protect items in your collection. Most notably used for posters and artwork, framing can also be used for display headers, card and box proofs, cromalins, photo art, animation cels, storyboards, and virtually any other two-dimensional collectible. There are three types of framing options available to choose from: basic, semiprofessional, and archival, and it's important to determine what style of framing will best suit your needs.

Basic framing offers an inexpensive way to display your collectibles and do-it-yourself style frames can be purchased at most major department stores. In most cases, basic frames do little to actually preserve an item and sometimes may actually do more harm to a collectible than good. Low-end, easily replaceable collectibles that you simply wish to display and not preserve would best suit this type of option.

Semiprofessional framing is typically offered by several arts and crafts chains and tends to offer a middle-of-the-road approach to framing. Items displayed this way may look aesthetically pleasing, but generally these types of framing outlets do not specialize in archival framing methods and some of the supplies they use, such as regular mattes and double sided tape, may actually damage the collectible over time. Like basic framing, low- to midrange collectibles would be best suited for this type of framing.

Archival framing involves taking your collectible to a professional framer who specializes in using methods and materials that are designed to ensure an item's preservation. Acid-free mattes prevent any discoloration of the item and clear, acid-free corner tabs eliminate the need for any double-sided tape. Most professional framers also offer UV resistant glass that helps prevent the occurrence of any unnecessary light damage. Professional framing can be expensive but when dealing with any range of collectibles, especially high-end pieces that aren't easily replaceable, many collectors believe that the piece of mind is definitely worth the price paid.

Coins

Collectible coins are not found in great numbers in most *Star Wars* collections, but a number of items have been produced over the decades that included exclusively minted collector coins.

Framed LGDE display header
(Image courtesy of Curtis Comeau)

While many chose to keep them intact with the packaging they came in, there are still many of these coins available loose, and as such should be stored appropriately.

Coin shops specialize in coin collecting supplies and offer a wide variety of preservation options. One of the most popular ways to store coins is in plastic binder sleeves. These sleeves have many individual coin pockets on each page that protect the coins and allow both sides to be seen. When stored in binders, they take up little space. Having a set of coins custom framed to show both sides of the coins is another effective way of both displaying and preserving a coin collection.

Comics

The science of comic book storage is nearly a half-century older than the first *Star Wars* collectible, and *Star Wars* collectors have always turned to the comic book community for help. There are three catalysts that cause damage to comic books: chemical degradation (caused by the inks and low-quality paper used in most comic books from the 1970s and 1980s), mechanical damage (from wear and tear through general handling), and environmental factors (such as those that will affect anything else in a *Star Wars* collection).

Because of production practices, chemical degradation is almost impossible to avoid. Thankfully, the dyes used in inks and the quality of paper have improved over the past decade, and this should mean that today's comic books will not be as susceptible to this kind of damage. However, because the timescale is still open, there is no way of knowing exactly how modern inks and paper will fare.

Mechanical damage is easier to prevent through correct techniques. The key to protecting comics from mechanical damage is to put them in plastic bags (Mylar is better than polythene, which degrades more quickly) with a card backboard. A collector would be hard pressed not to find a comic store that doesn't stock these. Bagged comic books should be stored in specially sized boxes, also available from most comic stores, and stored vertically rather than horizontally. Alternatively, comics can be stored in punched Mylar envelopes that can be clipped into three-ring binders (both made by Ultra-PRO, www.ultra-pro.com).

The same environmental enemies (sunlight, heat, moisture, etc.) that will damage plastic action toys will affect comic books as well and can be combated in the same way. With comic books, it is particularly important to store them away from moisture—but do not make the mistake of keeping them as dry as possible or else the paper will desiccate and become brittle.

Trading Cards

All trading cards, whether they are made by Topps, Decipher, or Wizards of the Coast, suffer from the same maladies as other paper products, and so they must be treated in the same way. Chemical biodegradation, mechanical damage, and the environment are all factors in the downfall of collectible cards, but luckily the same solutions used in comic book collecting can be employed with trading cards.

Individual cards can be displayed in top-loading hard cases. These cases allow both sides of the card to be seen and offer a great deal of protection for higher-end cards. Collectible cards can also be stored in special card boxes that are similar to comic book long boxes, although considerably smaller. These boxes are acid free and stack easily, thereby cutting down on the amount of storage space needed. Most comic stores stock trading card sleeves, and companies such as Ultra-PRO sell archival binder sleeves online. These sleeves allow both sides of the card to be seen and take up little space when stored.

Trading cards should be stored out of direct sunlight and be kept in climate-controlled environments—and most important—sugary gum residues should be wiped away with a dry cloth to prevent mold and pests from being attracted.

Small Items, Food Premiums, and Ephemera

What would *Star Wars* collecting be without all the small, unclassified items that litter our collections? Just because an item seems inconsequential doesn't mean it doesn't deserve the care and attention that every other *Star Wars* product receives.

Paper goods, buttons, and patches are all small items than can be difficult both to display and to keep track of. Storing these items in special binder sleeves, page protectors, and foam-backed display cases is the ideal solution for preserving and organizing these types of collectibles. Look to companies like Avery (www.avery.com) and Ultra-PRO for these items.

Food items should be emptied of any liquids and biodegradable or corrosive contents to prevent leakage, mold, and pests. If possible, containers coming in contact with food or drinks should be washed and rinsed thoroughly before being displayed or stored.

Long-Term Storage

One of the unfortunate facts of collecting is that at some point or another it may be impossible to display some or even all of our collectibles. When confronted with this prospect, it's important to know how to pack and store your collection. The following are a few basic rules:

Always keep your collection stored in a cool, dry place, and avoid rooms that have do not have climate control.

Avoid packing your collection in corrugated cardboard boxes for any extended period. These boxes are highly acidic and may damage your collectibles over time. Plastic tubs are one of the safest ways to store your collection. They are sturdier than cardboard boxes and offer protection from moisture and pests.

Plastic stacking drawers offer almost the same degree of protection as plastic tubs. While there is still a chance of moisture affecting your collection, these drawers have one advantage over the plastic tubs: accessibility.

Fishing tackle boxes and hardware bins are a great way to keep action figures sorted with their original weapons while taking up little space in storage. The drawer style of these cases also makes retrieving figures much easier than if they were tucked away inside a tub.

Insurance

After building up a personal collection, the last thing a collector would ever want is for something to happen to it. Unfortunately, unforeseen circumstances such as theft, floods, or fires can come out of nowhere and alter or destroy our collections. Although the outcomes of these events can be devastating, it's always better to be one step ahead, and looking into insurance for your collection might be a good idea.

Like every other collector in the world, you have built your collection in a unique way. The first thing you need to do is ask yourself is: Is my particular collection worth insuring?

Smaller collections that are made up of inexpensive or easily replaceable items are probably not worth obtaining specific collectibles insurance for and are most likely covered by homeowners or renters insurance policies for replacement value only. Unfortunately, these basic policies do not cover any specific collectibles and insurance companies will offer to replace the lost items with *like* items. This means that when ascertaining the value of a vintage 12 Back Luke Skywalker, your insurance company will likely want to value it the same as a modern Luke Skywalker action figure that can be purchased at retail. This is certainly not an appealing prospect for vintage collectors whose collections contain rare and irreplaceable items.

Fortunately, there are two other options open to collectors. The first is to add a blanket valuable items rider to an existing homeowners or renters policy. This type of rider will cover a collection but only for a certain, predetermined amount that generally is capped at $5,000 to $10,000. Additionally, if there is a loss, the owner will have to pay out a deductible before making a claim. This type of policy is ideal for smaller collections.

The second and most popular option for those with high-end collections is to get specific collectibles insurance known as inland marine or floater policies. Several groups such as State Farm and the Collectibles Insurance Agency (www.collectinsure.com) do offer special insurance policies specifically for *Star Wars* and other types of high-dollar collections. Collectors will have to provide extensive documentation and itemized lists and have an appraisal done on their collections before insurance will be provided. Of course, there are also annual fees, but should there be a loss, a deductible won't have to be paid when making a claim.

Whichever policy you chose for your collection, before settling on any type of insurance, it's best to talk to an agent at length, because he or she can answer any questions you may have and will be able to point you to the best available coverage.

Terminology

The following are the most commonly used phrases and acronyms in preserving *Star Wars* collectibles:

Backboards   Cardstock boards used to stiffen and support polybags.

Mylar   A polythene plastic made by DuPont and commonly used in film processing, and known for its anti-degradation properties.

Polybag   A sealable pouch typically made of polythene.

Star Case   A type of plastic clamshell case used to protect carded 3¾" action figures.

Ultra-PRO   A manufacturer of high-grade Mylar storage sleeves.

7 REPRODUCTION AND FAKE ITEMS

Prices for *Star Wars* memorabilia, like many other collectibles, are in a constant state of ebb and flow. Despite these fluctuations, certain items—based on rarity, mythos, general appeal, or a combination thereof—will always command premium prices. Because of these factors and the basic laws of supply and demand, these types of *Star Wars* collectibles have either become too difficult to locate or have simply become too expensive for the average collector to afford. As a result, the hobby has started to see a rise in the production and proliferation of reproductions and fakes.

From patches to props, posters to prototypes and even carded and loose vintage action figures and accessories, reproductions and fakes have infiltrated virtually every facet of the hobby. Certainly, in this global marketplace of e-collecting, where items trade hands without the buyers being physically present to inspect their purchases, never has the old adage "buyer beware" been more important. For collectors looking to add *authentic* items to their collections without being swindled by a fake or reproduction, truly, the most essential tool at their disposal is knowledge.

It's important to note that while the original intent of a reproduction piece may seem to have philanthropic purposes, future owners may alter or misrepresent a reproduction to deceive potential buyers. If this should happen, it is dangerous to the hobby. This makes it all the more important for the creators of reproductions to ensure that their items are clearly identified and not easily tampered with.

While fakes have wormed their way into numerous facets of the hobby, there is no area where they have become more abundant than within the vintage action figure line. The following section will identify and examine some of the more commonly faked vintage items and will provide information to help identify the real deal from a real disaster.

Fake Weapons and Accessories

The majority of the action figures made during the vintage era were packaged with tiny weapons, weapons that were easily lost down heating vents, swallowed by younger siblings, or sucked up by unassuming vacuum cleaners. Ultimately, from a collecting standpoint, these missing weapons left many figures in an incomplete state and finding replacement weapons became a daunting task for many collectors. As a result, some of the first fake vintage items to hit the market were created to replace the original weapons that were becoming harder and harder for collectors to find.

Unfortunately, the sheer volume of fake weapons that have been produced has created a market glut where seemingly there are more fake weapons available than originals. While some people are content to own these fake weapons as placeholders, more often than not, these weapons are being passed off as real either by unknowing sellers or by people looking to make a fast buck off unknowing buyers. Fortunately, the majority of weapons, whether original or fake, sell for relatively little money and while buying a fake by mistake may sting, it's often better to be taken for $2 instead of $200 or $2,000.

Fake and original weapons are made of different plastics. When learning to tell the difference between fake and original weapons, it's best to have examples of each on hand. Fake weapons tend to feel harder, while original weapons feel slightly softer and have a slight degree of flexibility.

Another effective way of determining fake weapons from originals is by using what has become known as the "drop test." Again, for this test you will need a weapon you know to be a fake and one you know to be original. When dropped on a solid surface, each weapon will make a distinctly different sound. By becoming familiar with the different sounds fakes and originals make, you will effectively be able to use the drop test at any time.

Naturally, if the weapon in question has been molded in incorrect colors or has been repainted to hide an incorrect mold color, it is a fake. Most reproductions have been cast off the originals and lack their detail. Check for blotches—especially in handle grips. Poorer production techniques often leave flash lines. Look for these in tight corners. Pieces customized from original toys are often used as reproductions.

Collectors should note that some foreign figures, such as those that were produced in Brazil by Glasslite, came with weapons that were molded in colors that were different from the ones produced by Kenner. When dealing with loose foreign figures and weapons, it's best to know your source or the history of the items before making a purchase.

While the bulk of the weapons on the market are relatively inexpensive, there is an exception to the rule, involving the infamous Double-Telescoping (DT) Lightsabers. The DT sabers were originally released by Kenner with only the earliest Luke Skywalker, Darth Vader, and Obi-Wan Kenobi figures and were quickly swapped out for the standard single-piece sabers as a cost-saving measure. Because of his inclusion in the Early Bird set, Luke's DT saber is the easiest to find, but each of the three sabers are quite scarce and therefore command premium prices. Like many other big-ticket collectibles, the high price point and sheer scarcity of the

DT sabers has led to the creation of several types of fakes. Buyers interested in obtaining original examples need to be extra cautious before spending their hard earned money.

There are several unique factors inherent to DT lightsabers that can help aide in authentication. Original sabers should have three different mold points along the top of the outer saber and many have one or two letters molded onto the handle. Most sabers will not be in mint condition. The Obi-Wan sabers are particularly brittle but the inner piece of all three DT sabers will most likely be bent or even broken. All three types of DT sabers may be slightly faded when compared to single sabers. Fake DT sabers may be made by drilling out the center of an existing single-piece saber and inserting a thin piece of plastic down the center, but in person, the drilled portion of the saber should be easy to spot.

Recently, there have been some incredibly well-made, injection-molded fake DT sabers originating from the United Kingdom, which have made the task of identifying authentic DT sabers even harder. The best way to ensure you're truly buying an authentic DT saber is to buy from a reputable dealer or at the very least, to be able to easily track the saber's history. When in doubt, select reputable dealers that offer authentication services.

In addition to small weapons, a few of the original figures released under the *Star Wars* and *Empire Strikes Back* banners were issued with vinyl capes. These capes are quite fragile under the best circumstances, and heavy play conditions often left them torn, tattered, or quite simply destroyed. While the fragility of the capes was one factor that eventually led to them being faked in later years, it was the scarcity and desirability of the vinyl-caped Jawa that ultimately led to the reproduction of vinyl capes. Initially, when Kenner released the Jawa figure, it was released with a vinyl cape, much like that of Darth Vader, Obi-Wan Kenobi, and the Tusken Raider, but it was promptly changed early on in the figure's production to the more aesthetic cloth cape. Subsequently, the vinyl-caped Jawa became one of the earliest documented variations and its scarce nature quickly made both mint on card and loose examples fairly valuable. Needless to say, it was only a matter of time before fake examples of both surfaced on the market.

Reproduction Capes

All of the authentic vinyl capes that were originally released with figures are made of a soft, pliable vinyl and have two distinct surfaces. One side of the cape will be smooth while the other side features a crosshatch pattern. Even though this pattern can be made out with the naked eye, it can easily be seen with a magnifying glass. Additionally, the armholes of an original cape should fit tightly around the arms of the corresponding figure.

Fake capes may often match the color of an original but are usually made of a stiffer vinyl that isn't as easy to manipulate. The crosshatching pattern is often missing on fake capes and the armholes are generally larger than the armholes found on original examples.

Perhaps the most faked cape of all vintage action figures is the vinyl Jawa cape that came with the original issue of this figure. While forgers are becoming more adept at reproducing these pieces, there are still a few ways to spot a dud.

The cape on a loose vinyl-caped Jawa should match all of the characteristics of other original vinyl capes and the color of the cape should be almost indistinguishable from that of the Jawa itself. (It should be noted that the Australian vinyl-caped Jawas came with capes that are closer in color to those found on Obi-Wan Kenobi and are harder to differentiate.) Fake examples are often made from cut down Obi-Wan Kenobi capes. As such, the color will not be correct and the cut itself may be crooked.

Imitation Action Figures (Loose)

It seems hard to believe that, with Kenner producing each figure from the vintage line in incredibly large quantities, there would exist the need for fake loose action figures. There are literally millions of original loose figures available on the market today, yet, disturbingly enough, there are an alarming number of fake figures coming out of the "plasticwork."

Due to the mythos surrounding them and the higher prices they command, the majority of the fake loose figures on the market seem to be of Yak Face and Blue Snaggletooth. With a little patience, original examples of these figures can easily be obtained, yet for some reason, a market for fakes exists. If this trend continues, it is possible that we could see fake examples of other, more common figures surface and this could be dangerous for the future of the hobby.

When creating fake vintage figures on a small scale, it's nearly impossible to re-create the production techniques Kenner used to make the originals. Fakes are usually made from crude molds of the original figures and as such, they are often lacking many minute details and may be slightly smaller than their true vintage counterparts. Additionally, the quality and color of the plastic will be different and the figures themselves will most likely be hand painted and hand glued.

Imitation Action Figures (Carded)

Collecting carded action figures (figures still in their original packaging) is one of the most popular forms of vintage collecting. Like any collectible, the prices and availability of vintage carded figures depend on rarity and desirability. Most *Return of the Jedi* carded figures are overly abundant and can be had for a few dollars, but 12 backs, obscure packaging variations, or early carded examples of popular characters are often difficult to find and can command premium prices. High-quality printing machines and the availability of fake bubbles has led to the creation of fake carded figures, which often can be difficult to detect, especially when the buyer is presented with only a photograph.

Throughout the vintage line, Kenner employed high standards when it came to printing the cardbacks. As such, the images on an original cardback will be clear and crisp and luckily, no matter how good the printing techniques used for fakes have gotten, they still can't match the quality of an original.

Some of the fake carded figures on the market use cardstock that has been made by simply printing out the images of both the front and back of a card on two separate sheets of paper that are then glued to the front and back of a thin piece of cardboard. These types of fakes may be difficult to spot in a photograph but when compared to the original cardstock used by Kenner, they are easy to identify in person—particularly along the edges where the cardstock that is sandwiched between the front and back covers is white.

Another way to identify fake figures is by the punch tab, where the figure would have hung from the store peg. No vintage figures have the punch in the center of the top of the card and any that do are fakes.

Original vintage figures have distinct bubbles and bubble patterns. Many of the fake bubbles that have been introduced to the market are of one size (which is usually too large) and do not fit the figure correctly. With the exception of the Tri-logo releases, all original figures come with unique bubbles that fit closely around each individual character. If the figure is loose in the bubble, chances are it's a fake. Additionally, original bubbles will feature a waffle-type pattern around the seal where the bubble is attached to the card.

While there are several telltale ways to spot fake figures, collectors also need to be on the lookout for resealed figures. These are figures that employ original cardbacks and bubbles that have been reattached to one another. Fortunately, when the bubble is removed from the card, there should almost always be damage to the cardback and it's next to impossible to completely eliminate all signs of damage when doing a reseal. When trying to spot a resealed figure, look closely around the bubble area. If there is any indication of damage or any place where the graphics don't line up perfectly, then there's a good chance the figure has been resealed.

Prototype Copies

Because prototypes generally exist in low quantities and frequently have high price tags associated with them, they are considered by many to be the high-end collectibles of the vintage Kenner line. Unfortunately, the factors mentioned earlier have long been a beacon for shady characters and fake items representing various stages of Kenner's preproduction process have been introduced to the marketplace. Collectors need to be careful when purchasing prototype material and should do considerable homework on the subject before making any purchases.

When in the market for prototypes, there really is only one solid tip that can be offered: know the item's provenance. It's been through the efforts of a core group of individuals that much of Kenner's preproduction material has been saved and many of these items can be traced back to the finds made by these collectors. Buying items that can be traced back to these finds, or better yet, from these collectors themselves is one way of ensuring you don't get swindled. Purchasing from a reputable dealer who has previous experience in dealing in preproduction material is also a solid bet.

Collectors looking to collect hardcopy prototypes need to be familiar with the term "blue harvest." In the mid-1990s, several blue urethane hardcopies—commonly Micro Collection 4-ups—surfaced from a Kenner source and were sold as original vintage hardcopies. After much investigation, it was determined that blue urethane was not used by Kenner until 1989, long after the vintage line had been put to bed. Ultimately, these hard copies are nothing more

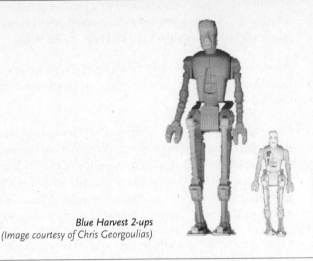

Blue Harvest 2-ups
(Image courtesy of Chris Georgoulias)

than fakes and any blue, vintage hardcopy on the market today is most likely from this blue harvest.

The previous list covers some of the more frequently faked *Star Wars* items, but collectors must remember that this list is by no means comprehensive. Much to the dismay of many in the hobby, new types of fakes and reproductions are turning up all the time and unfortunately they seem to be getting harder and harder to differentiate. It's up to the individual collector to stay on top of what kinds of fakes are surfacing, know how to spot them, and, most importantly, know how not to get ripped off. While this may seem an overwhelming prospect, there are avenues open to collectors that can aide in this task. Collecting graded items and buying from reputable dealers are two solid options that will ensure you don't end up buying a fake or reproduction. There are also numerous online forums where knowledgeable collectors from around the world network and are more than happy to help answer any questions you might have.

When it comes to fakes, remember, buyer beware, and if the deal seems too good to be true, it probably is.

Terminology

The following are the most commonly used words and acronyms in reproduction and fake *Star Wars* collectibles:

4-up   When Kenner developed the Micro Collection, it sculpted its models four times larger than they were intended to be produced at. The resulting hardcopies were therefore also four times the normal size and they are often referred to as 4-ups. They should not be confused with the original sculpt, which is never called a 4-up.

Blister   The plastic bubble that holds the toy to the cardback. (Also known as bubble.)

Blue harvest   The term used for a large number of fake prototype *Star Wars* items that appeared in the mid-1990s.

Bootleg   An unlicensed version of a preexisting, licensed product. Usually, a bootleg is a direct copy (albeit typically much shoddier in appearance) of its licensed counterpart. Unlike fakes or customs, bootlegs are made in factory environments to be sold in stores as *toys* and are not made specifically to mimic preexisting collectibles. Action figure toys are the most frequently bootlegged items.

Cardback   The cardboard packaging onto which a plastic blister containing the toy would be attached. Most often, these are action figures, but a few Mini Rigs were produced on cardbacks instead of boxes.

Cromalin   A color proof sheet of packaging is created using special colored powders on sensitized paper so that the copy and the balance of colors from the color separations can be studied and corrected, if necessary, before the actual press run.

Custom   Refers to a homemade toy and is commonly an action figure, vehicle, or play. Custom toys are made for the enjoyment of the individual and are not usually produced in larger quantities than one.

DT   Double-Telescoping Lightsaber: An early version of the $3^3/_4$-inch lightsaber accessory that had a double action of telescoping, meaning that there are two stages of extension. Not to be confused with the common single-telescoping lightsaber.

Fake   An item that is as near to a perfect copy of an original item and is made to deceive the buyer. Not to be confused with a reproduction item.

Flash lines   A thin trim that surrounds a plastic item resulting from a gap between the pieces of a mold.

Hardcopy   A hand-cast, -painted, and -assembled copy of the original wax sculpts made of polyurethane to demonstrate the functionality of the toy.

Reproduction   Items that are meant to look identical to one that has been produced under license. Typically, these are weapons and accessories (Double-Telescoping Lightsabers and blasters), blisters, dioramas, and cardbacks. Initially, they were meant to act as temporary replacements for missing parts, but nowadays they are used to dishonestly replace vintage parts and accessories. Also known as repro.

8 VINTAGE ACTION TOYS

Every saga has its defining moment, and for *Star Wars* collectors it was the fourth quarter of 1977, when a small toy company from Cincinnati, Ohio, sold us the promise of living *Star Wars*.

No one could have expected *Star Wars* to be the hit that it was, and as such many potential licensees were left behind. Kenner, the small American toy maker with the *Star Wars* license, knew it couldn't have its first collection of toys out in time for Christmas, so it did the next best thing: it sold envelopes containing a cardboard display for the forthcoming figures and a mail-in certificate that ensured the owner a set of the first four figures to be released.

Ultimately, these toys would become the backbone of this collecting genre. In the first quarter of 1978, Kenner fulfilled its pledge and shipped little mailer boxes containing a white tray with twelve little white foot pegs to go on the cardboard display along with four miniaction figures. In doing so, the toy maker successfully sealed the fates of hundreds of thousands *Star Wars* aficionados.

A quarter-century has passed since that moment, and as the case always is, the smaller events that fill any important historical era fade in the shadow of the milestones and are forgotten. This section will look at the complete history of not only Kenner's figure line, but also every *Star Wars* collectible Kenner, and its sister companies associated with the General Mills Fun Group, produced between 1977 and 1985.

The demand for *Star Wars* toys was overwhelming, and as such Kenner allowed subdistribution of the license for international markets. Therefore, *Star Wars* figures can be found on cardbacks distributed by Kenner (US), Kenner Canada—in conjunction with Irwin Toys (Canada)—Lili Ledy (Mexico), and many other distributors around the world. In most cases, the figures packaged for these different distributors were the same as the standard Kenner line, but some, like Lili Ledy, are a bit more distinctive to their countries of origin.

Of the distinct 116 figures, excluding sculpt, mold, and paint variations, produced in all the different lines, there were only two figures not released in the United States. The Yak Face figure saw release only in Europe on the Tri-logo card and in Australia (and possibly New Zealand) on a Kenner Canada Power of the Force card. (Inexplicably, Yak Face is the only known figure produced on a Kenner Canada Power of the Force card. It is believed that this figure was sold to Toltoys for distribution in Australia long before it would have had a chance to make it to Canadian collectors. Furthermore, despite a few catalogs advertising them, there currently is no substantial proof that the Power of the Force figures were sold domestically in Canada.) The Vlix figure from the Droids series only saw release in Brazil on a Glasslite card.

For North America, the toys were distributed by Kenner, Kenner Canada, and Lili Ledy, and with only a few exceptions, these three toy distributors released a representation of all the toys available worldwide, and in most cases, produced the most interesting variations in the line.

There are currently over 400 documented sculpt and mold variations on vintage *Star Wars* figures produced for the North American collections alone, but the majority are not noticeable at quick glance, and in most cases do nothing to increase the value of the figure since only the smallest fraction of collectors focus on variations. That being said, there are some popular variations that are often sought after by the average collector and therefore are exceptions that sell for a drastically increase premium.

Kenner USA

All the toys produced for American release were made and distributed by the Cincinnati, Ohio, based company Kenner, which was a division of the General Mills Fun Group at that time. The toys produced by Kenner set the standard on which all the collectibles were priced.

STAR WARS, 1977–1979

▶ 1977

The line began in the fourth quarter of 1977 with the release of the Early Bird Certificate Package, but not a single action figure saw release this year. As the near-legendary tale goes, Kenner was unable to get the toys ready for a Christmas 1977 release, and while under the gun grasping for ideas, the toy makers devised the Early Bird, which for all intents and purposes was nothing more than a promise with a suggested retail price attached. In actuality, the envelope included a cardboard backdrop, a little sticker sheet, a club membership card, and most importantly a certificate, which when mailed in would guarantee the sender the first four figures mailed to his or her house as soon as possible. Holding true to its promise, Kenner, shipped off small white mailer boxes containing a white tray that held Luke Skywalker, Princess Leia Organa, Artoo-Detoo (R2-D2), and Chewbacca action figures, as well as a little bag of twelve foot pegs to accompany the backdrop display stand that came with the certificate.

Also found on the earliest of carded figures, the vast majority of Early Bird Luke Skywalker figures included what collectors have dubbed as the Double-Telescoping Lightsaber (DT). This accessory featured a two-piece shaft that extended to almost 2 inches, and was quickly swapped out in favor of a one-piece accessory. The set also came with a green-molded version of Chewbacca's Bowcaster rifle accessory. This version has also been spotted on the first card-backs but in almost as limited quantities as the DT Lightsaber.

OTHER LINES

It takes a great deal of time to develop an action figure line. Being a conscientious company, Kenner was concerned that the lack of properly designed and constructed products would allow cheap counterfeit merchandise that could ruin the good name the license deserved. To respond to the increasing market, Kenner began to make other *Star Wars* (SW) products. One of the products Kenner produced was a set of six jigsaw puzzles:

- Luke Skywalker Meets R2-D2 (140-piece set)
- Trapped in the Trash Compactor! (140-piece set)
- Darth Vader and Ben Kenobi Duel with LightSabers! (500-piece set)
- Luke Skywalker and Princess Leia Leap for Their Lives! (500-piece set)
- Aboard the Millennium Falcon (1,000-piece set)
- Star Wars Adventure (1,000-piece set)

Tapping into the "kitchen table craft/project theme," Kenner also released *Star Wars* versions of Dip Dots Poster with felt markers and Dip Dots Poster with water color paints and brushes; plus, they released the first in a line of board games with the *Escape from the Death Star* game.

▶ 1978

ACTION FIGURES

In the first quarter of 1978, the line was in full swing with twelve carded (SW12bk cards) 3¾-inch figures:

- Luke Skywalker
- Princess Leia Organa
- Artoo-Detoo (R2-D2)
- Chewbacca
- See-Threepio (C-3PO)
- Han Solo
- Stormtrooper
- Ben (Obi-Wan) Kenobi
- Darth Vader

Loose Vintage: Luke Skywalker

Loose Vintage: Princess Leia Organa

Loose Vintage: Artoo-Deetoo

Loose Vintage: Chewbacca

Loose Vintage: See-Threepio

Loose Vintage: Han Solo

Loose Vintage: Stormtrooper

Loose Vintage: Ben (Obi-Wan) Kenobi

Loose Vintage: Darth Vader

Loose Vintage: Jawa

Loose Vintage: Death Squad Commander

Loose Vintage: Sand People

- Jawa

- Death Squad Commander

- Sand People

The SW12bk cards offered the *Star Wars* Action Collector's Stand as a premium and used phrases such as "Start your own collection of *Star Wars* Action Figures and Space Vehicles!" Kenner was quick to instill the collector mentality with the license. As such, these toys were immediately something special. There were few figure variations in the early line. Those include the Jawa going from having a vinyl cape to a material cloak, and Han Solo going from having a small head sculpt to a much larger head sculpt. There are, however, a few documented *The Empire Strikes Back* (TESB) carded examples of the small-head Han Solo, but this was likely the result of returned retail stock getting repackaged, or older factory stock that somehow got overlooked, or otherwise separated from the figures that were carded.

Although there are only a few examples known to exist, there were carded examples of Luke Skywalker, Darth Vader, and Ben (Obi-Wan) Kenobi with the DT Lightsaber. Of the three, there are far more documented examples of the carded DT Luke Skywalker than the other two considerably rarer figures.

Later that year, a series of action figure three-packs were introduced called the Special Action Figure Sets.

- Hero Set with Han Solo, Princess Leia Organa, and Ben (Obi-Wan) Kenobi

- Villain Set with Stormtrooper, Darth Vader, and Death Squad Commander

- Android Set with See-Threepio (C-3PO), Artoo-Detoo (R2-D2), and Chewbacca

Kenner: SW TIE Fighter
(Image courtesy of Curtis Comeau)

VEHICLES AND PLAY SETS

Kenner released four vehicles and two play sets to accompany the $3^3/4$-inch-scale figures:

- Land Speeder

- TIE Fighter

- X-Wing Fighter

- Radio Controlled Land Speeder (exclusive to JC Penney)

- Death Star Space Station Play Set

- Cantina Adventure Set (exclusive to Sears)

The Cantina Adventure Set was little more than a cardboard backdrop like the Early Bird, but it featured the only *Star Wars* action figure never to be released on a single card: the Blue Snaggletooth. As the story goes, while developing the play set, Kenner designers had only a black-and-white chest shot to use to create the figure, and they assumed the character would have been the same height as the other characters. They went on to produce a fairly substantial number of the blue figure before Lucasfilm informed them that Snaggletooth was meant to be short and outfitted in red. Kenner quickly retooled the figure and was able to swap over, without any visual indication on the package, to the new improved version in all the later releases of the play set and well before the planned single-carded release.

As the year progressed, Kenner added figure pack-in premiums for the Land Speeder (Luke Skywalker and See-Threepio) and Darth Vader TIE Fighter (Darth Vader and Stormtrooper). Both boxes featured large yellow stickers promoting the pack-ins.

OTHER LINES

Kenner also debuted figure and vehicle collectibles in different scales, creating the Diecast Collection (the carded Land Speeder, X-Wing Fighter, and TIE Fighter), and the Large Size Action Figure line debuted:

- Luke Skywalker
- Princess Leia Organa with "Beautiful Hairstyles for Princess Leia" book
- See-Threepio (C-3PO) (exclusive to JC Penney)
- Artoo-Detoo (R2-D2) (exclusive to JC Penney)
- Darth Vader
- Chewbacca

Though it is not a part of the Large Size Action Figure line, despite being a comparable scale, the Remote Controlled R2-D2, had more in common with the Remote Controlled Sandcrawler than any other toy.

Kenner even made the action figure with the release of "life-sized" role-playing weapons.

- Han Solo Laser Pistol
- Three Position Laser Rifle
- 35" yellow inflatable lightsaber
- Luke Skywalker AM Headset Radio

Kenner also gave a big push to some more unique items:

- Electronic Laser Battle
- X-Wing Aces Target
- *Star Wars* Give-a-Show Projector
- *Star Wars* Movie viewer
- *Star Wars* Super Sonic Power Vans (each sold separate and as a set)

    Heroes Van

    Darth Vader Van

- Play-Doh *Star Wars* Action Set
- Artoo-Detoo plush "Squeaking" doll
- Chewbacca plush doll
- Darth Vader Inflatable Bop Bag
- Artoo-Detoo (R2-D2) Inflatable Bop Bag

○ Adventures of R2-D2 board game

In addition, Kenner rereleased its four previously released jigsaw puzzles along with six new puzzles, all in uniform black boxes. The new puzzles included:

○ Luke and R5-D4 (140-piece set)

○ Trash Compactor (140-piece set)

○ Darth Vader and Obi-Wan (500-piece set)

○ Luke and Leia (500-piece set)

○ Falcon Cockpit (1,000-piece set)

○ Brothers Hildebrandt Painting (1,000-piece set)

MODELS

Model Products Corporation (MPC), a part of the General Mills Fun Group, began producing highly detailed *Star Wars* models this year. The first wave included:

○ Snap Together Luke Skywalker Van

○ Snap Together Darth Vader TIE Fighter

○ Snap Together Artoo-Detoo Van

○ Snap Together Darth Vader Action Model (bust)

○ Authentic R2-D2 (Artoo-Detoo) in wide box

○ Authentic C-3PO (See-Threepio) in wide box

○ Luke Skywalker's X-Wing Fighter in 8" × 14" box

○ Luke Skywalker's X-Wing Fighter in 10" × 14" box

○ Darth Vader TIE Fighter

▶ 1979

ACTION FIGURES

Following the initial release, there were eight more figures. All the eight were packaged with the original twelve figures on new cardbacks that showcased all twenty figures (SW20bk card). The new figures on this cardback consisted of:

○ Luke Skywalker X-Wing Pilot

○ Walrus Man

○ Power Droid

○ Snaggletooth

Loose Vintage: Luke Skwalker X-Wing Pilot

Loose Vintage: Walrus Man

Loose Vintage: Power Droid

Loose Vintage: Snaggletooth

Loose Vintage: Death Star Droid

Loose Vintage: Hammerhead

Loose Vintage: Arfive-Defour

Loose Vintage: Greedo

- Death Star Droid

- Hammerhead

- Arfive-Defour (R5-D4)

- Greedo

Shortly after the first SW20bk figures starting shipping, Kenner repackaged them all on card-backs, offering a special mail-in premium figure of Boba Fett. As it would turn out, the image used for the offer was that of a Boba Fett prototype that looked considerably different from the production version. This prototype featured a rocket-firing backpack, which was taken through many levels of development but was never produced. The produced Boba Fett that was shipped out included a little note explaining Kenner's safety concerns and why they opted to go without the feature. The cards offering the figure were quickly altered with a large sticker to conceal the rocket-firing feature. Immediately after the offer was over, the Boba Fett figure, accompanied by the other twenty figures, were shipped on the SW21bk card. During the release of these figures, Kenner offered a Free Secret Action Figure, which turned out to be Bossk. This figure, however, did not get carded on a *Star Wars* cardback.

The second series of Special Action Figure Sets, all of which included unique and exclusive cardboard backdrops, included:

- Hero Set with Luke X-Wing Pilot, Ben Kenobi, and Han Solo figures and the Yavin Hanger backdrop

- Villain Set with Sand People, Boba Fett, and Snaggletooth figures and the Tusken Raiders backdrop

- Droid Set with R5-D4, Death Star Droid, and Power Droid figures and the Jawa Droid Sale backdrop

- Creature Set with Hammerhead, Walrus Man, and Greedo figures and the Cantina Band backdrop

VEHICLES AND PLAY SETS

Other accessories made available at this time were:

- Land of the Jawas Play Set

- Creature Cantina Play Set

- Droid Factory Play Set

- Patrol Dewback beast figure

- Millennium Falcon

- Darth Vader TIE Fighter

- Imperial Troop Transporter

Kenner: SW Patrol Dewback
(Image courtesy of Curtis Comeau)

Kenner Canada: SW Death Star Playset
(Image courtesy of Curtis Comeau)

- Radio Controlled Jawa Sandcrawler

Though only in the most subtle ways, Kenner repackaged the X-Wing Fighter (swapped out images of the Luke Skywalker action figure on the box sides to feature the Luke Skywalker [X-Wing Pilot] action figure), and the TIE Fighter (now renamed as the Imperial TIE Fighter). The packages for these two vehicles, along with the Land Speeder and Death Star Space Station, no longer featured the small blue LP (Long Play) logo. Later that year, the Land of the Jawa play set was shipped with a yellow starburst rebate sticker promoting cash rebates for purchasing Kenner *Star Wars* products.

OTHER LINES

Keeping with the concept that the figures were collectibles, Kenner released a packaged version of the *Star Wars* Action Collector's Stand (the mailer from the previous year, but now with twenty-two individual name tags—two for Sand People—instead of a preformatted name label) and the vinyl *Star Wars* Mini-action Figure Collector's Case. An interesting variation of the vinyl case was produced and collectors are still eager to add it to their collections. All the collector's cases produced in the Kenner line had a cardstock insert depicting the figures (all sold separately) in the case's designated spaces. Because this was photographed early in production, the Boba Fett prototype ended up finding a home in one of the spaces. Kenner caught this and changed it, but only after the first shipment.

This year also saw additions to the Large Size Action Figures line with the following:

- Han Solo

- Stormtrooper

- Jawa

- Ben (Obi-Wan) Kenobi

- Boba Fett

- See-Threepio (C-3PO) (no longer an exclusive)

- Artoo-Detoo (R2-D2) (no longer an exclusive)

The Diecast Collection was expanded with:

- Darth Vader TIE Fighter (on a blister card)

- Imperial Cruiser (in shadow box)

- Y-Wing Fighter (in shadow box)

- Millennium Falcon (in shadow box)

There is a known variation of the Diecast Darth Vader TIE Fighter that is rare. The ship was produced with both short and long wings. Each version, to accommodate for their different sizes, required different sized blisters. The one with short wings is the more scarce version.

As suggested earlier, the sizing of the first wave of the new Diecast Collection vehicles would remain a problem. Meaning that Kenner couldn't find and maintain a consistent sizing scale. Shortly after the initial release, the shadowboxed vehicles were packed with mail-away offer stickers to get backdrops themed to each of the three toys. Kenner also released the Electronic Battle Command Game and added the Destroy the Death Star Game to its board games line.

As with preexisting lines in the Give-a-Show Projector line, the Give-a-Show Projector was repacked with a sticker promoting the addition of sixteen various non-*Star Wars* slide shows to the sixteen *Star Wars* ones already packed in.

Star Wars jigsaw puzzles exploded with ten new additions:

- Stormtroopers Stop the Land Speeder! (140-piece set)

- Attack of the Sand People (140-piece set)

- Jawas Capture R2-D2 (140-piece set)

- The Banta (140-piece set)

- Victory Celebration! (500-piece set)

- X-Wing Fighters Prepare to Attack (500-piece set)

- The Selling of Droids (500-piece set)

- The Cantina Band (500-piece set)

- Millennium Falcon in Hyper-Space (1,500-piece set)

- Corridor of Lights (1,500-piece set)

Ending 1978, Bop Bags saw the addition of the Chewbacca and the Jawa Bop Bags.

MODELS

New MPC models were added in 1979:

- R2-D2 (Artoo-Detoo) repackaged in a slim box

- C-3PO (See-Threepio) repackaged in a slim box

- Darth Vader with glow in the dark lightsaber

- Han Solo's Millennium Falcon with light up feature

THE EMPIRE STRIKES BACK, 1980–1982

▶ 1980

ACTION FIGURES

Kenner started promoting *The Empire Strikes Back* (TESB) with the offer of the Boba Fett figure on the SW20bk cards, and later with Bossk on the SW21bk cards. But it was on the late shipping of the first twenty-one figures that we saw the new film's logo on the packaging (TESB21bk card).

Boba Fett

The first ten figures produced from the new film were released in the first quarter of 1980. These figures, shipped on TESB31bk cards, included:

- Lando Calrissian

- Bespin Security Guard (I)

- Luke Skywalker (Bespin Fatigues)

- Rebel Soldier (Hoth Battle Gear)

- Imperial Stormtrooper (Hoth Battle Gear)

- FX-7 (Medical Droid)

- Leia Organa (Bespin Gown)

- Han Solo (Hoth Outfit)

- IG-88 (Bounty Hunter)

- Bossk (Bounty Hunter)

Shortly thereafter, the Yoda figure was rereleased (TESB32bk card), but was notorious for not selling.

- Yoda

The third series of Special Action Figure Sets included:

Loose Vintage: Boba Fett

Loose Vintage: Lando Calrissian

Loose Vintage: Bespin Security Guard (I)

Loose Vintage: Luke Skywalker (Bespin Fatigues)

Loose Vintage: Rebel Soldier (Hoth Battle Gear)

Loose Vintage: Imperial-Stormtrooper (Hoth Battle Gear)

Loose Vintage: FX-7

Loose Vintage: Leia Organa (Bespin Gown)

Loose Vintage: Han Solo (Hoth Outfit)

Loose Vintage: IG-88 (Bounty Hunter)

Loose Vintage: Bossk (Bounty-Hunter)

Loose Vintage: Yoda

- Imperial Forces with Bossk, IG-88, and Stormtrooper

- Bespin Alliance with Bespin Security Guard (I), Lando, and Luke Skywalker (Bespin Fatigues)

- Hoth Rebels with Han Solo (Hoth Outfit), Rebel Soldier, and FX-7

In 1980, for reasons undisclosed, the figure names in the year's assortment were all shortened to the character's first names.

This year Kenner also introduced an action figure Six Pack (Rebel Soldier, C-3PO, R2-D2, Han Solo [Hoth Battle Gear], Darth Vader, and Stormtrooper [Hoth Battle Gear]). Do note that this pack features the first versions of the Droids, since the later versions were not yet available. This pack used different names for the Han Solo and Snowtrooper, but both were identical to the ones packed on single cards.

VEHICLES AND PLAY SETS

A new movie brought new vehicles and accessories. With the tremendous success of the *Star Wars* assortment, it was obvious that Kenner didn't have to deviate far from the original to create the same excitement again. There were three new vehicles, one beast, and two new play environments created:

- Darth Vader's Star Destroyer

- Twin-Pod Cloud Car

- Rebel Armored Snowspeeder

- Tauntaun

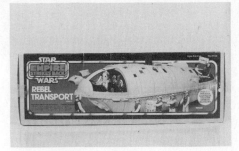

Kenner: TESB Rebel Transport
(Image courtesy of Curtis Comeau)

Kenner Canada: TESB DV Star Destroyer
(Image courtesy of Curtis Comeau)

- Hoth Ice Planet Adventure Set

- Cloud City Play Set with four previously unreleased figures: Han Solo (Bespin Outfit), Lobot, Ugnaught, and Dengar (exclusive to Sears)

Kenner repackaged the X-Wing Fighter, Imperial TIE Fighter, Imperial Troop Transporter, Droid Factory, and Millennium Falcon in boxes using the previous images, but with the TESB logo instead of the SW logo. Darth Vader TIE Fighter, though still sporting the original logo, featured a special offer sticker and included a cardboard Battle Scene Setting backdrop pack-in premium.

The *Star Wars* Action Display Stand had one of the shortest rereleases in Kenner history when it was repackaged as the Special Action Display Stand with six pack-in figures: Luke Skywalker (Bespin Fatigues), Leia Organa (Bespin gown), Lando Calrissian, Bossk, Snowtrooper, and FX-7. As of 2005, there are only five documented examples of this known, and even though one of the five has a price tag on it, there is nothing known of its distribution. It was offered to retailers in 1980, but it is only speculation that it was shipped in that year.

As the year continued, Kenner included a Rebel Soldier figure pack-in with the Rebel Armored Snowspeeder, a Snowtrooper with the Hoth Ice Planet Adventure Set, and a Bespin Security Guard (I) with the Twin-Pod Cloud Car. These figure pack-in premiums were promoted with a yellow special offer sticker.

OTHER LINES

Switcheroos was the only other new line introduced this year. The line consisted of light switch covers designed to "make it fun" to turn things on and off. There were only three released, R2-D2, Darth Vader, and C-3PO. It was short lived and saw no additions or packaging upgrades. The fact that it was discontinued has never been commented on officially. You can guess that someone, somewhere, realized that it wasn't cool for kids to play with electricity.

The previously released "life-sized" role-playing weapons were repackaged to promote the new film. Replacing the Three Position Laser Rifle was the Electronic Laser Rifle, now packaged without the folding stock from the original toy and with the box art featuring a Snowtrooper on Hoth, and instead of the Han Solo Laser Pistol there was the Laser Pistol featuring box art of Luke on Dagobah. Both were packaged in Empire Strikes Back shadow boxes, and sported new TESB logo stickers where SW stickers once were. Besides these weapons, Kenner also introduced The Force Lightsaber. This new lightsaber was sold individually with yellow and red blades and replaced the rather flimsy inflatable lightsaber. The new weapon sported a hollow PVC blade, that when swung, made a swooshing sound meant to mimic the noise their movie counterparts made.

Kenner also added the twelfth and final figure to the Large Size Action Figure line (with the 15-inch-scale IG-88 [Bounty Hunter] action figure) as well as the final Diecast Collection ships:

∘ Rebel Armored Snowspeeder (on blister card)

∘ Slave I (on blister card)

∘ Twin-Pod Cloud Car (on blister card)

∘ TIE Bomber (in shadow box)

Kenner made two new additions to its Collector's Cases assortment with a reissue of the first vinyl Mini-action Figure Collector's Case that now featured the TESB logo where the SW logo was previously, and the Darth Vader Collector's Case, which was first available in a white mailer box through retail catalogs and then as a shelf-stock item with a printed cardboard covering the lower half of the case. The new plastic figural case easily surpassed the simpler vinyl design, but not enough to destroy the consumer appeal of the more cost efficient vinyl case. Before the year was over, the Darth Vader Collector's Case shipped with a three-figure pack-in premium (Boba Fett, Bossk, and IG-88). Though featuring different fronts, the backsides of both versions of this case were TESB31bk.

Other additions to preexisting lines included:

∘ Hoth Planet Adventure [Board] Game

∘ ESB Movie Viewer

∘ Give-a-Show Projector

∘ Play-Doh Empire Strikes Back Action Set

In addition, Kenner introduced the Coloring Books line. The first assortment included:

∘ Luke Skywalker Bespin cover

∘ Bespin Hallway cover

○ Leia and Chewbacca cover

○ R2-D2 cover

Craft Master, a smaller Kenner subsidiary company, introduced a selection of craft items that included:

Acrylic Paint by Number sets

○ Hoth AT-AT Attack

○ Leia and Han Hoth Rebel Base

○ Darth Vader Bespin Freezing Chamber

○ Luke Bespin Control Room

Figurines

○ Boba Fett

○ Han Solo

○ Luke Skywalker (on Tauntaun)

○ Princess Leia

MODELS

New MPC models added in 1980:

○ Star Destroyer

○ Luke Skywalker's Snowspeeder

▶ 1981

ACTION FIGURES

Kenner introduced nine more figures, including:

○ Han Solo (Bespin Outfit)

○ Imperial Commander

○ AT-AT Driver

○ Rebel Commander

○ Princess Leia Organa (Hoth Outfit)

○ Lobot

○ 2-1B (Too-Onebee)

Loose Vintage: Han Solo (Bespin Outfit)

Loose Vintage: Imperial Commander

Loose Vintage: AT-AT Driver

Loose Vintage: Rebel Commander

Loose Vintage: Princess Leia Organa (Hoth Outfit)

Loose Vintage: Lobot

Loose Vintage: 2-1B

Loose Vintage: Dengar

Loose Vintage: Ugnaught

○ Dengar

○ Ugnaught

The new (TESB41bk) cardbacks originally promoting the *Star Wars* Action Figure Survival Kit send-in premium offer was well received. This premium contained a small assortment of previously released weapons along with some unique accessories that were not previously available. Later on, different pieces were offered in smaller sets, but this premium never saw retail distribution as a complete set. The premium included a Dengar/ Snowtrooper rifle, an IG-88/ Imperial Commander Blaster, the AT-AT Driver rifle, a Rebel Commander rifle, a Bespin blaster, Luke Skywalker's AT-AT Grappling Hook Belt, a Jedi Training Harness, two Hoth Backpacks, and three Asteroid Gas Masks

The addition to the Special Action Figure Sets in 1981 included:

○ Rebel Set with 2-1B, Leia (Hoth Outfit), and Rebel Commander

○ Bespin Set with Han Solo (Bespin Outfit), Ugnaught, and Lobot

○ Imperial Set with Imperial Commander, Dengar (Bounty Hunter), and AT-AT Driver

Kenner released the second Six Pack with Darth Vader, Stormtrooper (Hoth Battle Gear), AT-AT Driver, Rebel Soldier (Hoth Battle Gear), IG-88, and Yoda. As seen previously, some of the character names from the multipacks differ from their single-carded counterparts; the figures themselves are identical. This line was not produced beyond this set.

VEHICLES AND PLAY SETS

There were three vehicles and four environments this year:

○ AT-AT (All Terrain Armored Transport)

○ Slave I (Boba Fett's Spaceship vehicle)

○ Imperial Cruiser (exclusive to Sears)

○ Turret and Probot Play Set

○ Imperial Attack Base Play Set

○ Dagobah Action Play Set

○ Rebel Command Center Adventure Set with previously unreleased AT-AT Commander, Luke Skywalker (Hoth Battle Gear), and Artoo-Detoo (R2-D2) (with sensorscope) figures (exclusive to Sears)

Kenner used some of its old molds with its products this year: The Imperial Cruiser was a reissue of 1979's Troop Transport with new stickers and an orange battery cover instead of the red one found on the original toy. This version was produced without the electronics. The Rebel Command Center was the third and final reissue of 1978's Land of the Jawa Action Play Set.

Kenner: TESB AT-AT
(Image courtesy of Curtis Comeau)

Kenner: TESB Slave I
(Image courtesy of Curtis Comeau)

Possibly the result of rushed production, Kenner made a few subtle, yet substantial changes in the packaging of two of its environment play sets. The earliest packages for the Turret and Probot Play Set actually called the toy Turret/Probot Play Set. The title was changed in the late first quarter or early second quarter of 1981. In addition, the Dagobah Action Play Set had minor packaging variation with the logos on the printed portions of the box. The first version had a black-and-white TESB logo, which was changed to incorporate the appropriate red that was found on all other TESB logos

Kenner spruced up the images on the packages of the Millennium Falcon (Bespin Cloud City scene) and the X-Wing Fighter (Dagobah scene) to help cross-promote the old toys for the newer film. As an added bonus later in 1981, identified by the yellow special offer sticker on its boxes, both the Darth Vader TIE Fighter and Slave I were shipped with special cardboard Hanger Bay backdrops. The backdrop was identical with both, but different from the one that shipped previously with the Darth Vader TIE Fighter.

OTHER LINES

1981 was the year of Yoda, with some great toys based on the diminutive Jedi Master. Besides Yoda the Jedi Master Board Game, Kenner released the incredible Yoda Hand Puppet, and the quirky Yoda the Jedi Master fortune-telling toy.

A new vinyl Mini-action Figure Collector's Case was introduced, featuring new Empire Strikes Back-inspired art on the cover, and the Darth Vader Collector's Case, now featuring TESB41bk packaging, was available with and without the three-figure pack-in premium of Darth Vader, Luke Skywalker (Bespin Fatigues), and Yoda.

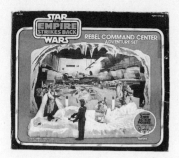

Kenner: Rebel Command Center
(Image courtesy of Curtis Comeau)

In the absence of the Diecast Collection and the Large Size Action Figure lines, Kenner introduced a line of "just off camera" 3³/₄-inch-scale vehicles. The line, called the Mini Rigs, was introduced with three small vehicles with price points low enough that anyone could afford to purchase them. The first line included:

- MTV-7 (Multi-terrain Vehicle)
- PDT-8 (Personnel Deployment Transport)
- MLC-3 (Mobile Laser Cannon)

This proved to be quite successful. All three vehicles were released in flap-boxes that showed all three vehicles on the backside of the flap (MR3bk box). The entire set of Mini Rigs was later shipped with pack-in premium figures that were promoted using yellow special stickers, unique to each of the toys, and featured an image of the figure included (MRS03bk). The MTV-7 included the AT-AT Driver, the PDT-8 included 2-1B, and the MLC-3 included the Rebel Commander.

This year, Craft Master added Yoda to their Acrylic Paint by Number line.

MODELS

New MPC models added in 1981 were:

- Snap Action Scene Battle on Ice Planet Hoth
- Snap Action Scene Encounter with Yoda on Dagobah
- AT-AT All-Terrain Armored Transport

▶ 1982

ACTION FIGURES

1982 was the last year Kenner produced TESB figures. Its release was unusual; it released what, by cardback count (TESB45bk card), would seem like four new figures but were actually six new figures because the original See-Threepio (C-3PO) and Artoo-Detoo (R2-D2) figures were taken out of the collection permanently in favor of newer versions. The new figures premiering on this cardback included:

- Bespin Security Guard (II)
- (Twin-Pod) Cloud Car Pilot
- Luke Skywalker (Hoth Battle Gear)
- AT-AT Commander
- See-Threepio (C-3PO) (Removable Limbs)
- Artoo-Detoo (R2-D2) (With Sensorscope)

The TESB45bk card promoted a premium called *The Empire Strikes Back* Display Arena, which were four interlocking white plastic L-shaped display stands (with enough foot pegs to display up to fourteen figures) and four double-sided backdrop images:

- Yoda and Purchase of the Droids
- Death Star Hanger and Asteroid Chase
- Trash Compactor and AT-AT Attack
- Bespin Platform 327 and Medical Bay

Shortly after, Kenner released Zuckuss and the Imperial TIE Fighter Pilot on a card promoting the final TESB figure mail-in offer—the last of the Bounty Hunters, 4-LOM (TESB47bk card). It wasn't long, however, until 4-LOM was shipped out (TESB48bk card).

- Zuckuss
- TIE Fighter Pilot
- 4-LOM

For a brief time, TESB48bk was shipped without promoting any premium, but the vast majority of TESB48bk cards were printed or stickered to promote a mail-in offer for the first figure from the new movie. The offer was for Admiral Ackbar, but the movie was listed as *Revenge of the Jedi*. Inadvertently, this offer made it near impossible to find a 4-LOM figure on an TESB card without the offer, and therefore it created a fairly sought-after piece. Shortly after that, the first TESB48bk cards with Zuckuss and Imperial TIE Fighter Pilot were shipped without a mail-in offer before the cards were printed with *Return of the Jedi* logos.

Loose Vintage: Bespin Security Guard (II)

Loose Vintage: (Twin-Pod) Cloud Car Pilot

Loose Vintage: Luke Skywalker (Hoth Battle Gear)

Loose Vintage: AT-AT Commander

Loose Vintage: See-Threepio (Removable Limbs)

Loose Vintage: Artoo-Deetoo (with Sensorscope)

Loose Vintage: Zuckuss

Loose Vintage: TIE Fighter Pilot

Loose Vintage: 4-LOM

This year's Special Action Figure Sets included:

- Rebel Set with Princess Leia Organa (Hoth Outfit), Artoo-Detoo (R2-D2) (with sensorscope), and Luke Skywalker (Hoth Battle Gear)

- Bespin Set with See-Threepio (C-3PO) (with removable limbs), Ugnaught, and Cloud Car Pilot

- Imperial Set with Zuckuss, AT-AT Driver, and Imperial TIE Fighter Pilot

Although a few pictures have been shown and they have been mentioned in other price guides, this line was not continued beyond this point. Any sets featuring *Return of the Jedi* logos are either in-house mock-ups or fakes.

VEHICLES AND PLAY SETS

Even though this year saw no new play sets, Kenner kept up with its traditional assortment of three new vehicles with the release of the following:

- "Battle Damaged" X-Wing Fighter

- Rebel Transport

- Scout Walker

Technically, the "Battle Damaged" X-Wing Fighter is the same toy as the original X-Wing Fighter. This version, besides a body molded in light gray and a dark smoke gray canopy, featured a sheet of battle scar stickers that could be applied to the vehicle to create a battle-damaged appearance. Despite the differences on this version, the lasers blasters and landing gear were identical to those on the original toy.

The Rebel Transport had an odd packing variation. The first version had a yellow background, which was altered to a blue background for later releases. In both cases, the same photograph was used, and both packages included an offer for the four Asteroid Gas Masks and five Hoth Backpacks (originally from the previous year's *Star Wars* Action figure Survival Kit Offer).

The Tauntaun was revisited this year, but now as the Tauntaun with Open Belly Rescue Feature. This new version, packaged in boxes both with and without the printed rebate promotion, featured a soft plastic underside that split down the center to house "wounded" figures until their rescuers could get a shelter set up. To accommodate for the new soft belly, the saddle was retooled and featured a much wider strap.

To make the new Tauntaun's life hard, Kenner also released the Wampa Snow Creature from Hoth in a package showing the toy dragging the Rebel Commander figure away from a felled Tauntaun. This package was quickly replaced by a version that renamed the toy Hoth Wampa. This newer package featured new photo art to include Luke Skywalker (Hoth Battle Gear) in the Rebel Commander's place. This version of the packaging was available both with and without the printed rebate promotion.

Kenner repacked the Rebel Armored Snowspeeder in a box that featured new photo art with a more appropriate blue background in place of the original pink background. The new package was also shipped with a yellow rebate program sticker on it.

The AT-AT (All Terrain Armored Transport) was shipped in a package with a printed premium pack-in offer. The offer was for a bagged set of accessories based on the *Star Wars* Action Figure Survival Kit Offer from the previous year. This version included only the four Hoth Backpacks, two Luke Skywalker AT-AT Grappling Hook Belts, a Dengar/Snowtrooper rifle, a long IG-88 rifle, an AT-AT Driver rifle, and a Rebel Commander rifle.

To complete the distribution of former Survival Kit items, the 1982 version of the Dagobah Action Play Set was repacked featuring the Jedi Training Harness premium pack-in. This offer started being promoted using stickers applied to both of the boxes the toy shipped in the previous year (with another sticker promoting the rebate program) before being printed on new boxes that featured a new image. This version of the packaging is easiest to spot by noting the Luke Skywalker (Bespin Fatigues) figure carrying Yoda in the Jedi Training Harness and the Artoo-Detoo (R2-D2) (with sensorscope) figure in the swamp; the original photo art featured the regular Artoo-Detoo (R2-D2) figure.

OTHER LINES

There were two new additions to the Mini Rigs collection:

- CAP-2 (Captivator)
- INT-4 (Interceptor).

These two Mini Rigs were packaged in gatefold boxes that pictured all five Mini Rigs on the backside of the flap (MR5bk boxes). The first three Mini Rigs were also reshipped in this package. As the year went on, all five vehicles featured the figure pack-in premium, just like the year before. Like the MRS03bk premiums, the new ones promoted the pack-ins using yellow special stickers featuring an image of the figure that was uniquely offered with each toy (MRS05bk). The CAP-2 included Bossk, and the INT-4 came with the AT-AT Commander. The reissued Mini Rigs from 1981 offered the same figures as they did the year earlier, but now featured new stickers that, though similar to their predecessors, were unique to the 1982 offer. Later on, all five were packed without the figure premiums in packages promoting the rebate program. The CAP-2 and INT-4 promoted the program with printed Rebate boxes, whereas the other three used stickers.

Similar in size to the Mini Rigs, Kenner released three accessories outside of that line that were based on equipment actually seen in the films. This set included:

- Vehicle Maintenance Energizer Toy
- Tri-pod Laser Cannon Toy
- Radar Laser Cannon Toy

Kenner: Micro Collection Bespin Gantry
(Image courtesy of Curtis Comeau)

Kenner Canada: Micro Collection Hoth
Generator Attack
(Image courtesy of Curtis Comeau)

Though similar to the accessory that was included in the Hoth Ice Planet Adventure Set from 1980, the Radar Laser Cannon Toy is almost twice as large and features an "explosive" battle-damage button for added playability.

1982 also saw the release of a new vinyl Mini-action Figure Collector's Case. Though similar to the previously released TESB case, this one featured a new illustration that subtly promoted the toys that were released in 1982. The Darth Vader Collector's Case was repackaged with a TESB47bk package promoting the rebate program.

The Coloring Book line continued with the addition of two books: the Darth Vader with Stormtroopers cover and the Yoda cover.

In 1982, Kenner released what is arguably their best concept. The ill-received line was called the *Star Wars* Micro Collection, and it offered what no other scale could: Functioning play environments. The line was based on a 1-inch-figure scale, and offered three different environments: Hoth, Bespin, and the Death Star. Each set, sold as "Worlds" and as individual play sets, included nonarticulated painted figures made of die cast metal.

- Death Star World Action Play Sets: This World included two play sets, which were also sold separately:
- Death Star Escape with six figures
- Death Star Trash Compactor with eight figures
- Bespin World Action Play Sets: This World comprised of three smaller sets:
- Bespin Gantry with four figures
- Bespin Freeze Chamber with eight figures

Kenner Canada: Micro Collection Hoth
Turret Defense
(Image courtesy of Curtis Comeau)

Kenner Canada: Micro Collection X-Wing
(Image courtesy of Curtis Comeau)

- Bespin Control Room with four figures

- Hoth World Action Play Sets: This World includes three of the four produced Hoth sets:

- Hoth Ion Cannon with eight figures

- Hoth Wampa Cave with five figures (including the plastic Probot figure)

- Hoth Generator Attack with six figures

- Hoth Turret Defense with six figures (never sold with a World)

To accompany the play sets, the line also included four vehicles:

- X-Wing Fighter Vehicle with one figure

- Imperial TIE Fighter Vehicle with one figure

- Millennium Falcon Vehicle with six figures (exclusive to Sears)

- Snowspeeder Vehicle with two figures (exclusive to JC Penney)

The packages promoted the Build Your Armies mail-in offer that included three Rebel Soldiers and three Imperial Snowtroopers die cast figures to add to the Hoth environments.

Sadly, this line didn't last long enough to truly blossom. It was a line that was ahead of its time and couldn't find a market. It was discontinued before any additional sets could be released. Craft Master slightly altered some of its packaging, but did not release anything new in 1982.

MODELS

New MPC models added in 1982:

- Boba Fett's Slave I

- It's a Snap Action Scene Rebel Base

RETURN OF THE JEDI, 1983–1984

▶ 1983

ACTION FIGURES

With *Return of the Jedi* (ROTJ), the last episode of the *Star Wars* trilogy, hitting theaters, Kenner began its largest campaign. Just before new figures were shown, Kenner released the ROTJ48bk card with an offer for the Nien Nunb action figure. This cardback only shipped with figures that were released before 1983. The first single card ROTJ line (ROTJ65bk card) included a staggering seventeen new figures:

- Admiral Ackbar

- Nien Nunb

- Bib Fortuna

- General Madine

- Squid Head

- Logray

- Chief Chirpa

- Gamorrean Guard

- Lando Calrissian (Skiff Guard Disguise)

- Biker Scout

- Rebel Commando

- Klaatu

- Weequay

- Ree-Yees

- Luke Skywalker (Jedi Knight Outfit)

- Princess Leia Organa (Boushh Disguise)

- Emperor's Royal Guard

Having a record-breaking first assortment notwithstanding, the ROTJ line also featured some card image variations. Later versions of the ROTJ65bk cards featured a send-away offer for the Emperor action figure.

Even though it has been common practice for Kenner to rerelease almost every figure onto its current cardback, up until the ROTJ65bk cards, all the card front photos have remained unaltered. Sporting new images were:

Loose Vintage: Admiral Ackbar

Loose Vintage: Nien Nunb

Loose Vintage: Bib Fortuna

Loose Vintage: General Madine

Loose Vintage: Squid Head

Loose Vintage: Logray

Loose Vintage: Chief Chirpa

Loose Vintage: Gamorrean Guard

*Loose Vintage: Lando Calrissian
(Skiff Guard Disguise)*

Loose Vintage: Biker Scout

Loose Vintage: Rebel Commando

Loose Vintage: Klaatu

Loose Vintage: Weequay

Loose Vintage: Ree-Yees

Loose Vintage: Luke Skywalker
(Jedi Knight Outfit)

Loose Vintage: Princess Leia
Organa (Boushh Disguise)

Loose Vintage: Emperor's Royal
Guard

- Luke Skywalker (Gunner Station)
- Darth Vader (pointing)
- Ben (Obi-Wan) Kenobi (hood up)
- Han Solo (Death Star)
- Chewbacca (Endor)
- Yoda (standing)
- Boba Fett (Tatooine)

All seven of these figures could be found on ROTJ65bk cards with both the new and old photos.

As an interesting side note, Kenner blacked out Logray and Chief Chirpa from all first-run ROTJ65bk cards, but this did little to keep the characters secret, since both figures shipped on the blacked out cards.

VEHICLES AND PLAY SETS

Despite the bumper crop of figures that came out this year, Kenner stuck with its three-vehicles-a-year mantra, offering only the following:

- "Battle-Damaged" Imperial TIE Fighter
- Y-Wing Fighter
- Speeder Bike

Since the "Battle-Damaged" Imperial TIE Fighter was little more than the original TIE Fighter molded in blue plastic with a sheet of transparent "damage" stickers similar to the previous year's "Battle-Damaged" X-Wing fighter, and the Speeder Bike was a small-scale vehicle, it was a rather inexpensive vehicle year. That didn't mean that the *Star Wars* enthusiast saved a lot of money, it just meant that he or she had more money to spend on the newly released play environments:

- Jabba the Hutt Action Play Set
- The Jabba the Hutt Dungeon Action Play Set with yet-to-be-released Klaatu (in Skiff Guard Outfit), 8D8, and Nikto action figure pack-in premiums
- Ewok Village Action Play Set

Many times described as a reissue of the Droid Factory, the Jabba the Hutt Dungeon Action Play Set was actually created using a sculpt inspired by the former and used a different mold. They share only their basic shapes.

Only three previously released vehicles were repackaged in ROTJ boxes. To promote its place in the new film, the Millennium Falcon was repackaged with a new photo of it surrounded by

Kenner: ROTJ Speeder Bike
(Image courtesy of Curtis Comeau)

Kenner: ROTJ Jabba The Hutt
(Image courtesy of Curtis Comeau)

Kenner: ROTJ Jabba The Hutt Dungeon
(Image courtesy of Curtis Comeau)

Kenner Canada: ROTJ Ewok Village
(Image courtesy of Curtis Comeau)

Kenner Canada: ROTJ Millennium Falcon
(Image courtesy of Curtis Comeau)

new action figures on a sandy Tatooine-like environment. The "Battle-Damaged" X-Wing Fighter and Scout Walker Vehicle were both released with the ROTJ logo instead of the TESB logo. Later that year, the Scout Walker Vehicle was again repackaged with new photo art that featured new figures interacting with it in an Endor-esque environment.

OTHER LINES

Similar to the previous year, there were two additions to the Mini Rigs line. As before, the new vehicles, the ISP-6 (Imperial Shuttle Pod) and the AST-5 (Armored Sentinel Transport), were designed to be off-camera vehicles that fit perfectly in the environments of the new film. All but the earlier released Mini Rigs, minus the PDT-8, were put out with the two new ones in MR6bk gatefold boxes.

Kenner was certainly not slouching this year in terms of the Collector's Cases. To accommodate all seventeen additions to the figure line this year, Kenner released not only a new vinyl Mini-action Figure Collector's Case sporting an all-new ROTJ logo and image, it also introduced the See-Threepio (C-3PO) Collector's Case, and the (ill-conceived) Chewbacca Bandolier Strap to go on the shelf right beside the Darth Vader Collector's Case, which was repackaged with the ROTJ logo and ROTJ65bk.

The Laser Pistol saw rerelease in a ROTJ package, which sported a different picture of Luke on Dagobah. Like the previous releases of this toy, the logo sticker was updated to reflect the new film. Also released was an updated set of the Force Lightsabers. The yellow blade was swapped out with a green one, and with the red blade, labeled with the ROTJ logo where the TESB logo was on the earlier release.

Kenner started pushing the animated version of the Ewoks with some of its other product lines, such as the ROTJ Ewok Play-Doh Set, which hit the shelves alongside two coloring books (Wicket's World Coloring Book and Wicket the Ewok Coloring Book), a series of ROTJ Ewok Plush Dolls (Wicket, Wiley, and Nippet), and the Sew 'N Show Cards (from Craft Master).

There were additions to two other previously existing lines that include two coloring books (the Leia, Chewbacca, and C-3PO on Endor cover and the Max Rebo Band cover), and the Jabba the Hutt Play-Doh Set.

The puzzles came back with a passion this year through Kenner's affiliate, Craft Master. These puzzles were released with ROTJ and Wicket and Friends (WAF)/Wicket the Ewok (WTE) logos:

- ROTJ Darth Vader (15-piece set)
- ROTJ Gamorrean Guard (15-piece set)
- ROTJ Leia and Wicket (15-piece set)
- ROTJ Wicket (15-piece set)

- ROTJ Death Star Scene (70-piece set)
- ROTJ Friends of Jabba (70-piece set)
- ROTJ Jabba's Throne Room (70-piece set)
- ROTJ Battle on Endor (170-piece set)
- ROTJ B-Wings on Attack (170-piece set)
- ROTJ Ewok Leaders (170-piece set)
- ROTJ Match Box Puzzle
- WTE Kneesaa and Baga (15-piece set)
- WTE Wicket and Kneesaa on Gliders (15-piece set)
- WTE Wicket and R2-D2 (15-piece set)
- WTE Ewok Village (15-piece set)
- WAF Fishing (boxed) (35-piece set)
- WAF Swimming Hole (boxed) (35-piece set)
- WAF Nature Lesson (boxed) (35-piece set)
- WTE Match Box Puzzle

Besides the puzzles, Craft Master also released the following craft sets in 1983:

Fast Drying Acrylic Paint by Number sets:

- R2-D2 and C-3PO Ewok Village
- Jabba the Hutt
- Boushh and Lando Jabba's Palace
- Sy Snootles and the Max Rebo Band

WTE Watercolor Painting sets:

- Ewok Glider
- Wicket Hanging on to Vine
- Wicket and Baga

Fast Drying Acrylic Paint Figurines:

- Admiral Ackbar
- R2-D2 and C-3PO
- Wicket the Ewok

MODELS

For the ROTJ line, MPC spared no expense and produced considerably more models than in previous years. Packaged in uniform silver packages featuring the ROTJ logo, the twelve models included:

- X-Wing Fighter
- Speeder Bike
- Shuttle Tydirium
- Millennium Falcon without light-up feature
- AT-AT (All-Terrain Armored Transport)
- R2-D2
- C-3PO
- It's a Snap X-Wing Fighter
- It's a Snap TIE Interceptor
- It's a Snap B-Wing Fighter
- It's a Snap A-Wing Fighter
- It's a Snap Jabba the Hutt Throne Room Action Scene

▶ 1984

ACTION FIGURES

1984 marked the last year that Kenner would release action figures on a film-specific card with the ROTJ77bk and ROTJ79bk cards. The new figures on the ROTJ77bk card included:

- Nikto
- Klaatu (in Skiff Guard Outfit)
- 8D8
- B-Wing Pilot
- Han Solo (in Trench Coat)
- Teebo
- AT-ST Driver
- Prune Face
- Wicket W. Warrick

Loose Vintage: Nikto

Loose Vintage: Klaatu (in Skiff
Guard Disguide)

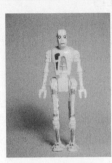

Loose Vintage: 8D8

Loose Vintage: B-Wing Pilot

Loose Vintage: Han Solo
(in Trench Coat)

Loose Vintage: Teebo

Loose Vintage: AT-ST Driver

Loose Vintage: Prune Face

Loose Vintage: Wicket W.
Warwick

- Rancor Keeper

- Princess Leia Organa (in Combat Poncho)

- The Emperor

The ROTJ79bk card, which shipped later that year, featured only two new figures:

- Paploo

- Lumat

Later versions of the ROTJ79bk card featured a printed action figure send-away offer for Anakin Skywalker. This offer was also promoted on other ROTJ65bk, ROTJ77bk, and ROTJ79bk cards using stickers. In the case of the ROTJ65bk cards, some Anakin Skywalker offers were placed over the older offer for the Emperor figure.

VEHICLES AND PLAY SETS

New vehicles to come out this year included:

- TIE Interceptor

- B-Wing Fighter

- Imperial Shuttle

Although there weren't any new play sets this year, Kenner compensated with the release of two creature sets:

- Rancor Monster Figure

- Sy Snootles and the Rebo Band Action Figures three-pack

The Jabba the Hutt Dungeon Action Play Set was repackaged with three new never-before-released figures (Barada, EV-9D9, and Amanaman). The package was changed with new text and a new photo to reflect the change.

This year also marked the short-lived commemorative rereleases of the Land Speeder, the Darth Vader TIE Fighter, and the Patrol Dewback. The set, called the Collector's Series, offered a second chance to acquire toys that had not been available for a few years. The packaging on these items was designed to perfectly match the original designs, but with the addition of a red starbursts identifying them as Collector's Series editions. The line was not continued past these three toys.

OTHER LINES

The Mini Rigs line was wrapped up this year with the release of the Desert Sail Skiff and Endor Forest Ranger vehicles. Packaged with the ISP-6 and AST-5 from the previous year in gatefold boxes that only promoted the four toys (MR4bk). All earlier released Mini Rigs were discontinued and did not see production in 1984.

Loose Vintage: Rancor Keeper

Loose Vintage: Princess Leia Organa (in Combat Poncho)

Loose Vintage: The Emperor

Loose Vintage: Paploo

Loose Vintage: Lumat

Kenner: ROTJ Imperial Shuttle (Image courtesy of Curtis Comeau)

Kenner: ROTJ TIE Interceptor (Image courtesy of Curtis Comeau)

There is no surprise that the Darth Vader Collector's Case made it right to the end of the movie-specific portion of the Kenner line. Wrapping up with its ROTJ77bk packaging, the case was placed on the shelves right beside the last addition to the Collector's Case line: the Laser Rifle Carry Case, which also doubled as a role-playing toy.

Exceeding the previous year, Kenner focus a great deal of time and energy in the expansion of the Ewok-related toy products with the release of the Wicket the Ewok Preschool line. Preschool was a line that produced popular toys for a younger audience. Preschool's *Star Wars*-influenced items included:

- Give-a-Show Projector
- Sit 'n Spin
- Ewok Family Hut
- Ewok Woodland Wagon
- Ewok Fire Cart
- Ewok Toothbrush
- Ewok Music Box Radio
- Ewok Talking Phone
- Ewok Teaching Clock

MODELS

1984 saw the last additions to the vintage MPC line, even though the models would be available for many years after. This year, MPC introduced Structures, which were models with wind up walking mechanisms, and the Mirr-a-Kits, which were essentially half of a vehicle attached to a mirror to create the illusion of a full ship. Besides these two new lines, MPC also released two final It's a Snap kits.

Structures Action Walkers:

- C-3PO
- AT-ST (All-Terrain Scout Transport)
- AT-AT (All-Terrain Armored Transport)

Mirr-a-Kits:

- AT-ST (All-Terrain Scout Transport)
- Shuttle Tydirium
- Speeder Bike
- TIE Interceptor

- X-Wing Fighter

- Y-Wing Fighter

It's a Snap:

- AT-ST (All-Terrain Scout Transport)

- Y-Wing Fighter

THE POWER OF THE FORCE, 1985

ACTION FIGURES

With the *Star Wars* trilogy finished and no new movies planned in the near future, Kenner tried a new approach to keep the 3³/₄-inch line alive: exclusive coin pack in premiums. Sadly, the addition of the coins wasn't enough to carry the line forward. The Power of the Force (POTF) line included fourteen new figures:

- EV-9D9

- Artoo-Detoo (R2-D2) (with pop-up lightsaber)

- Han Solo (in Carbonite Chamber)

- Warok

- Imperial Dignitary

- Romba

- Barada

- Lando Calrissian (General Pilot)

- Luke Skywalker (Imperial Stormtrooper Outfit)

- Imperial Gunner

- Anakin Skywalker

- Luke Skywalker (in Battle Poncho)

- A-Wing Pilot

- Amanaman

Besides the new figures, Kenner repackaged some of the previously released figures, but unlike other packaging changes, only nineteen of them were released domestically:

- Darth Vader (with original photo art)

- Imperial Stormtrooper

- Jawa

- Luke Skywalker (X-Wing Fighter Pilot)

Loose Vintage: EV-9D9

Loose Vintage: Artoo-Detoo
(With Pop-Up Lightsaber)

Loose Vintage: Han Solo
(In Carbonite Chamber)

Loose Vintage: Warok

Loose Vintage: Imperial Dignitary

Loose Vintage: Romba

Loose Vintage: Barada

Loose Vintage: Lando Calrissian
(General Pilot)

Loose Vintage: Luke Skywalker
(Imperial Stormtrooper Outfit)

Loose Vintage: Imperial Gunner

Loose Vintage: Anakin Skywalker

Loose Vintage: Luke Skywalker (Battle Poncho)

Loose Vintage: A-Wing Pilot

Loose Vintage: Amanaman

- Imperial Commander Empire
- Lando Calrissian Rebel General (Bespin)
- Logray Ewok
- Luke Skywalker Rebel Hero
- Luke Skywalker Rebel Leader
- Luke Skywalker Jedi Knight (Dagobah)
- Princess Leia Rebel Leader (with R2-D2)
- Princess Leia Boushh

- See-Threepio (C-3PO) (with removable limbs)

- Chewbacca

- Ben (Obi-Wan) Kenobi

- Yoda, the Jedi Master

- Luke Skywalker (Jedi Knight Outfit)

- Biker Scout

- Princess Leia Organa (in Combat Poncho)

- Wicket W. Warrick

- The Emperor

- B-Wing Pilot

- AT-ST Driver

- Han Solo (in Trench Coat)

- Teebo

- Lumat

- Paploo

Kenner ran a send-away premium offer during this period, using large yellow stickers applied to old stock offering one randomly selected coin (of a total of sixty-two coins) in exchange for the sticker cut—not peeled—from the card, the proof of purchase stamp from the card's back, and the original cashiers receipt. Excluding the specific coins included with the previous thirty-two figures, the remaining coins in the set included:

- Anakin Skywalker Jedi

- Bib Fortuna Major Domo

- Boba Fett Bounty Hunter

- Chief Chirpa Ewok Leader

- Emperor's Royal Guard Empire

- FX-7 Medical Droid

- Gamorrean Guard Palace Sentry

- Greedo Bounty Hunter

- Han Solo Rebel Fighter

- Han Solo Rebel Hero

- Hoth Stormtrooper
- Star Destroyer Commander Empire
- *Star Wars* AT-AT
- *Star Wars* Creatures
- *Star Wars* Droids
- *Star Wars* Millennium Falcon (spelled incorrectly) (available with two different write ups on the back side)
- *Star Wars* Sail Skiff
- TIE Fighter Pilot Empire
- Too-Onebee medical Droid
- Tusken Raider Sand People
- Yak Face Bounty Hunter
- Zuckuss Bounty Hunter

To support the comic books and animated television programs of the same names, Kenner released figures and accessories under the titles Droids and Ewoks. These two lines, with only two exceptions, were all exclusive sculpts to represent the character's animated design. Both of these lines featured character-specific collector's coins packaged exclusively with each figure. The lines included:

DROIDS

- See-Threepio C-3PO
- Artoo-Detoo R2-D2
- Thall Joben
- Jord Dusat
- Kea Moll
- Kez-Iban
- Uncle Gundy
- Jann Tosh
- Tig Fromm
- Sise Fromm
- A-Wing Pilot
- Boba Fett

Kenner: Droids ATL Interceptor
(Image courtesy of Curtis Comeau)

EWOKS

- Wicket W. Warrick (unique animated sculpt)
- Logray Ewok Medicine Man (unique animated sculpt)
- King Gorneesh
- Urgah Lady Gorneesh
- Dulok Scout
- Dulok Shaman

The Droids See-Threepio (C-3PO) figure was packed with a coin variation; one version was Droids specific, while the other was a bronze version of the coin that packed out with the POTF See-Threepio (C-3PO) (with removable limbs). Both the Boba Fett and A-Wing Pilot figures featured bronze versions of the POTF coins. There was a Droids Vlix figure produced, but it only saw release in Brazil.

VEHICLES AND PLAY SETS

There were slim pickings for large-scale accessories this year, with only two vehicles being offered in the POTF packaging.

- Ewok Battle Wagon Vehicle
- Tatooine Skiff Vehicle

The Droids line did make up for the POTF drought with the release of three large-scale vehicles:

- A-Wing Fighter Vehicle

- Side Gunner

- ATL Interceptor

There were no large-scale accessories released under the Ewoks banner.

OTHER LINES

With sales dropping drastically, Kenner didn't release much under the POTF banner and nothing was repackaged. The items released were the POTF small-scale "off camera" vehicles, similar to the Mini Rigs, but packed out on blister cards instead of in boxes. The three released were:

- Security Scout Vehicle

- Imperial Sniper Vehicle

- One Man Sail Skimmer Vehicle

Another new item that was released this year was the Droids Battery Operated Lightsaber Accessory. Though drastically out of scale, the light up, spring-loaded blade was a good idea that could have been better had Kenner spent more time developing it. The toy was available with both green and red blades.

And finally, Kenner released one final Ewoks coloring book and two more board games (Ewoks Save the Trees! and Wicket the Ewok) before closing the door on the first era of *Star Wars* collecting.

Kenner Canada

At quick glance, Kenner Canada seems virtually identical to its parent company, but on close inspection the subtle differences become obvious. Created through a fifty-fifty partnership between Kenner and Irwin Toys, Kenner Canada produced and distributed *Star Wars* products exclusively for the Canadian market. Kenner Canada produced its items at roughly 10 percent the quantity of its American counterpart and in some cases chose to bring in items that were not available to American collectors. Because of the large number of similarities, this section will examine only the major differences between Kenner Canada and Kenner (U.S.).

Canada has two official languages, and Canadian bilingual laws dictate that both English and French have to be represented on consumer products. Even though there are examples of this being over looked, virtually ever *Star Wars* collectible released in Canada adheres to the law.

The easiest way to identify a Kenner Canada carded figure or toy package is to peek below the "Ages 4 and up" marking on the upper right hand corner. Following the laws of the land, almost every Canadian *Star Wars* toy has "Pour 4 ans et plus," "A Partir de 4 ans," or simply "4 ans et Plus" printed below it. When it isn't visible on the front of the package, it always turns up on the back. Many of the boxed items split the languages up to offer both English and

French sides for display. The hardest Canadian boxes to spot are the Large Size Action Figures, which have no indication of French anywhere on the front. Unlike other boxes, the gatefold design of these figures didn't lend itself to the flip-the-box method that worked well with all other toys.

Many early Canadian toys sported a *La Guerre des Etoiles* (*Star Wars*; LGDE) pyramid logo prominently on the photo art, and for a time even the figures displayed the logo proudly on the front of the card. The LGDE logo on the 12 back cards (KCLGDE12bk) was a late edition to the 1978 figure line and was quickly dropped. The first twelve figures were sold on LGDE cards. In addition, packaging for both TESB and ROTJ products featured film title logos that presented the French translations using the same layout as the English logos.

LA GUERRE DES ÉTOILES, 1977–1979

▶ **Action Figures**

Canadian collectors didn't see the same number of cardbacks as American collectors, so in some instances the debut card is different from that of the Kenner (U.S.) line. The Canadian line didn't include SW21bk, TESB48bk, or ROTJ79bk cards. The following is a list of all figures that had different debut cardback; all other Canadian figures were released on the same cardback numbers as their American counterparts:

◦ Boba Fett (KCSW20bk)

◦ C-3PO with removable limbs (KCTESB45bk)

◦ 4-LOM (KCROTJ65bk)

◦ Klaatu (Skiff Guard) (KCROTJ65bk)

◦ Prune Face (KCROTJ65bk)

◦ 8D8 (KCROTJ65bk)

◦ Nikto (KCROTJ65bk)

◦ Paploo (KCROTJ77bk)

◦ Lumat (KCROTJ77bk)

Though there are no known examples of the 4-LOM figures shipping in Canada on a TESB logo card, there is a chance that this figure may have been shipped on a KCTESB47bk card.

MULTIPACKS

Canada did not have nearly as many multifigure sets as America, but what was made available was fairly well received, and in today's marketplace is considered extremely rare and collectible:

◦ Special Action Figure Set

◦ SW Creature Set: Hammerhead, Walrus Man, and Greedo

○ SW Droid Set: R5-D4, Death Star Droid, and Power Droid

○ SW Hero Set: Luke X-Wing Pilot, Ben Kenobi, and Han Solo

○ SW Hero Set: Princess Leia, Ben Kenobi, and Han Solo

○ SW Villain Set: Sand People, Boba Fett, and Snaggletooth

○ SW Android Set: C-3PO, Chewbacca, and R2-D2

○ SW Villain Set: Darth Vader, Stormtrooper, and Death Squad Commander

○ TESB Bespin Alliance: Bespin Security Guard (I), Lando, and Luke (Bespin Fatigues)

○ TESB Hoth Rebels Set: Han (Hoth), Rebel Soldier, and FX-7

○ TESB Imperial Forces Set: Bossk, IG-88, and Stormtrooper (Snowtrooper)

○ TESB Bespin Set: Han (Bespin), Ugnaught, and Lobot

Though listed in other price guides, there are currently no known examples of either of the *Star Wars* Hero Sets in Canadian packing. Considering the fact that these two sets were produced as part of the Kenner (U.S.) line, and Kenner Canada released every other set with the *Star Wars* logo available in the United States, it stands to reason that these should have been produced for the Canadian market as well.

SPECIAL 12 MINI-FIGURES SET (EXCLUSIVE TO SEARS)

○ Contained the first twelve *Star Wars* figures. It is believed that they were all on the KCSW20bk card, but it is possible, however unlikely, that the set may have contained some KCSW12bk or KCSWLGDE12bk cards as well.

○ Special 9 Mini-figures Set (exclusive to Sears)

○ Contained Luke Skywalker (X-Wing Fighter Pilot), Power Droid, Arfive-Defour (R5-D4), Death Star Droid, Boba Fett, Hammerhead, Greedo, Walrus Man, and Snaggletooth on KCSW20bk cards

○ TESB Special 7 Mini Action Figure sets (exclusive to Sears)

○ Jawa, Greedo, Snaggletooth, Sand People, Hammerhead, Walrus Man, and Ben (Obi-Wan) Kenobi

○ Luke Skywalker (X-Wing Fighter Pilot), Star Destroyer Commander, Han Solo (Hoth Outfit), Princess Leia Organa, Darth Vader, Stormtrooper, and Ugnaught CSW

○ Bossk, Chewbacca, Rebel Soldier, Snowtrooper, Luke Skywalker (Bespin Fatigues), Leia Organa (Bespin Gown), and Han Solo (Cloud City Outfit) CSW

○ Death Star Droid, FX-7, See-Threepio (C-3PO), Artoo-Detoo (R2-D2), Power Droid, Arfive-Defour (R5-D4), and Dengar

○ Boba Fett, Lando Calrissian, Bespin Security Guard (I), IG-88, Han Solo, Luke Skywalker, and Lobot (Lando's Aid)

- TESB Special 4 Mini Action Figure sets (exclusive to Sears)

- Lobot, Chewbacca, See-Threepio (C-3PO), and Han Solo (Cloud City Outfit) CSW

- Bossk, Luke Skywalker, Princess Leia Organa, and General Veers CSW

- Stormtrooper, IG-88, Leia (Hoth Outfit), and Luke Skywalker (Hoth Outfit) CSW

- AT-AT Driver, Dengar, Han Solo (Hoth Outfit), and R2-D2 (with Periscope) CSW

- Darth Vader, Ben (Obi-Wan) Kenobi, Luke Skywalker (Bespin fatigues), and Yoda

- TESB Special 3 Mini Action Figure sets (Exclusive to Sears)

- Zuckuss, Rebel Soldier, and Imperial TIE Fighter Pilot

- Snowtrooper, AT-AT Driver, and (Twin-Pod) Cloud Car Pilot

A number of Canadian multipack figures were sold not in blisters but with vacuum-formed skins and became known as Canadian skin wrapped (CSW) figures. They were produced for Sears Canada and were included as exclusive bonus figures in the multipacks just listed. Since these figures had not yet been released on card backs, Kenner Canada produced them vacuum-sealed on lower quality cards that featured all the elements that regular Canadian TESB cards had except for an actual character image or the individual colors on the name plate and behind the figure itself. The card back was completely unprinted. Though in some cases renamed from the mass-released versions, the skin wrapped figures were: Dengar, Ug-naught, Lobot (Lando's Aid), Han Solo (Cloud City Outfit), General Veers, Luke Skywalker (Hoth Outfit), and R2-D2 with periscope. Though intended to be exclusive to these sets, there are documented examples of Han Solo (Cloud City Outfit), General Veers, Luke Skywalker (Hoth Outfit), and R2-D2 with periscope figures with ROTJ transition stickers on them.

Like the Kenner line, Kenner Canada ventured forward by promoting the Droids and Ewoks cartoons and comics with a line of action figures, but as a way to cut costs, the Canadian versions of these figures were released on generic cardbacks. The Canadian Droids cardback featured an illustration of the Droids running away from bad guys Vlix and Boba Fett, while the Ewoks cardback featured an illustration of Wicket and Princess Kneesaa climbing a vine. The figures released on these cardbacks were as follows:

DROIDS

- See-Threepio (C-3PO)

- Artoo-Detoo (R2-D2)

- Thall Joben

- Jord Dusat

- Kea Moll

- Kez-Iban

- Uncle Gundy

- Jann Tosh

Kenner Canada: Sears Han Solo CSW
(Image courtesy of Curtis Comeau)

Kenner Canada: Sears General Veers CSW
(Image courtesy of Curtis Comeau)

Loose Vintage: Yak Face
(Image courtesy of Curtis Comeau)

EWOKS

- King Gorneesh
- Urgah Lady Gorneesh
- Dulok Shaman
- Dulok Scout

Wicket W. Warrick and Logray were only offered domestically through a special Sears two pack, which was little more than the two American-carded figures in a white mailer.

There is a great deal of mystery surrounding the distribution of the POTF action figures in Canada. The only figure from the POTF line that Kenner Canada produced on a Canadian card was Yak Face, but all evidence suggests that most of the available stock of this figure was sold to Toltoys for distribution in Australia (and possibly New Zealand). For the most part, the POTF figure assortment was available in Canada, but in extremely limited quantities. Sadly for Canadian collectors, the distribution of this line was questionable at best and many collectors looking for these figures went without ever finding any of them in retail stores.

LARGE SIZE ACTION FIGURES

The Canadian line was identical in most respects to the American figures, except for the French text on the backside of the boxes. Except for IG-88, all the figures produced in this line saw release in Canada. While not technically a part of the Large Size Action Figure line, the Remote Controlled R2-D2 was also released in a Canadian package, albeit a cluttered box with an unfortunately large amount of text. All these toys were released with only the SW logo.

▶ Vehicles and Play Sets

Like the action figures, Kenner Canada's vehicles and environment toys were not that different from their American counterparts. In the same fashion as the figure line, most of the *Star Wars* vehicles and play sets featured the LGDE logo:

- Land Speeder
- Millennium Falcon
- X-Wing Fighter
- TIE Fighter
- Darth Vader TIE Fighter
- Land of the Jawa
- Creature Cantina (featuring LGDE in standard *Star Wars* font)
- Death Star (chipboard) (LGDE logo on the back of the package)

The only *Star Wars* environment not to feature the LGDE logo was the Death Star Space Station Playset.

In the case of the Land Speeder, where the first shipments featured the toy made in the United States, all later shipped versions (1979–1980) were actually imported from Australian *Star Wars* toy distributors Toltoys and featured stickers instead of paint details on the vehicle body.

L'EMPIRE COUNTRE-ATTAQUE (TESB), 1980–1982

When the time came to promote *The Empire Strikes Back*, Kenner Canada repackaged only three preexisting toys and took the opportunity to release some late-shipping toys with the new films logo. The TESB line, including the previously mentioned items, consisted of the following:

- Millennium Falcon (original photo art, new TESB logo)
- TIE Fighter (original photo art, new TESB logo)
- X-Wing Fighter (new Dagobah photo art, new TESB logo)
- Patrol Dewback (package only with TESB logo)
- Droid Factory (package only with TESB logo)
- Radio Controlled Sandcrawler (package only with TESB logo)
- Imperial Troop Transport (packaged only with TESB logo)
- Rebel Armored Snow Speeder (produced with pink photo art only)
- Twin-Pod Cloud Car
- Slave I

Kenner Canada: LGDE Millennium Falcon
(Image courtesy of Curtis Comeau)

Kenner Canada: LGDE Landspeeder
(Image courtesy of Curtis Comeau)

Kenner Canada: LGDE Creature Cantina
(Image courtesy of Curtis Comeau)

Kenner Canada: LGDE X-Wing
(Image courtesy of Curtis Comeau)

Kenner Canada: LGDE Darth Vader TIE Fighter
(Image courtesy of Curtis Comeau)

Kenner Canada: TESB Twin-Pod Cloud Car
(Image courtesy of Curtis Comeau)

Kenner Canada: TESB X-wing
(Image courtesy of Curtis Comeau)

Kenner Canada: TESB Patrol Dewback
(Image courtesy of Curtis Comeau)

- Rebel Transport (produced with blue photo art only)
- AT-AT (All-Terrain Armored Transport) (packed both with and without the Survival Pack premium pack in)
- Scout Walker
- "Battle-Damaged" X-Wing Fighter
- Tauntaun (with open belly rescue feature)
- Wampa
- Gun Turret and Probot Playset (note toy name, which was unique to Canadian packaging.)
- Darth Vader's Star Destroyer Action Playset
- Imperial Attack Base
- Dagobah Action Playset
- Ice Planet Hoth Adventure Set
- Cloud City Playset (with Han Solo, Lando Calrissian, Boba Fett, and Ugnaught figures)

LE RETOUR DU JEDI (ROTJ), 1983–1984

By the time the *Return of the Jedi* line hit Canada, it was apparent that things were winding down. While all the earlier released items were in Canadian packages, vehicles released in the following two years like the Imperial Shuttle, Tatooine Skiff, Ewok Battle Wagon, and A-Wing Fighter were sold in American packaging. Vehicles, Environment, and Beasts for the ROTJ line produced in Canadian packaging included:

- Millennium Falcon (original photo art, new ROTJ logo)

- "Battle-Damaged" X-Wing Fighter (original photo art, new ROTJ logo)

- Rebel Armored Snow Speeder (original photo art, new ROTJ logo)

- B-Wing Fighter Vehicle

- Speeder Bike Vehicle

- "Battle-Damaged" Imperial TIE Fighter Vehicle

- Y-Wing Fighter Vehicle

- Jabba The Hutt Action Playset

- Ewok Village Action Playset

- Rancor monster Figure

- Sy Snootles and the Rebo Band Action Figure Set

Interestingly, the "Battle-Damaged" Imperial TIE Fighter Vehicle is the only Kenner-produced item to be released to retail with a ROTJ logo, it can be found with the French version of the logo. The Millennium Falcon, the "Battle-Damaged" X-Wing Fighter, and the Rebel Armored Snow Speeder were the only previously released toys to be repackaged with a ROTJ logo.

COLLECTOR'S SERIES

Undocumented until just recently, Kenner Canada did participate in the Collector's series reissues like Kenner (U.S.) did. Thus far, only the Darth Vader TIE Fighter has turned up, but chances are good that the other two (Landspeeder and Patrol Dewback) may also have been available in Canadian packaging. The Canadian version features the LGDE pyramid logo, making it even more uniquely Canadian. Interestingly enough, the "Guerre" is misspelled as "Querre." It is unknown if this typo is unique to the Darth Vader TIE Fighter, or if it made it onto the other boxes as well.

MINI RIGS AND SMALL-SCALE ACCESSORIES

Just like their American counterparts, the Canadian Mini Rigs and small-scale accessories allowed the *Star Wars* generation with fixed budgets to enjoy the toys in a whole new way. Identical in all ways save packaging, the Canadian version of these toys included:

The Empire Strikes Back

- Cap-2 (Captivator)

- Int-4 (Interceptor)

- MLC-3 (Mobile Laser Cannon)

- MTV-7 (Multi-terrain Vehicle)

- PDT-8 (Personnel Deployment Transport)

Return of the Jedi

- AST-5

- Desert Sail Skiff

- Endor Forest Ranger

- ISP-6

Small-Scale Accessories

- Radar Laser Cannon

- Tri-pod Laser Cannon

- Vehicle Maintenance Energizer

PACK IN ACTION FIGURE PREMIUMS (AFP)

The United States wasn't the only county to include pack in premiums to promote the larger, sometimes slower moving items in the *Star Wars* line. The Canadian line relied on these just as heavily as the American line. The premiums were:

- Land Speeder AFP (Luke Skywalker)

- Millennium Falcon AFP (TESB package Han Solo and Chewbacca, yellow starburst sticker)

- Land of the Jawa AFP (Jawa, yellow sticker)

- Creature Cantina AFP (Yoda and 8-by-11-inch photo of Yoda, white sticker)

- Death Star AFP (chipboard version) (2x Stormtroopers, yellow sticker)

- Radio Controlled Sandcrawler AFP (2x Jawas)

- Patrol Dewback AFP (Stormtrooper, printed on box, most featuring an orange sticker promoting the offer)

- Rebel Armored Snow Speeder AFP1 (Rebel Soldier, white sticker)

- Rebel Armored Snow Speeder AFP2 (Luke X-Wing, white sticker)

- Twin-Pod Cloud Car AFP1 (1x Cloud Car Pilot, white sticker)

- Twin-Pod Cloud Car AFP2 (2x Cloud Car Pilots, white sticker)

- Slave I AFP (Boba Fett)

- AT-AT AFP1 (AT-AT Driver, white sticker)

- AT-AT AFP2 (AT-AT Driver, AT-AT Commander, Stormtrooper, white sticker)

- Scout Walker AFP (Stormtrooper, white sticker—possibly a Snowtrooper)

- "Battle-Damaged" X-Wing Fighter AFP (Luke X-Wing)

- Ice Planet Hoth AFP1 (Snowtrooper, white sticker)

- Ice Planet Hoth AFP2 (Rebel Soldier, Luke X-Wing, and Snowtrooper, white sticker)

COLLECTOR'S CASES

There were only five collector's cases released in Canada with bilingual packaging:

- *Star Wars* Mini Action Figure Collector's Case

- TESB Mini Action Figure Collector's Case (same as SW version, but with the TESB logo)

- TESB Mini Action Figure Collector's Case (same as Kenner's [U.S.] first version TESB illustration)

- TESB Darth Vader Collector's Case

- ROTJ Chewbacca, Bandolier Strap

Interestingly enough, the *Star Wars* Mini Action Figure Collector's Case featured bilingual text on the actual cover art. All other vinyl cases were identical to the American versions.

DIECAST COLLECTION

Except for the TIE Bomber, Kenner Canada released every Diecast vehicle sold in the United States. The packaging, though bilingual, was identical to the American designs. There are no known examples of the Darth Vader TIE Fighter with small wings on a Canadian card.

MICRO COLLECTION

This line sold as poorly in Canada as it did in the United States, so it wasn't much of a surprise that the line was short lived. All the items sold in the United States, save the Millennium Falcon and Snow Speeder, which were available in Canadian packaging. Besides the duel-language text, another telltale sign to identify the Canadian packaging was its color. Unlike the American versions in their dark crimson boxes, the Canadian Micro Collection stood out in pink boxes.

OTHER LINES

Though they pale in comparison to the sea of products released in the United States, Kenner Canada offered its customers a wide selection of items that did not directly fit into previous categories. These items included:

STAR WARS

- SW Give-a-Show Projector

- SW Movie Viewer

- SW Play-Doh Action Set

- SSP Heroes Van (slightly different mold from U.S. version)

- SSP Darth Vader Van

The Empire Strikes Back

- Yoda Hand Puppet

Unlike the gatefold box used on the American version, the Canadian *Star Wars* Give-a-Show Projector was packaged in a two-piece package. Furthermore, the projector itself was molded in opposite colors of the American version, with a red body instead of blue, and a blue lens instead of red.

▶ Role-Playing Toys

Here is one of the areas where Kenner Canada shone. Even in the cases where the toy didn't see production in Canadian packaging, Kenner Canada ensured Canadian kids that they had the choice to buy every role-playing weapon available to American kids and then some. The following are all that were released in Canadian packaging:

STAR WARS

- 35-inch Inflatable Lightsaber

- Laser Pistol

- Three Position Laser Rifle

- Darth Vader Utility Belt

- Luke Skywalker Utility Belt

- Princess Leia Organa Utility Belt

THE EMPIRE STRIKES BACK

- Electronic Laser Rifle

RETURN OF THE JEDI

- The Force Lightsaber (red and green versions)

The three utility belts were produced exclusively for the Canadian market and were readily available for a time at most retail outlets. It's been speculated that in 1978 Lucasfilm requested a recall on these items. If this is in fact true, retailers paid little attention to it, as these sets were available for some time and never abruptly disappeared. In fact, they were slow to sell out and in some cases were found on store shelves right up until 1980.

The utility belts were based on sets previously released in North America by a toy company called Remco to promote other licenses. Since Kenner Canada imported and sold toys on behalf of other toy companies outside of Canada, it was no problem for Kenner Canada to create SW versions. Kenner (U.S.), on the other hand, could not use designs from a rival toy company and resell them in the United States.

▶ Coloring Books, Puzzles, and Board Games

Well before Kenner (U.S.) introduced its Coloring Books line (1980), Kenner Canada had produced a series of coloring books. Unlike the American line that began promoting *The Empire Strikes Back*, the Canadian series printed four *Star Wars*–themed books. Except for these four (listed below), all the other Canadian books featured the same photo art as the American versions but with bilingual text.

- *Star Wars* Han and Chewbacca cover

- *Star Wars* R2-D2 cover

- *Star Wars* Luke and C-3PO cover

- *Star Wars* Chewbacca and Luke cover

Kenner Canada released all 140- and 500-piece puzzles available to the American market place, besides three puzzles exclusively offered in Canada. Besides the bilingual text, the 500-piece sets all sported a large Parker Brothers logo, a Kenner subsidiary, in the bottom left corner. Unlike the American versions, the Canadian puzzles were never switched over to the black packaging, therefore all Canadian *Star Wars* puzzles were packaged in blue or purple boxes. Like the American line, there were no TESB puzzles, but there was a large push for ROTJ and Wicket the Ewok puzzles. The following is a list of all known Canadian packaged puzzles:

STAR WARS

- Artoo-Detoo/See-Threepio (140-piece) blue box

- Banta (140-piece) blue box

- Han and Chewbacca (140-piece) blue box

- Jawas (140 piece)

- Land Speeder Group (140-piece) blue box

- Luke/C3-PO (140-piece) blue box (exclusive to Canada)

- Luke, R2-D2, Jawas (140-piece) blue box

- Sand People (140-piece) blue box

- Stormtroppers (140-piece) blue box (exclusive to Canada)

- Trash Compactor (140-piece) blue box

- Cantina Band L'Orchestre de la Taverne (500-piece) purple box

- Death Star (500-piece) purple box (exclusive to Canada)

- Leia/Luke (500-piece) purple box

Kenner Canada: Death Star
jigsaw
(Image courtesy of Mike Chomyn)

Kenner Canada: Luke & Threepio
jigsaw
(Image courtesy of Mike Chomyn)

Kenner Canada: Stormtropper
jigsaw
(Image courtesy of Mike Chomyn)

- Lightsaber Duel (500-piece) purple box
- Luke Skywalker (500-piece) set
- Rebel Base (500-piece) purple box
- Selling of Droids La Vente des Droides (500-piece) purple box
- Space Battle (500-piece) purple box
- Victory (500-piece) purple box

An interesting note: there are more than a handful of spelling mistakes on the box art including "Stormtroppers" and "Banta." None of these errors were ever corrected.

RETURN OF THE JEDI

- Darth Vader (15-piece set)
- Gamorrean Guard (15-piece set)
- Leia and Wicket (15-piece set)
- Wicket (15-piece set)
- Death Star Scene (70-piece set)
- Friends of Jabba (70-piece set)
- Jabba's Throne Room (70-piece set)
- Battle on Endor (170-piece set)
- B-Wings on Attack (170-piece set)

- Ewok Leaders (170-piece set)
- ROTJ Match Box Puzzle

WICKET AND FRIENDS

- Kneesaa and Baga (15-piece set)
- Wicket and Kneesaa on Gliders (15-piece set)
- Wicket and R2-D2 (15-piece set)
- Fishing (boxed) (35-piece set)
- Swimming Hole (boxed) (35-piece set)
- Wicket the Ewok Match Box Puzzle

Every board game sold in Canada had to be reworked from the ground up. It was with these items, which were all rather text heavy, that Canada's bilingualism laws had its strongest influence. As such, this line was distinctly Canadian. The Canadian line of board games included:

- Escape from Death Star Game
- SW Destroy the Death Star Game
- SW Adventures of R2-D2 Game
- TESB Hoth Ice Planet Adventure Game
- TESB Yoda the Jedi Master Adventure Game
- ROTJ Battle at Sarlacc's Pit Game
- ROTJ Ewoks Save the Trees! Game
- ROTJ Wicket the Ewok Game

TAKARA IMPORTS

Kenner Canada, through Irwin's connections with overseas toy makers, was able to offer Canadian *Star Wars* fans a popular toy available only in Japan. This item is of course the infamous Walking Wind Up R2-D2 (on the only KCSW18back card).

Lily Ledy

In a similar fashion to the Canadian distribution of *Star Wars* products, Kenner (U.S.) farmed the license out to other international toy companies to bring the toys to almost everyone in the world who could ever want them. For Mexico, the toy company that exclusively distributed *Star Wars* items to the masses was Lili Ledy. The Lili Ledy line is considerably smaller than even the Canadian collection, but considering the rarity of virtually everything it produced, the Mexican line is an expensive collection to complete.

ACTION FIGURES

▶ *La Guerra de las Galaxias* (LGDLA), 1978–1979

Like Kenner and Kenner Canada, 1978 was the year Lili Ledy got the wheels rolling with its *Star Wars* line. Straying from all other distributors with the coveted *Star Wars* license, Lili Ledy didn't focus immediately on the 3³/₄-inch action figure line. Instead, the toy maker released a line of 12-inch figures like none other. Utilizing its own sculpts and molds, Lili Ledy released seven large-scale figures over two years. All of the figures were a strong contrast to their Kenner counterparts, and for years were thought to be poorly constructed bootlegs.

That all changed in 1996, after a warehouse find produced a small quantity of these figures in sealed boxes in mint condition. As an odd twist of fate, most of the figures found were sold for roughly $50 each. Less than a decade later, a loose complete figure runs in the lower triple digits. The line of seven large-scaled figures included:

1978

- Princess Leia Organa
- Luke Skywalker
- Darth Vader
- Han Solo
- Ar-Tu-Ri-To (R2-D2)

1979

- Hombre de las Dunas (Tusken Raider)
- Jawa

▶ *El Imperio Contraataca* (EIC), 1982

The first 3³/₄-inch figures shipped in Mexico came out in 1982 and were packed on generic cards sporting the *El Imperio Contraataca* (LLEIC12bk) logo. These cardbacks featured a poorly laid out illustration of the Millennium Falcon with X-Wing Fighters in space on the front and an illustration of ten figures on the back. Of the ten figures promoted on the cardback, two were not released: Han Solo (Hoth Outfit) and Snowtrooper. The figures that shipped on this cardback were as follows:

- Leia Organa (Bespin Gown)
- Luke Skywalker (Bespin Fatigues)
- Rebel Soldier (called "Comandante Rebelde")
- Darth Vader
- See-Threepio (C-3PO)

- Artoo-Detoo (R2-D2)

- Chewbacca

- Yoda

These ten figures were imported from Spain and were shipped in extremely small quantities. This gamble helped Lili Ledy test the water before diving in headfirst. The line, however limited, proved to be a success. From that point forward, Lili Ledy began producing *Star Wars* collectibles right in Mexico.

▶ *El Retorno De Jedi* (ERetDJ)

Once the production of toys began in Mexico, the figures were released on cardbacks sporting an *El Retorno De Jedi* (LLERetDJ12bk) logo. The title was based on a direct translation of *Return of the Jedi*, but used a word (Retorno) not commonly spoken. This cardback was featured only for the first wave of Mexican-made figures, and included:

- Squid Head (Hombre Calamar)

- Ree-Yees

- Lando Calrissian (Skiff Guard Disguise)

- Klaatu

- Gamorrean Guard (Guardia Gamorrian)

- Luke Skywalker (Bespin Fatigues)

- Han solo (Bespin Outfit)

- Darth Vader

- Yoda the Jedi Master (Yoda con su Sierpe)

- See-Threepio (C-3PO) (CI-TRI-PI-O)

- Artoo-Detoo (R2-D2) (AR-TU-RI-TO)

All these figures' card fronts featured the same photo art as their Kenner counterparts except Artoo-Detoo (R2-D2), whose card sported a shot of the droid in Bespin, and See-Threepio (C-3PO), whose card had the droid standing in the Millennium Falcon as photo art.

▶ *El Regreso Del Jedi* (ERegDJ)

Lili Ledy switched the card logo out in favor of *El Regreso del Jedi* (LLERegDJ14bk), which though not a direct translation was a more contemporary phrase. Following this, Lili Ledy released the LLREG14bk card, which added three new figures to the collection:

- Nien Nunb (featured on LLERetDJ12bk cardback, but not released until now)

- Chief Chirpa (as Cacique Chirpa)

- Logray

Proving incredibly popular with *Star Wars* fans, Lili Ledy added sixteen figures to the line (LLERegDJ30bk). This cardback featured an odd variation. Some cardbacks were printed with black ink on raw cardboard, while others were found with a predominantly black cardback with the figures printed in negative. The sixteen figures included:

- Princess Leia Organa (Bespin Gown)

- Chewbacca

- Ben (Obi-Wan) Kenobi

- Stormtrooper

- Boba Fett

- General Madine

- Weequay

- Emperor's Royal Guard

- Imperial TIE Fighter Pilot (Piloto Imperial)

- Bib Fortuna

- Princess Leia Organa (Boushh Disguise) (Disfraz de Boushh)

- Biker Scout

- Star Destroyer Commander

- Imperial Commander

- Admiral Ackbar

- Luke Skywalker (Jedi Knight Outfit)

Finally, Lili Ledy released its last cardback (LLERegDJ50bk) with twenty new figures including:

- Paploo

- Wicket W. Warrick

- Lumat

- The Emperor (El Emperador)

- AT-ST Driver

- Prune Face

- Lando Calrissian

- Teebo

- Han Solo (in Trench Coat) (Con Gabardina de Camuflaje)

- Jawa

- Klaatu (Skiff Guard Outfit) (Guardia del Velero del Desierto)

- Rebel Commander (El Comandante Rebelde)

- Princess Leia Organa (in Combat Poncho)

- 8D8

- B-Wing Pilot (Piloto de la Nave de Combate)

- Cloud Car Pilot (Piloto del Vehiculo de las Nubes)

- Rancor Keeper (El Guardia del Monstruo Rancor)

- Zuckuss

- Nikto

- See-Threepio (C-3PO) (with Removable Limbs) (Ci-Tri-Pi-O con extremidades desmontables)

VEHICLES, PLAY SETS, AND ACCESSORIES

The Lili Ledy line tended to shy away from expensive accessories, so there weren't many vehicles or play sets produced.

▶ Vehicles

- B-Wing Fighter (Nave de Combate B)

- Darth Vader TIE Fighter (Nave Imperial) (LLRET and LLREG logos produced)

- Imperial Shuttle (El Transbordador Iimperial)

- Millennium Falcon (Halcon Milenario Vehiculo)

- Rebel Armored Snowspeeder (Halcon De Las Nieves)

- Scout Walker (Nave Exploradora)

- Y-Wing Fighter (Nave de Combate Y)

▶ Small-Scale Vehicles

- Ewok Assault Catapult (Catapulta de Asalto)

- Ewok Combat Glider Vehicle (Planeador de Combate)

- Speeder Bike (Velociclo)

- Tri-pod Laser Cannon (Canon Laser de Tripie)

- Vehicle Maintenance Energizer (Unidad Movil Reactivadora)

▶ **Minirigs**
- AST-5 (Astronave Sideral de Transporte)
- CAP-2 (Capturador)
- MLC-3 (called CLM-3 Canon Laser Movil)
- INT-4 (Interceptor)

▶ **Beasts**
- Rancor Monster (El Monstruo Rancor)
- Sy Snootles and the Rebo Band (Sy Snootles y la Banda Rebo)

▶ **Play Sets**
- Jabba the Hutt Action Playset

▶ **Role-playing Toys**
- Biker Scout Laser Pistol (Pistola Laser)

▶ **Collector's Cases**
- Darth Vader Collector's Case (Casco Colector de Darth Vader)

OTHER LINES

▶ **Super Masa**

The only Play-Doh set sold in Mexico was the Jabba the Hutt Set, which was identical to the American version.

▶ **Figure Art**

Based on the Craft Master figurine and paints sets sold by Kenner and Kenner Canada, the Lili Ledy set contained only three figurines:

- Admiral Ackbar (Almirante Ackbar)
- R2-D2 and C-3PO
- Wicket (Wicket el Ewok)

▶ **Rompecabezas**

Lili Ledy produced a small assortment of puzzles based on the Craft Master ROTJ puzzles sold by Kenner and Kenner Canada. The line of six puzzles included:

- Darth Vader Rompecabezas (15-piece set)
- Wicket Rompecabezas (15-piece set)

- ○ Gamorrean Guard Rompecabezas (15-piece set)

- ○ Friends of Jabba (Grupo de Aliens) Rompecabezas (70-piece set)

- ○ Jabba the Hutt Rompecabezas (70-piece set)

- ○ Death Star Scene (Destructor Imperial) Rompecabezas (70-piece set)

▶ **Modelo Para Armar De La Nave**

Based on the MPC models produced by Kenner and Kenner Canada, the Lili Ledy line was considerably more modest with the release of only two iconic vehicles:

- ○ The Authentic Luke Skywalker X-Wing Fighter (Nave Supersonica de Luke Skywalker)

- ○ The Authentic Darth Vader TIE Fighter (Nave Imperial de Darth Vader)

Terminology

The following are the most commonly used words and acronyms for vintage action *Star Wars* collectibles:

CSW	Canadian Skin Wrapped: The term used for a number of Sears Canada–exclusive figures that were vacuum wrapped instead of placed in blisters.
EIC	*El Imperio Contraataca:* The first Lili Ledy line of *Star Wars* action figures based on Kenner's *The Empire Strikes Back* collections.
ERegDJ	*El Regreso del Jedi:* The third Lili Ledy line of *Star Wars* action figures based on Kenner's *Return of the Jedi* collections.
ERetDJ	*El Retorno de Jedi:* The second Lili Ledy line of *Star Wars* action figures based on Kenner's *Return of the Jedi* collections.
GMFG	General Mills Fun Group: The parent group that owned Kenner, Model Products Corporation, and a number of other subsidiaries that had *Star Wars* licenses.
IT	Irwin Toys: A Canadian company that merged with Kenner to create Kenner Products (Canada) Ltd.
KC	Kenner Canada: The abbreviated name for Kenner's Canadian counterpart. Its full name was Kenner Products (Canada) Ltd.
LGDE	*La Guerre des Etoiles*: French translation of *Star Wars*, and commonly used on Kenner Canada products.
LGDLA	*La Guerra de las Galaxias*: Spanish translation of *Star Wars*, and commonly used on Lili Ledy products.

LL   Lili Ledy: The toy manufacturer that held the *Star Wars* action toy (and accessories) license in Mexico.

Micro Collection   The packaging toy line of 1-inch-scale miniatures produced by Kenner between 1982 and 1983.

MPC   Model Products Corporation: The plastic modeling arm of the General Mills Fun Group.

POTF   Power of the Force: The packaging toy line produced by Kenner in 1985 that encompassed characters and vehicles from the original *Star Wars* trilogy.

ROTJ   *Return of the Jedi*: The third movie in the original *Star Wars* trilogy. Also the packaging toy line made by Kenner between 1983 and 1984.

SW   *Star Wars*: The original and alternate title used to refer to *A New Hope*. Also the packaging toy line made by Kenner between 1978 and 1979.

Takara   The toy manufacturer that held the *Star Wars* action toy (and accessories) license in Japan.

TESB   *The Empire Strikes Back*: The second movie in the original *Star Wars* trilogy. Also the packaging toy line produced by Kenner between 1980 and 1982.

WAF   Wicket and Friends: A collection of children's book, puzzles, and toys marketed alongside the animated *Ewoks* cartoon.

WTE   Wicket the Ewok: A collection of children's book, puzzles, and toys marketed alongside the animated Ewoks cartoon.

xback   The term used to define the cardback type based on the number of $3^{3}/_{4}$-inch action figures displayed on the rear of the card.

9 TRADING CARDS

Initially, the Topps Company Inc. was a gum company famous for Bazooka bubble gum. In the 1940s, it attempted to increase sales by wrapping the gum in a comic strip that could be redeemed for merchandise. In 1950, Topps realized it could sell even more gum by packaging it with trading cards. These first trading cards were related to the television series Hopalong Cassidy and American football. The first baseball cards followed them in 1951. Eventually, the cards were the main attraction secondary to the gum and Topps began to concentrate on trading cards even though every pack still included a stick of gum. By 1991, card collectors complained that the gum made the cards sticky and left imprints on the cards, so the hard sticks were eliminated altogether.

Topps's involvement in entertainment cards expanded with Davy Crockett, Elvis Presley, the Beatles, Star Trek, and others. In 1977, it was natural for Topps to produce a set for *Star Wars*. Topps trading cards were one of the very first licensed products for *Star Wars*. Producing card sets almost every year since 1977, it is also the only license holder, except Del Rey, that has survived and continued to produce licensed *Star Wars* merchandise to the present. To date, there are thirty-five series of cards, each with new features and incentives to collect.

Vintage Trading Cards, 1977–1983

Vintage *Star Wars* consists of twelve series of cards. They are similar in that several cards and one sticker are wrapped with a stick of hard gum in a wax wrapper. These original cards are printed on gray card stock with a photo on the front and either a photo that was part of a larger puzzle or a descriptive text on the back. The images on these cards could be blurry or the printing offset. They were also typically coated with remnants of the wax wrapping or stained by pink bubble gum. What's special about them? They were the first.

Topps: SW series 1

Topps: SW series 2

Topps: SW series 3

Topps: SW series 4

Topps: SW series 5

STAR WARS

In 1977, there were five *Star Wars* sets produced: blue, red, yellow, green, and orange. Each set builds on each other for a total of 330 cards and 55 stickers. Starting with the orange set, each wrapper sported an ad, either for Kenner action figures or a redemption offer.

- Series 1 (blue) card set 1 to 66

- Series 1 (blue) sticker set 1 to 11

- Series 2 (red) card set 67 to 132

- Series 2 (red) sticker set 12 to 22

- Series 3 (yellow) card set 133 to 198

○ Series 3 (yellow) sticker set 23 to 33

○ Series 4 (green) card set 199 to 264

○ Series 4 (green) sticker set 34 to 44

○ Series 5 (orange) card set 265 to 330

○ Series 5 (orange) sticker set 45 to 55

There are no cards in this series more rare than the green #207, C-3PO. There are two versions of this card. The first has C-3PO sporting more male anatomy than usual. The second is a corrected version with the extra part removed. The origin of how the first print of this card came into being has transcended fact into myth. One story tells of a disgruntled Topps employee who thought to exact his revenge on the company. The other that a simple trick of the light led to the effect. Either way, the so-called "x-rated" C-3PO card typically sells for $20 and the corrected version for $5. Facts are, however, that the "x-rated" version is much more common than the reissue because it was corrected very late in production.

STAR WARS SUGAR-FREE GUM

After the first five Star Wars sets, at the request of George Lucas, Topps made sugar-free gum in 1978. These are single pieces of hard gum wrapped in foil and then with paper. There are no trading cards or stickers, however, the back of each paper wrapper contains a photo, deemed a "Movie Photo Pin-Up." There are fifty-six photos to collect on the backs of four different wrappers: Luke Skywalker, Princess Leia, Darth Vader, and Han Solo. There are seven "subsets" of photos and photos from only one set are included in a box of thirty-six packs. Therefore, any hope of getting the complete set requires opening a minimum of seven boxes of gum.

○ Series 1 photo set 1 to 56

THE EMPIRE STRIKES BACK

Three series of cards were released for The Empire Strikes Back: red, blue, and yellow, for a total of 352 cards and 88 stickers. Similar in style to the Star Wars cards except the wax wrappers began to sport ads for an uncut press sheet, the newly formed Star Wars fan club, candy, and a special collector's box to hold the cards. A favorite component to these sets are the stickers that came in the form of alphabet letters filled with scenes from the movie. The sticker card backs sport photos that can be placed together to form a larger puzzle.

○ Series 1 (red) card set 1 to 132

○ Series 1 (red) sticker set 1 to 33

○ Series 2 (blue) card set 133 to 264

○ Series 2 (blue) sticker set 34 to 66

○ Series 3 (yellow) card set 265 to 352

○ Series 3 (yellow) sticker set 67 to 88

Topps: TESB series 1

Topps: TESB series 2

Topps: TESB series 3

GIANT MOVIE PHOTOCARDS

In addition, Topps made a series of thirty cards called Photocards. These are a larger size, approximately 5-by-7 inches and there are two variations of the series. A "test" version was produced with line drawings on the back. Test series were typically limited in number and geographical area to test the popularity of a set. There is also a "production" series with full black-and-white photos on the back. The test set is difficult to find while the production set is more common.

○ Test series 1 to 30

○ Production series 1 to 30

RETURN OF THE JEDI

The release of *Return of the Jedi* in 1983 saw the release of two series of 220 cards and 55 stickers: red and blue. The stickers are similar to *The Empire Strikes Back* sets in that they have puzzle photos on their backs.

○ Series 1 (red) card set 1 to 132

○ Series 1 (red) sticker set 1 to 33

○ Series 2 (blue) card set 133 to 220

○ Series 2 (blue) sticker set 34 to 55

Classic Trading Cards, 1993–1997

The dark years for trading cards were between 1983 and 1993, when there were no new sets produced. Starting in 1993, Topps began to create card concepts that would become the mainstay of modern card collecting.

Topps: ROTJ series 1

Topps: ROTJ series 2

STAR WARS GALAXY

Between 1993 and 1995, Topps created the first *Star Wars* trading card sets in ten years with three new series called Galaxy. These are entirely art cards featuring images produced by the best comic book artists, novel illustrators, and others. These drawings and paintings are the basis for the 365-card Galaxy Series 1, 2, and 3.

- Series 1 card set 1 to 140
- Series 2 card set 141 to 275
- Series 3 card set 276 to 365

With these sets, Topps also introduced promotional cards and chase cards for the *Star Wars* line. Promotional cards are typically in the same format as the card line and are inserted in other publications such as Dark Horse comic books or given away at conventions to advertise and promote the upcoming cards. Promotional cards have been used for every series since.

The most valuable card from the Galaxy series is the Levitating Yoda card, P3 from Galaxy Series 2. This card was pulled from production by Lucasfilm because it felt the card had too much religious overtone. A few made it to the public and each one sells for between $500 and $1,000.

Chase cards, chasers, or special insert cards were introduced as a way of getting more sales. Collectors chase after special cards that are, for example, inserted one in every thirty-six packs. Chase cards are usually extra special in that they include a foil stamp and can be made entirely out of foil or some other material. Since Galaxy, chase card collecting has become the main directive for serious card collectors. They have become more elaborate and unique over the

Topps: Galaxy series 1

Topps: Galaxy series 2

years, and many are highly prized and valuable. Chase cards for the Galaxy series include etched foil, hologram, prism, clear, autograph, and foil-stamped.

WIDEVISION

Produced between 1994 and 1997, widevision cards, measuring 2.5-by-4.6 inches, showed more of the image similar to that of a movie scene. There are five sets:

- *Star Wars* series 1 to 120
- *The Empire Strikes Back* series 1 to 144
- *Return of the Jedi* series 1 to 144
- *Star Wars* Trilogy series 1 to 72
- *Star Wars* Trilogy Special Edition series 1 to 72

Chase cards for the widevision series include standard, chromium, mini poster, laser cut, and hologram.

MASTERVISIONS

The Mastervisions series, released in 1995, was a large (approximately 6-by-10 inch) format card set that could be purchased as a complete set of thirty-six cards in one box. There were two promos and no chasers.

- Series 1 card set 1 to 36

STAR WARS CAPS

In order not to be left out of the Pogs milkcap craze, Topps created *Star Wars* Caps in 1995. While technically not trading cards, they were usually found in Topps card collections. They are round cardboard discs that can be played in a game. There are seventy caps and eight plastic chase "slammers" that come in gold, silver, or black.

○ Series 1 caps set 1 to 70

SHADOWS OF THE EMPIRE

This 100-card set, to celebrate the first expanded universe novel, technically didn't have chase cards. Instead, there was one "Case Topper" set on the top of a case of eight boxes.

○ Series 1 card set 1 to 100

STAR WARS 3D WIDEVISION

The first series to really break away from the standard card format was the *Star Wars* 3D widevision set. These sixty-three lenticular cards show a three-dimensional image. They are plastic on card stock and quite expensive with only three cards per pack. The one chase card in the series also pushed the boundaries: a multimotion card. If tilted back and forth, several images in a row appear as if they are moving.

○ Series 1 card set 1 to 100

STAR WARS FINEST

Finest is a series of ninety chromed paintings and drawings from the Galaxy sets. The entire series is duplicated as a refractor set that has gold backs instead of the silver chrome. A refractor card can be found one in every twelve packs, thereby making an entire set extremely difficult to acquire.

○ Series 1 card set 1 to 90

Chase cards for the Finest series include embossed foil, matrix, chromium, refractor, and redemption cards.

STAR WARS VEHICLES

Vehicles is a seventy-two-card set featuring nothing but ships and vehicles from the *Star Wars* galaxy. These cards are on extra heavy card stock and are foil-stamped.

○ Series 1 card set 1 to 72

Chase cards for Vehicles include a unique cut-away technology where a flap with a photo of the vehicle can be lifted to reveal the inside of the vehicle. Other chase cards include 3D, chromium, and refractor promo cards.

STAR WARS CHROME ARCHIVES

The Chrome Archives is a set of ninety chromed cards with images taken from the vintages series.

○ Series 1 card set 1 to 90

Chase cards include clear and double-sided versions.

Topps: Star Wars Widescreen   Topps: Finest   Topps: Vehicles

Modern Trading Cards, 1999–2004

The modern era of trading card collecting started with the release of *The Phantom Menace* in 1999. At this time, Topps began to distribute two different kinds of card boxes. One to mass-market retailers and one to hobby retailers. This has long been the tradition in sports cards and allows different types of consumers to enjoy the cards. The retail market typically consists of younger fans and the chase cards included in retail boxes cater to this type of buyer; an example is stickers. Hobby boxes are directed toward more sophisticated collectors who expect to chase special cards such as those that have been previously mentioned. Hobby boxes can also typically be sold as an entire thirty-six-pack box to more serious collectors who want to increase their chances of finding chasers by buying entire boxes.

THE PHANTOM MENACE

For the release of *The Phantom Menace* in 1999, the eighty-card set sent to retailers included chasers, foil cards, and stickers, while the hobby edition included chrome cards and an entire forty-card, foil-stamped extension set. In addition, there were five tin boxes, with each containing a large-sized box topper card. *The Phantom Menace* eighty-card set is similar to the hobby set in that there are two editions. Each of these editions has a set of chrome and embossed foil cards, but different images. There is a third *The Phantom Menace* set, directed at hobby retailers, a forty-six-card 3D set with two multimotion chasers.

- Series 1 card set 1 to 80

- Series 1 sticker set 1 to 16

- Series 1 widevision card set 1 to 46

Topps: TPM series 1

Topps: TPM series 2

Topps: Evolution

EVOLUTION

Between *The Phantom Menace* and *Attack of the Clones*, Topps introduced *Star Wars* Evolution. This ninety-card set was meant to bridge the gap between the two movies by showing the evolution of characters from the original trilogy, through *The Phantom Menace* and finally to *Attack of the Clones*. The *Attack of the Clones* images were the first images viewable on trading cards before the movie was released.

  ○ Series 1 card set 1 to 90

The chasers are what make this set special. Topps contacted twenty-five stars from the *Star Wars* saga to autograph special cards with their characters' picture. Although autograph chasers had been available before, this was the first time top-star autographs were included on an officially licensed product and advertised as indisputably authentic. Autograph cards for Carrie Fisher and Anthony Daniels were inserted 1:3,677, with only 100 total cards available for each. The after-market price of these cards reached over $1,000 on eBay.

ATTACK OF THE CLONES

The first set of 100 *Attack of the Clones* cards has a retail edition (twenty-four packs/box) and a hobby edition (thirty-six packs/box), but the inserts are the same for both. The chasers include prismatic foil, silver foil, and panoramic foldout cards. Another five tin boxes are available to match those from *The Phantom Menace*, with each containing a large-sized box topper card. The second *Attack of the Clones* series includes eighty widevision cards and twenty-four autographed chasers from the stars of the movie.

  ○ Series 1 card set 1 to 100

  ○ Series 2 widevision card set 1 to 80

Topps: Clone Wars Cartoon   Topps: Clone Wars Animated   Topps: Heritage

CLONE WARS

In 2004, Topps topped even the popularity of the autograph cards with a chaser called the Artist Sketch Card. The Clone Wars set was inspired by the Cartoon Network microseries of the same name. Thirteen artists known in the *Star Wars* community, including Genndy Tartakovsky and Paul Rudish, the creators of the cartoon, were chosen to do small sketches on these cards to be included at a maximum of one in thirty-six packs, or one per box. Each card is completely unique and signed by the artist, thereby making it not only prized by card collectors, but also by those who collect original art. Dave Dorman is the rarest artist with cards found one in 1,945 packs. Tartakovsky and Rudolfo Migliari are found one in 606 packs. Each of these sketch cards fetches up to $300, depending on the quality of the drawing. At least one box of cards must be opened to acquire one of the 7,000 to 8,000 different sketch cards. Consequently, there is an excess of the ninety-card sets available for sale or trade at very low prices due to the popularity of the sketch cards.

∘ Series 1 card set 1 to 90

∘ Series 2 battle motion card set 1 to 10

HERITAGE

The Heritage set was released to coincide with the sale of the original trilogy on DVD in 2004. This set is unique in that it brings the love of the vintage cards and the modern appeal of popular chasers like the Artist Sketch Cards together. The 120-card Heritage set contains new images from all six films, including previews for *Revenge of the Sith*, and is printed on gray card stock and includes a cellophane-wrapped piece of gum in each package.

∘ Series 1 card set 1 to 120

The sticker chasers available with the retail edition are similar to the alphabet stickers from the original *The Empire Strikes Back* set complete with an image from a larger puzzle on the back. The hobby edition features a second round of Artist Sketch Cards from over twenty-five artists from the *Star Wars* universe. Again, one of the 16,000 available sketch cards for the United States and Europe are found approximately one per box. Other chase cards for the hobby edition include six etched foil cards drawn by Jan Duursema and inked by Dan Parsons. These special cards fit together to make a larger two-by-three card collage; they also happen to fit with the Walt Simonson-etched foil cards from the Galaxy series.

The Future

As one of the longest running license holders for *Star Wars*, Topps cards are sure to be treasured into the future. There are two sets in the works for *Revenge of the Sith*, while there may be encores for Clone Wars, Evolution, and Galaxy. Also look for new, different, and exciting inserts to fuel the chase.

Terminology

The following are terms commonly associated with *Star Wars* trading cards:

Chase card	These are bonus cards that are not considered to be part of the basic set, and because they are produced in smaller quantities than regular cards they are more valuable. (Also known as insert cards.)
Hobby edition	A set of trading cards sold to specialist hobby retailers (such as comic book stores), and usually contains a series of regular cards as well as extended cards such as chasers.
Lenticular	A trading card printed on special plastic, which displays a short animation when tilted from top to bottom.
Milkcap	A small disc, usually made of cardboard, that features an image on one side and is blank or numbered on the other.
Photo card	Large-sized trading cards, which are manufactured to look like standard photographs.
Promo card	A limited-edition card that is designed to advertise a new trading card series and is often given away as a free gift at collector's exhibitions and in trading card and movie magazines.
Regular card	A standard trading card that forms part of a basic set.
Retail edition	A set of trading cards sold to general retailers, and usually only contains a series of regular cards.
Set	A collection of all the regular cards manufactured for a particular series. A basic set never includes chase cards. (Also known as series.)
Widevision	A card that is printed wider than a regular card's dimensions to portray widescreen (usually 16:9) aspect ratios.

10 COMICS

Comic books have been important throughout the history of *Star Wars*. With the film having been inspired by the comic book style of movie serials, it's no surprise that Lucasfilm chose to have its film adapted in the four-color medium.

Marvel Comics Group acquired the exclusive license to publish *Star Wars* comics beginning in 1977 and published their monthly titles until 1986. There were several years without *Star Wars* comics, until Dark Horse Comics picked up the license in 1991. It began publishing a handful of titles, and over twelve years later they are still going strong, having produced dozens of titles and hundreds of issues.

The *Expanded Universe*, which details events and situations that occur within the *Star Wars* universe, has grown with the publication of the comic books. What began as a small film adaptation by a predominantly superhero-driven publisher has blossomed, in a quarter of a century, to allow an even smaller comic publisher to compete with the largest comic publishers.

With over 650 issues published to date, and more coming out each month, there are plenty of *Stars Wars* comic books to keep fans entertained far into the future.

Canon and Continuity

In the beginning, except for the movie adaptations of *Star Wars*, *The Empire Strikes Back*, and *Return of the Jedi*, what happened in the *Star Wars* comic universe stayed in the *Star Wars* comic universe. The *Star Wars* canon was limited to the films and the books. The comics seemed to be an afterthought, or lesser medium. There were no crossovers with books, the events of one story line did not influence another, and the time line progressed, unaffected, forward from film to film. For many years, fandom at large as well as Lucasfilm denounced the early comic works as noncanon material.

When the publishing of comics and novels resumed in the early 1990s, there was a concerted effort to relate all the stories into one universe and into one time line that stemmed from the films themselves. But as the *Expanded Universe* grew, so did the embracing of all things comic related.

Current comics make use of years of continuity and time line notes, expanded histories of the least-glimpsed character, and have even led to the appearance of an *Expanded Universe* character in a *Star Wars* film.

Marvel Comics Group

In their second decade of publishing super hero comics, Marvel Comics put effort into film adaptations. *Logan's Run*, *2001: A Space Odyssey*, and *Star Wars* made up some of the titles published. Only one of these film titles initiated in the 1970s took off and is still being published today!

- ### Monthly Issues (107 issues; 1977 to 1986)

  Originally published in early 1977, the first six issues of *Star Wars* was an adaptation of the film by Roy Thomas, Howard Chaykin, and Steve Leialoha. These six issues were published in a variety of ways during the late 1970s and early 1980s, including direct reprints of the issues (noted by the diamond-shaped icon around the issue number or the text "Reprint" on the cover image), as "Treasury Sized" editions or in black-and-white paperback book form.

  Issue #1 also features several other variations that are worth noting. At that point in time, Marvel was in the process of switching from 30¢ comics to 35¢ comic books. Copies of issue #1 were printed with both the 30¢ and 35¢ prices, with the 35¢ issue being the rarer of the two. Both versions of these were reprinted, which caused some confusion among collectors.

  The authors of the comic books that followed the film adaptation were allowed relatively free reign to create characters and situations not predicated by the films. Many people remember the Marvel issues for their outlandish story lines, colorful characters, and strange situations. Some of the most memorable characters show up in the first story line that moves beyond the films. Issues #7-10, which featured Han Solo and Chewbacca, introduced readers to Crimson Jack the space pirate, Amaiza a sexy, scantily clad gunslinger, and Jaxxon the six-foot-tall green rabbit, all characters that are still discussed among fans today. Roy Thomas, Howard Chaykin, and Tom Palmer proved that classic characters can exist outside of the movies.

  The next batch of issues, #11-15, include adventures with Luke and the droids on a water planet in the system of Drexel. These issues begin a long run by noted comic artist Carmine Infantino, whose art continued nearly uninterrupted until the adaptation of *The Empire Strikes Back* in 1980.

  Issues that followed introduced readers to the Cyborg bounty hunter Valance, the gambling establishment The Wheel, Senator Greyshade, and Commander Strom. Issue #23 marked the return of Darth Vader to the pages of the comic.

Marvel Comics: Star Wars
monthly issue 1

Marvel: Star Wars
monthly issue 28

Marvel: Star Wars
monthly issue 70

The story lines that led up to *The Empire Strikes Back* involved the rebels evading any number of Imperial factions, including the Tagge family. Readers also got to see the return and final fate of Valance, explore an untold tale of Obi-Wan Kenobi during the Clone Wars, and met with Jabba the Hut (who appears as a character very unlike the large slug that would show up in *Return of the Jedi*). The Jabba and Obi-Wan stories seem apocryphal now, given the fact that the Jabba the Hutt scenes were reinstated into the Special Edition, and the Clone Wars are being well explored in current Dark Horse comics.

The Empire Strikes Back was adapted into the regular monthly series with issues #39–44. After the film, Lando became a regular member of the cast as the Star Warriors searched for a new base. On the way, they had several Solo stories, including Luke versus an Imperial Prove Droid, R2-D2 and C-3PO exploring "Droid World," and Leia outwitting Vader on the banking planet of Aargau in issue #48.

Issue #50 was a double-sized issue, as many milestone issues were, and featured a flashback to an untold Han Solo story. It also began a run of issues with Walt Simonson as the artist in residence. Simonson worked through the establishment of a base on Arba, with those loveable furry Hoojibs, Lando's return to Bespin in issues #56 and 57, and the hunt for Han Solo, which led right up to the film adaptation of Jedi in its own minicomic book series.

The publication of the *Return of the Jedi* miniseries was followed by the Rebellion, which stayed on Endor under the artwork of Cynthia Martin. Standout stories include #81 with Boba Fett escaping from the sarlacc, only to end up back in the creature by the issue's end. The major antagonists during these final twenty-some issues were the Nagai and Lumiya, who was actually Imperial Agent Shira Brie, bent on revenge.

The series' run came to an end with issue #107, September 1986. While the comic book titles of *Droids* and *Ewoks* would last another year and a set of three-dimensional comics would be published the following year, fans would need to wait five more years to relive the continuing adventures of Luke Skywalker and crew.

- ### Pizzazz (16 issues; 1977 to 1978)

These two comic strips seemed to have been missed by many people. They appeared in Marvel's *Pizzazz Magazine* between 1977 and 1978, and were serialized at three pages per issue. The first issue featured a cover with R2-D2 and C-3PO, and issue #7 had Darth Vader on the cover with other science-fiction characters, but as a whole, these issues were not geared to the *Star Wars* reader, but to the younger superhero fans.

- ### Return of the Jedi Miniseries (4 issues; 1983)

Breaking tradition, the comic book adaptation of Episode 4 was set outside the issues of the monthly series in their own four-issue limited series.

- ### Annuals (3 issues; 1979, 1982, and 1983)

Annuals were a staple of the comics industry during the silver age of comics. These issues usually would be one-shot stories and not part of the existing continuity or story lines, and were usually published during the summer months. Annuals were also notorious for not coming out on an actual annual schedule.

Annual #1, written by X-Men scribe Chris Claremont, further develops the characters of Luke and Leia, plus the history and mystery of the Jedi in "The Long Hunt." "Shadeshine" returns Han Solo to the series, having been frozen for "months" in carbonite, with a story from his past. "The Apprentice," the final issue in the series, features Flint, Vader, and the planet Belderone entitled.

- ### Ewoks (14 issues; 1985 to 1987)

- ### Droids (8 issues; 1986 to 1987)

Based on the Nelvana-animated series of the same names, these bimonthly series were released under Marvel's Star Comics line. Designed with the younger reader in mind, the *Ewok* stories followed the adventures of Wicket, Princess Kneesa, and the tribe of Ewoks, while the *Droids* stories followed the adventures of R2-D2 and C-3PO. *Ewoks* #10 is of particular interest, as it was a special crossover with *Droids* #4.

Los Angeles Times

Between 1979 and 1984, the Los Angeles Times Press syndicated daily and weekend strips by Russ Manning, Archie Goodwin, and Al Williamson. The Archie Goodwin strips were collected into three hardcover books produced by Russ Cochran Publishing. These strips were also reprinted by Dark Horse Comics in the *Classic Star Wars* and *Classic Star Wars: The Early Adventures* series that was reedited, colored, and given new art to combine the daily comic strip style into a more flowing comic book style. However, two strips, one by Manning and one by Goodwin (under the pseudonym Russ Helm) have yet to be reprinted.

Marvel Comics: Ewoks   *Blackthorne Pub.:* Star Wars 3D

- **Russ Manning (9 strips; 1979 to 1980)**

  The Russ Manning strips were reprinted in *Classic Star Wars: The Early Years* #1–9 and *The Constancia Affair* by Dark Horse Comics. The untitled July to September 1979 story, commonly referred to as "The Kashyyyk Depths," has yet to be reprinted.

- **Archie Goodwin (18 strips; 1980 to 1984)**

  The Archie Goodwin and Al Williamson strips were reprinted in *Classic Star Wars* #1–20, while the 1980 strip adapting Brian Daley's *Han Solo at Stars End* was reprinted in the title *Classic Star Wars: Han Solo at Stars End*. The strip credited to Russ Helm, titled *Planet of Kadril*, has yet to be reprinted.

Blackthorne Publishing

- ***Star Wars 3D* (3 issues; 1987 to 1988)**

  Blackthorne was a publisher of various *3D* comics as well as *Laffin Gas*, *Dick Tracy*, and parody comics such as *Hamster Vice* and *Failed Universe*. It also produced three issues of *Star Wars 3-D* between 1987 and 1998. These issues dealt with Luke returning to Tatooine and the Rebels looking for a new base after evacuating Yavin IV in *A New Hope*.

Dark Horse Comics

Five years after it started publishing, Dark Horse Comics managed to grab the brass ring by securing the comic book publishing rights to the *Star Wars* franchise. At the time, it was a small publisher with titles such as *Concrete* and *Boris the Bear*. It had begun a small revolution in the independent world with its *Aliens* comic series and was working with artists and writers to develop creator-owned properties. December 1991 signaled the beginning of the new age of *Star Wars* comics—an age when readers could enjoy continuity between the various publication arms of Lucasfilm.

As Dark Horse continued to grow, and the number of *Star Wars* titles published increased, Lucasfilm began utilizing its monthly comic book publishing franchise to a stronger advantage in the fan community. The year 1996 featured the *Shadows of the Empire* multimedia crossover event in which the comic book series was a focal point. Besides telling great stories in and around the time lines of the films, the comics have also been used to retroactively fix continuity glitches between the book publications and other sources.

Most recently, the comics have been used, along with novels, short stories, and animated shows, to tell the expanded tale of the Clone Wars. Dark Horse also has a pivotal role in the lead-in to *Episode 3: Revenge of the Sith*, tying its monthly issues and miniseries into the continuity of the novels and, eventually, the film itself.

Most Dark Horse series have been collected into trade paperbacks for distribution through noncomic shops. However, several series have not been republished in this format to date, most notable the first arc of *X-Wing Rogue Squadron* "The Rebel Opposition" and the *River of Chaos* miniseries.

- **Dark Empire (6 issues; 1991)**

Appearing a few months after the release of Timothy Zahn's *Heir to the Empire* novel, this series ushered in the new era of comic publication. The art style of Cam Kennedy was a major departure from previous renditions of the classic characters. The issues feature the return of a clone emperor and the introduction of several characters from Han's past. Fans also relished the return of Boba Fett to the comics with issue #4, necessitating a backstory to be developed on how the character may have escaped from the sarlacc's maw.

- **Classic Star Wars (20 reprint issues; 1992)**

This series reprinted the Archie Goodwin and Al Williamson strips published during the early 1980s. The strips were reformatted, colored, and in some cases new art was drawn by Al Williamson to transform the stories from the repetitive nature of a daily comic strip into the more prosaic comic book format.

- **Dark Horse Insider (8 issues; 1993)**

This free black-and-white preview comic featured a sneak peek at the Ulic Qel-Droma story line from the first *Tales of the Jedi* series in issues #15–20. Issues #33–34 featured previews of art and covers from *Dark Lords of the Sith*.

- **Dark Horse Comics (6 issues; 1993)**

Two separate story lines in this anthology series, #7–9 and #17–19, feature *Star Wars* characters. The first story line previewed the Nomi Sunrider issues of *Tales of the Jedi*, and the second story line contained a *Droids* story line to be reprinted in the *Droids Special*.

Dark Horse: Dark Empire

Dark Horse: Classic Star Wars

Dark Horse: Droids

- *Tales of the Jedi* **(5 issues; 1993)**

  Culling stories previewed in *Dark Horse Insider* and the monthly anthology *Dark Horse Comics*, *Tales of the Jedi* launched stories told in the distant past, when the birth of hyperspace travel was just beginning. Set in such a distant time as to avoid continuity conflicts, Tom Veitch's story line revolves around Nomi Sunrider and Ulic Qel-Droma as two young Jedi Knights thrust into the spotlight of galactic conflict. The series would continue in several in-carnations, introducing characters that would show up in novels and other sources, finally cul-minating in 1998 with the Redemption story line.

- *Tales of the Jedi: Freedon Nadd Uprising* **(2 issues; 1994)**

  A direct sequel to the original *Tales of the Jedi* series, these issues provided some backstory on the Sith (or what the Sith were before the prequels) and their ties to the Jedi.

- *Classic Star Wars: The Early Adventures* **(9 reprint issues; 1994)**

  The Early Adventures reprinted most of the Russ Manning *Los Angeles Times* daily comic strips. The strips were reformatted, colored, and in some cases new art was drawn to transform the stories from the repetitive nature of a daily comic strip into the more prosaic comic book for-mat. This series is significant as it features the first chronological appearance of Boba Fett months before the release of *The Empire Strikes Back*.

- *Droids* **(6 issues; 1994)**

  A new series featuring R2-D2 and C-3PO and their adventures with Olag Greck and C-3PX before joining Princess Leia in *A New Hope*.

- *Classic Star Wars: Movie* (ANH, TESB, and ROTJ reprints—2 issues per movie; 1994)

The square-bound books reprinted the Marvel movie adaptations. Each film adaptation was divided between two issues and featured new colorization of the existing art, plus additional end papers with original trilogy production artwork.

- *Tales of the Jedi: Dark Lords of the Sith* (6 issues; 1994)

Prolific author Kevin J. Anderson joined Tom Veitch on this series, which introduced Exar Kun and the teachings of the Sith. Exar Kun would also show up in Anderson's *Jedi Academy* book trilogy.

- *Dark Empire II* (6 issues; 1994)

A sequel to the hugely successful *Dark Empire*. This series continues Luke's quest for information on the Jedi and their teachings, plus the wrath of the clone Emperor Palpatine continues.

- *Droids Special* (1995)

Reprints the pages that originally appeared in the anthology title *Dark Horse Comics*, issues #17–19, in which the droids face off against the assassin droid IG-88.

- *Classic: Vandelhelm Mission* (1 issue reprints; 1995)

Reprints the classic Marvel story "Supply and Demand" from *Star Wars* #98, August 1985. This issue, by Archie Goodwin and Al Williamson, was chosen to be reprinted because of the large number of reprints already published by these creators.

- *Droids*, volume 2 (6 issues; 1995)

A second series featuring R2-D2 and C-3PO and their adventures with another set of masters, including Boonda the Hutt before joining Princess Leia in *A New Hope*.

- *Jabba the Hutt* (4 issues; 1995)

The *Jabba* series was published as individual one-shot comics over two years and consists of "The Gaar Suppoon Hit," "The Hunger of Princess Nampi," "The Dynasty Trap," and "Betrayal."

- *River of Chaos* (4 issues; 1995)

River of Chaos was a Princess Leia miniseries that took place just after the Battle of Yavin. Trapped behind enemy lines, can Leia unite a divided people while staying one step ahead of Imperial search parties?

- *X-Wing Rogue Squadron* (35 issues; 1995-1998)

Rogue Squadron featured continuing tales of Wedge Antilles and his rebel pilots. The series was divided into four-issue or smaller story arcs that could be easily collected. This series introduced characters such as Tycho Celchu, Winter, Sate Pestage, and Baron Fell, all who would show up in other novels. Other X-Wing stories appear in an *Apple Jacks X-Wing Special*, which was available as a mail-in offer from the popular breakfast cereal, and a special half-issue published in conjunction with Wizard Press.

Dark Horse: The Sith War

- **Tales of the Jedi: The Sith War (6 issues; 1995)**

  Continuing the story begun in previous *Tales of the Jedi* comics, Exar Kun and Ulic Qel-Droma battle into the heart of Yavin IV and provide a backstory to the already published *Jedi Academy* book trilogy.

- **Empire's End (2 issues; 1995)**

  The *Dark Empire* story line concludes with the destruction of the Galaxy Gun and the final clone emperor.

- **The Mixed-Up Droid (1 issue; 1995)**

  Released as a companion piece to the audiobook *The Mixed-Up Droid*, this issue follows the events of the audiotape in an abridged fashion, as C-3PO deals with some faulty wiring.

- **Heir to the Empire: Adaptation (6 issues; 1995)**

  This series adapted the Timothy Zahn novel into the comics medium, in which a new Imperial grand admiral begins striking at the New Republic, and the clone of a long-deceased Jedi returns to torment Luke Skywalker, Han Solo, and Princess Leia.

- **Boba Fett (5 issues; 1995)**

  The *Boba Fett* series was published as individual one-shot comics over five years and consists of "Bounty on Bar-Kooda," "When the Fat Lady Swings," "Murder Most Foul," "Agent of Doom," and a special half-issue published in conjunction with Wizard Press.

- **Splinter of the Mind's Eye: Adaptation (4 issues; 1995)**

  This series adapts the classic Alan Dean Foster story from 1978, where Luke and Leia travel to the Planet Mimban to find the mysterious Kaiburr Crystal.

- **Shadows of the Empire (6 issues; 1996)**

  This six-issue miniseries was created by Lucasfilm to tell the story between *The Empire Strikes Back* and *Return of the Jedi*. It featured characters and situations from a perspective unique to the comics.

- **Tales of the Jedi: Golden Age of the Sith (6 issues; 1996)**

  Readers were catapulted an additional 1,000 years into the past with this series that explored the origins and factions of the Sith.

- **A Decade of Dark Horse (1996)**

  Celebrating its tenth anniversary, Dark Horse published three issues of an anthology series. Only issue #2 featured a short story about everyone's favorite Kowakian monkey-lizard, called "This Crumb for Hire."

- **Classic: Devilworlds (2 issue reprints; 1996)**

  This two-issue series reprinted some hard-to-find, and never-before reprinted stories from the 1980s Marvel United Kingdom weekly series.

- **A New Hope: Special Edition (4 issues; 1997)**

  A brand new adaptation of *A New Hope* was created for the 1997 releases of the *Star Wars: Special Editions*. This featured the extra added scenes and creatures as seen in that version of the film.

- **Classic: Han Solo at Stars End (3 issue reprints; 1997)**

  This series reprints the 1980–1981 comic strip adaptation of the Brian Daley novel *Han Solo at Stars End*. As with other comic strip reprints, these issues were reedited and colored for the new format.

- **Dark Force Rising: Adaptation (6 issues; 1997)**

  This series adapted the Timothy Zahn novel into the comics medium, which continued the story from *Heir to the Empire*, with the discovery of a long lost fleet of Imperial ships and the secrets they hold that can destroy the New Republic.

- **Dark Forces: Soldier for the Empire (HC; 1997)**
- **Dark Force: Rebel Agent (HC; 1998)**
- **Dark Forces: Jedi Knight (HC; 1998)**

  These direct-to-market hardcovers for the high-end comic reader were not technically comics but illustrated novels. They were still published by Dark Horse and featured characters and situations created by LucasArts in the *Dark Forces* and *Jedi Knight* video games.

- **Tales of the Jedi: Fall of the Sith Empire (5 issues; 1997)**

  Continuing the story line from *Golden Age of the Sith*, readers discovered the power of the Sith as events set the stage for the already published *Tales of the Jedi* series.

Dark Horse: The Last Command   Dark Horse: Crimson Empire

- **The Protocol Offensive (PF; 1997)**

  This prestige format one-shot collaboration between Brian Daley and Anthony Daniels sees C-3PO and R2-D2 trying to prevent a plot that could tip the people of Tahlboor into chaos.

- **The Last Command: Adaptation (6 issues; 1997)**

  This series adapted the Timothy Zahn novel into the comics medium, and concluded the *Thrawn* trilogy with the final showdown between Mara Jade, Luke Skywalker, and Joruus C'Baoth.

- **Crimson Empire (6 issues; 1997)**

  Readers get a glimpse of the always impressive and mysterious Emperor's Royal Guard in this series that deals with a rogue member of the guard, Kir Kanos, who is forced to go after another of his kind. This story features ties to the old Marvel series with the inclusion of the planet Yinchorr.

- **Shadows of the Empire: Evolution (5 issues; 1998)**

  A sequel to the *Shadows of the Empire* series featuring Guri, the human-replica droid.

- **Dark Forces: Soldier for the Empire (TPB; 1998)**

- **Dark Force: Rebel Agent (TPB; 1998)**

- **Dark Forces: Jedi Knight (TPB; 1998)**

  These direct-to-market paperbacks were reprints of the original Dark Horse–illustrated hardcover novels.

- **Star Wars Handbook Volume 1: X-Wing Rogue Squadron** (1998)

- **Star Wars Handbook Volume 2: Crimson Empire** (1999)

- **Star Wars Handbook Volume 3: Dark Empire** (2000)

  Acting as guides to the characters and technology of several different *Star Wars* comic series, these single edition handbooks covered bios on the characters with some extra behind-the-scenes notes and descriptions of vehicles and planets.

- **Tales of the Jedi: Redemption** (5 issues; 1998)

  The conclusion to the successful *Tales of the Jedi* series features the final redemption of Ulic Qel-Droma.

- **A New Hope: Manga** (4 issues; 1998)

  The original script of *Star Wars* adapted into the Japanese animation style by artist Tamaki Hisao.

- **Mara Jade** (6 issues; 1998)

  Fan favorite Mara Jade, a character to break the bounds of her literary beginnings, gets her own miniseries written by Timothy Zahn and Michael Stackpole.

- **Jedi Academy: Leviathan** (4 issues; 1998)

  A spin-off from the *Jedi Academy* book trilogy by Kevin J Anderson, this series concentrates on several graduates from Luke's Jedi Academy.

- **Crimson Empire II: Council of Blood** (6 issues; 1998)

  The sequel to *Crimson Empire* featuring the first appearance of Nom Anor, who would grow to fame and fortune in the *New Jedi Order* series of novels.

- **Star Wars** (45 issues; 1998 to 2002)

  The first regular monthly series to bear only the name *Star Wars* since the Marvel series concluded in 1986. This series had story arcs that were broken over four or six issues and featured the first appearance of Ki-Adi-Mundi several months before the release of *The Phantom Menace*. This series dealt with characters, mostly Jedi Council members for its early issues, such as Ki-Adi-Mundi and Mace Windu. Lucasfilm utilized issue #13 to explain why some preproduction photos of Mace Windu had one lightsaber style, while photos after the film was released had a different model.

  Issue #19 introduced readers to Quinlan Vos (a background extra seen in *The Phantom Menace*), a Jedi with amnesia. Shortly after that, Vos' padawan Aayla Secura was introduced. She marks the only character to make the leap from a comic book into one of the films, with her appearance in *Attack of the Clones*.

  The series "ended" with issue #45 when it underwent a name change to *Star Wars: Republic* and jumped ahead two years in the continuity to deal with Episode 2-related story lines.

- **The Empire Strikes Back: Manga** (4 issues; 1999)

  A Japanese animation adaptation by Toshiki Kudo, based on the screenplay by Leigh Brackett and Lawrence Kasdan.

- **Boba Fett: Enemy of the Empire** (4 issues; 1999)

  This series teams up two of the best villains in the *Star Wars* universe, as Darth Vader hires Boba Fett to retrieve a small box from a remote planet. An apparently easy job for such a notorious bounty hunter, or is it?

- **Vader's Quest** (4 issues; 1999)

  How did Darth Vader find out the name of the Rebel that destroyed the Death Star? Darko Macan and Dave Gibbons fit this story into the ever-increasing dense time line between *A New Hope* and *The Empire Strikes Back*.

- **Classic: Long Time Ago V1** (6 issue reprints; 1999)

  These black-and-white, digest-sized reprints of various Marvel issues were released exclusively through comic specialty shops and remain difficult issues to locate.

- **The Phantom Menace** (4 issues; 1999)

  The official adaptation of the prequel movie that everyone was waiting for. These issues were release about one month before the film. Spin-off issues that focused on individual characters in and around the events of the film were also published at this time. These included "Anakin Skywalker," "Qui-Gon Jinn," "Obi-Wan Kenobi," and "Queen Amidala." There was also a special half-issue published in conjunction with Wizard Press.

- **Bounty Hunters** (3 issues; 1999)

  A series of three one-shot issues that feature Aurra Sing, Dengar, 4-LOM, Bossk, and Kenix Kil. Aurra Sing's story occurs after the events of *The Phantom Menace* with the bounty hunter tracking down a renegade Jedi. Dengar, 4-LOM, and Bossk appear in "Scoundrel's Wages" tracking down the captain of the Millennium Falcon. Not quite as easy as it sounds. And finally Kenix Kil, who is actually Kir Kanos from the *Crimson Empire* issues, is featured in his own title.

- **Dark Horse Presents Annual** (1999)

  This anthology annual, subtitled *DHP Jr.*, features stories of Dark Horse characters as kids. The *Star Wars* tale features Luke and Windy on a Tatooine adventure that turns dangerous, until Ben Kenobi saves them.

- **Return of the Jedi: Manga** (4 issues; 1999)

  A Japanese animation adaptation of the original screenplay by Shin-Ichi Hiromoto.

- **Tales** (20+ issues; 1999 to present)

  This quarterly anthology series was intended to showcase new artists and writers to the Dark Horse stables. It proved to be a place where short *Star Wars* stories could be told. It was also a

Dark Horse: Tales

Dark Horse: Union

Dark Horse: Jedi Council *issue 4*

place of fan contention because of the Infinities nature of some of the stories. Infinities is the seal that Dark Horse places on those stories that are felt to be out of continuity with the rest of the comic issues. The on-again, off-again Infinities labeling confused and upset many fans. The series was reportedly cancelled with issue #20. It actually marked a turning point, as the title was revamped for better continuity and larger stories.

- ### *Union* (4 issues; 1999)

  What began as a feud between Luke Skywalker and Mara Jade way back in *Heir to the Empire* has turned into love, and this issue celebrates their marriage. It includes appearances by many characters from the *Star Wars* novels including Booster Terrik, Talon Karrde, and Corran Horn.

- ### *The Phantom Menace: Manga* (2 issues; 1999)

  Animation retelling of the prequel by Japanese artist Kia Asamiya.

- ### *Sergio Aragonés Stomps Star Wars* (2000)

  A spoof issue, in the vein of *Fred Hembeck Destroys the Marvel Universe*. Dark Horse allows the creator of Groo the Wanderer a little fun in a galaxy far, far away.

- ### *Chewbacca* (4 issues; 2000)

  Designed as a memorial issue to Chewbacca, who was killed in Vector Prime. Following the first novel in the *New Jedi Order* series, each issue allows a different set of writers and artists to tell stories from Chewbacca's past.

- ### *Dark Horse Extra* (11 issues; 2000)

  This direct market, newspaper-styled Dark Horse tabloid contained three short comic strips based on various Dark Horse properties. Eleven of these issues featured *Star Wars* characters over three separate strips, "Hard Currency," a preview of the canceled *Crimson Empire III* comic, in issues #21–24, "Heart of Fire," which features Quinlan Vos from issues #35–37, and "Poison Moon," with Anakin and Obi-Wan in issues #44–47.

- **Jedi Council (4 issues; 2000)**

A series that takes place shortly before *The Phantom Menace*, it explores the characterizations of the members of the council. Includes a previous council member, Micah Giiett, who sacrifices himself to save his fellow Jedi, thus providing the seat for Ki-Adi-Mundi in the "Prelude to Rebellion" story in *Star Wars* #1–6.

- **Darth Maul (4 issues; 2000)**

Jan Duursema explores that fury and power that is Darth Maul in this four-issue series. The story line of this series leads into the novel *Darth Maul: Shadow Hunter* with the inclusion of characters and situations hinted at in that story.

- **Qui-Gon and Obi-Wan: Last Stand on Ord Mantell (3 issues; 2000)**

This three-issue miniseries explores the master/padawan relationship between Qui-Gon Jinn and Obi-Wan Kenobi as they track down a rogue Jedi on the planet of Ord Mantell.

- **Underworld: Yavin Vasilika (5 issues; 2000)**

This pre–*A New Hope* story line features Han Solo and Chewbacca, as well as Lando and a number of bounty hunter characters in a race to find a secret and prized treasure: the Yavin Vasilika.

- **Dark Horse Presents Annual (2000)**

The second *DHP Annual* to feature *Star Wars* characters. Aurra Sing gets a chance to shine in this issue, with the story "Aurra's Song," which features a historical account of one of her early adventures.

- **Jedi Vs Sith (6 issues; 2001)**

With the release of the prequels and the apocryphal alteration of the Sith backstory, Darko Macan and Ramon F. Bachs provide some retrocontinuity to bring the *Tales of the Jedi Sith* and the prequel Sith together into a seamless time line.

- **Infinities: A New Hope (4 issues; 2001)**

A series that looks at the possibilities and alternate realities that can happen when something within the films does not happen as expected. Based on the *What If . . . ?* series published by Marvel, this particular story line explores what would happen if Luke missed his shot on the Death Star.

- **Jedi Quest (4 issues; 2001)**

This miniseries explores the early relationship between Obi-Wan Kenobi and his padawan, Anakin Skywalker. This story line eventually continues in the *Jedi Quest* young-adult novels by Scholastic.

Dark Horse: Underworld   *Dark Horse:* Tag & Bink Are Dead

- **Tag and Bink Are Dead (2 issues; 2001)**

  A humorous look at the events of two inept Rebel spies as they work their way in, around, and behind the events of the classic trilogy. Based on the play *Rosencrantz and Guildenstern Are Dead* and written by Troops director Kevin Rubio.

- **Starfighter: Crossbones (3 issues; 2002)**

  A spin-off from a video game series for PlayStation 2 featuring Nym and used to tie the *Starfighter* and *Jedi Starfighter* game story lines together.

- **Qui-Gon and Obi-Wan: The Aurorient Express (2 issues; 2002)**

  This two-issue miniseries explores the master/padawan relationship between Qui-Gon Jinn and Obi-Wan Kenobi as they investigate the mysterious sinking of a luxury passenger liner.

- **Jango Fett/Zam Wessel Specials (2 issues; 2002)**

  Two square-bound one-shots that share a common story thread. Released around the time of Episode 2, these issues provide some additional backstory on the two bounty hunters of *Attack of the Clones*.

- **Attack of the Clones (4 issues; 2002)**

  The official adaptation of the film was released shortly before the movie in both individual issues and a trade paperback.

- **Jango Fett: Open Seasons (4 issues; 2002)**

  The Episode 2 bounty hunter gets his own miniseries that explores his origins and expands on story possibilities developed in *Attack of the Clones* and the *Bounty Hunter* console videogame.

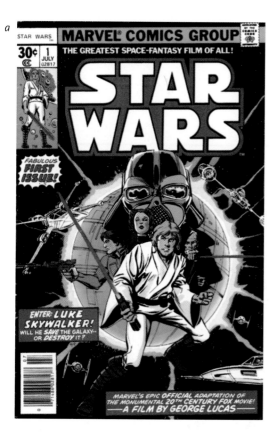

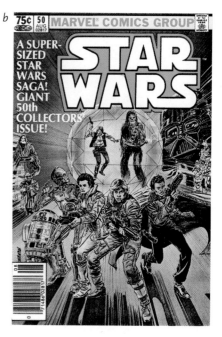

a. *Marvel* Star Wars Monthly #1 *comic book cover*

b. *Marvel* Star Wars Monthly #50 *comic book cover*

c. *Kenner Body Rigs original promotional art work*

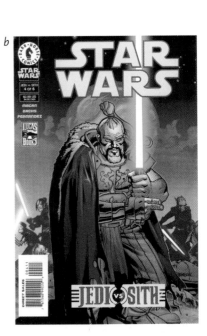

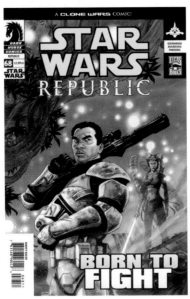

a. *Dark Horse* Boba Fett: Agent of Doom *trade paperback cover*

b. *Dark Horse* Jedi versus Sith *trade paperback cover*

c. *Dark Horse* Republic #68 *comic book cover*

d. *Dark Horse* The Phantom Menace *trade paperback cover*

a

b

c

a. *Kenner loose Ewoks unreleased
   second wave*

b. *Kenner loose Droids unreleased
   second wave*

c. *Kenner Canada boxed* La Guerre des
   Étoiles *special 12 mini-figures set*

a. *Kenner Canada boxed* Star Wars: *Station Spatiale de L'Étoile de la Mort*

b. *Kenner Canada Droids Thall Joben card front*

c. *Kenner Canada carded Sears exclusive Canadian skin-wrapped General Veers*

d. *Pride Displays loose action figure display diorama*

a

b

c

a. Topps Heritage signed Darth Vader trading card

b. Topps Heritage signed Luke Skywalker trading card

c. Topps Heritage signed Princess Leia trading card

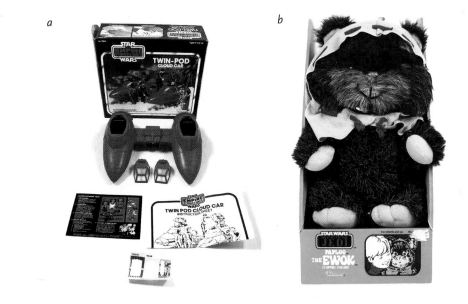

a. *Kenner boxed* The Empire Strikes Back *Twin-Pod Cloud Car (complete with inserts)*

b. *Kenner boxed plush* Return of the Jedi *Paploo the Ewok doll*

c. *Kenner Canada boxed* Star Wars Death Star

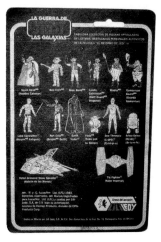

a. Topps Star Wars C-3PO X-rated trading card

b. Lily Ledy El Returno de Jedi 12-back card reverse

c. Lily Ledy loose 12-inch Tusken Raider

a. *Kenner packaged* Star Wars Young Jedi *mail-away kit*

b. *Kenner Canada boxed* The Empire Strikes Back *Rebel Transport*

c. *Kenner boxed* The Empire Strikes Back *Rebel Transport*

Dark Horse: Open Season

Dark Horse: Republic *issue 49*

Dark Horse: Jedi

- **Infinities: Empire Strikes Back (4 issues; 2002)**

  A series that looks at the possibilities and alternate realities that can happen when something within the films does not happen as expected. Based on the *What If . . . ?* series published by Marvel, this particular story line explores what would happen if Luke had died on the icy plains of Hoth.

- **Republic (24+ issues; 2002 to present)**

  This series continued the numbering of *Star Wars* but jumped further up the time line to include stories from the *Attack of the Clones* era. With issue #49, the issues began the Clone Wars story lines that continue up to Episode 3.

- **Empire (25+ issues; 2002 to present)**

  Spun off from the *Star Wars* monthly series and restarting with issue #1, this title focuses on stories from the time of *A New Hope*. Highlights of this series include the Biggs Darklighter story arc, and the story line involving Lt. Sunber and the Amanaman.

- **Jedi (5 issues; 2002)**

  A series of one-shot super-sized (sixty-four-page) comics that serve as explorative pieces on different Jedi during the Clone Wars. These issues integrate with the *Republic* issues and are reprinted in the Clone Wars trade paperbacks. The individual issues include "Mace Windu," "Shaak Ti," "Aayla Secura," "Dooku," and "Yoda."

- **A Valentine's Story (2003)**

  This pre–*Empire Strikes Back* one-shot explores a growing affection between Leia and Han, and what a coincidence—it was published in time for Valentine's Day.

- **Infinities: Return of the Jedi (4 issues; 2003)**

  A series that looks at the possibilities and alternate realities that can happen when something within the films does not happen as expected. Based on the *What If . . . ?* series published by Marvel, this particular story line explores what would happen if C-3PO had been unable to translate properly for Jabba the Hutt.

- **Clone Wars Adventures (2 issues; 2004)**

  This digest-sized series tells tales of the Clone Wars in the style of the Cartoon Network Clone Wars animated shows. One of the stories from issue #2, "Hide in Plain Sight," was originally published as a stand-alone comic for Free Comic Books Day 2004.

Hasbro/Toys "R" Us Exclusives

These four minicomics were handed out as promotional material during May and June 2002 at Toys "R" Us stores, and were nothing more than advertisements for Hasbro's *Attack of the Clones* toy line.

- Issue 1: *Full of Surprises* (2002)

- Issue 2: *Most Precious Weapon* (2002)

- Issue 3: *Practice Makes Perfect* (2002)

- Issue 4: *Machines of War* (2002)

The Topps Company Inc.

Topps, the trading card company, was given permission to reprint a number of short Dark Horse stories in its quarterly magazines as two- to four-page comic strips that would eventually be reprinted by Dark Horse in individual one-shot issues or trade paperback collections.

- **Star Wars Galaxy Magazine (13 issues; 1994 to 1997)**
  - Issue 1: "Artoo's Day Out"

  - Issue 2: "Tales of the Mos Eisley Cantina" (part 1)

  - Issue 3: "Tales of the Mos Eisley Cantina" (part 2)

  - Issue 4: "Tales of the Mos Eisley Cantina" (part 3)

  - Issue 5: "Boba Fett: Twin Engines of Destruction" (part 1)

  - Issue 6: "Boba Fett: Twin Engines of Destruction" (part 2)

  - Issue 7: "Boba Fett: Twin Engines of Destruction" (part 3)

  - Issue 8: "Boba Fett: Twin Engines of Destruction" (part 4)

  - Issue 9: "Shadow Stalker" (part 1)

  - Issue 10: "Shadow Stalker" (part 2)

    ◦ Issue 11: "Shadow Stalker" (part 3)

    ◦ Issue 12: "Shadow Stalker" (part 4)

    ◦ Issue 13: "The Jabba Tape" (part 1)

Galaxy Magazine was cancelled in 1997, with only the first chapter of "The Jabba Tapes" published. When Topps began publishing its *Galaxy Collector* magazine in 1998, it included the last three parts of the story.

- **Star Wars Galaxy Collector (3 issues; 1998)**

    ◦ Issue 1: "The Jabba Tape" (part 2)

    ◦ Issue 2: "The Jabba Tape" (part 3)

    ◦ Issue 3: "The Jabba Tape" (part 4)

Trade Paperbacks

Frequently, comic books are collected together and bound in a single, or series, of paperback books and published with the mass market in mind. The following are those *Star Wars* comics that have been printed as trade paperbacks.

    ◦ *Dark Empire* (1993)

    ◦ *Classic Star Wars, Vol. 1: In Deadly Pursuit* (1994)

    ◦ *Tales of the Jedi: Knights of the Old Republic* (1994)

    ◦ *Droids: The Kalarba Adventures* (1995)

    ◦ *Classic Star Wars, Vol. 2: The Rebel Storm* (1995)

    ◦ *Dark Empire II* (1995)

    ◦ *Classic Star Wars: A New Hope* (1995)

    ◦ *Classic Star Wars: The Empire Strikes Back* (1995)

    ◦ *Classic Star Wars: Return of the Jedi* (1995)

    ◦ *Classic Star Wars, Vol. 3: Escape to Hoth* (1996)

    ◦ *Tales of the Jedi: Dark Lords of the Sith* (1996)

    ◦ *Tales of the Jedi: The Sith War* (1996)

    ◦ *Heir to the Empire* (1996)

    ◦ *Splinter of the Mind's Eye* (1996)

    ◦ *Droids: Rebellion* (1997)

    ◦ *A New Hope: The Special Edition* (1997)

    ◦ *The Empire Strikes Back: The Special Edition* (1997)

- *Return of the Jedi: The Special Edition* (1997)

- *Shadows of the Empire* (1997)

- *Classic Star Wars: The Early Adventures* (1997)

- *Tales of the Jedi: The Golden Age of the Sith* (1997)

- *Empire's End* (1997)

- *Classic Star Wars: Han Solo at Stars' End* (1997)

- *X-Wing Rogue Squadron: The Phantom Affair* (1997)

- *Tales of the Jedi: The Freedon Nadd Uprising* (1997)

- *Boba Fett: Death, Lies, and Treachery* (1998)

- *Dark Force Rising* (1998)

- *X-Wing Rogue Squadron: Battleground Tatooine* (1998)

- *Tales of the Jedi: The Fall of the Sith Empire* (1998)

- *Jabba the Hutt: The Art of the Deal* (1998)

- *Dark Forces: Soldier for the Empire* (1998)

- *X-Wing Rogue Squadron: The Warrior Princess* (1998)

- *Crimson Empire* (1998)

- *X-Wing Rogue Squadron: Requiem for a Rogue* (1999)

- *Dark Forces: Rebel Agent* (1999)

- *X-Wing Rogue Squadron: In the Empire's Service* (1999)

- *Episode I: The Phantom Menace* (1999)

- *The Last Command* (1999)

- *X-Wing Rogue Squadron: Blood and Honor* (1999)

- *Mara Jade: By the Emperor's Hand* (1999)

- *Boba Fett: Enemy of the Empire* (1999)

- *Dark Forces: Jedi Knight* (1999)

- *Crimson Empire: Council of Blood* (1999)

- *Vader's Quest* (1999)

- *Shadows of the Empire: Evolution* (2000)

- *Episode I: The Phantom Menace Adventures* (2000)

- *Prelude to Rebellion* (2000)

- *X-Wing Rogue Squadron: Masquerade* (2000)
- *Jedi Academy: Leviathan* (2000)
- *Union* (2000)
- *The Bounty Hunters* (2000)
- *X-Wing Rogue Squadron: Mandatory Retirement* (2000)
- *Chewbacca* (2001)
- *Outlander* (2001)
- *Darth Maul* (2001)
- *Jedi Council: Acts of War* (2001)
- *Tales of the Jedi: Redemption* (2001)
- *Emissaries to Malastare* (2001)
- *Underworld* (2001)
- *Twilight* (2001)
- *Infinities: A New Hope* (2002)
- *Star Wars Tales Volume 1* (2002)
- *Episode II: Attack of the Clones* (2002)
- *Jedi vs. Sith* (2002)
- *Star Wars Tales Volume 2* (2002)
- *A Long Time Ago . . . Volume 1: Doomworld* (2002)
- *A Long Time Ago . . . Volume 2: Dark Encounters* (2002)
- *Star Wars: The Hunt for Aurra* (2002)
- *Star Wars: Darkness* (2002)
- *A Long Time Ago . . . Volume 3: Resurrection of Evil* (2002)
- *A Long Time Ago . . . Volume 4: Screams in the Void* (2003)
- *Jango Fett: Open Seasons* (2003)
- *Star Wars Tales Volume 3* (2003)
- *A Long Time Ago . . . Volume 5: Fool's Bounty* (2003)
- *Infinities: The Empire Strikes Back* (2003)
- *A Long Time Ago . . . Volume 6: Wookie World* (2003)
- *Clone Wars Volume 1: The Defense of Kamino* (2003)

- *A Long Time Ago . . . Volume 7: Far, Far Away* (2003)

- *Empire Vol. 1* (2003)

- *The Stark Hyperspace War* (2003)

- *Clone Wars Volume 2: Victories and Sacrifices* (2003)

- *Star Wars Tales Volume 4* (2004)

- *The Rite of Passage* (2004)

- *Clone Wars Volume 3: Last Stand on Jabiim* (2004)

- *Empire Vol. 2* (2004)

- *Clone Wars Volume 4: Light and Dark* (2004)

- *Clone Wars Adventures Vol. 1* (2004)

- *Infinities: Return of the Jedi* (2004)

The Future

The *Republic, Empire*, and *Tales* titles will continue to be published. In anticipation of *Episode 3: Revenge of the Sith*, Dark Horse is releasing a five-issue series called *Obsession* that will tie up loose ends from the Clone Wars as well as dovetail story lines from the Cartoon Network–animated shows and the novel *Labyrinth of Evil*. There are also plans for a *General Grievous* miniseries to begin in April 2005, plus the *Episode 3* film adaptation.

Dark Horse will also be releasing two other titles that deal with the comics and artwork of the *Star Wars* universe. *Panel to Panel*, the first book, published in late 2004, will reprint some of the greatest covers and artwork from over a decade of publishing *Star Wars* stories. The second book, *Visionaries*, will contain comic stories utilizing characters and designs from the *Episode 3* art department.

The *Expanded Universe* may have originated in the novels of Timothy Zahn, but thanks to the hard work of many artists and writers, those characters and situations have been allowed to grow and continue to live. They have also become a useful tool to repair continuity errors within the *Star Wars* universe. Fans continue to record and alter homemade time lines to encompass information presented monthly by comic publishers that further weaves the web of continuity throughout the fictional universe. Where *Star Wars* films were once inspired by the comic medium, *Star Wars* comics now benefit from George Lucas's visions and continue to inspire millions of fans monthly.

With the wealth of characters and the continued interest in comic stories, there's no reason that these titles won't continue well after the films are completed.

Terminology

The following are terms and acronyms commonly associated with *Star Wars* comics:

GN   Graphic Novel: A self-contained comic that is not an installment of a series, generally between sixty-four and ninety-five pages in length.

IN   Illustrated Novel: A novel that includes large graphics to illustrate the story line.

One-shot   A self-contained comic that is not an installment of a series, generally no more than sixty-four pages in length.

PF   Prestige Format: Similar in length and style to a one-shot but printed on higher quality paper and bound using glue instead of staples.

Strip   A sequence of drawings telling a story in a newspaper or comic book.

TPB   Trade Paperback: A book that is typically of better production quality, larger size, and higher price than a mass-market edition and is intended for sale in bookstores. Specifically, it is a bound collection of comic books to encompass all or part of a story line.

11 PROTOTYPES

Prototype and variation collecting are at different ends of the hobby's spectrum and require considerable amounts of effort to collect. For some collectors, the thought of having one of everything is not enough, so they spend a great deal of time and energy tracking down the earliest examples of *Star Wars* collectibles or different versions with subtle changes.

This chapter focuses on an area of the hobby that is more concerned with the developments and changes an item goes through in its life cycle, from a designer's drawing board to the shelf in a toy store, rather than the actual item itself. Since *Star Wars* collecting is dominated by Kenner/Hasbro, this chapter will look at toys, but the same is true for almost any other piece of *Star Wars* memorabilia.

Put simply, a prototype is the original model of an item from the initial stages of product development. A variation on the other hand is a product that has endured postproduction running changes during its shelf life and is identified by the alterations to the original release.

The Life of a Toy

The attraction of prototype and variation collecting is closely linked to a collector's knowledge of the life cycle of a product, whether it is a vintage *Star Wars* action figure or an *Attack of the Clones* shampoo bottle. For most products, the steps from drawing board to store shelf are the same.

DEVELOPMENT

The first stage of development always begins on paper. A product designer draws sketches from reference material from the license owner, in this case Lucasfilm. In the past, these would be production stills taken at the studio or in a carpenter's, costume, or creature workshop. It was done this way because often character, vehicle, and set design wasn't completed until a camera was about to shoot the subject in question. Today, the importance of accurate merchandise is well known, and production departments are keyed up to supply art, photographs, and other references as early as possible to prevent delays or mistakes from happening.

A well-known example of this is Kenner's original blue Snaggletooth figure that was included with the Sears-exclusive Cantina Adventure. Lucasfilm provided only a head shot of the character and Kenner toy designers made up the rest of the body themselves. They made Snaggletooth taller and gave him boots and a silver outfit to wear. When more reference photos arrived, the toy was corrected to the short, bootless, red-suited Snaggletooth.

From this source material come a series of sketches showing how the subject could be adapted into toy form. For instance, what movie features could and could not be reproduced, and what changes would have to be made to certain elements to make the toy feasible? A good example of this would be Kenner's decision to use 3¾-inch figures instead of its usual 12-inch dolls, which would have made vehicles like the Millennium Falcon unfeasibly large and expensive.

There are instances where product designers employed the use of model makers to build concept models to demonstrate the toy. Concept models were often used in vehicles and play sets. Model makers often used existing toys (even from other lines or different companies), model kits, and random pieces of plastic to construct this earliest of prototype. Concept models were only meant to be used for demonstration (and sometimes exhibition), so they were quickly destroyed. Thus, there are few examples surviving from the vintage years but the practice is known to have continued at Hasbro through to the present.

Once down on paper, Lucasfilm has the right to approve or decline any licensed item. Assuming that the product in question gets a green light, detailed schematics are drawn to determine the mechanics of the pieces such as how many parts to the finished product, assembly patterns, and annotations to sculptors. It is from these blueprints that the sculptor works.

PROTOTYPING

To create an action figure, a sculptor will build a 1:1-scale replica of what is intended to be the final product. In some instances, the model is made twice (2:1) or four times (4:1) the size of the finished product to provide additional detail on intricate parts or small-scale products. Such was the case of EV-9D9 and the Kenner Micro Collection. If it is a vehicle or play set, it is a model maker who takes over and builds a mock-up that is as true to the design as possible. Often, action figures are constructed from the parts of existing figures to save time and expense.

In vintage times, most sculptors based their first efforts on a metal skeleton clad in clay. Using the tools of their trade, they built up the general shape of the character and then added rough details such as clothing, fixed accessories (belts and holsters), and facial detail. Typically, clay was used because it allowed both subtractive and additive sculpting. After that, a clay mold of the sculpt was made, and then a cast made from wax was produced. This wax casting was then detailed further to closer resemble the desired outcome. The final stage was to take the wax cast apart, such as removing limbs and other articulated appendages to separate each part of the final product.

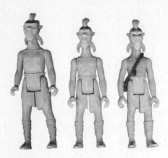

Kez Iban Wax and Acetate Sculpt
(Image courtesy of Chris Georgoulias)

Y-wing Landing Gear Proto-mold
(Image courtesy of Chris Georgoulias)

In the case of a play set or vehicle, particularly ones with large mechanical details, the original was not sculpted from clay but carved from wood, and was often several times larger than the intended finished product. Fine detail was made from putty while larger pieces of detail such as paneling or engines were made from separate pieces of wood and glued on to the pattern. This allowed extra detail to be included without risking damage to the pattern. A mold is made from the pattern and finally a polyurethane cast is made, which is known as the tooling master, from which the production mold is made. Because the molds made in the early stages of prototyping aren't durable, a toy designer will often get a protomold milled from a block of aluminum so that a number of identical parts can be cast over and over again to test a product in development.

Advancements in prototyping techniques have almost done away with clay sculptures and wax castings. A three-dimensional scanning laser, such as that devised by Gentle Giant Studios, which constructed digital models for Lucasfilm's digital library during the filming of *Attack of the Clones* and *Revenge of the Sith*, is commonly used on actors, models, scenery, and props. In the case of 3³/₄- and 12-inch action figures, this method allowed Hasbro to avoid the long sculpting process by selecting poses for performers in full costume and then having them scanned.

Today, rapid prototyping, a method that utilizes computer-aided design (CAD) software and a three-dimensional printer, has shortened the process of producing a physical replica from days to hours. The three-dimensional printer builds up microlayers of liquid photosensitive polymers that solidify when exposed to ultraviolet (UV) light to construct a facsimile at any chosen scale.

The most common rapid prototyping technique is with a stereolithographer. Using this device, the cast is built on a platform that is situated just below the surface in a vat of liquid epoxy or acrylate resin. A low-power highly focused UV laser traces out the first layer, so-

International Toy Center

lidifying the model's cross section while leaving excess areas liquid. Next, an elevator incrementally lowers the platform into the liquid polymer. A sweeper recoats the solidified layer with liquid, and the laser traces the second layer atop the first. This process is repeated until the prototype is complete. Afterward, the solid part is removed from the vat and rinsed clean of excess liquid. Supports are broken off and the model is then placed in an ultraviolet oven for complete curing. Early stereolithography prototypes were fairly brittle and prone to curing-induced warping and distortion, but recent modifications have largely corrected these problems.

The next stage in the process is to make a silicon mold of the wax or resin sculpt, and then to hand cast each part separately in polyurethane to produce a hardcopy, which is then articulated using simple wooden dowels. The hardcopy is hand painted so that it can serve as a paint master, and is accompanied by paint swatches that have a note of the manufacturer and pantone number for later stages of the production process.

SELLING

In general, it takes ten to twelve months to go from concept to collectible. But the manufacturer must begin to promote to retailers months before the finished product is ready. This usually happens at trade fairs, though the larger manufacturers will sometimes also take promotional material on tour to potential retailers. The bulk of *Star Wars* collectibles are toys, so the most important trade fair is the American International Toy Fair (also known simply as Toy Fair) in New York.

Toy Fair has been running for over 100 years and is traditionally held in February, which marks the start of the Christmas buying season. Though there are many toy fairs around the world throughout the year, the New York Toy Fair is the biggest. It is where nearly all major and minor manufacturers will present most, if not all, of the coming year's line up of toys.

Manufacturers need to have enough orders to produce an item. It is crucial that the toy creates excitement and a good impression on buyers and the trade press when a product line is tied to a movie because the success of the movie is an unknown. And that was the problem that faced Lucasfilm when Charles Lippincott began selling *The Star Wars* to potential licensees.

In most cases, the smaller companies like Master Replicas, Kenner (of old), Code 3, Gentle Giants, Rubies, Galoob, and other Lucasfilm license holders rented out show suites at the International Toy Center, while the giants of the toy industry (LEGO and Hasbro Inc.) hired their own show rooms or even buildings. The purpose of a toy fair is to present the product in the best possible light, so a great deal of effort goes into decorating the exhibition area with displays, dioramas, stands, and demonstration areas.

The lead time on a product line can be immense, so manufacturers generally send specially prepared prototypes in packaging mock-ups, as well as promotional campaign material such as posters, flyer, television advertisements, store displays, and planograms. Often, toy fair products, packaging, displays, and promotional prototypes are thrown away at the end of the toy fair, but sometimes they are saved and become collectibles themselves.

If there is enough interest from buyers, then the line is commissioned and orders are sent to the manufacturer's production factories. If there aren't enough orders placed, the product is canceled. This has been the fate of many *Star Wars* collectibles throughout the decades, including Kenner's Holiday Special figures, extended Power of the Force range, the second series of *Droids* and *Ewoks* action figures, a number of play sets from their Micro Collection, Hasbro's Trophy Edition sets, the second generation of Commtech chips, many MicroMachines toys, plus a number of vehicle and pack-in figures that were intended to be retailer exclusives.

PRODUCTION

When the decision is made to manufacture a toy, production molds are made. This is done with a pantograph mill, a device that has a stylus at one end and a router on a mount with three axes of movement (horizontal, lateral, and vertical). The stylus is used to copy the casting while the router mills an aluminum or steel block to create a negative of the cast. The choice of metal is based on the type of plastic that will be used in the injection process, as well as the number of casts it is expected to cast. In predigital times, the pantograph would have been operated by hand, but today's automated machines can interface with CAD software and be fed the dimensions of the mold instead of having to trace them out from the original casting. (Future advancements in mold making will see devices using metal ink built up in layers.) Once the mold has been milled, it is polished to remove any burrs or metal shavings.

What follows is the creation of the first shot, whereby molten plastic is pumped into the different parts of the mold to test its fabrication, the different kinds of plastics, the suitability of the paint, and the various paint schemes. Because first shots are only intended as production test pieces, any kind of plastic is used, so these prototypes tend to be made of incorrect colors and multicolored plastic. If there are difficulties with the mold, extra first shots will be made. Nowadays, most prototypes on the market are just first shots from the many production facilities in China. From these first shots, the type of plastic that will be used is determined and a

First Shot prototype (left) and
production figure (right)
(Image courtesy of Chris Georgoulias)

Walrusman Photoart
(Image courtesy of Chris Georgoulias)

number of examples will be kept with plastic swatches identifying the make and stock number of the material to be used. Once the mold has been passed for production, the final adjust-
ments are made, such as adding the ball and socket joints, copyright dates, manufacturer's
stamps, and peg holes in action figures.

From here, the creation process is turned over to the mass-production plant at whatever plastics company that has won the contract. It should be noted that in few cases is an entire figure,
play set, or vehicle made at one factory. Rather, parts are molded in separate locations and
brought together at an assembly and packing facility before they are sent to the transport
agency whose job it is to distribute them around the world to their ultimate destinations.

PACKAGING

Almost as soon as a new product goes into its prototype stage work begins on developing
packaging that is visually attractive, practical to manufacture, and appropriate for both retailer and consumer. Early Kenner graphic artists had a tough time coming up with a suitable
card design for the never-before-produced 3³/₄-inch action figure. They were designing a new
item for a new market.

The first step in designing a range of packaging is coming up with sketches that depict various concepts of the *Star Wars* logo and themes, bubble/window shape and location, product
title, and captions. When beginning to experiment with the logo and theme, many decisions
have to be made concerning colors, product positioning, graphic locations, and countless other
small but equally important elements. In the case of packaging that does not incorporate a display window, a product shot is used instead. It is the norm to picture products in a play situation—photoart—so that consumers can picture the toy better (though legislation in some
countries has prohibited this). Once these factors are determined, the company's artists, or an
outside team of design experts, produce a range of concepts for review.

Walrusman Proof Card
(Image courtesy of Cloud City Collectibles)

Sears Exclusive Cloud City Playset Chromalin
(Image courtesy of Jim McCallum)

To demonstrate item dimensions to interested retailers so that they can devise their planograms, short-listed designs are produced. They are produced as packaging mock-ups, proof cards, and carded samples to illustrate the design clearly.

Meanwhile, staff at the manufacturer compose the copy that goes on the product, such as an explanation of what the item does, a synopsis of the movie, a description of the scene it is in, and character biographies (such as history, planet of origin, favorite weapon, etc.). Normally, Lucasfilm provides a style guide that includes the basic information, but if material has to be expanded on, it is usually passed onto licensing staff at Lucasfilm to ensure that plot spoilers are not included and that there are no conflicts of *Star Wars* time line continuity.

Once all the packaging has been finalized, the designs are sent to the printers, who then produce a number of proofs to provide a near-exact replica, called a chromalin, so that any final tweaks can be made before the print run is started.

Assuming all goes to plan, the printed sheets of card are passed through a die cutter, a precision cutting machine with a number of predetermined blades that press down to incise the card, which is then fed into a folding machine and hand glued before putting in the inserts and the product.

Occasionally, there are mistakes, the most common being spelling mistakes in captions that appear on the packaging (such as a product description or a *Star Wars* character biography), running changes made to the design (such as a close-up character shot being replaced by a long shot), or alterations to copy included on the packaging.

VARIATIONS

In many cases, a product will be changed almost immediately after it is first made available to correct a defect or fix a spelling or printing mistake or a production error. It is these first changes that make the early variations so desirable.

It is worth remembering that when tens of thousands of a single item are mass-produced, mistakes often occur. There are many cases of figures being put on the wrong cards, body parts being assembled incorrectly, and accessories being mixed up. Such production errors are not highly sought after and aren't considered real variations, but are collected by some just for the novelty factor.

A true variation is an alteration to a product made by the manufacturer rather than at the production facility to correct a mistake or defect not spotted in the design and prototyping phases. Changes to toys are easier to observe, while packaging variations (design layout, spelling corrections, and graphic alterations) are much harder to discern and track; as such, these subtle differences can command larger values. In many cases, because of tight release schedules simple errors aren't observed until they are already on the shelves at local toy stores. Often, it is collectors who observe these errors and inconsistencies and alert fan Web sites to spread the news. Because manufacturers monitor certain Web sites, they are able to correct their errors before large quantities are produced.

Variations have existed since Kenner began making *Star Wars* toys in 1978, and have been a staple part of vintage collecting since the arrival of the Early Bird figures. With the return of *Star Wars* action figures in 1995, variation hunting resumed when the glove on the POTF2 Boba Fett was incorrectly painted, and a change to the length of the lightsabers packed with Darth Vader, Ben (Obi-Wan) Kenobi, Luke Skywalker, Luke Skywalker (X-wing Fighter Pilot Gear), and Luke Skywalker (Dagobah Fatigues) created a blip on the *Star Wars* collecting radar.

These last examples serve to illustrate that variation hunting, especially with the modern toys, can have short-lived price peaks. Using the lightsaber variations as a case in point, prices on these variations rocketed to several hundred dollars at the time. Less than a handful of years later, they can be bought at a tenth of their original secondary market value. On the other hand, vintage variations have maintained a slow increase in value over the decades mostly because collectors have a better idea of the known quantity of these figures.

So, if you do get involved in variation collecting, it would be wise to wait out the initial rush over the minor changes and see what comes of prices as the excitement abates.

RERELEASE AND REHASH

After a period, many companies will look over older toys and consider ways to redistribute them to get rid of redundant stock or to allow new entrants to the *Star Wars* collecting hobby a chance to get items that haven't been available for many years.

A common way to do this is to create a new brand line but with rereleased figures to attract new interest to the market, as was done with the Original Trilogy Collection line in 2004 when the *Star Wars* trilogy was released on DVD. Another method is to make a small change to the packaging to create a side line to the main packaging brand. This was practiced by Hasbro in 2004 when it released the Hall of Fame line up, a series of rehashed figures that had previously been available a number of months before in plain Saga cards.

Glamour Gals display stand
(Image courtesy of Carol Roth)

RECYCLING

When a particular line has been retired it does not mean that fans won't get to see their favorite play things again, because many companies recycle items from one line to another. There are plenty of examples when Kenner has resurrected its previous products for *Star Wars*. Kenner was also proficient at finding ways of reusing old *Star Wars* molds to make new ranges of toys that had absolutely nothing to do with *Star Wars* or even science fiction. This opens up a whole new field of collecting.

In 1977, Kenner was in a rush to get its new licensed *Star Wars* toy line off the ground and because of the narrow time margin it had to cut corners. Instead of developing new products, it decided to use toys it had already developed and had the molds for. The most notable instances of recycled toys include a number of toys from the Six Million Dollar Man line. The CB Radio Headset Receiver made by Kenner and released in 1977 was later rebranded and repackaged in 1978 as the Luke Skywalker AM Radio. And the Six Million Dollar Man/Bionic Woman electric toothbrush was given the slightest of makeovers to fit in with the new *Star Wars* theme. Kenner also recycled some strange items to make good on the latest cash cow. Two SPP (Super Sonic Power) vans had their flashy 1970s stickers removed and replaced with stock *Star Wars* art to convince a Luke-and-Han crazy public that their celluloid heroes cruised around in suped-up vans instead of star ships. A similar fate met Kenner's 1977 *Aerial Aces* dog fight game. Instead of shooting down World War I biplanes, Imperial TIE Fighters were the target and the toy was imaginatively renamed X-Wing Aces. And much like Kenner Canada's Utility Belt sets, which were recycled Super-Hero Utility Belts made by Remco in the early 1970s, they weren't popular with retailers and were soon retired from toy store shelves.

It is a natural law of physics that what goes up must come down and *Star Wars* was no exception, but the practice started long before the bubble popped in 1985. Both the *Star Wars* mail-away action display stand and the Creature Cantina were recycled into other Kenner lines in the early 1980s. One became a Glamour Gals mail-away display stand and the other was converted into The Real West "Western Café Action Playset," which was part of the abortive tie-in line to *Butch and Sundance: The Early Years* movie that sank without a trace. Undaunted, Kenner continued to acquire movie rights and in 1990 and 1992 picked up licenses for two blockbusters, *Batman* and *Robin Hood: Prince of Thieves*. Despite *Batman* being a toy designer's dream job, Kenner decided not to go bat-crazy on utility belts but instead brought out the old *Star Wars* Three Position Laser Rifle, known to fans as a Stormtrooper blaster, and reissued it with a Batman logo and called it a Sonic Neutralizer. The *Robin Hood* toys relied heavily on old *Star Wars* molds and included an action figure, the Gamorrean Guard was turned into Friar Tuck, a Playset (the vintage Ewok Village had plastic tree branches added and became the Sherwood Forest Playset), and the Ewok Battle Wagon, a late Power of the Force entrant, had some work done on its body to appear as a Battle Wagon.

With the return of *Star Wars* action figures in 1995, collectors were soon crying out for vehicles and Hasbro didn't keep them waiting because a month or two later the X-Wing Fighter was released. While collectors were hoping to get updated toys with better features and correct scales, except for the Millennium Falcon, they were disappointed to find that Hasbro was recycling old molds and producing vintage toys with minor changes to stickers and plastic colorings. This practice became so prevalent that it was accepted that Hasbro/Kenner would just rerelease vintage toys to a modern market, but in 1996 the first original vehicle to come out of Kenner since 1985 was Dash Rendar's Outrider from the *Shadows of the Empire*, proving that there was some interest in creating new large-sized toys.

Unproduced Vintage Toys

Between 1978 and 1985, Kenner produced a huge range of toys in a variety of scales and themes. To see these toys through from inception to completion, Kenner had a huge design department, which took care of the bulk of the developmental process. Of course, there were times when many of Kenner's ideas were never fully implemented for reasons of cost, lack of interest in a particular line, or simply because the idea was squashed by Lucasfilm. Many of these ideas were scrapped early on in the conceptual phase and while others made it close to final production, all these ideas ultimately went unproduced. Today, the prototype and pre-production items from these lines exist in extremely limited numbers and are considered by many collectors to be the Holy Grails of Kenner's vintage line.

3³/₄-INCH ACTION FIGURE LINE

By the time the 3³/₄-inch line was finally extinguished in 1985, Kenner produced well over 100 individual figures and a myriad of vehicles and play sets. During that time, it also conceived and designed several other 3³/₄-inch-scale toys that never made it into production. One of the earliest unproduced prototypes, and possibly the most infamous, was actually released, albeit in a slightly scaled-down form. First promoted as a mail-away figure, Boba Fett was originally designed to come with a spring-loaded rocket that fired from his backpack. Even though a considerable amount of development and promotion went into this feature, the idea was eventually abandoned because of an unfortunate incident involving a young boy who died from choking on the spring-loaded missile from Mattel's Battlestar Galactica Colonial Viper toy. Contrary to popular belief, no Rocket Fetts were ever mailed out to consumers, however, many prototypes have been found from Kenner sources in various stages of prepro-duction. Two different types of Rocket Fetts are known to exist, one with a J-slot style of launcher and one with an L-slot style and despite the high price tag associated with them, there are approximately fifty known Rocket Fetts in existence—far more than any other fig-ural prototype.

In 1978, the world was still much abuzz over *Star Wars* and many people were expecting great things from the Holiday Special that aired that Thanksgiving. Kenner was no exception and before the film aired it had started developing toys based on the show's central characters: Chewbacca's Wookiee family. The Holiday Special was certainly memorable, if not for all the wrong reasons, and when the show received terrible reviews, plans for this line were ulti-mately canceled. To date, only one set of prototypes for Chewbacca's family has ever surfaced.

After the Holiday Special debacle, things rolled along fairly smoothly for Kenner and few concepts were abandoned until 1985. Kenner had planned to release at least two more figures under its POTF banner—Luke in Robes and Gargan, the six-breasted dancer from Jabba's palace—but plans for both went unfulfilled. The Luke in Robes figure in particular is a bit of an enigma. Two premiered gray hardcopies of this figure are known to exist as are a small amount of hardcopy parts but without any of them being painted. No one is sure if this figure was meant to represent Luke in Jedi robes or Luke in medical robes.

When it came to Gargan, the idea of an action figure of a six-breasted dancing slave didn't go over too well with Lucasfilm executives and for obvious reasons the Gargan figure was scrapped early on in it's design process. It's not known whether this figure was originally slated to be produced within the first wave of the POTF line or with a second, unproduced se-ries and to this day, only a coin sketch and a handful of prototypes exist in hardcopy and wax form. Both the Luke in Robes figure and Gargan are an interesting look at where Kenner's POTF may have ended up had it not been canceled.

The *Star Wars* property was, of course, a major moneymaker for Kenner and by the time 1985 rolled around *Star Wars* toy sales had dwindled to an all-time low and even two Saturday morning cartoon shows couldn't do much to remedy the situation. Without the prospect of another feature film to keep the momentum of the line going forward, several Kenner design-ers, who had become fond of working on the *Star Wars* line and who were reluctant to let it die, came up with an Expanded Universe type story line and Kenner's toys were to serve as the basis for it.

A new villain named Atha Prime was created for this story. Deemed the "architect of the Clone Wars," Atha Prime, with his loyal droid Blue-Four and his army of Clone Warriors, terrorized the galaxy and it was up to our favorite band of heroes to save the Alliance from certain destruction. Kenner's team put a lot of effort into conceptualizing, designing, and even building kit-bashed mock-ups of all the different toys that could be included within this range.

Kitbash: POTF85 All Terrain Ion Cannon
(Image courtesy of Vic Wertz and Lisa Stephens)

Kitbash: POTF85 XP-38 Landspeeder
(Image courtesy of Vic Wertz and Lisa Stephens)

Several new figures were proposed including Atha Prime, Blue-Four, the Clone Warriors, a Mongo Beefhead Tribesman, and new versions of both Luke and Han. Of course, the Imperial Army hadn't been completely decimated and several Imperial droids were designed, as was a figure based on Grand Moff Tarkin, who, according to the new story line, had survived the destruction of the first Death Star and had come back to lead the Imperials to victory.

And what fun would new figures be without new vehicles? Kenner's designers came up with an assortment of no less than fifteen new vehicle and play set concepts and while most supported this new story line, a handful were based on movie favorites that had not previously been made into toys.

All-Terrain Ion Cannon: What would happen if you cut away the back-half of an AT-AT and placed a big gun back there instead? Well, you'd get the All-Terrain Ion Cannon! This new version of the classic AT-AT featured the gun from Kenner's Death Star play set and would have been an effective way to knock out space ships from the ground.

Annihilator: Atha Prime's warship. This behemoth of a spaceship looks like two Star Destroyers fused together, one on top of the other.

Apex Invader: This unique ship was to serve as Atha Prime's personal vessel, and when not engaged in battle it could be found docked high atop Prime's warship, the Annihilator.

Bantha: Why Kenner never made a Bantha toy during the initial *Star Wars* run we may never know, but the existence of conceptual artwork indicates it was poised to correct that error in 1986.

Kitbash: POTF85 Rebel
Sandspeeder
(Image courtesy of Vic Wertz and
Lisa Stephens)

Kitbash: POTF85 MF Cargo
Handler
(Image courtesy of Vic Wertz and
Lisa Stephens)

Concept Sketch: POTF85 SRV-1
(Image courtesy of Vic Wertz and
Lisa Stephens)

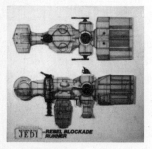

Concept Sketch: POTF85
Blockade Runner
(Image courtesy of Vic Wertz and
Lisa Stephens)

Concept Sketch: POTF85
Imperial Outpost
(Image courtesy of Vic Wertz and
Lisa Stephens)

Blockade Runner: The idea to turn the Rebel Blockade runner, as seen in the first few minutes of *A New Hope*, into a toy was actually considered for the *Return of the Jedi* line. Photos of both the conceptual artwork and a scratch-built mock-up have been found and indicate this would have been a fairly elaborate toy.

Imperial Outpost: Possibly the coolest and largest idea Kenner's designers ever had. This monster play set incorporated several Imperial themes as seen in the movies, including a landing pad for the shuttle and the guns found in the Death Star trenches. While some think that the size of this piece would have been too immense to produce, it looked to be similar in size to many of the large GI Joe play sets being made by Hasbro at the time and its production would have been feasible. Unfortunately, all that exists for this toy is the conceptual artwork.

Millennium Falcon Cargo Hauler: Designed to fit in between the forward mandibles of the Millennium Falcon, this little vehicle was designed for the quick loading and unloading of smuggled goods.

Rebel Scout and Retrieval Vehicle: The SRV-1 was essentially a tow truck for downed rebel aircraft. Kenner had originally designed and mocked up this toy in previous years but decided to resurrect the idea for this range of toys.

Sand speeder: This Rebel vehicle was similar to the snow speeder and would have been used in desert environments. Designers actually built a kit-based model from a snow speeder to help visualize this toy.

Skyhopper: Like the TIE Bomber, no real development had taken place on this toy. A copy of Joe Johnston's sketch was all that was included.

Sniper Fighter: This vehicle was a one-man craft that looked similar to many of the early conceptual designs for the speeder bikes seen in *Return of the Jedi*.

Tandem X-Wing: Almost a super X-Wing, this new version of an old favorite had two cockpits and was painted black.

TIE Bomber: No formal plans for this *Empire Strikes Back* craft were developed, but a copy of Joe Johnston's sketch was presented, indicating it would have been considered for production.

XP-36 and XP-38: Two new land speeder toys were designed by Kenner, one of which was mentioned by Luke in *A New Hope*. The XP-36 was a bulkier, almost a souped-up version of Luke's original land speeder, sleeker, and a more aerodynamic looking speeder.

All these ideas, photos of the mock-ups, and copies of the artwork were placed into a binder titled *Star Wars Is Forever*, which was then pitched to Lucasfilm. It was most impressed with the ideas presented and the time it took to develop them, but in the end the ideas were not approved and the *Star Wars* line ended in 1985.

Besides extending the POTF line and the *Star Wars Is Forever* concept, Kenner also had high hopes for the toys based on Nelvana's *Droids* and *Ewoks* cartoons. The first series of these toys was released in 1985 to a mildly receptive audience and by the time the decision was made to cancel the line, a great deal of work had already been put into developing the second series. Out of all the lines that Kenner had planned, none made it further into development than this second series of unproduced *Droids* and *Ewoks* (UDE) figures.

Eight new figures were planned for the *Droids* line—Jessica Meade, Mungo Baobab, Governor Koong, Admiral Screed, Gaff, Vlix, Mon Julpa, and Kleb Zellock—and several companion *Droids* figures were also in development. Six more figures were in the works for the *Ewoks* line: Bondo, Morag, Paploo, Weechee, Chief Chirpa, and Chituhr.

All these figures have turned up as fully painted hardcopies and some production-quality first shots have surfaced for some characters as well. Additionally, many cromalins, packaging proofs, and even carded mock-ups have been discovered, which indicate this line was ready to go into full production just before the plug was ultimately pulled.

Figures certainly weren't the only *Droids* and *Ewoks* items on order for 1986. Kenner was also planning on releasing a *Droids* version of the C-3PO carrying case as well as two vehicles, Thall Joben's White Witch and a *Droids* version of the POTF Skiff. Catalog photography shows that the Max Rebo band was also slated to be rereleased in *Droids* packaging, but unfortunately the physical mock-up has never been found. No new Ewoks vehicles were planned, but photographic evidence suggests that the Ewok Village and Battle Wagon, as well as several plush Ewoks, were planned to be reissued in the animated *Ewoks* packaging.

12-INCH ACTION FIGURE LINE

Kenner had many ideas for the Large Size Action Figure line that it released in 1979. Unfortunately, poor sales and lack of interest in the first series ultimately meant that the line was cut short before all the ideas were ever produced. One of the first plans Kenner hatched to extend the 12-inch line was to make fashion-savvy accessory sets for both the Princess Leia and Luke Skywalker dolls and three different outfits were created for each character. For Luke, designers made a ceremonial outfit as seen at the end of *A New Hope*, an X-Wing outfit, and a fatigue suit. Leia's new outfits included a flight suit, a snow bunny-type Arctic outfit, and a poncho that would have been perfect for traipsing through the jungles of Yavin IV. The accessory packs were eventually aborted because of the slow sales of the line itself, but thankfully many of the original prototypes as well as some packaging comps have been found by collectors.

Kenner also planned to release four new dolls under the *Empire Strikes Back* banner: Luke Skywalker in Bespin fatigues, Han Solo in his Hoth outfit, Leia in her Bespin gown, and Lando Calrissian. These dolls are striking and while it's rather unfortunate that none ever made into production, various examples and stages of the dolls, outfits, and packaging have since been discovered by collectors and are highly prized.

MICRO COLLECTION LINE

Kenner's Micro Collection line, while wildly popular with today's collectors, was by no means a commercial success when it first landed on toy shelves in 1982. By that time, most parents had already made a considerable investment in Kenner's 3³/₄-inch line and were reluctant to purchase a whole new range of toys in an entirely different scale. Kenner had planned to further the Micro Collection line but poor sales of the initial sets inevitably lead to the line's demise. Extensions to the Bespin, Hoth, and Death Star sets were in the works, as were new environments based on Dagobah, Endor, and Jabba's Dungeon. Today, a great deal of preproduction material from these sets has been uncovered, thereby providing collectors with an in-depth look at what could have been.

Unproduced concept: Micro
Collection Darth Vader
(Image courtesy of Jeffrey Correll)

Unproduced concept: Micro
Collection Bespin Torture
Chamber
(Image courtesy of Anonymous)

Unproduced concept: Micro
Collection Chewbacca (Torture
Chamber)
(Image courtesy of Jeffrey Correll)

Unproduced concept: Micro
Collection Luke (Bacta Chamber)
(Image courtesy of Jeffrey Correll)

Unproduced concept: Micro
Collection Yoda

Except for the Sears cardboard set, the Micro line was the only venue where Bespin received full toy treatment. To add to the already existing Bespin World, Kenner designed the Bespin Torture Chamber, where kids could reenact tiny scenes from the interrogation room, prison cell, and furnace area with six new micro figures: Han Solo, Chewbacca, C-3PO, two Bespin guards, and an Ugnaught. To date, several 4-ups and 1:1-scale die-cast versions of the figures have been uncovered in both painted and unpainted form. Two complete versions of the play set and a mock-up box all reside in private collections.

Even though the Micro Hoth World was the largest of the Micro worlds, it, too, was slated for an additional play set: the Hoth Bacta Chamber. Four new figures were to be added for this environment: FX-7, 2-1B, C-3PO, and a half-naked Luke Skywalker who could be fixed up just as he was after the Wampa attack in the film. All the figures exist in 4-up and 1:1-scale prototype form as do a mock-up box, box proofs, and a complete play set.

Like both the Bespin and Hoth Worlds, there was also another set in the works for the Death Star environment: the Throne Room. Unfortunately, only a conceptual painting and a smattering of photographs are known to exist for this set and it largely remains a mystery. Everything about this toy is unknown, except for the title and one single picture.

There were also three other "world" play sets proposed by Kenner—Jabba's Palace, Dagobah, and Endor—and only a handful of prototypes are known to exist from these lines. A few 4-ups and a complete example of Jabba's Boiler Room and its accompanying blueprints are all that have been found from Jabba's Palace, although it is surmised that a Throne Room and Rancor Pit may also have been in development. No play set has been discovered for the Dagobah World, but several 4-ups for exclusive Darth Vader, R2-D2, Luke Skywalker in X-Wing gear, and Yoda figures have been found, indicating that the set would have included at least four new die-cast figures. Little is known about the Endor set, but it would have most likely included Ewok Village play environments, an Endor Bunker, and several new die-cast figures.

It's unfortunate that none of these unproduced Micro Collection play sets were ever released. The ultimate demise of the Micro Collection seems to be more of an issue of timing than anything else, as this scale eventually proved to be incredibly successful for Galoob and its Action Fleet line over a decade later.

OTHER CONCEPTS

Besides its 3³/₄-, 12-inch, and Micro Collection lines, several ideas for a variety of Kenner's other toy properties were tossed around and eventually scrapped. From plush toys to preschool playthings, there were a myriad of concepts that stayed on Kenner's proverbial cutting room floor and a few of the more popular designs will be further discussed here.

STAR TOTS

Long before the release of the Ewoks preschool line, Kenner was poised to make a line of preschool figures based on the characters and vehicles seen in *A New Hope*. Prototypes for this Star Tots line, so named for their resemblance to Kenner's Tree Tots preschool toys, indicate that cute little versions of Luke, Leia, C-3PO, and R2-D2 would have been released alongside even cuter versions of an X-Wing Fighter and Luke's Land speeder. Conceptual artwork shows that several other figures may also have been planned. Only one set of these prototypes is known to have been designed and it currently resides in a private collection.

TALKING YODA DOLL

From the moment when Yoda made his first on-screen appearance, fans couldn't get enough of his quirky speech pattern. Kenner wanted to capitalize on this by releasing a talking Yoda doll that was designed to say eight different Yoda-isms at the pull of a cord. The talking Yoda doll made it through several stages of development before it was finally canceled. It is not known why Kenner decided not to make this toy. Luckily, several full dolls as well as a variety of first shot heads have been discovered and preserved by collectors.

PLUSH SALACIOUS CRUMB

Those cute and cuddly Ewoks sure made adorable plush toys, didn't they? Unfortunately, Salacious Crumb, Jabba the Hutt's Kowakian counterpart, didn't have the universal appeal of the Ewoks, despite how cute Kenner designers actually made him. In the end, the plans to immortalize Crumb in plush form were aborted. To date, two sizes of plush Salacious prototypes have been found: two large ones and one smaller example.

COINS

Actually, the POTF Coin Album and the sixty-third coin could also be covered under the 3¾-inch section, but because they are not specifically action figures, they have been included in this section instead. When Kenner produced its POTF line in 1985, a new series of figures and several existing ROTJ-era figures were repackaged with special collector's coins. Sixty-two coins were released in total, either with figures or via mail-away promotions. Kenner had also planned on making an exclusive sixty-third coin. This coin would have been available only in a mail-away promotion and would have been included with a POTF coin album. Needless to say, the offer never came to fruition. Several prototype examples of the sixty-third coin exist, but only one example of the album has been uncovered.

It should be noted that this chapter is by no means comprehensive in its coverage of unproduced items. There were many more ideas abandoned by Kenner but covering them all would require a book unto itself. Readers interested in learning more on the subject are encouraged to visit the *Star Wars* Collector's Archive (www.toysrgus.com).

While many collectors may place a high amount of importance on certain unproduced pieces, truly, *all* the unproduced prototypes that have been found and saved by collectors should be held in the highest esteem. All these items are an irreplaceable part of toy history and provide unique look at what might have been in Kenner's vintage repertoire.

Starting a Prototype Collection

For most who collect prototype items, whether it be artwork, production proofs, or concept modes, it is often the case that they have reached the end of the road, but for others it is a chance to own a unique piece of *Star Wars* memorabilia.

This is a difficult area to break into—not just because of the expense but also because it requires having a great deal of knowledge about the market and some good connections. Most vintage prototype collectors started in the mid-1990s when there were, relatively, a great number of deals to be had.

One section of this area of the hobby that is still inexpensive is Micro Collection toys, which are still in abundance because the line was so badly received by retailers. Unpainted figures, basically plain metal figurines, can be bought for around $5—The Earth Collectible Toy Mall (www.theearthtoymall.com) in Cincinnati has plenty of these, as well as unproduced Micro Collection figurines from the Hoth Bacta Chamber and Bespin Torture Chamber.

Cardback and packaging prototypes are another popular area of collecting. Proof cards from the terminated *Revenge of the Jedi* line are not as uncommon as would be believed, and more than a handful of collectors have put together a full set. Considering that these were meant to be destroyed when George Lucas changed the title to *Return of the Jedi*, there are hundreds, including some proof sheets, still in existence—presumably because Kenner employees realized that the fledgling collector's market would one day snap them up. Occasionally, they do appear on eBay; *Revenge* cardbacks can go for less than $100. Harder to find are Power of the Force cardbacks, which range in price from $500 to $1,500, depending on how much interest there is in the character. The entire $3^3/4$-inch action figure range was planned to be rereleased on these cards, but because Kenner wrapped up its *Star Wars* toy line in 1986, over half the POTF figures never saw the light of day.

From here, the next logical step is on to production prototypes such as concept models, wax and acetate sculpts, and first shots. Getting into this area of prototype collecting requires a great deal of specialist knowledge. Because these kinds of prototypes often have unclear provenances, they have long been a beacon for shady characters. Fake items representing various stages of Kenner's preproduction process have been introduced to the marketplace. Collectors need to be careful when purchasing prototype material and should do considerable homework on the subject before making any purchases.

Getting into the higher end of *Star Wars* prototype collecting can cost thousands—sometimes even tens of thousands—of dollars and requires specialized knowledge. When buying high-end prototypes, one piece of advice that should always be followed is to ask for provenance (proof of authenticity). To be completely satisfactory, this should be more than a printed piece of paper purporting to be a certificate of authenticity. Ask to see any paper work, past receipts, and any previous correspondence to do with the item. If the seller can't supply these, then request that the item be verified by an independent expert.

If you aren't interested in vintage prototype collecting, then the modern toys are much easier to find and less expensive. A quick search for "star wars prototype" on eBay will net you scores of auctions for such items. One popular avenue to tread is collecting prototypes of toys that were never produced, such as the Episode 1 Trophy Series and many Hasbro MicroMachines prior to their *Star Wars* line getting shelved in 2000. Rebelscum staff member Mark Hurray has a large collection of these online at Rebelscum.com, as well as write-ups about the history of each piece. Unproduced samples of the second version of the Episode 1 Commtech chip are also easy to find, but represent the higher end of the modern prototype market, as one of these pieces can reach several hundred dollars.

Be warned, however, because the *Star Wars* collector's proclivity for rare and interesting pieces is well known in China, where the bulk of plastic toys are made, and while many of the first shots being sold on eBay are genuinely from the Hasbro production facilities, they are often not really first shots and are nothing more than pirate toys made from leftover plastic by factory staff members who are aware of the market. This is not the case with all such modern first shots, but anyone wanting to get into modern prototypes should fist look at the large numbers of preproduction samples that are flooding the market and ask why there should be dozens of prototypes of the same figure available at any one time.

Terminology

The following are the most commonly used terms and acronyms in collecting prototype and variation *Star Wars* collectibles:

4-up　　　　　When Kenner developed the Micro Collection, it sculpted its models four times larger than they were intended to be produced at. The resulting hardcopies were therefore also four times the normal size and they are often referred to as 4-ups. They should not be confused with the original sculpt, which is never called a 4-up.

Carded sample　　An action figure placed on a cardback to represent a finished example. Many times, the action figure did not match the art of the cardback.

Casting　　　　The solid object made using a mold.

Concept model　　A hand-built mock-up generally made from preexisting toys or model kits to demonstrate the notion of the item.

Copy　　　　　The textual product or character description that is suitable material to print on packaging.

Cromalin　　　A color proof sheet of packaging is created using special colored powders on sensitized paper so that the copy and the balance of colors from the color separations can be studied and corrected, if necessary, before the actual press run.

First shot　　　A preliminary piece made as part of the production process in an effort to determine the accuracy of the mold being used. They are typically made of different colors of plastic and lack details.

Hardcopy　　　A hand-cast, -painted, and -assembled copy of the original wax sculpts made of polyurethane to demonstrate the functionality of the toy.

Kit-bash　　　A model maker's term used to denote an item that has been constructed of parts taken from other toys. These are often used in the early stages of product development for designers to illustrate the basic concept of the toy.

Mock-up　　　A full-sized model of an item, built to scale and with working parts, used especially for testing or research.

Mold　　　　A container that gives a shape to a molten or liquid substance poured into it to harden.

Packaging　　　The wrapping or container in which an item is presented for sale.

Paint master　　A casting whose purpose is to illustrate the correct paint colors to be used for production and is accompanied by the swatches painted in the appropriate colors and annotated.

Photoart   The master image used on packaging for a toy.

Plastic master   A casting whose purpose is to illustrate the correct plastic colors to be used for production and is accompanied by swatches of the correct plastic.

Plastic swatch   A sample piece of square plastic of the correct type/color to be used on each part of the figure.

Production error An item that has been incorrectly painted, manufactured, assembled, or packaged because of a mistake during the mass-production process. Not to be considered a variation.

Proof card   An early master of a card of packaging example, printed on thin card in matt inks. Typically, they are single sided and hand cut.

Proof sheet   An entire sheet that is printed with several individual proof cards with both front and back images.

Prototype   Any item resulting from preproduction processes. Not to be confused with first shots, which are part of the production process.

Variation   A running change to packaging or an item that makes it different from previously released versions of the same piece of merchandise.

12 BOOTLEGS AND KNOCK-OFFS

With all the licensed *Star Wars* merchandise that has been produced around the world since 1977, there has also been a steady stream of unlicensed *Star Wars* products trying to undercut the market. While one certainly does not want to condone the act of piracy or bootlegging, as it defrauds both the legal licensee and Lucasfilm of money, the fact remains that these misfits of the *Star Wars* galaxy do exist and have considerable and interesting histories. So it becomes important to acknowledge their existence as secondary-market collectibles and to be able to differentiate between them, as these items are both collected by adult collectors and have been played with and used by children worldwide.

All the *Star Wars* items that have been produced without the consent of Lucasfilm are considered unlicensed products, but these items can be further divided into two distinct categories: bootlegs and knock-offs.

Early Material

When the *Star Wars* phenomenon hit the world in the spring of 1977, many potential licensees were caught unaware. This, coupled with Kenner's inability to manufacture the toy line in a timely manner, left a huge void in a marketplace that was hungry for all things *Star Wars*. Many manufacturers recognized the potential for immediate profit and instead of going through the proper, time-consuming legal channels to acquire licenses, they decided to throw caution to the wind and produced their own unlicensed *Star Wars*-esque merchandise. From buttons to jewelry, toys to apparel, there was a plethora of unlicensed merchandise unleashed on the market in 1977. Naturally, there were heavy legal issues surrounding these items (and in some cases serious safety concerns as well) and this meant that many of these unlicensed goodies experienced a short shelf life, thus making them quite collectible in today's marketplace.

Some of the more unique, non-toy products made without a license include, but are by no means limited to, a series of campy buttons that were sold through a *Star Trek* magazine and three ceramic lamp kits (Darth Vader, R2-D2, and Chewbacca) that were made by Windmill Ceramics. While many of these types of items certainly are interesting and kitschy, it is the unlicensed toys that capture most collectors' attention and they will be the focus of this chapter.

Long before the advent of Kenner's Micro line of die-cast figures, a company known as Heritage produced a series of small, pewter figures that were sold in both painted and unpainted form as well as with nickel and gold plating. These were the first figural representations of many of the characters to ever hit the market and essentially look like crude versions of their licensed Micro Series successors. The complete set consists of Han Solo, Chewbacca, Luke Skywalker, Princess Leia, C-3PO, R2-D2, Darth Vader, Stormtrooper, Obi-Wan Kenobi, Jawa, Garindan (the Imperial snitch), the Cantina Band, a Tusken Raider in attack position, and two sitting Tusken Raiders, which were to be perched on a pewter Bantha. It should be noted that many of these Heritage figures were also turned into jewelry.

One of the earliest and simplest unlicensed toys to hit the market in 1977 was the Force Beam toy, which shared a rather uncanny resemblance to a lightsaber and was made from a flashlight and a translucent plastic tube manufactured by Jack A. Levin and Associates. In Canada, Campus Craft made a similar toy called the Light Beam saber. While both toys were somewhat blatant in their misuse of *Star Wars*-styled graphics, Campus Craft's Light Beam saber took it a bit further with the words "The Force Is with You" along the bottom of its logo. Both of these toys were quickly pulled from the shelves for safety reasons.

Reliable, another Canadian company known for making vinyl dolls, in an effort to not be outdone by Campus Craft, manufactured a coin bank in the image of the lovable little droid, R2-D2. While safe enough, these bulky banks were in clear copyright violation and were soon removed from Canadian store shelves.

In 1977, a time when most kids wanted to be Han Solo, what better way was there to emulate the galaxy's greatest smuggler than with your own blaster pistol? Unfortunately, there weren't any licensed blasters on the market until 1978, so several companies saw fit to produce toy guns that looked like they could fit right in with the *Star Wars* galaxy. Several manufacturers made many different styles of these toy guns throughout the run of *Star Wars'* popularity. Most of the guns themselves aren't easily distinguishable as *Star Wars* knock-offs, but much of the packaging for these guns did feature unlicensed *Star Wars* imagery.

One of the more interesting toys produced under the guise of a *Star Wars* toy was the hybrid Galaxy Warrior robot. This neat piece featured a classic robot body with the head of an Imperial Stormtrooper and came packaged in a campy science-fiction box. These robots were produced in 1979 and have turned up in both silver and black colors.

Once Kenner got the ball rolling on its action figure line, a brand new opportunity opened up for manufacturers looking to cash in on the *Star Wars* craze. Several unlicensed carrying cases were produced to compete with Kenner's vinyl *Star Wars* cases. The Space Case and the Star World Vinyl Case were compatible with Kenner's *Star Wars* action figures and are nearly identical to each other, with both featuring funky space graphics. In Canada, Sears produced the Cryotron carrying case, which was made to "accommodate most *Star Wars* figures." The Cryotron case held forty action figures and was made to resemble a large, flying saucer type space ship. But, as interesting as these carrying cases are, it was of course the Kenner figures themselves that led to the most fascinating unlicensed products—the bootleg figure.

Most of the vintage bootleg action figures on the market today have been produced in foreign markets and many of the countries that have spawned these lines did so for a variety of reasons. Generally, the licensed products were not available for importation because of trade embargos and political instability. Also, the economic conditions of a country sometimes made the licensed products unaffordable to the people who wanted to buy them for their children. To satisfy the growing demand for *Star Wars* toys in these markets, companies in countries such as Turkey, Hungary, Poland, and Brazil inevitably created some of the most infamous lines of bootleg toys during the vintage era.

The Turkish line of Uzay bootleg figures is without a doubt the most well-known line of *Star Wars* bootlegs in the world. A company known as SB Products released the line in the late 1980s in Turkey. The allure of this line is due, in part, to the ultra cheesy packaging artwork, but collectors are also drawn to the rarity of each of the figures and tracking them all down is challenging. The Uzay line consists of fourteen different figures with some variations and off-the-wall names.

In terms of oddity and rarity, the two "gems" of the Uzay line are Blue Stars, basically a blue Hoth Stormtrooper with a white gun and the ultra rare Headman, which is an Emperor's Royal Guard figure with a chromed head and a shield. Both of these figures are difficult to find even loose and so far only one carded Headman has surfaced in known collecting circles.

In Brazil in the mid-1980s, U.S. licensed *Star Wars* products were not available in stores and there was no Brazilian company with the *Star Wars* license. To answer to the growing the demand for *Star Wars* toys in Brazil, Model Trem, a Brazilian company known for making parts and scenery for model trains, produced its line of bootleg *Star Wars* figures. In total, thirty-four figures were produced for this line and believe it or not, the figures were made from lead, which is not exactly the safest material for children to play with. The figures were released in at least three different styles of generically colored boxes. Some came with the character's name and number, some with just the number on a sticker on the front of the box, and still others with stickered box tops that either read "Model Trem" and provided company information or simply read "Aventura na Galáxia." They were sold in stores for the equivalent of $1.50 U.S. and while they lack the "high-quality" card art of an Uzay Turkish bootleg, the figures themselves are visually one of the more accurate bootleg lines to have been produced. Each figure was detailed as closely to its licensed counterpart as possible and most figures came with the appropriate weapon for each character. There are also several mold and paint variations in the line. Model Trem stopped producing its line of *Star Wars* figures after Glasslite had secured the Brazilian license to produce *Star Wars* products. Brazilian sources claim that both Glasslite and Lucasfilm had threatened Model Trem with legal action if it did not cease production.

Uzay bootleg: Arfive-Defour

Uzay bootleg: Artoo-Detoo

Uzay bootleg: AT-Driver

Uzay bootleg: Blue Stars

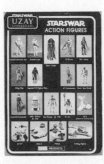

Uzay bootleg: Cardback

Uzay bootleg: Chewbacca (Aslan)

Uzay bootleg: Chewbacca (Maymum)

Uzay bootleg: Darth Vader

Uzay bootleg: Death Star Droid

Uzay bootleg: Emperor's Royal Guard (1)

Uzay bootleg: Emperor's Royal Guard (2)

Uzay bootleg: Head Man

Uzay bootleg: Imperial Gunner

Uzay bootleg: Imperial Stormtroper

Uzay bootleg: See-Threep (1)

Uzay bootleg: See-Threep (2)

Uzay bootleg: Stormtroper

Uzay bootleg: Imperial TE Fighter Pilot

The Hungarian "Csillagok Haboruja" bootleg line consists of ten figures. The rarest figures from this line are Darth Vader and Boba Fett and conversely, the Princess Leia and Wicket figures are reasonably priced and relatively easy to find on the collector's market. Most of the Hungarian figures currently in American collections were imported by toy dealers who bought them from Hungarian stores in the late 1980s.

Although Kenner's *Star Wars* figures were sold in Hungary, for many people, the bootlegs were a more affordable alternative and were sold mostly through smaller stores and market-places. They are made from rigid injection-molded plastic and their limb joints are loosely attached to their bodies, making it hard for loose examples to stand upright. The quality of the backer cards and bubbles on these bootlegs is shoddy as well. The card art is a photocopied image from the style-C movie poster with a bare nameplate in the bottom section and the bubbles are stapled onto the card, not glued. Sometimes, the bubbles on these have actually taken on the shape of the figure inside.

The figures themselves are slightly smaller than their licensed counterparts, and the most significant differences are in the Luke and Darth Vader figures. Luke and Darth both have hands and not the slide-in lightsabers that the licensed figures had. The sabers that they come with resemble the saber from the Luke Jedi figure.

The depth of the Polish variety of bootleg figures is rivaled only by Mexico's vast stockpile of unlicensed products, but the Polish lines are definitely less random than most of the Mexican one or two-off item lines. We'll start with the "Original" series of five Polish bootlegs, which came out in the early 1980s: Han, Leia, Ben, Chewbacca, and a Tusken Raider. According to Polish sources, these came bagged (similar to many Mexican pieces) with a weapon. To date, none have been found still in their original bag and in fact these are so rare that there are only three full sets of these in known collections. The figures themselves are articulated, and in many ways look and feel similar to the Hungarian line of bootleg figures.

The "Original" set was certainly not the end of bootlegs in Poland—it was just the beginning. The next known series of bootlegs from Poland consists of twenty articulated figures broken down into three distinct waves. All had either Biker Scout limbs, Tie Pilot limbs, or AT-AT Driver limbs. The first-generation figures came carded on a generic backer card and were sold in stores in Poland in the mid- to late 1980s.

For the most part, the second generation of Polish-articulated bootlegs visually resembles the first-generation figures in paint and color decoration. There are two different package styles for the second generation of Polish-articulated figures. The first style has a photo of a Stormtrooper, while the second has a Biker Scout photo and is definitely more reminiscent of the first-generation card.

The third generation of Polish bootlegs originally came shrink-wrapped to their cardbacks, but they are next to impossible to find in this condition today and are usually found loose. The company that made the third-generation *Star Wars* bootlegs also made a series of GI Joe bootlegs, which are actually harder to find than their *Star Wars* counterparts. The *Star Wars*

Bootleg: Polish carded 2nd generation

Bootleg: Polish carded 2nd generation

Bootleg: Polish carded 3rd generation

Bootleg: Polish IG-88

Bootleg: Polish Deluxe Gamorrean Guard

line was distributed with various weapons (including some from the bootleg GI Joe line) and they are much different in paint and decoration than the first- and second-generation figures. The third-generation Polish bootlegs were made in the early to mid-1990s and are the most common to find of the Polish bootleg lines.

The next series of Polish bootleg figures are unarticulated. They are molded in one piece directly from Kenner figures and some still have the LFL copyrights on their legs! They came in a variety of colors ranging from direct copies to color schemes so absurd they make you wonder why people are drawn to these ugly misfit toys in the first place. There are nineteen figures in this Polish line, with color variations galore and collecting just a few figures from this line is challenging enough, let alone trying to collect one figure in every color scheme!

Next, we have unarticulated Polish figures that seem to have been cast from the first-generation bootlegs as evidenced by them having the same Biker Scout, Tie Pilot, or AT-AT Driver limbs. Bootlegged bootlegs—it doesn't get much better than that for a bootleg collector! These are great bootlegs but are also hard to find, even for the most advanced of bootleg collectors.

The last and probably rarest of the Polish figure lines is the "deluxe" series. These figures were sold in a vinyl baggie with the appropriate weapons for their characters. They are articulated and are directly cast from the Kenner figures. There are four figures in the deluxe line, with the most common of the four being the AT-AT Driver. The other three, Yoda, Gamorrean Guard, and Ree Yees, are all difficult to find.

No other country in the world can match Mexico for bootleg production. Much of this can be attributed to the economic situation in Mexico, as well as to the lack of licensed 3³/₄-inch products during the early years of the *Star Wars* line. But even moving beyond that, throughout the POTF2 era, many modern bootleg figures have been made in Mexico. There has been a seemingly inexhaustible supply of bootleg *Star Wars* merchandise produced in Mexico since the early 1980s. And even despite coming from different time lines and factories, many of these items are similar. As a result, trying to determine the origins and histories of Mexican bootlegs is a daunting task. The easiest way for collectors to categorize these items has been to break down bootlegs with similar features into several distinct groups.

Some of the earliest Mexican bootlegs were based on one of the first series of *Star Wars* toys to be released there: the Lili Ledy 12-inch figures. Twelve-inch Mexican bootlegs include a 12-inch Darth Vader and Stormtrooper, as well as a 12-inch-scale R2-D2. One of the more well known and hard to find early Mexican bootlegs is a large C-3PO. C-3PO was never released by Lili Ledy in the 12-inch form, so this particular 12-inch bootleg was based on a model kit and was meant to fit in with the other Lili Ledy 12-inch dolls that were sold during the same time frame.

Other early Mexican bootlegs include Land Speeders, which were molded from the Kenner die-cast vehicle and were available in a few different colors.

Like most bootleg lines, it's the cheesy duplications of Kenner's 3³/₄-inch line that attracts collectors and there were many different vintage 3³/₄-inch bootleg figures available in Mexico. Some are fully articulated, while others are totally unarticulated. Some even used parts from Lili Ledy figures. Some came bagged with a header card and many others came loose in bins that were sold at flea markets and assorted marketplaces. Some come in all the colors of the rainbow, but all are unlicensed treasures.

The first that are shown here are among the most interesting ones, as they have "googley" eyes that move when you move the figure. So far, only three different googley-eyed figures have shown up—two different Ewoks and a Yoda. The only known Ewoks are loose and the only known Yoda is still in its original bag. The figures themselves are unarticulated (one piece) and are solid rubbery plastic.

Bootleg: Mexican google-eyed Ewoks

Bootleg: Mexican LL hybrid

Next up are what are referred to as static figures. They are unarticulated with solid colors and are generally unpainted. Often, you will find these figures bagged but usually, these static figures are found loose. Even the same character can be found in many different color plastics and it's surmised that these figures were actually used as prizes inside of piñatas for children. Other vintage unarticulated figures include a series of all-black unarticulated rubber figures and it is not known if these were distributed in any packaging or just loose in a bin.

In the mid-1980s when the Lili Ledy toy company closed its doors, a large amount of complete figures was donated to orphanages. The orphanages repackaged these Ledy figures in bootleg packaging and sold them to buy items better suited for survival than toys. Factory overstock of Lili Ledy body parts also made their way into bootleggers' hands. The bootleggers cast parts to complete the figures and created hybrid figures that were part licensed product and part bootleg.

The most popular and common "vintage" bootleg figures from Mexico consist of a line that has a base of sixteen figures, as well as at least six more that share the same manufacturing style but are often sold separately from the base line. Most of the figures from this line are articulated in the arms, but have one-piece-molded torsos and legs. There are many color and paint variations in this line and the basic line consists of the following sixteen figures: Bib Fortuna, Yoda, Weequay, Ugnaught, Chewbacca, Gamorrean Guard, Admiral Ackbar, Klaatu, Klaatu Skiff, the Emperor, Bossk, Emperors Royal Guard, C-3PO, Greedo, AT-AT Driver, and Logray. The aforementioned six additional figures that are made in the same plastics and share the same articulation include: Luke Bespin, Leia Bespin, Darth Vader, Hoth Stormtrooper, Tie Pilot, and the Biker Scout, who is rarest of the lot. While these bootlegs have a vintage style, and the earliest versions of them are definitely vintage, there have been many castings of them, and the most recent ones are still easily found in Mexico.

Modern Bootlegs

The POTF 2 era saw a renewed interest in *Star Wars* product, and with it came a renewed, worldwide interest in bootlegging it. Mexico was certainly no exception. Like the vintage bootlegs, there has been a considerable amount of styles and sizes of modern Mexican bootlegs unleashed on the populace. One of the first modern Mexican bootleg lines to surface were the bagged bootleg two packs, which included two POTF figures (or one figure and one vehicle). Some sets even use vintage molds for one figure and a modern mold for the other, in the same multipack, or the same type of blister packaging.

This series of bagged figures consists of Vader and a Stormtrooper. But here the bootleggers decided to change their colors around as well as alter their poses to create different variations. The figures themselves are unarticulated and cast directly from the POTF figures.

Modern 3³/₄-inch bootlegs also include many unarticulated figures—the figures from this five-pack being the most prevalent. The five-pack includes an R2-D2, a C-3PO, Darth Vader, Chewbacca, and a Death Star Gunner. These figures have also been found carded on mini-POTF2 cards, as well as loose in unmarked baggies, most likely sold in bins. The Vader has a couple of paint variations and the C-3PO and R2-D2 were available in a variety of colors as shown below.

Despite the tight control Lucasfilm tried to have surrounding the release of Episode 1, in Mexico bootlegs were flowing even before the movie opened. The bagged two packs containing Qui-Gon and Darth Maul in one and a Battle Droid and Watto in the other are regarded by many collectors as some of the worst-made bootlegs to have ever come out of Mexico.

One of the best things about collecting Mexican bootlegs has to be the constant flow of items still being discovered. There seems to be no limit or end to just how many bootleg items were made in Mexico for both the modern and vintage lines. The constant learning process combined with the rush of finding that one piece that's never been seen before makes Mexico a favorite source for bootlegs for many collectors.

When the POTF2 line was released in 1995, the floodgates for a whole slew of new bootleg toys were also opened. Although modern *Star Wars* bootlegs are found in virtually every country of the world, most of these figures have originated from factories in China and finding import stickers on these figures is not uncommon. A veritable plethora of bootlegs in all shapes, sizes, and colors are made in China and for the most part these modern bootlegs are found in places such as flea markets, dollar stores, and ethnic import shops, often alongside other knock-off items such as purses and watches.

One of the earliest modern *Star Wars* knock-off lines made in China was the Galaxy Cops series, which was released in both 6- and 12-inch formats. The 6-inch figures had generic Power Ranger-type bodies and Darth Vader and Stormtrooper masks that fit over the figures' heads and shoulders. The 12-inch versions had removable helmets that had a generic human head underneath and they were released in two different box styles.

Bootleg: Mexican bagged POTF2

Bootleg: Mexican bagged
Episode 1

Bootleg: Mexican bagged
Episode 1

Bootleg: China Galaxy Cop

Bootleg: China POTF2

The most commonly seen Chinese bootleg figures are reprinted on Kenner/Hasbro's orange and green POTF2 cardbacks and the character photo on the package rarely matches the figure inside. A variety of different generic character photos can be found in this series including Luke Skywalker (Tatooine outfit), Luke Jedi, Luke Dagobah, Luke Stormtrooper, Luke X-Wing, and C-3PO. There are also two additional sets that used the purple Shadows of the Empire cardbacks with photos of the AT-ST Driver and Stormtrooper on the front of the cardback. While there are many packaging variations, the figures themselves are rather crude and are poorer quality renditions of their licensed counterparts. Besides the basic POTF2 figures, there is also a bootleg set of the Deluxe figures that were released by Kenner/Hasbro in 1996.

In staying with the POTF2 cardback theme, bootleggers thought another fun idea would be to make the figures two times the size of the regular 3³/₄-inch versions. There are two different series of these two-up bootlegs and like the 3³/₄-inch bootlegs, these figures came on generic character photo cardbacks—an orange Luke Jedi card and a green AT-ST Driver card.

The most well-known style of POTF2, 2-up bootlegs is the Galaxy Empire line. These figures were distributed in various countries throughout the world but seem to have been released in heavier quantities in Europe. The line consists of seven figures. Luke Skywalker, Han Solo, Darth Vader, Stormtrooper, Chewbacca, Chewbacca in Snoova disguise (from the Shadows of the Empire line), and, of course, everyone's favorite bounty hunter, Boba Fett. The packages of these figures are rather flimsy and the artwork features an image of the Millennium Falcon being chased by a Star Destroyer under the rather jovial Galaxy Empire logo.

Another large-sized figure set is the "versus" two-pack series. These figures were released around the same time as the Galaxy Empire line but are more difficult to find. The line has six different two packs to its credit: Lando (white) versus Hammerhead, Han Hoth versus Leia Boussh, Dash Rendar versus Han Solo, Chewie Snoova versus Tie Pilot, Luke Jedi versus Prince Xizor, and Luke Imperial Guard Disguise versus Boba Fett.

Soon after the first licensed Episode 1 figures hit the retail shelves, flea markets, small stores, and toy dealers knew that a secondary market existed for bootlegs, so they imported enough pirated merchandise to fill the needs that existed for both children and collectors alike.

These bootlegged Episode 1 figures were released in similar fashion to the POTF2 bootlegs—most on a single character cardback and in both 3³/₄ and 2-up sizes. Some even had fake Commtech chips inside the packaging to make them resemble even more their licensed counterparts.

Most of the Episode 1 bootlegged figures came on either Darth Maul cards with a fake Commtech chip or on two different Queen Amidala cards—one with the original release eight-back photo on the back of the card and one with eighteen figures listed on the back. Other 3³/₄-inch Episode 1 bootlegs came on Anakin or C-3PO cards. One particular line even went so far as to have each figure on its correct individual cardback; this line was packaged with a fake Commtech chip as well.

Besides the aforementioned single-carded Episode 1 figures, bootleggers also created a deluxe set. This line of eleven figures has an odd mixture of both Episode 1 characters and Original Trilogy figures and each comes packaged with a large role-playing lightsaber toy.

Another style of Episode 1-era bootlegs are those released under the *Space Wars* moniker. These were found worldwide in the typical places where bootlegs are sold and they come packaged in a variety of ways. There are a variety of *Space Wars* four packs and single-carded figures and one of the more oddball figure sets are those that were released with Sith Speeders. These sets came on two different header cards: one with the popular *Space Wars* logo and one set with an Episode 1 logo. You'll notice in the photos that on the vehicle side, the opposite logo is there, meaning that if the figure/speeder is in a *Space Wars* package, the vehicle will say *Star Wars* Episode 1, and if the vehicle is in an Episode 1 package, the vehicle will have *Space Wars* on its side.

Bootleg: *China Galaxy Empire*   Bootleg: *China Kubricks*

A popular fad in the Asian toy and model markets are superdeformed toys. These particular toys are shorter, fatter versions of pop culture characters and are often distinguished by their rather large heads. Of course, *Star Wars*, being the worldwide phenomenon that it is, has seen many of its popular characters from both the Original Trilogy and Episode 1 released as several types of unlicensed superdeformed toys. A series of wind-up toys packaged in plastic baggies has been released and many different variations of each character can be found. A similar line of superdeformed figures has also been released and each character comes in both glow-in-the-dark and standard paint schemes. All these items can still be found in stores in China for affordable prices. None of these toys have licensed counterparts but Hasbro did try to capitalize on the superdeformed craze in 2001 with its line of "palm talker" toys.

In recent years, one of the biggest licensed collectibles trends has involved Tomy's line of Kubrick character toys. Of course, when something becomes popular, it's sure to be bootlegged and Kubricks are no exception. Tomy did eventually secure the license to produce *Star Wars* Kubricks, but interestingly enough, there were unlicensed *Star Wars* Kubrick-esque toys on the market long before the licensed versions appeared. These knock-off lines consist of three different boxed sets: Boba Fett and a Biker Scout; Han in Carbonite, an Episode 1 Darth Maul, and Qui Gon-Jinn in a two-pack; and an Episode 2 Clone Trooper multipack.

It's no secret that licensed Episode 1 overstock left retailers reeling and reluctant to buy into the hype surrounding Episode 2. Perhaps bootleggers also felt this pinch because there were few Episode 2 bootleg items released. A series of carded figures and a multipack of bagged Clone Trooper figures (which are great for building an unlicensed army of clone troopers!) are all that are known to exist.

When it comes right down to it, no one condones the act of piracy or bootlegging, but one also can't ignore that these items are an integral part of *Star Wars* toy history. It seems that almost every day a new bootleg line or a new variation to an existing one, both vintage and modern, is discovered. It's this kind of diversity and exhaustive range that make bootleg collecting so challenging and appealing to collectors. Well, that and something also has to be said for being one of the few owners of some of the most appalling toys ever made—bootleg collectors often follow the motto "the uglier the better!" It's also important to note that while bootleg toys are fun to collect, they should not be given to small children to play with. The construction and quality of these items is usually suspect. If the licensed products are available to you, it's best to let children play with those, as they have met the strict safety standards that are needed for a child's safety.

Terminology

The following are terms commonly associated with *Star Wars* collecting accessories:

Bootleg An unlicensed version of a preexisting, licensed product. Usually, a bootleg is a direct copy (albeit typically much shoddier in appearance) of its licensed counterpart. Unlike fakes or customs, bootlegs are made in factory environments to be sold in stores as toys and are not made specifically to mimic preexisting collectibles. Action figure toys are the most frequently bootlegged items.

Knock-off Almost the same as a bootleg, but the major difference is that knock-offs are items that bear resemblance to a licensed property but are not exact in their appearance.

Reproduction Items that are meant to look identical to one that has been produced under license. Typically, these are weapons and accessories (Double-Telescoping Lightsabers and blasters), blisters, dioramas, and card-backs. Initially, they were meant to act as temporary replacements for missing parts, but nowadays they are used to dishonestly replace vintage parts and accessories. Also known as repro.

13 ACCESSORIES

This section deals with the extra items that can be bought to enhance a collection from display stands to protective cases. None of these items are licensed by Lucasfilm, but they are considered to be staples of the *Star Wars* collecting hobby.

REAL Action Figure Stands

These are a very popular brand of display stands that were specially designed for *Star Wars* action figures when one collector was unsatisfied with how the rereleased 1995 figures failed to remain upright. REAL stands are made of a scratch-resistant polycarbonate and come in two formats, one for modern action figures measuring just under $2^{1}/_{2}$ inches with 2 foot-pegs, and a smaller one (measuring $1^{3}/_{4}$ inches) for vintage action figures. They also have a glasslike appearance in order to not detract from displays.

ProTech Star Cases

These are considered to be the best protective clamshell cases currently available today, and they come in a variety of sizes and shapes to protect both loose and packaged action figures. ProTech also makes soft and hard cases, single figure blister cases, and loose figure display cylinders.

The Star Case most commonly found in *Star Wars* collections is the soft case that holds modern carded figures snuggly and securely without risking the cardstock or the blister. ProTech also produced a slightly larger version to accommodate the deeper bubble since the new Saga packaging came out with the release of *Attack of the Clones*. It also developed a third variety to hold Saga carded Deluxe figures.

REAL Display Stands
(Image courtesy of Tim Roberts)

Ultarama

This modular display system was also created by a *Star Wars* collector who wanted to make quick dioramas and easily adaptable play sets. Ultarama action figure display systems is a tiered, semicircular shelving system that can be stacked several tiers high and holds up to eighty action figures. They are designed so that they can be easily decorated in any style, which makes them especially convenient for collectors.

Ultra-PRO Mylar Sleeves

Ultra-PRO is the leading manufacturer of long-term storage products for printed materials such as trading cards, comics, and photos. Its range of products includes pouches made of Mylar for the safe storage of comic books, multipocketed sleeves for trading cards, and card deck boxes for CCG/TCG players. It also stocks folders suitable for its various Mylar sleeve products.

Terminology

The following are terms commonly associated with *Star Wars* collecting accessories:

Action stands   A type of plastic display base used to mount 3³/₄-inch action figures.

Blister   The plastic bubble that holds the toy to the cardback. (Also known as bubble.)

Clamshell   A hinged plastic case used for protecting carded 3³/₄-inch action figures.

Mylar   A polythene plastic made by DuPont that is commonly used in film processing and that is known for its antidegradation properties.

Polybag   A sealable pouch typically made of polythene.

Star Case   A type of plastic clamshell case used to protect carded $3^3/4$-inch action figures.

Ultra-PRO   A manufacturer of high-grade Mylar storage sleeves.

Part Two
Price Guide

ABOUT THIS PRICE GUIDE

There is a certain amount of risk in fixing values to goods for a price guide for any collectible, but especially in a market that is as variable as *Star Wars*. Because so many of the values placed on *Star Wars* collectibles are linked to eBay, the prices in this guide are based upon a long-term average that should iron out any highs and lows as the market changes. The prices contained in the *Official Price Guide to Star Wars Memorabilia* are considered to be a snapshot of prices at the time of publication and should be used as a measuring stick, rather than as a definitive means of valuation.

Even though over 250 million action figures were produced by Kenner in the vintage era, many of these toys are now rare due to limited distribution or production runs, and changes to design such as the Double-telescoping Lightsabers that came in the earliest wave of $3^3/_4$-inch figures. A good example of a rare toy would be Yak Face. Some items were never produced to be kept, like Dixie bathroom cups from American Can Co., Drawing Board Greeting Cards Inc.'s party favors, and wallpaper by Wallpaper To Go Inc. Consequently many such disposable goods were thrown out once they were used. In some cases over-produced goods were stockpiled and forgotten about. In the late 1980s and early '90s there were a number of warehouse finds that delivered large numbers of vintage goods to the market and deflated the value of many items. Rapid price reductions aren't just constrained to vintage merchandise either: in recent years there have been more than one occasion when a limited edition item worth hundreds of dollars one week was released to the mass market through popular retailers the next.

The price guide is broken up into broad categories of content to make it easy to use, and from there is further broken down into increasing detail dependent on the level of interest from the collecting community. Thus causing Kenner/Hasbro toys to receive the greatest amount of attention.

Each item is listed with three values: RRP (Recommended Retail Price), which is the sticker price of the item when it was originally produced; Loose, the value of the item without any packaging but complete in every other respect; and finally MISB (Mint In Sealed Box), where the item is in mint condition in a sealed box (or other suitable packaging) that is also in mint condition. Even though this price guide is aimed at readers in Mexico and Canada, as well as the USA, all prices are in US dollars for simplicity. Using a single currency helps to level the playing field and avoids the problem of fluctuating foreign currency markets. Since the advent of online stores and eBay, the US dollar has become the international currency for the *Star Wars* collecting hobby. Each item in the Price Guide is linked to a reference number (for example, "Ref. No.: 3836"). The reference number can be used to find out more information on the product through the collecting database at Rebelscum (www.rebelscum.com/swdb).

Vintage Action Toys

A NEW HOPE

Chewbacca with Bandolier
Ref. No.:	4353
Retail Price:	$4.99
Loose Price:	$8
MISB:	$15

Give-A-Show Projector
Ref. No.:	42536
Retail Price:	N/A
Loose Price:	$8
MISB:	$15

Luke Skywalker AM Headset Radio
Ref. No.:	12177
Retail Price:	$19.99
Loose Price:	$250
MISB:	$400 to $1250

Movie Viewer
Ref. No.:	42537
Retail Price:	N/A
Loose Price:	$12
MISB:	$50

Play-Doh Action Set

Star Wars
Ref. No.:	12328
Retail Price:	N/A
Loose Price:	$18
MISB:	$30

The Empire Strikes Back
Ref. No.:	N/A
Retail Price:	N/A
Loose Price:	$65
MISB:	$25

Return of the Jedi
Ref. No.:	N/A
Retail Price:	N/A
Loose Price:	$15
MISB:	$25

R2-D2 (Squeaking)
Ref. No.:	5349
Retail Price:	$4.99
Loose Price:	N/A
MISB:	$20

12″ Action Figures

A NEW HOPE

Artoo-Detoo (R2-D2)
Ref. No.:	4099
Retail Price:	$9.99
Loose Price:	$36
MISB:	$110

Ben (Obi-Wan) Kenobi
Ref. No.:	4101
Retail Price:	$9.99
Loose Price:	$35
MISB:	$130

Boba Fett
Ref. No.:	4102
Retail Price:	$9.99
Loose Price:	$60
MISB:	$380

Chewbacca
Ref. No.:	4104
Retail Price:	$9.99
Loose Price:	$30
MISB:	$110

Darth Vader
Ref. No.:	4105
Retail Price:	$9.99
Loose Price:	$35
MISB:	$240

Han Solo
Ref. No.:	4106
Retail Price:	$9.99
Loose Price:	$50
MISB:	$300

Jawa
Ref. No.:	4100
Retail Price:	$9.99
Loose Price:	$25
MISB:	$100

Luke Skywalker
Ref. No.:	4108
Retail Price:	$9.99
Loose Price:	$35
MISB:	$150

Princess Leia Organa
Ref. No.:	4109
Retail Price:	$9.99
Loose Price:	$30
MISB:	$200

See-Threepio (C-3PO)
Ref. No.:	4110
Retail Price:	$9.99
Loose Price:	$26
MISB:	$100

Stormtrooper
Ref. No.:	4111
Retail Price:	$9.99
Loose Price:	$32
MISB:	$110

THE EMPIRE STRIKES BACK

Boba Fett
Ref. No.:	4103
Retail Price:	$12.99
Loose Price:	$60
MISB:	$250

Chewbacca
Ref. No.:	6634
Retail Price:	$11.99
Loose Price:	$30
MISB:	N/A

Darth Vader
Ref. No.:	6621
Retail Price:	$14.99
Loose Price:	$30
MISB:	N/A

IG-88 (Bounty hunter)
Ref. No.:	4107
Retail Price:	$9.99
Loose Price:	$100
MISB:	$225

3³/₄" Action Figures

MAIL AWAY

4-LOM
Ref. No.:	3456
Retail Price:	N/A
Loose Price:	N/A
MISB:	$25

Admiral Ackbar
Ref. No.:	17427
Retail Price:	N/A
Loose Price:	N/A
MISB:	$15

Anakin Skywalker
Ref. No.:	17430
Retail Price:	N/A
Loose Price:	N/A
MISB:	$20

Boba Fett
Ref. No.:	3583
Retail Price:	N/A
Loose Price:	N/A
MISB:	$90

Bossk (Bounty hunter)
Ref. No.:	3591
Retail Price:	N/A
Loose Price:	N/A
MISB:	$15

Nien Nunb
Ref. No.:	17428
Retail Price:	N/A
Loose Price:	N/A
MISB:	$12

The Emperor
Ref. No.:	17429
Retail Price:	N/A
Loose Price:	N/A
MISB:	$20

A NEW HOPE

Artoo-Detoo (R2-D2)
Ref. No.:	3477
Retail Price:	$1.99
Loose Price:	$7
MISB:	$220 to $280

12 Back
Ref. No.:	3477

20 Back
Ref. No.:	3481

21 Back
Ref. No.:	3489

Ben (Obi-Wan) Kenobi
Ref. No.:	3527
Retail Price:	$1.99
Loose Price:	$10
MISB:	$115 to $280

12 Back, side view picture
Ref. No.:	3527

12 Back, side view picture, Double-Telescoping Lightsaber
Ref. No.:	3526

20 Back
Ref. No.:	3549

21 Back
Ref. No.:   3554

Boba Fett
Ref. No.:   6525
Retail Price: $1.99
Loose Price: $20
MISB: $600

20 Back
Ref. No.:   6525

21 Back

Chewbacca
Ref. No.:   3603
Retail Price: $1.99
Loose Price: $7
MISB: $120 to $350

12 Back
Ref. No.:   3603

20 Back
Ref. No.:   3610

21 Back
Ref. No.:   3615

Darth Vader
Ref. No.:   3632
Retail Price: $1.99
Loose Price: $7
MISB: $125 to $420

12 Back, saber picture
Ref. No.:   3632

12 Back, saber picture, Double-Telescoping Lightsaber
Ref. No.:   3630

20 Back
Ref. No.:   3639

21 Back
Ref. No.:   3644

Death Squad Commander
Ref. No.:   3653
Retail Price: $1.99
Loose Price: $10
MISB: $95 to $315

12 Back
Ref. No.:   3653

20 Back
Ref. No.:   3660

21 Back
Ref. No.:   3666

Death Star Droid
Ref. No.:   6230
Retail Price: $1.99

Loose Price: $7
MISB: $85 to $150

20 Back
Ref. No.:   6230

21 Back
Ref. No.:   6527

Greedo
Ref. No.:   6240
Retail Price: $1.99
Loose Price: $7
MISB: $95 to $160

20 Back
Ref. No.:   6240

21 Back
Ref. No.:   6529

Hammerhead
Ref. No.:   6248
Retail Price: $1.99
Loose Price: $7
MISB: $100 to $160

20 Back
Ref. No.:   6248

21 Back
Ref. No.:   6531

Han Solo
Ref. No.:   3733
Retail Price: $1.99
Loose Price: $15
MISB: $225 to $620

12 Back, large head
Ref. No.:   3733

12 Back, small head
Ref. No.:   3717

20 Back
Ref. No.:   3726

21 Back
Ref. No.:   3732

Jawa
Ref. No.:   3780
Retail Price: $1.99
Loose Price: $7
MISB: $90 to $2500

12 Back, cloth cape
Ref. No.:   3780

12 Back, vinyl cape
Ref. No.:   3779

20 Back
Ref. No.:   3787

21 Back
Ref. No.:   3793

Luke Skywalker

Ref. No.:	3836
Retail Price:	$1.99
Loose Price:	$25
MISB:	$250 to $3500

12 Back, blond hair

Ref. No.:	3836

12 Back, blond hair, Double-Telescoping Lightsaber

Ref. No.:	3835

20 Back

Ref. No.:	3843

21 Back

Ref. No.:	3849

Luke Skywalker: X-Wing Pilot

Ref. No.:	6543
Retail Price:	$1.99
Loose Price:	$7
MISB:	$125 to $200

20 Back

Ref. No.:	6543

21 Back

Ref. No.:	6539

Power Droid

Ref. No.:	6260
Retail Price:	$1.99
Loose Price:	$7
MISB:	$85 to $150

20 Back

Ref. No.:	6260

21 Back

Ref. No.:	6533

Princess Leia Organa

Ref. No.:	3903
Retail Price:	$1.99
Loose Price:	$7
MISB:	$190 to $425

12 Back

Ref. No.:	3903

20 Back

Ref. No.:	3910

21 Back

Ref. No.:	3916

R5-D4

Ref. No.:	6267
Retail Price:	$1.99
Loose Price:	$7
MISB:	$125 to $180

20 Back

Ref. No.:	6267

21 Back

Ref. No.:	6270

Sand People

Ref. No.:	3963
Retail Price:	$1.99
Loose Price:	$12
MISB:	$165 to $335

12 Back

Ref. No.:	3963

20 Back

Ref. No.:	3970

21 Back

Ref. No.:	3976

See-Threepio (C-3PO)

Ref. No.:	3980
Retail Price:	$1.99
Loose Price:	$7
MISB:	$155 to $300

12 Back

Ref. No.:	3980

20 Back

Ref. No.:	3987

21 Back

Ref. No.:	3993

Snaggletooth (blue)

Ref. No.:	N/A
Retail Price:	N/A
Loose Price:	$55
MISB:	N/A

Snaggletooth (red)

Ref. No.:	6275
Retail Price:	$1.99
Loose Price:	$7
MISB:	$125 to $150

20 Back

Ref. No.:	6275

21 Back

Ref. No.:	6534

Stormtrooper

Ref. No.:	4014
Retail Price:	$1.99
Loose Price:	$10
MISB:	$115 to $280

12 Back

Ref. No.:	4014

20 Back

Ref. No.:	4021

21 Back

Ref. No.:	4027

Walrus Man

Ref. No.:	6282
Retail Price:	$1.99
Loose Price:	$7
MISB:	$115 to $180

20 Back
Ref. No.:	6282

21 Back
Ref. No.:	6536

MULTIPACKS

Android Set: C-3PO, R2-D2, Chewbacca

Ref. No.:	17433
Retail Price:	N/A
Loose Price:	N/A
MISB:	$750 to $1500

Creature Set with Backdrop: Hammerhead, Walrus Man, Greedo

Ref. No.:	17437
Retail Price:	N/A
Loose Price:	N/A
MISB:	$1250 to $2250

Droid Set with Backdrop: R5-D4, Death Star Droid, Power Droid

Ref. No.:	17435
Retail Price:	N/A
Loose Price:	N/A
MISB:	$1250 to $2250

Early Bird Figure Set: Luke Skywalker, Princess Leia, Chewbacca, R2-D2 with stand

Ref. No.:	3684
Retail Price:	N/A
Loose Price:	N/A
MISB:	$350 to $500

Hero Set with Backdrop: Luke X-Wing Pilot, Ben Kenobi, Han Solo

Ref. No.:	17434
Retail Price:	N/A
Loose Price:	N/A
MISB:	$1250 to $2250

Hero Set: Han Solo, Princess Leia, Ben (Obi-Wan) Kenobi

Ref. No.:	17432
Retail Price:	N/A
Loose Price:	N/A
MISB:	$750 to $1500

Villain Set with Backdrop: Sand People, Boba Fett, Snaggletooth

Ref. No.:	17436
Retail Price:	N/A
Loose Price:	N/A
MISB:	$1250 to $2250

Villain Set: Darth Vader, Stormtrooper, Death Squad Commander

Ref. No.:	17431
Retail Price:	N/A
Loose Price:	N/A
MISB:	$750 to $1500

THE EMPIRE STRIKES BACK

2-1B

Ref. No.:	7385
Retail Price:	$2.49
Loose Price:	$7
MISB:	$85 to $105

41 Back
Ref. No.:	7385

45 Back
Ref. No.:	4887

47 Back
Ref. No.:	3454

4-LOM

Ref. No.:	4888
Retail Price:	$2.49
Loose Price:	$7
MISB:	$100

Artoo-Detoo (R2-D2)

Ref. No.:	3492
Retail Price:	$2.49
Loose Price:	$7
MISB:	$90 to $155

21 Back
Ref. No.:	3492

31 Back
Ref. No.:	5462

32 Back
Ref. No.:	5461

42 Back
Ref. No.:	11667

Artoo-Detoo (R2-D2) (Sensorscope)

Ref. No.:	4905
Retail Price:	$2.49
Loose Price:	$7
MISB:	$65 to $70

45 Back
Ref. No.:	4905

47 Back
Ref. No.: 3498

48 Back
Ref. No.: 4908

AT-AT Commander
Ref. No.: 3502
Retail Price: $2.49
Loose Price: $7
MISB: $25 to $40

45 Back
Ref. No.: 3502

47 Back
Ref. No.: 3503

48 Back
Ref. No.: 4912

AT-AT Driver
Ref. No.: 7388
Retail Price: $2.49
Loose Price: $7
MISB: $30 to $50

41 Back
Ref. No.: 7388

45 Back
Ref. No.: 3509

47 Back
Ref. No.: 3510

48 Back
Ref. No.: 4916

Ben (Obi-Wan) Kenobi
Ref. No.: 3557
Retail Price: $2.49
Loose Price: $10
MISB: $85 to $175

21 Back
Ref. No.: 3557

31 Back
Ref. No.: 5463

32 Back
Ref. No.: 4919

41 Back
Ref. No.: 7433

45 Back
Ref. No.: 4925

47 Back
Ref. No.: 3560

48 Back
Ref. No.: 4922

Bespin Security Guard (II)
Ref. No.: 3570
Retail Price: $2.49

Loose Price: $7
MISB: $40 to $60

45 Back
Ref. No.: 3570

47 Back
Ref. No.: 4857

48 Back
Ref. No.: 4928

Bespin Security Guard (I)
Ref. No.: 4926
Retail Price: $2.49
Loose Price: $7
MISB: $30 to $65

31 Back
Ref. No.: 4926

32 Back
Ref. No.: 3566

41 Back
Ref. No.: 7398

45 Back
Ref. No.: 4856

47 Back
Ref. No.: 4858

48 Back
Ref. No.: 4930

Boba Fett
Ref. No.: 4934
Retail Price: $2.49
Loose Price: $20
MISB: $145 to $280

21 Back
Ref. No.: 4934

31 Back
Ref. No.: 4949

32 Back
Ref. No.: 4938

41 Back
Ref. No.: 7403

45 Back
Ref. No.: 4941

47 Back
Ref. No.: 11862

48 Back
Ref. No.: 4933

Bossk (Bounty Hunter)
Ref. No.: 4942
Retail Price: $2.49
Loose Price: $7
MISB: $40 to $90

31 Back
Ref. No.: 4942

32 Back
Ref. No.:   4944

41 Back
Ref. No.:   7406

45 Back
Ref. No.:   4946

47 Back
Ref. No.:   3594

48 Back
Ref. No.:   4948

C-3PO (Removable Limbs)

Ref. No.:   4960
Retail Price: $2.49
Loose Price: $7
MISB: $55 to $115

45 Back
Ref. No.:   4960

47 Back
Ref. No.:   3599

48 Back
Ref. No.:   4957

Chewbacca

Ref. No.:   3618
Retail Price: $2.49
Loose Price: $7
MISB: $95 to $270

21 Back
Ref. No.:   3618

31 Back
Ref. No.:   5332

32 Back
Ref. No.:   5370

41 Back
Ref. No.:   7381

45 Back
Ref. No.:   5333

47 Back
Ref. No.:   5012

48 Back
Ref. No.:   5015

Cloud Car Pilot

Ref. No.:   4879
Retail Price: $2.49
Loose Price: $7
MISB: $35 to $70

45 Back

47 Back

48 Back

Darth Vader

Ref. No.:   3647
Retail Price: $2.49
Loose Price: $7
MISB: $65 to $165

21 Back
Ref. No.:   3647

31 Back
Ref. No.:   5023

32 Back
Ref. No.:   5025

41 Back
Ref. No.:   7414

45 Back
Ref. No.:   5029

47 Back
Ref. No.:   5030

48 Back
Ref. No.:   5033

Death Squad Commander

Ref. No.:   3667
Retail Price: $2.49
Loose Price: $10
MISB: $240

21 Back
Ref. No.:   3667

Death Star Droid

Ref. No.:   5034
Retail Price: $2.49
Loose Price: $7
MISB: $60 to $140

21 Back
Ref. No.:   5034

31 Back
Ref. No.:   5036

32 Back
Ref. No.:   5038

41 Back
Ref. No.:   7417

45 Back
Ref. No.:   5039

47 Back
Ref. No.:   3671

48 Back
Ref. No.:   5042

Dengar

Ref. No.:   7420
Retail Price: $2.49
Loose Price: $7
MISB: $40 to $90

41 Back
Ref. No.: 7420

45 Back
Ref. No.: 3677

47 Back
Ref. No.: 5467

48 Back
Ref. No.: 5470

FX-7 (Medical Droid)
Ref. No.: 5346
Retail Price: $2.49
Loose Price: $7
MISB: $40 to $90

31 Back
Ref. No.: 5346

32 Back
Ref. No.: 5376

41 Back
Ref. No.: 3696

45 Back
Ref. No.: 5379

47 Back
Ref. No.: 5441

48 Back
Ref. No.: 5473

Greedo
Ref. No.: 5043
Retail Price: $2.49
Loose Price: $7
MISB: $75 to $165

21 Back
Ref. No.: 5043

31 Back
Ref. No.: 5054

32 Back
Ref. No.: 5049

41 Back
Ref. No.: 7426

45 Back
Ref. No.: 5053

47 Back
Ref. No.: 3708

48 Back
Ref. No.: 5046

Hammerhead
Ref. No.: 5055
Retail Price: $2.49
Loose Price: $7
MISB: $65 to $145

21 Back
Ref. No.: 5055

31 Back
Ref. No.: 5057

32 Back
Ref. No.: 5059

41 Back
Ref. No.: 7428

45 Back
Ref. No.: 5063

47 Back
Ref. No.: 3714

48 Back
Ref. No.: 5066

Han Solo
Ref. No.: 3734
Retail Price: $2.49
Loose Price: $7
MISB: $155 to $280

21 Back
Ref. No.: 3734

31 Back
Ref. No.: 3735

31 Back
Ref. No.: 3720

32 Back
Ref. No.: 5069

41 Back
Ref. No.: 7430

45 Back
Ref. No.: 5073

47 Back
Ref. No.: 5074

48 Back
Ref. No.: 5077

Han Solo (Bespin Outfit)
Ref. No.: 7435
Retail Price: $2.49
Loose Price: $7
MISB: $50 to $70

41 Back
Ref. No.: 7435

45 Back
Ref. No.: 4869

47 Back
Ref. No.: 4870

48 Back
Ref. No.: 5080

Han Solo (Hoth Outfit)
Ref. No.: 5131
Retail Price: $2.49
Loose Price: $7
MISB: $50 to $100

31 Back
Ref. No.:   5131

32 Back
Ref. No.:   5381

41 Back
Ref. No.:   7432

45 Back
Ref. No.:   5398

47 Back
Ref. No.:   6961

48 Back
Ref. No.:   6964

IG-88 (Bounty Hunter)
Ref. No.:   5335
Retail Price: $2.49
Loose Price: $7
MISB: $40 to $90

31 Back
Ref. No.:   5335

32 Back
Ref. No.:   5385

41 Back
Ref. No.:   7453

45 Back
Ref. No.:   4849

47 Back
Ref. No.:   3758

48 Back
Ref. No.:   5475

Imperial Commander
Ref. No.:   7460
Retail Price: $2.49
Loose Price: $7
MISB: $25 to $65

41 Back
Ref. No.:   7460

45 Back
Ref. No.:   5399

47 Back
Ref. No.:   5442

48 Back
Ref. No.:   5445

Imperial Stormtrooper (Hoth Battle Gear)
Ref. No.:   5337
Retail Price: $2.49
Loose Price: $7
MISB: $40 to $90

31 Back
Ref. No.:   5337

32 Back
Ref. No.:   5336

41 Back
Ref. No.:   11690

45 Back
Ref. No.:   5391

47 Back
Ref. No.:   5554

48 Back
Ref. No.:   5557

Imperial Tie Fighter Pilot
Ref. No.:   3775
Retail Price: $2.49
Loose Price: $7
MISB: $50 to $90

47 Back
Ref. No.:   3775

48 Back
Ref. No.:   5457

Jawa
Ref. No.:   3795
Retail Price: $2.49
Loose Price: $7
MISB: $70 to $165

21 Back
Ref. No.:   3795

31 Back
Ref. No.:   5081

32 Back
Ref. No.:   5083

41 Back
Ref. No.:   7465

45 Back
Ref. No.:   5087

47 Back
Ref. No.:   5091

48 Back
Ref. No.:   5090

Lando Calrissian
Ref. No.:   5478
Retail Price: $2.49
Loose Price: $7
MISB: $40 to $90

31 Back, without teeth
Ref. No.:   5478

32 Back, without teeth
Ref. No.:   5479

41 Back, without teeth
Ref. No.:   7467

45 Back, with teeth
Ref. No.:   4898

47 Back, with teeth
Ref. No.:   3813

48 Back, with teeth
Ref. No.:   4903

Leia (Hoth Outfit)
Ref. No.:   11669
Retail Price: $2.49
Loose Price: $7
MISB: $40 to $90

41 Back
Ref. No.:   11669

45 Back
Ref. No.:   5173

47 Back
Ref. No.:   5174

48 Back
Ref. No.:   5450

Leia Organa (Bespin Gown)
Ref. No.:   3820
Retail Price: $2.49
Loose Price: $7
MISB: $70 to $180

31 Back
Ref. No.:   3820

32 Back, crew neck
Ref. No.:   3821

32 Back, turtleneck
Ref. No.:   3925

41 Back
Ref. No.:   11672

41 Back
Ref. No.:   5413

45 Back
Ref. No.:   5543

47 Back
Ref. No.:   5546

47 Back
Ref. No.:   5723

Lobot
Ref. No.:   3824
Retail Price: $2.49
Loose Price: $7
MISB: $45 to $70

41 Back
Ref. No.:   3824

45 Back
Ref. No.:   3826

47 Back
Ref. No.:   3827

48 Back
Ref. No.:   5447

Luke Skywalker
Ref. No.:   3851
Retail Price: $2.49
Loose Price: $25
MISB: $115 to $250

21 Back
Ref. No.:   3851

31 Back
Ref. No.:   5097

32 Back
Ref. No.:   5099

41 Back, blond hair
Ref. No.:   5101

41 Back, brown hair
Ref. No.:   3838

45 Back, blond hair
Ref. No.:   5400

45 Back, brown hair
Ref. No.:   3844

47 Back, blond hair
Ref. No.:   3852

47 Back, brown hair
Ref. No.:   3845

48 Back, blond hair
Ref. No.:   5105

48 Back, brown hair
Ref. No.:   3850

Luke Skywalker (Bespin Fatigues)
Ref. No.:   5110
Retail Price: $2.49
Loose Price: $7
MISB: $90 to $165

31 Back
Ref. No.:   5110

32 Back, blond hair
Ref. No.:   3863

32 Back, brown hair
Ref. No.:   5114

41 Back, blond hair
Ref. No.:   7473

41 Back, brown hair
Ref. No.:   6955

45 Back
Ref. No.:   5118

47 Back
Ref. No.:   3861

48 Back
Ref. No.:   5689

Luke Skywalker (Hoth Battle Gear)

Ref. No.:	3867
Retail Price:	$2.49
Loose Price:	$7
MISB:	$60 to $115

45 Back
Ref. No.:	3867

47 Back
Ref. No.:	4860

48 Back
Ref. No.:	5109

Luke Skywalker (X-Wing Pilot)

Ref. No.:	7471
Retail Price:	$2.49
Loose Price:	$7
MISB:	$75 to $155

21 Back
Ref. No.:	5093

31 Back
Ref. No.:	5120

32 Back
Ref. No.:	5107

41 Back
Ref. No.:	7471

45 Back
Ref. No.:	5121

47 Back
Ref. No.:	3882

48 Back
Ref. No.:	5096

Power Droid

Ref. No.:	5125
Retail Price:	$2.49
Loose Price:	$7
MISB:	$60 to $120

21 Back
Ref. No.:	5125

31 Back
Ref. No.:	5338

32 Back
Ref. No.:	5402

41 Back
Ref. No.:	5362

45 Back
Ref. No.:	5406

47 Back
Ref. No.:	3900

48 Back
Ref. No.:	7482

Princess Leia Organa

Ref. No.:	3918
Retail Price:	$2.49
Loose Price:	$7
MISB:	$130 to $160

21 Back
Ref. No.:	3918

31 Back
Ref. No.:	5407

32 Back
Ref. No.:	5409

41 Back
Ref. No.:	11674

45 Back
Ref. No.:	5412

47 Back
Ref. No.:	3919

48 Back
Ref. No.:	5542

R5-D4

Ref. No.:	4884
Retail Price:	$2.49
Loose Price:	$7
MISB:	$475 to $155

21 Back
Ref. No.:	4884

31 Back
Ref. No.:	5415

32 Back
Ref. No.:	5416

41 Back
Ref. No.:	11676

45 Back
Ref. No.:	4890

47 Back
Ref. No.:	3942

48 Back
Ref. No.:	4895

Rebel Commander

Ref. No.:	11678
Retail Price:	$2.49
Loose Price:	$7
MISB:	$30 to $65

41 Back
Ref. No.:	11678

45 Back
Ref. No.:	4863

47 Back
Ref. No.:	4864

48 Back
Ref. No.:	5364

Rebel Soldier (Hoth Battle Gear)

Ref. No.: 5417
Retail Price: $2.49
Loose Price: $7
MISB: $40 to $90

31 Back
Ref. No.: 5417

32 Back
Ref. No.: 5418

41 Back
Ref. No.: 11680

45 Back
Ref. No.: 5421

47 Back
Ref. No.: 3955

48 Back
Ref. No.: 5550

Sand People

Ref. No.: 3978
Retail Price: $2.49
Loose Price: $12
MISB: $90 to $175

21 Back
Ref. No.: 3978

31 Back
Ref. No.: 5428

32 Back
Ref. No.: 5430

41 Back
Ref. No.: 11682

45 Back
Ref. No.: 5433

47 Back
Ref. No.: 3979

48 Back
Ref. No.: 5553

See-Threepio (C-3PO)

Ref. No.: 3995
Retail Price: $2.49
Loose Price: $7
MISB: $95 to $175

21 Back
Ref. No.: 3995

31 Back
Ref. No.: 4951

32 Back
Ref. No.: 4953

41 Back
Ref. No.: 7410

Snaggletooth (Red)

Ref. No.: 5126
Retail Price: $2.49
Loose Price: $7
MISB: $65 to $145

21 Back
Ref. No.: 5126

31 Back
Ref. No.: 5422

32 Back
Ref. No.: 5424

41 Back
Ref. No.: 11684

45 Back
Ref. No.: 5427

47 Back
Ref. No.: 4005

48 Back
Ref. No.: 6277

Star Destroyer Commander

Ref. No.: 4961
Retail Price: $2.49
Loose Price: $7
MISB: $60 to $105

31 Back
Ref. No.: 4961

32 Back
Ref. No.: 5281

41 Back
Ref. No.: 5283

45 Back
Ref. No.: 5284

47 Back
Ref. No.: 5286

48 Back
Ref. No.: 4962

Stormtrooper

Ref. No.: 4029
Retail Price: $2.49
Loose Price: $10
MISB: $90 to $175

21 Back
Ref. No.: 4029

31 Back
Ref. No.: 5341

32 Back
Ref. No.: 5434

41 Back
Ref. No.: 11688

45 Back
Ref. No.: 5326

47 Back

Ref. No.:	5327

48 Back

Ref. No.:	5330

(Twin Pod) Cloud Car Pilot

Ref. No.:	4855
Retail Price:	$2.49
Loose Price:	$7
MISB:	$30 to $60

45 Back

Ref. No.:	4855

47 Back

Ref. No.:	4052

48 Back

Ugnaught

Ref. No.:	11692
Retail Price:	$2.49
Loose Price:	$7
MISB:	$45 to $70

41 Back

Ref. No.:	11692

45 Back

Ref. No.:	4056

47 Back

Ref. No.:	5451

48 Back

Ref. No.:	5454

Walrus Man

Ref. No.:	5127
Retail Price:	$2.49
Loose Price:	$7
MISB:	$65 to $145

21 Back

Ref. No.:	5127

31 Back

Ref. No.:	5342

32 Back

Ref. No.:	5344

41 Back

Ref. No.:	11694

45 Back

Ref. No.:	5440

47 Back

Ref. No.:	5559

48 Back

Ref. No.:	5562

Yoda

Ref. No.:	5351
Retail Price:	$2.49

Loose Price:	$20
MISB:	$100 to $165

32 Back

Ref. No.:	5351

41 Back

Ref. No.:	36602

41 Back

Ref. No.:	9058

45 Back

Ref. No.:	36603

47 Back

Ref. No.:	36604

48 Back

Ref. No.:	5354

Zuckuss

Ref. No.:	5460
Retail Price:	$2.49
Loose Price:	$12
MISB:	$100

48 Back

Ref. No.:	5460

MULTIPACKS

Bespin Alliance: Bespin Security Guard (White), Lando Calrissian, Luke Skywalker (Bespin Fatigues)

Ref. No.:	17444
Retail Price:	N/A
Loose Price:	N/A
MISB:	$700 to $900

Bespin Set: Han Solo (Bespin Outfit), Ugnaught, Lobot

Ref. No.:	16918
Retail Price:	N/A
Loose Price:	N/A
MISB:	$700 to $900

Bespin Set: See-Threepio (C-3PO) with Removable Limbs, Ugnaught, Cloud Car Pilot

Ref. No.:	17441
Retail Price:	N/A
Loose Price:	N/A
MISB:	$700 to $800

Darth Vader, Stormtrooper (Hoth), AT-AT Driver, Rebel Soldier, IG-88, Yoda

Ref. No.:	17447
Retail Price:	N/A
Loose Price:	N/A
MISB:	$700 to $900

Hoth Rebels: Han Solo (Hoth), Rebel Soldier, FX-7

Ref. No.:	17443
Retail Price:	N/A
Loose Price:	N/A
MISB:	$700 to $900

Imperial Forces: Bossk, Imperial Stormtrooper (Hoth Battle Gear), IG-88

Ref. No.:	17445
Retail Price:	N/A
Loose Price:	N/A
MISB:	$700 to $900

Imperial Set: Imperial Commander, Dengar, AT-AT Driver

Ref. No.:	17439
Retail Price:	N/A
Loose Price:	N/A
MISB:	$700 to $900

Imperial Set: Zuckuss, AT-AT Driver, Imperial TIE Fighter Pilot

Ref. No.:	17442
Retail Price:	N/A
Loose Price:	N/A
MISB:	$800 to $1000

Rebel Set: 2-1B, Princess Leia Organa (Hoth Outfit), Rebel Commander

Ref. No.:	17438
Retail Price:	N/A
Loose Price:	N/A
MISB:	$700 to $900

Rebel Set: Princess Leia Organa (Hoth Outfit), Artoo-Detoo (R2-D2) with Sensorscope, Luke Skywalker (Hoth Battle Gear)

Ref. No.:	17440
Retail Price:	N/A
Loose Price:	N/A
MISB:	$800 to $1050

Rebel Soldier: C-3PO, R2-D2, Han Solo (Hoth), Darth Vader, Stormtrooper (Hoth)

Ref. No.:	17446
Retail Price:	N/A
Loose Price:	N/A
MISB:	$700 to $900

RETURN OF THE JEDI

4-LOM

Ref. No.:	5144
Retail Price:	$2.99
Loose Price:	$12
MISB:	$155 to $300

48 Back
Ref. No.:	5144

65 Back
Ref. No.:	3458

77 Back
Ref. No.:	5147

79 Back
Ref. No.:	5149

8D8

Ref. No.:	5157
Retail Price:	$2.99
Loose Price:	$7
MISB:	$20 to $40

77 Back
Ref. No.:	5157

79 Back
Ref. No.:	5159

Admiral Ackbar

Ref. No.:	3466
Retail Price:	$2.99
Loose Price:	$7
MISB:	$25 to $45

65 Back
Ref. No.:	3466

77 Back
Ref. No.:	5162

79 Back
Ref. No.:	4968

Arfive-Defour (R5-D4)

Ref. No.:	3475
Loose Price:	$7
MISB:	$60 to $115

48 Back
Ref. No.:	3475

65 Back
Ref. No.:	5738

77 Back
Ref. No.:	5741

79 Back
Ref. No.:	5743

Artoo-Detoo (R2-D2) with Sensorscope

Ref. No.:	5730
Retail Price:	$2.99
Loose Price:	$7
MISB:	$25 to $50

48 Back
Ref. No.:	5730

77 Back
Ref. No.:   5734

79 Back
Ref. No.:   5735

AT-AT Commander
Ref. No.:   3505
Retail Price: $2.99
Loose Price: $7
MISB: $20 to $40

48 Back
Ref. No.:   3505

65 Back
Ref. No.:   5165

77 Back
Ref. No.:   5168

79 Back
Ref. No.:   5170

AT-AT Driver
Ref. No.:   3511
Retail Price: $2.99
Loose Price: $7
MISB: $25 to $40

48 Back
Ref. No.:   3511

65 Back
Ref. No.:   5176

77 Back
Ref. No.:   5179

79 Back
Ref. No.:   5181

AT-ST Driver
Ref. No.:   5182
Retail Price: $2.99
Loose Price: $7
MISB: $15 to $35

77 Back
Ref. No.:   5182

79 Back
Ref. No.:   5183

B-Wing Pilot
Ref. No.:   5186
Retail Price: $2.99
Loose Price: $7
MISB: $25 to $40

77 Back
Ref. No.:   5186

79 Back
Ref. No.:   5185

Ben (Obi-Wan) Kenobi
Ref. No.:   5187

Retail Price: $2.99
Loose Price: $10
MISB: $15 to $75

48 Back
Ref. No.:   5187

65 Back, front-view picture
Ref. No.:   5192

65 Back, side-view picture
Ref. No.:   5188

77 Back
Ref. No.:   5190

79 Back
Ref. No.:   5189

Bespin Security Guard I
Ref. No.:   5193
Retail Price: $2.99
Loose Price: $7
MISB: $25 to $50

48 Back
Ref. No.:   5183

65 Back
Ref. No.:   5194

77 Back
Ref. No.:   5195

79 Back
Ref. No.:   5196

Bespin Security Guard II
Ref. No.:   3568
Retail Price: $2.99
Loose Price: $7
MISB: $30 to $45

48 Back
Ref. No.:   3568

65 Back
Ref. No.:   3573

77 Back
Ref. No.:   5200

79 Back
Ref. No.:   5204

Bib Fortuna
Ref. No.:   5206
Retail Price: $2.99
Loose Price: $7
MISB: $20 to $40

65 Back
Ref. No.:   5206

77 Back
Ref. No.:   5209

79 Back
Ref. No.:   5211

Biker Scout

Ref. No.:	3580
Retail Price:	$2.99
Loose Price:	$7
MISB:	$30 to $55

65 Back

Ref. No.:	3580

77 Back

Ref. No.:	5215

79 Back

Ref. No.:	5217

Boba Fett

Ref. No.:	3587
Retail Price:	$2.99
Loose Price:	$20
MISB:	$145 to $280

48 Back

Ref. No.:	3587

65 Back, action picture

Ref. No.:	5223

65 Back, drawing picture

Ref. No.:	5219

77 Back

Ref. No.:	5221

77 Back

Ref. No.:	5220

Bossk (Bounty Hunter)

Ref. No.:	5684
Retail Price:	$2.99
Loose Price:	$7
MISB:	$40 to $75

48 Back

Ref. No.:	5684

65 Back

Ref. No.:	3596

77 Back

Ref. No.:	5685

79 Back

Ref. No.:	5687

Chewbacca

Ref. No.:	5262
Retail Price:	$2.99
Loose Price:	$7
MISB:	$90 to $175

48 Back

Ref. No.:	5262

65 Back, gun picture

Ref. No.:	5266

65 Back, scruffy picture

Ref. No.:	7255

77 Back

Ref. No.:	5267

79 Back

Ref. No.:	3621

Chief Chirpa

Ref. No.:	5270
Retail Price:	$2.99
Loose Price:	$7
MISB:	$25 to $45

65 Back

Ref. No.:	5270

77 Back

Ref. No.:	5272

79 Back

Ref. No.:	5273

Cloud Car Pilot

Ref. No.:	5275
Retail Price:	$2.99
Loose Price:	$7
MISB:	$35 to $65

48 Back

Ref. No.:	5275

65 Back

Ref. No.:	3628

77 Back

Ref. No.:	5278

79 Back

Ref. No.:	5280

Darth Vader

Ref. No.:	3649
Retail Price:	$2.99
Loose Price:	$7
MISB:	$35 to $70

48 Back

Ref. No.:	3649

65 Back, close-up picture

Ref. No.:	7262

65 Back, saber picture

Ref. No.:	5252

77 Back

Ref. No.:	5253

79 Back

Ref. No.:	5248

Death Star Droid

Ref. No.:	5287
Retail Price:	$2.99
Loose Price:	$7
MISB:	$35 to $60

48 Back

Ref. No.:	5287

65 Back
Ref. No.:   5574

77 Back
Ref. No.:   5594

79 Back
Ref. No.:   3673

Dengar
Ref. No.:   3678
Retail Price: $2.99
Loose Price: $7
MISB: $35 to $55

48 Back
Ref. No.:   3678

65 Back
Ref. No.:   5290

77 Back
Ref. No.:   5293

79 Back
Ref. No.:   5295

Emperor's Royal Guard
Ref. No.:   3687
Retail Price: $2.99
Loose Price: $7
MISB: $30 to $50

65 Back
Ref. No.:   3687

77 Back
Ref. No.:   5303

79 Back
Ref. No.:   5305

FX-7
Ref. No.:   3693
Retail Price: $2.99
Loose Price: $7
MISB: $35 to $60

48 Back
Ref. No.:   3693

65 Back
Ref. No.:   5596

77 Back
Ref. No.:   5599

79 Back
Ref. No.:   5601

Gamorrean Guard
Ref. No.:   5307
Retail Price: $2.99
Loose Price: $7
MISB: $20 to $40

65 Back
Ref. No.:   5307

77 Back
Ref. No.:   4969

79 Back
Ref. No.:   5306

General Madine
Ref. No.:   3702
Retail Price: $2.99
Loose Price: $7
MISB: $20 to $40

65 Back
Ref. No.:   3702

77 Back
Ref. No.:   5315

79 Back
Ref. No.:   5317

Greedo
Ref. No.:   5318
Retail Price: $2.99
Loose Price: $7
MISB: $35 to $60

48 Back
Ref. No.:   5318

65 Back
Ref. No.:   5320

77 Back
Ref. No.:   5322

79 Back
Ref. No.:   5323

Hammerhead
Ref. No.:   5577
Retail Price: $2.99
Loose Price: $7
MISB: $35 to $60

48 Back
Ref. No.:   5577

65 Back
Ref. No.:   5579

77 Back
Ref. No.:   5583

79 Back
Ref. No.:   5582

Han Solo
Ref. No.:   3736
Retail Price: $2.99
Loose Price: $7
MISB: $150 to $250

48 Back
Ref. No.:   3736

65 Back, action picture
Ref. No.:   5603

65 Back, standing picture
Ref. No.:   5604

77 Back, action picture
Ref. No.:   3737

77 Back, standing picture
Ref. No.:   3727

79 Back
Ref. No.:   5607

79 Back
Ref. No.:   3721

Han Solo (Bespin Outfit)
Ref. No.:   3741
Retail Price: $2.99
Loose Price: $7
MISB: $55 to $70

48 Back
Ref. No.:   3741

65 Back
Ref. No.:   5609

77 Back
Ref. No.:   5612

79 Back
Ref. No.:   5614

Han Solo (Hoth Battle Gear)
Ref. No.:   5615
Retail Price: $2.99
Loose Price: $7
MISB: $35 to $60

48 Back
Ref. No.:   5615

65 Back
Ref. No.:   5616

77 Back
Ref. No.:   5619

79 Back
Ref. No.:   5621

Han Solo In Trench Coat
Ref. No.:   5232
Retail Price: $2.99
Loose Price: $7
MISB: $25 to $40

77 Back
Ref. No.:   5232

79 Back
Ref. No.:   5230

IG-88
Ref. No.:   3754
Retail Price: $2.99
Loose Price: $7
MISB: $30 to $60

48 Back
Ref. No.:   3754

65 Back
Ref. No.:   5623

77 Back
Ref. No.:   5626

79 Back
Ref. No.:   5628

Imperial Commander
Ref. No.:   3761
Retail Price: $2.99
Loose Price: $7
MISB: $30 to $55

48 Back
Ref. No.:   3761

65 Back
Ref. No.:   5630

77 Back
Ref. No.:   5633

79 Back
Ref. No.:   5635

Imperial Stormtrooper (Hoth Battle Gear)
Ref. No.:   5782
Retail Price: $2.99
Loose Price: $7
MISB: $40 to $70

48 Back
Ref. No.:   5782

65 Back
Ref. No.:   5783

77 Back
Ref. No.:   5786

79 Back
Ref. No.:   5788

Imperial Tie Fighter Pilot
Ref. No.:   5792
Retail Price: $2.99
Loose Price: $7
MISB: $35 to $65

48 Back
Ref. No.:   5792

65 Back
Ref. No.:   3776

77 Back
Ref. No.:   5798

79 Back
Ref. No.:   5800

Jawa
Ref. No.:   3797
Retail Price: $2.99

Loose Price: $7
MISB: $35 to $60

48 Back
Ref. No.:   3797

65 Back
Ref. No.:   5637

77 Back
Ref. No.:   5640

79 Back
Ref. No.:   5642

Klaatu
Ref. No.:   3805
Retail Price: $2.99
Loose Price: $7
MISB: $25 to $50

65 Back
Ref. No.:   3805

77 Back
Ref. No.:   5647

79 Back
Ref. No.:   5649

Klaatu (In Skiff Guard Outfit)
Ref. No.:   5134
Retail Price: $2.99
Loose Price: $7
MISB: $20 to $35

77 Back
Ref. No.:   5134

79 Back
Ref. No.:   5136

Lando Calrissian
Ref. No.:   5652
Retail Price: $2.99
Loose Price: $7
MISB: $30 to $60

48 Back
Ref. No.:   5652

65 Back
Ref. No.:   5653

77 Back
Ref. No.:   5656

79 Back
Ref. No.:   5658

Lando Calrissian (Skiff Disguise)
Ref. No.:   5659
Retail Price: $2.99
Loose Price: $7
MISB: $35 to $60

65 Back
Ref. No.:   5659

77 Back
Ref. No.:   5662

79 Back
Ref. No.:   5664

Lobot
Ref. No.:   3828
Retail Price: $2.99
Loose Price: $7
MISB: $40 to $60

48 Back
Ref. No.:   3828

65 Back
Ref. No.:   5666

77 Back
Ref. No.:   5669

79 Back
Ref. No.:   5671

Logray (Ewok Medicine Man)
Ref. No.:   5296
Retail Price: $2.99
Loose Price: $7
MISB: $25 to $50

65 Back
Ref. No.:   5296

77 Back
Ref. No.:   5299

79 Back
Ref. No.:   5297

Luke Skywalker
Ref. No.:   3853
Retail Price: $2.99
Loose Price: $25
MISB: $140 to $245

48 Back
Ref. No.:   3853

48 Back
Ref. No.:   3858

65 Back, gunner picture
Ref. No.:   5683

65 Back
Ref. No.:   12816

65 Back
Ref. No.:   5754

77 Back, gunner picture
Ref. No.:   36639

79 Back, gunner picture
Ref. No.:   36642

Luke Skywalker (Bespin Fatigues)
Ref. No.:   5692
Retail Price: $2.99

Loose Price: $7
MISB: $65 to $110

48 Back
Ref. No.:   5692

65 Back
Ref. No.:   5694

77 Back
Ref. No.:   5690

79 Back
Ref. No.:   3837

Luke Skywalker (Hoth Battle Gear)

Ref. No.:   14609
Retail Price: $2.99
Loose Price: $7
MISB: $45 to $80

48 Back
Ref. No.:   14609

65 Back
Ref. No.:   38305

77 Back
Ref. No.:   12843

79 Back
Ref. No.:   35977

Luke Skywalker (Jedi Knight Outfit)

Ref. No.:   3872
Retail Price: $2.99
Loose Price: $7
MISB: $25 to $140

65 Back, blue lightsaber
Ref. No.:   3872
Loose Price: $30

65 Back
Ref. No.:   3874

77 Back
Ref. No.:   5696

79 Back
Ref. No.:   5698

Luke Skywalker (X-Wing Fighter Pilot)

Ref. No.:   5699
Retail Price: $2.99
Loose Price: $7
MISB: $40 to $70

48 Back
Ref. No.:   5699

65 Back
Ref. No.:   5700

77 Back
Ref. No.:   5703

79 Back
Ref. No.:   5705

Lumat

Ref. No.:   5672
Retail Price: $2.99
Loose Price: $25
MISB: $35 to $60

79 Back
Ref. No.:   5672

Nien Nunb

Ref. No.:   3888
Retail Price: $2.99
Loose Price: $7
MISB: $30 to $50

65 Back
Ref. No.:   3888

77 Back
Ref. No.:   5676

79 Back
Ref. No.:   5678

Nikto

Ref. No.:   5679
Retail Price: $2.99
Loose Price: $7
MISB: $25 to $45

77 Back
Ref. No.:   5679

79 Back
Ref. No.:   5681

Paploo

Ref. No.:   5673
Retail Price: $2.99
Loose Price: $25
MISB: $35 to $45

79 Back
Ref. No.:   5673

Power Droid

Ref. No.:   7310
Retail Price: $2.99
Loose Price: $7
MISB: $35 to $60

48 Back
Ref. No.:   7310

65 Back
Ref. No.:   3901

77 Back
Ref. No.:   7314

79 Back
Ref. No.:   7316

Princess Leia Organa

Ref. No.:   3920
Retail Price: $2.99
Loose Price: $7
MISB: $250 to $450

48 Back
Ref. No.:   3920

65 Back
Ref. No.:   5713

77 Back
Ref. No.:   7317

79 Back
Ref. No.:   7318

Princess Leia Organa (Bespin Gown)

Ref. No.:   5724
Retail Price: $2.99
Loose Price: $7
MISB: $60 to $105

48 Back
Ref. No.:   5724

65 Back
Ref. No.:   3923

77 Back
Ref. No.:   3926

79 Back
Ref. No.:   5727

Princess Leia Organa (Boushh Disguise)

Ref. No.:   3928
Retail Price: $2.99
Loose Price: $7
MISB: $40 to $70

65 Back
Ref. No.:   3928

77 Back
Ref. No.:   5707

79 Back
Ref. No.:   5709

Princess Leia Organa (Hoth Outfit)

Ref. No.:   5716
Retail Price: $2.99
Loose Price: $7
MISB: $55 to $70

48 Back
Ref. No.:   5716

65 Back
Ref. No.:   5717

77 Back
Ref. No.:   5720

79 Back
Ref. No.:   5718

Princess Leia Organa (in Combat Poncho)

Ref. No.:   5710
Retail Price: $2.99
Loose Price: $7
MISB: $30 to $50

77 Back
Ref. No.:   5710

79 Back
Ref. No.:   5711

Prune Face

Ref. No.:   3938
Retail Price: $2.99
Loose Price: $7
MISB: $20 to $30

77 Back
Ref. No.:   3938

79 Back
Ref. No.:   13611

Rancor Keeper

Ref. No.:   5744
Retail Price: $2.99
Loose Price: $7
MISB: $15 to $25

77 Back
Ref. No.:   5744

79 Back
Ref. No.:   5746

Rebel Commander

Ref. No.:   17015
Retail Price: $2.99
Loose Price: $7
MISB: $30 to $50

48 Back
Ref. No.:   17015

65 Back
Ref. No.:   31681

77 Back
Ref. No.:   36606

79 Back
Ref. No.:   36641

Rebel Commando

Ref. No.:   5747
Retail Price: $2.99
Loose Price: $7
MISB: $25 to $45

65 Back
Ref. No.:   5747

77 Back
Ref. No.:   5749

79 Back
Ref. No.:   5751

Rebel Soldier (Hoth Battle Gear)
Ref. No.:   3956
Retail Price: $2.99
Loose Price: $7
MISB: $35 to $60

48 Back
Ref. No.:   3956

65 Back
Ref. No.:   5760

77 Back
Ref. No.:   5763

79 Back
Ref. No.:   5765

Ree-Yees
Ref. No.:   3957
Retail Price: $2.99
Loose Price: $7
MISB: $25 to $45

65 Back
Ref. No.:   3957

77 Back
Ref. No.:   3959

79 Back
Ref. No.:   5769

See-Threepio (C-3PO)
Ref. No.:   5566
Retail Price: $2.99
Loose Price: $7
MISB: $55 to $80

48 Back
Ref. No.:   5566

65 Back
Ref. No.:   3999

77 Back
Ref. No.:   5570

79 Back
Ref. No.:   5572

Snaggletooth (Red)
Ref. No.:   5591
Retail Price: $2.99
Loose Price: $7
MISB: $35 to $65

48 Back
Ref. No.:   5591

65 Back
Ref. No.:   5589

77 Back
Ref. No.:   5587

79 Back
Ref. No.:   5585

Squid Head
Ref. No.:   5770
Retail Price: $2.99
Loose Price: $7
MISB: $20 to $35

65 Back
Ref. No.:   5770

77 Back
Ref. No.:   5772

79 Back
Ref. No.:   5774

Star Destroyer Commander
Ref. No.:   4964
Retail Price: $2.99
Loose Price: $7
MISB: $35 to $60

48 Back
Ref. No.:   4964

65 Back
Ref. No.:   4965

77 Back
Ref. No.:   5018

79 Back
Ref. No.:   5019

Stormtrooper
Ref. No.:   5775
Retail Price: $2.99
Loose Price: $7
MISB: $45 to $80

48 Back
Ref. No.:   5775

65 Back
Ref. No.:   5776

77 Back
Ref. No.:   5779

79 Back
Ref. No.:   5781

Sy Snootles and the Rebo Band
Ref. No.:   4035
Retail Price: $2.99
Loose Price: $20
MISB: $35 to $70

77 Back
Ref. No.:   4035

79 Back
Ref. No.:   5789

Teebo

Ref. No.:   5790
Retail Price: $2.99
Loose Price: $7
MISB: $20 to $35

77 Back
Ref. No.:   5790

79 Back
Ref. No.:   5791

The Emperor

Ref. No.:   5301
Retail Price: $2.99
Loose Price: $7
MISB: $30 to $45

77 Back
Ref. No.:   5301

79 Back
Ref. No.:   4045

Too-Onebee (2-1B)

Ref. No.:   3455
Retail Price: $2.99
Loose Price: $7
MISB: $35 to $70

48 Back
Ref. No.:   3455

65 Back
Ref. No.:   5151

77 Back
Ref. No.:   5154

79 Back
Ref. No.:   5156

Tusken Raider (Sand People)

Ref. No.:   3972
Retail Price: $2.99
Loose Price: $12
MISB: $55 to $75

48 Back
Ref. No.:   3977

65 Back
Ref. No.:   3972

77 Back
Ref. No.:   3971

79 Back
Ref. No.:   3965

Ugnaught

Ref. No.:   5801
Retail Price: $2.99
Loose Price: $7
MISB: $30 to $55

48 Back
Ref. No.:   5801

65 Back
Ref. No.:   5802

77 Back
Ref. No.:   5804

79 Back
Ref. No.:   5806

Walrus Man

Ref. No.:   5807
Retail Price: $2.99
Loose Price: $7
MISB: $35 to $65

48 Back
Ref. No.:   5807

65 Back
Ref. No.:   5814

77 Back
Ref. No.:   5817

79 Back
Ref. No.:   5819

Weequay

Ref. No.:   4073
Retail Price: $2.99
Loose Price: $7
MISB: $25 to $50

65 Back
Ref. No.:   4073

77 Back
Ref. No.:   5811

79 Back
Ref. No.:   5613

Wicket W. Warrick

Ref. No.:   5481
Retail Price: $2.99
Loose Price: $7
MISB: $25 to $50

77 Back
Ref. No.:   5481

79 Back
Ref. No.:   5483

Yoda

Ref. No.:   5355
Retail Price: $2.99
Loose Price: $7
MISB: $95 to $160

48 Back
Ref. No.:   5355

Yoda, The Jedi Master

Ref. No.: 5565
Retail Price: $2.99
Loose Price: $7
MISB: $100 to $160

65 Back, looking left picture
Ref. No.: 5565

65 Back, looking right picture
Ref. No.: 11696

77 Back
Ref. No.: 11508

79 Back
Ref. No.: 9132

Zuckuss

Ref. No.: 4091
Retail Price: $2.99
Loose Price: $7
MISB: $35 to $60

48 Back
Ref. No.: 4091

65 Back
Ref. No.: 5753

77 Back
Ref. No.: 5756

79 Back
Ref. No.: 5758

MULTIPACKS

Admiral Ackbar, General Madine, Rebel Commando

Ref. No.: 17448
Retail Price: N/A
Loose Price: N/A
MISB: $300 to $500

Gamorrean Guard, Squid Head, Bib Fortuna

Ref. No.: 17449
Retail Price: N/A
Loose Price: N/A
MISB: $300 to $500

Imperial Set: Biker Scout, Emperor's RoyalGuard, Bib Fortuna

Ref. No.: 17451
Retail Price: N/A
Loose Price: N/A
MISB: $300 to $500

Rebel Set: Admiral Ackbar, Leia (Boushh), Chief Chirpa

Ref. No.: 17450
Retail Price: N/A
Loose Price: N/A
MISB: $300 to $500

The Power of the Force

CARD WITH COIN

A-Wing Pilot

Ref. No.: 3463
Retail Price: $2.99
Loose Price: $30
MISB: $60 to $80

92 Back
Ref. No.: 3463

Amanaman

Ref. No.: 3469
Retail Price: $2.99
Loose Price: $50
MISB: $130 to $200

92 Back
Ref. No.: 3469

Anakin Skywalker

Ref. No.: 3472
Retail Price: $2.99
Loose Price: $15
MISB: $1000 to $2800

92 Back
Ref. No.: 3472

Artoo-Detoo (R2-D2) with Pop-Up Lightsaber

Ref. No.: 3495
Retail Price: $2.99
Loose Price: $85
MISB: $100 to $150

92 Back
Ref. No.: 3495

AT-ST Driver

Ref. No.: 3517
Retail Price: $2.99
Loose Price: $7
MISB: $40 to $65

92 Back
Ref. No.: 3517

B-Wing Pilot

Ref. No.: 3521
Retail Price: $2.99
Loose Price: $7
MISB: $25 to $50

92 Back
Ref. No.: 3521

Barada

Ref. No.: 6605
Retail Price: $2.99
Loose Price: $30
MISB: $55 to $80

92 Back
Ref. No.:   6605

Ben (Obi-Wan) Kenobi
Ref. No.:   3563
Retail Price: $2.99
Loose Price: $7
MISB: $65 to $120
92 Back
Ref. No.:   3563

Biker Scout
Ref. No.:   3581
Retail Price: $2.99
Loose Price: $7
MISB: $60 to $100
92 Back
Ref. No.:   3581

Chewbacca
Ref. No.:   3622
Retail Price: $2.99
Loose Price: $7
MISB: $85 to $120
92 Back
Ref. No.:   3622

Darth Vader
Ref. No.:   3651
Retail Price: $2.99
Loose Price: $7
MISB: $65 to $115
92 Back
Ref. No.:   3651

EV-9D9
Ref. No.:   3691
Retail Price: $2.99
Loose Price: $35
MISB: $100 to $150
92 Back
Ref. No.:   3691

Gamorrean Guard
Ref. No.:   3699
Retail Price: $2.99
Loose Price: $7
MISB: $750 to $1200
92 Back
Ref. No.:   3699
MISB: $380

Han Solo (in Carbonite Chamber)
Ref. No.:   3745
Retail Price: $2.99
Loose Price: $50
MISB: $160 to $230

92 Back
Ref. No.:   3745

Han Solo (in Trench Coat)
Ref. No.:   3749
Retail Price: $2.99
Loose Price: $7
MISB: $250 to $360
92 Back
Ref. No.:   3749

Imperial Dignitary
Ref. No.:   3763
Retail Price: $2.99
Loose Price: $30
MISB: $50 to $80
92 Back
Ref. No.:   3763

Imperial Gunner
Ref. No.:   3765
Retail Price: $2.99
Loose Price: $30
MISB: $75 to $120
92 Back
Ref. No.:   3765

Imperial Stormtrooper
Ref. No.:   17014
Retail Price: $2.99
Loose Price: $7
MISB: $150 to $260
92 Back
Ref. No.:   17014

Jawa
Ref. No.:   3798
Retail Price: $2.99
Loose Price: $7
MISB: $65 to $85
92 Back
Ref. No.:   3798

Lando Calrissian (General Pilot)
Ref. No.:   3816
Retail Price: $2.99
Loose Price: $35
MISB: $65 to $105
92 Back
Ref. No.:   3816

Luke Skywalker (Imperial Stormtrooper Outfit)
Ref. No.:   3868
Retail Price: $2.99
Loose Price: $40
MISB: $230 to $375

92 Back
Ref. No.:   3868

Luke Skywalker (in Battle Poncho)
Ref. No.:   3870
Retail Price: $2.99
Loose Price: $40
MISB: $60 to $85
92 Back
Ref. No.:   3870

Luke Skywalker (Jedi Knight Outfit)
Ref. No.:   3875
Retail Price: $2.99
Loose Price: $7
MISB: $100 to $195
92 Back
Ref. No.:   3875

Luke Skywalker (X-Wing Fighter Pilot)
Ref. No.:   3878
Retail Price: $2.99
Loose Price: $7
MISB: $85 to $130
92 Back
Ref. No.:   3878

Lumat
Ref. No.:   3884
Retail Price: $2.99
Loose Price: $7
MISB: $35 to $60
92 Back
Ref. No.:   3884

Nikto
Ref. No.:   3893
Retail Price: $2.99
Loose Price: $7
MISB: $550 to $1300
92 Back
Ref. No.:   3893

Paploo
Ref. No.:   3896
Retail Price: $2.99
Loose Price: $7
MISB: $35 to $60
92 Back
Ref. No.:   3896

Princess Leia Organa (in Combat Poncho)
Ref. No.:   3933
Retail Price: $2.99
Loose Price: $7
MISB: $55 to $80

92 Back
Ref. No.:   3933

Romba
Ref. No.:   3961
Retail Price: $2.99
Loose Price: $30
MISB: $25 to $55
92 Back
Ref. No.:   3961

See-Threepio (C-3PO) (Removable Limbs)
Ref. No.:   4000
Retail Price: $2.99
Loose Price: $7
MISB: $55 to $80
92 Back
Ref. No.:   4000

Teebo
Ref. No.:   4039
Retail Price: $2.99
Loose Price: $7
MISB: $60 to $120
92 Back
Ref. No.:   4039

The Emperor
Ref. No.:   4046
Retail Price: $2.99
Loose Price: $7
MISB: $65 to $115
92 Back
Ref. No.:   4046

Warok
Ref. No.:   4070
Retail Price: $2.99
Loose Price: $30
MISB: $30 to $70
92 Back
Ref. No.:   4070

Wicket W. Warrick
Ref. No.:   4077
Retail Price: $2.99
Loose Price: $7
MISB: $70 to $115
92 Back
Ref. No.:   4077

Yoda, the Jedi Master
Ref. No.:   4088
Retail Price: $2.99
Loose Price: $7
MISB: $370 to $920

92 Back

Ref. No.: 4088

Droids

CARD WITH COIN

A-Wing Pilot

Ref. No.: 3465
Retail Price: $2.99
Loose Price: $30
MISB: $80 to $150

Artoo-Detoo (R2-D2) with pop-up Lightsaber

Ref. No.: 3494
Retail Price: $2.99
Loose Price: $75
MISB: $60 to $110

Boba Fett

Ref. No.: 3590
Retail Price: $2.99
Loose Price: $20
MISB: $600 to $1200

Jann Tosh

Ref. No.: 3778
Retail Price: $2.99
Loose Price: $15
MISB: $25 to $30

Jord Dusat

Ref. No.: 3800
Retail Price: $2.99
Loose Price: $15
MISB: $25 to $35

Kea Moll

Ref. No.: 3801
Retail Price: $2.99
Loose Price: $20
MISB: $30 to $40

Kez-Iban

Ref. No.: 3802
Retail Price: $2.99
Loose Price: $20
MISB: $30 to $40

Hyphenated coin
Ref. No.: 3802

Non-hyphenated coin
Ref. No.: 38667

See-Threepio (C-3PO)

Ref. No.: 14615
Retail Price: $2.99

Loose Price: $70
MISB: $75 to $125

Droids coin
Ref. No.: 14615

Protocol droid coin
Ref. No.: 3997

Sise Fromm

Ref. No.: 4787
Retail Price: $2.99
Loose Price: $65
MISB: $175 to $225

Thall Joben

Ref. No.: 4041
Retail Price: $2.99
Loose Price: $20
MISB: $25 to $30

Tig Fromm

Ref. No.: 4048
Retail Price: $2.99
Loose Price: $60
MISB: $80 to $120

Uncle Gundy

Ref. No.: 4060
Retail Price: $2.99
Loose Price: $30
MISB: $35 to $40

Ewoks

CARD WITH COIN

Dulok Scout

Ref. No.: 3681
Retail Price: $2.99
Loose Price: $20
MISB: $25 to $30

Dulok Shaman

Ref. No.: 3682
Retail Price: $2.99
Loose Price: $15
MISB: $20 to $30

King Gorneesh

Ref. No.: 3803
Retail Price: $2.99
Loose Price: $15
MISB: $20 to $30

Logray (Ewok Medicine Man)

Ref. No.: 3834
Retail Price: $2.99

Loose Price: $15
MISB: $20 to $30

Urgah Lady Gorneesh
Ref. No.: 4061
Retail Price: $2.99
Loose Price: $15
MISB: $20 to $30

Wicket W. Warrick
Ref. No.: 4079
Retail Price: $2.99
Loose Price: $20
MISB: $30 to $45

3³/₄″ Scale Accessories

THE EMPIRE STRIKES BACK

Action Figure Survival Kit
Ref. No.: 2557
Retail Price: N/A
Loose Price: N/A
MISB: $10

Hoth Survival Pack
Ref. No.: 2558
Retail Price: N/A
Loose Price: N/A
MISB: $5

Radar Laser Cannon
Ref. No.: 4506
Retail Price: $4.99
Loose Price: $5
MISB: $10 to $15

Tri-Pod Laser Cannon
Ref. No.: 4523
Retail Price: $4.99
Loose Price: $5
MISB: $10 to $15

Vehicle Maintenance Energizer
Ref. No.: 4526
Retail Price: $4.99
Loose Price: $5
MISB: $10 to $15

MTV-7 Mini Rig
Ref. No.: N/A
Retail Price: $4.99
Loose Price: $4
MISB: $15 to $20

Special Offer with AT-AT Driver
Ref. No.: N/A
MISB: $200 to $600

3 vehicles on back
Ref. No.: N/A

5 vehicles on back
Ref. No.: N/A

MLC-3 Mini-Rig
Ref. No.: 4495
Retail Price: $4.99
Loose Price: $4
MISB: $15 to $20

Special Offer with Rebel Commander
Ref. No.: N/A
MISB: $250 to $750

3 vehicles on back
Ref. No.: N/A

5 vehicles on back
Ref. No.: N/A

PDT-8 Mini Rig
Ref. No.: 4503
Retail Price: $4.99
Loose Price: $4
MISB: $15 to $20

Special Offer with 2-1B
Ref. No.: N/A
MISB: $250 to $600

3 vehicles on back
Ref. No.: N/A

5 vehicles on back
Ref. No.: N/A

INT-4 Mini Rig
Ref. No.: 4486
Retail Price: $4.99
Loose Price: $4
MISB: $15 to $20

Special Offer with AT-AT Commander
Ref. No.: N/A
MISB: $400 to $1300

CAP-2 Mini Rig
Ref. No.: 4464
Retail Price: $4.99
Loose Price: $4
MISB: $15 to $20

Special Offer with Bossk
Ref. No.: N/A
MISB: $250 to $800

RETURN OF THE JEDI

MTV-7 Mini Rig

Ref. No.:   13207
Retail Price: $4.99
Loose Price: $4
MISB: $5 to $20

MLC-3 Mini-Rig

Ref. No.:   4497
MISB: $5 to $20

INT-4 Mini Rig

Ref. No.:   4488
Retail Price: $4.99
Loose Price: $4
MISB: $15 to $20

CAP-2 Mini Rig

Ref. No.:   4467
Retail Price: $4.99
Loose Price: $4
MISB: $15 to $20

AST-5 Mini Rig

Ref. No.:   4457
Retail Price: $4.99
Loose Price: $4
MISB: $15 to $20

  4 vehicles on back
  Ref. No.:   N/A
  6 vehicles on back
  Ref. No.:   N/A

ISP-6 Mini Rig

Ref. No.:   4489
Retail Price: $4.99
Loose Price: $4
MISB: $15 to $20

  4 vehicles on back
  Ref. No.:   N/A
  6 vehicles on back
  Ref. No.:   N/A

Desert Sail Skiff

MISB: $15 to $20

Ewok Combat Glider

Ref. No.:   4477
Retail Price: $4.99
Loose Price: $10
MISB: $15 to $20

Ewok Assault Catapult

Ref. No.:   4474
Retail Price: $4.99
Loose Price: $10
MISB: $15 to $20

Radar Laser Cannon

Ref. No.:   4506
Retail Price: $4.99
Loose Price: $6
MISB: $8 to $12

Tri-Pod Laser Cannon

Ref. No.:   4523
Retail Price: $4.99
Loose Price: $6
MISB: $8 to $12

Vehicle Maintenance Energizer

Ref. No.:   4526
Retail Price: $4.99
Loose Price: $6
MISB: $8 to $12

3³/₄" Scale Carrying Cases

A NEW HOPE

Mini-Action Figure Collector's Case

Ref. No.:   2492
Retail Price: $5.99
Loose Price: $20
MISB: $35 to $50

THE EMPIRE STRIKES BACK

Darth Vader

Ref. No.:   6820
Retail Price: $5.99
Loose Price: $15
MISB: $30 to $200

  41 Back
  Ref. No.:   6820
  47 Back
  Ref. No.:   13197
  with IG-88, Bossk and Boba Fett
  Ref. No.:   2489
  Loose Price: $15
  MISB: $2500 to $6500
  with Luke Bespin, Darth Vader and Yoda
  Ref. No.:   2490
  Loose Price: $15
  MISB: $1500 to $4000

SW Case Art with TESB Logo

Ref. No.:   13262
Retail Price: $9.99
Loose Price: $5
MISB: $10 to $15

Vinyl

Ref. No.: 17462
Retail Price: N/A
Loose Price: $15
MISB: $45 to $150

with ESB pictures
Ref. No.: 17462

with ESB pictures, Centered Logo
Ref. No.: 17463

with SW pictures
Ref. No.: 2493

RETURN OF THE JEDI

C-3PO

Ref. No.: 2487
Retail Price: $12.99
Loose Price: $20
MISB: $50 to $100

65 Back
Ref. No.: 2487

Chewbacca Bandolier Strap

Ref. No.: 2488
Retail Price: $3.99
Loose Price: $5
MISB: $15 to $20

Laser Rifle

Ref. No.: 2491
Retail Price: $14.99
Loose Price: $20
MISB: $30 to $45

Vinyl

Ref. No.: 2495
Retail Price: $9.99
Loose Price: $25
MISB: $50 to $70

3³/₄″ Scale Creatures

A NEW HOPE

Patrol Dewback

Ref. No.: 7135
Retail Price: $11.99
Loose Price: $10
MISB: $50 to $70

Collector's Series
Ref. No.: 7149

THE EMPIRE STRIKES BACK

Hoth Wampa

Ref. No.: 4132
Retail Price: $8.99
Loose Price: $5
MISB: $15 to $30

Luke Skywalker in Hoth Gear Pictured on box
Ref. No.: 4132

Rebel Commander Pictured on box
Ref. No.: 4131

Tauntaun

Ref. No.: 4138
Retail Price: $8.99
Loose Price: $10
MISB: $15 to $20

Tauntaun with Open Belly Rescue Feature

Ref. No.: 5092
Retail Price: $8.99
Loose Price: $10
MISB: $20 to $25

$1 Coupon Offer
Ref. No.: 5092

No Offer
Ref. No.: 4139

RETURN OF THE JEDI

Jabba the Hutt Playset

Ref. No.: 4134
Retail Price: $12.99
Loose Price: $15
MISB: $30 to $55

Line Art Box
Ref. No.: 4134

Photo Box
Ref. No.: 4133

Rancor Monster

Ref. No.: 4137
Retail Price: $12.99
Loose Price: $10
MISB: $15 to $25

3³/₄″ Scale Displays

A NEW HOPE

Action Display Stand

Ref. No.: 17457
Retail Price: N/A

Loose Price: $50
MISB: $100 to $300

mailer box
Ref. No.:   17457

picture box
Ref. No.:   17458

Early Bird Certificate Package, Backdrop, Stickers, Certificate, Club Card, Pictures

Ref. No.:   3680
Retail Price: N/A
Loose Price: $150
MISB: $500 to $1000

THE EMPIRE STRIKES BACK

Display Arena

Ref. No.:   17460
Retail Price: N/A
Loose Price: $20
MISB: $35 to $60

3³/₄" Scale Play Sets

A NEW HOPE

Cantina Adventure Set

Ref. No.:   4307
Retail Price: $9.99
Loose Price: $50
MISB: $120 to $600

with Greedo, Hammerhead, blue Snaggletooth and Walrus Man
Ref. No.:   4307

with Greedo, Hammerhead, red Snaggletooth and Walrus Man
Ref. No.:   N/A

Creature Cantina

Ref. No.:   4309
Retail Price: $7.99
Loose Price: $40
MISB: $150 to $250

Death Star Space Station

Ref. No.:   4313
Retail Price: $24.99
Loose Price: $40
MISB: $70 to $130

Droid Factory

Ref. No.:   4314
Retail Price: $10.99
Loose Price: $20
MISB: $40 to $90

Land of the Jawas

Ref. No.:   13205
Retail Price: $9.99
Loose Price: $25
MISB: $40 to $55

$3 Offer Sticker on front
Ref. No.:   13205

original release
Ref. No.:   4319

THE EMPIRE STRIKES BACK

Cloud City Playset with Han Solo Bespin, Lobot, Dengar, and Ugnaught

Ref. No.:   4308
Retail Price: $9.99
Loose Price: $60
MISB: $280 to $330

Dagobah Action Playset

Ref. No.:   13181
Retail Price: $12.99
Loose Price: $25
MISB: $35 to $50

Droid Factory

Ref. No.:   13196
Retail Price: $11.99
Loose Price: $20
MISB: $80 to $240

Hoth Ice Planet Adventure Set

Ref. No.:   4316
Retail Price: $10.99
Loose Price: $20
MISB: $35 to $70

Special Offer with Hoth Stormtrooper
Ref. No.:   N/A
MISB: $1600 to $3200

Imperial Attack Base

Ref. No.:   4318
Retail Price: N/A
Loose Price: $10
MISB: $25 to $35

base has bridge pins
Ref. No.:   4318

base is flat
Ref. No.:   4317

Rebel Command Centre Adventure Set with AT-AT Commander, R2-D2 with Sensorscope, and Luke Skywalker in Hoth Gear

Ref. No.:   4321
Retail Price: $10.99

Loose Price: $45
MISB: $60 to $125

Turret and Probot

Ref. No.: 4324
Retail Price: $11.99
Loose Price: $15
MISB: $25 to $35

RETURN OF THE JEDI

Ewok Village

Ref. No.: 4315
Retail Price: N/A
Loose Price: $35
MISB: $50 to $85

The Jabba the Hutt Dungeon with Ev-9D9, Amanaman, and Barada

Ref. No.: 4323
Retail Price: N/A
Loose Price: $200
MISB: $75 to $350

The Jabba the Hutt Dungeon with Klaatu (Skiff Guard), Nikto and 8D8

Ref. No.: 4322
Retail Price: N/A
Loose Price: $35
MISB: $60 to $95

3³/₄″ Scale Vehicles

A NEW HOPE

Darth Vader TIE Fighter

Ref. No.: 4468
Retail Price: $14.99
Loose Price: $20
MISB: $35 to $70

Collector Series
Ref. No.: 7148

standard
Ref. No.: 4468

Special Offer with battle scene setting
Ref. No.: 4469
MISB: $400 to $1150

Imperial TIE Fighter

Ref. No.: 4483
Retail Price: $14.99
Loose Price: $15
MISB: $30 to $65

Special Offer with Darth Vader and Imperial Stormtrooper
Ref. No.: N/A
MISB: $450 to $1500

Imperial Troop Transporter (Talking)

Ref. No.: 4485
Retail Price: $9.99
Loose Price: $25
MISB: $40 to $80

Land Speeder

Ref. No.: 7147
Retail Price: $9.99
Loose Price: $10
MISB: $25 to $55

Collector Series
Ref. No.: 7147

standard
Ref. No.: 4490

Special Offer with R2-D2 and C-3PO
Ref. No.: 4491
MISB: $450 to $1250

Millennium Falcon

Ref. No.: 4492
Retail Price: $34.99
Loose Price: $45
MISB: $120 to $350

Radio Controlled Sand Crawler

Ref. No.: 4508
Retail Price: $49.99
Loose Price: $125
MISB: $300 to $500

Sonic Controlled Land Speeder

Ref. No.: 4517
Retail Price: $14.99
Loose Price: $30
MISB: $280 to $350

X-Wing Fighter

Ref. No.: 13188
Retail Price: $14.99
Loose Price: $20
MISB: $40 to $70

Special Offer with Tatooine Luke Skywalker & Han Solo Figures
Ref. No.: 13188
MISB: $550 to $1100

w/LP on front & Tatooine Luke on side
Ref. No.: 4528

w/LP on front & Luke X-Wing on side
Ref. No.: 13187

THE EMPIRE STRIKES BACK

AT-AT (All Terrain Armored Transport)

Ref. No.:   4458
Retail Price: $54.99
Loose Price: $55
MISB: $70 to $140

standard release
Ref. No.:   4458

w/Accessory Kit
Ref. No.:   5558

w/Accessory Kit & $1 Offer
Ref. No.:   13189

Battle Damaged X-Wing Fighter

Ref. No.:   4462
Retail Price: $14.99
Loose Price: $30
MISB: $35 to $80

Darth Vader's Star Destroyer

Ref. No.:   4470
Retail Price: $24.99
Loose Price: $35
MISB: $55 to $70

Imperial Cruiser (Non-Talking)

Ref. No.:   4479
Retail Price: $9.99
Loose Price: $40
MISB: $30 to $55

Sears Exclusive
Ref. No.:   4479

Imperial TIE Fighter

Ref. No.:   4484
Retail Price: $14.99
Loose Price: $15
MISB: $30 to $55

Millennium Falcon Spaceship

Ref. No.:   13202
Retail Price: $34.99
Loose Price: $45
MISB: $50 to $100

Cloud City box
Ref. No.:   13202

Rebel Armored Snowspeeder

Ref. No.:   4510
Retail Price: $14.99
Loose Price: $20
MISB: $35 to $60

pink box
Ref. No.:   4510

Special Offer with Rebel Soldier
Ref. No.:   N/A
MISB: $600 to $2250

blue box
Ref. No.:   N/A
MISB: $35 to $60

Rebel Transport

Ref. No.:   4511
Retail Price: $29.99
Loose Price: $20
MISB: $30 to $50

blue box
Ref. No.:   N/A

yellow box
Ref. No.:   N/A

Scout Walker

Ref. No.:   4512
Retail Price: $12.99
Loose Price: $15
MISB: $35 to $45

Slave I Boba Fett's Spaceship

Ref. No.:   4516
Retail Price: $19.99
Loose Price: $25
MISB: $40 to $75

Special Offer with backdrop
Ref. No.:   N/A
MISB: $650 to.$1200

Twin-Pod Cloud Car

Ref. No.:   4525
Retail Price: $12.99
Loose Price: $15
MISB: $25 to $55

Special Offer with Bespin Security Guard (White)
Ref. No.:   N/A
MISB: $600 to $2250

X-Wing Fighter

Ref. No.:   13186
Retail Price: $14.99
Loose Price: $20
MISB: $55 to $170

Dagobah picture on box
Ref. No.:   13186

no picture
Ref. No.:   4529

RETURN OF THE JEDI

AT-AT (All Terrain Armored Transport)

Ref. No.:   4459
Retail Price: $54.99

Loose Price: $55
MISB: $65 to $120

B-Wing Fighter

Ref. No.:   4460
Retail Price: $24.99
MISB: $60 to $110

Battle Damaged Imperial TIE Fighter

Ref. No.:   4461
Retail Price: $14.99
Loose Price: $30
MISB: $45 to $80

Battle Damaged X-Wing Fighter

Ref. No.:   4463
Retail Price: $14.99
Loose Price: $30
MISB: $45 to $80

Desert Sail Skiff

Ref. No.:   4471
Retail Price: $4.99
Loose Price: $10
MISB: $20 to $25

Endor Forest Ranger

Ref. No.:   4472
Retail Price: $4.99
Loose Price: $10
MISB: $20 to $25

Imperial Shuttle

Ref. No.:   4480
Retail Price: $39.99
Loose Price: $70
MISB: $100 to $150

Millennium Falcon Vehicle

Ref. No.:   4494
Retail Price: $34.99
Loose Price: $45
MISB: $50 to $100

with desert scene
Ref. No.:   N/A

Scout Walker

Ref. No.:   4513
Retail Price: $12.99
Loose Price: $15
MISB: $20 to $35

Speeder Bike

Ref. No.:   4518
Retail Price: $4.99
Loose Price: $10
MISB: $20 to $25

TIE Interceptor

Ref. No.:   4521
Retail Price: $19.99
Loose Price: $40
MISB: $55 to $80

Y-Wing Fighter

Ref. No.:   4530
Retail Price: $18.99
Loose Price: $50
MISB: $65 to $105

THE POWER OF THE FORCE

Ewok Battle Wagon

Ref. No.:   4476
Retail Price: $24.99
Loose Price: $55
MISB: $75 to $220

Tatooine Skiff

Ref. No.:   4519
Retail Price: $24.99
Loose Price: $90
MISB: $100 to $250

Imperial Sniper Vehicle Body-Rig

Ref. No.:   4481
Retail Price: $6.99
Loose Price: $15
MISB: $60 to $150

One-Man Sand Skimmer Vehicle Body-Rig

Ref. No.:   4501
Retail Price: $4.99
Loose Price: $15
MISB: $60 to $150

Security Scout Vehicle Body-Rig

Ref. No.:   4514
Retail Price: $4.99
Loose Price: $15
MISB: $60 to $150

DROIDS

A-Wing Fighter

Ref. No.:   4533
Retail Price: $19.99
Loose Price: $110
MISB: $200 to $450

ATL Interceptor Vehicle

Ref. No.:   4534
Retail Price: $11.99
Loose Price: $45
MISB: $60 to $75

Side Gunner Vehicle

Ref. No.:   4535
Retail Price: $10.99
Loose Price: $45
MISB: $60 to $75

Die Cast

A NEW HOPE

Darth Vader TIE Fighter

Ref. No.:   2506
Retail Price: $4.99
Loose Price: $50
MISB: $60 to $350

12 Back Small wings
Ref. No.:   2506

Large wings
Ref. No.:   2507

Imperial Cruiser

Ref. No.:   2508
Retail Price: $8.99
Loose Price: $10
MISB: $40 to $150

no background
Ref. No.:   2508

with background
Ref. No.:   2509

Land Speeder with Removable Windshield

Ref. No.:   6826
Retail Price: $2.99
Loose Price: $10
MISB: $20 to $120

Mailer Box
Ref. No.:   6826

Standard Box
Ref. No.:   2511

Millennium Falcon

Ref. No.:   2512
Retail Price: $8.99
Loose Price: $10
MISB: $50 to $90

no background
Ref. No.:   2512

with background
Ref. No.:   2513

TIE Fighter

Ref. No.:   2510
Retail Price: $4.99

Loose Price: $10
MISB: $30 to $50

X-Wing Fighter

Ref. No.:   2519
Retail Price: $4.99
Loose Price: $10
MISB: $50 to $70

Y-Wing Fighter

Ref. No.:   2520
Retail Price: $8.99
Loose Price: $10
MISB: $40 to $130

no background
Ref. No.:   2520

with background
Ref. No.:   2521

THE EMPIRE STRIKES BACK

Millennium Falcon

Ref. No.:   2514
Retail Price: $8.99
Loose Price: $10
MISB: $40 to $75

Slave I

Ref. No.:   2515
Retail Price: $4.99
Loose Price: $10
MISB: $20 to $100

Snowspeeder

Ref. No.:   2516
Retail Price: $4.99
Loose Price: $10
MISB: $50 to $75

TIE Bomber

Ref. No.:   2517
Retail Price: $8.99
Loose Price: $55
MISB: $175 to $325

Twin-Pod Cloud Car

Ref. No.:   2518
Retail Price: $4.99
Loose Price: $10
MISB: $20 to $75

Inflatable Bop Bags

A NEW HOPE

Artoo-Detoo (R2-D2)
Ref. No.: 42539
Retail Price: N/A
Loose Price: $45
MISB: $60 to $90

Chewbacca
Ref. No.: 42556
Retail Price: N/A
Loose Price: $45
MISB: $60 to $90

Darth Vader
Ref. No.: 42538
Retail Price: N/A
Loose Price: $45
MISB: $60 to $90

Jawa
Ref. No.: 42557
Retail Price: N/A
Loose Price: $45
MISB: $60 to $90

Lightsabers

A NEW HOPE

Inflatable Lightsaber
Ref. No.: 4389
Retail Price: $7.99
Loose Price: $45
MISB: $65 to $220

THE EMPIRE STRIKES BACK

"The Force" Lightsaber
Ref. No.: 4397
Retail Price: $4.99
Loose Price: $30
MISB: $45 to $120
  Red
  Ref. No.: 4397
  Yellow
  Ref. No.: 4398

RETURN OF THE JEDI

"The Force" Lightsaber
Ref. No.: 4388
Retail Price: $4.99

Loose Price: $30
MISB: $45 to $100
  Green
  Ref. No.: 4388
  Red
  Ref. No.: 4396

DROIDS

Battery-Operated Lightsaber Accessory
Ref. No.: 4387
Retail Price: $9.99
  Green
  Ref. No.: 4387
  Loose Price: $80
  MISB: $120 to $160
  Red
  Ref. No.: 4395
  Loose Price: $65
  MISB: $100 to $135

Micro Collection

THE EMPIRE STRIKES BACK

Bespin Control Room
Ref. No.: 2522
Retail Price: $8.99
Loose Price: $10
MISB: $15 to $20

Bespin Freeze Chamber
Ref. No.: 2523
Retail Price: $14.99
Loose Price: $20
MISB: $20 to $35

Bespin Gallery
Ref. No.: 16570
Retail Price: N/A
Loose Price: $10
MISB: $15 to $20

Bespin World
Ref. No.: 2524
Retail Price: $24.99
Loose Price: $40
MISB: $50 to $75

Build Your Armies Mail Away 6 pc Set
Ref. No.: 2525
Retail Price: N/A
Loose Price: $10
MISB: $15 to $25

Death Star Escape

Ref. No.:	2526
Retail Price:	$5.99
Loose Price:	$20
MISB:	$40 to $60

Death Star Trash Compactor

Ref. No.:	2527
Retail Price:	$9.99
Loose Price:	$20
MISB:	$40 to $60

Death Star World

Ref. No.:	2528
Retail Price:	$19.99
Loose Price:	$40
MISB:	$75 to $120

Hoth Generator Attack

Ref. No.:	2529
Retail Price:	$9.99
Loose Price:	$10
MISB:	$15 to $20

Hoth Ion Cannon

Ref. No.:	2530
Retail Price:	$9.99
Loose Price:	$20
MISB:	$20 to $35

Hoth Turret Defense

Ref. No.:	2531
Retail Price:	$9.99
Loose Price:	$10
MISB:	$15 to $20

Hoth Wampa Cave

Ref. No.:	2532
Retail Price:	$9.99
Loose Price:	$10
MISB:	$15 to $20

Hoth World

Ref. No.:	2533
Retail Price:	$29.99
Loose Price:	$50
MISB:	$65 to $105

Imperial TIE Fighter

Ref. No.:	2534
Retail Price:	$8.99
Loose Price:	$20
MISB:	$25 to $155

no background

Ref. No.:	2534

Special Offer with background

Ref. No.:	2535

Millennium Falcon

Ref. No.:	2536
Retail Price:	$19.99
Loose Price:	$40
MISB:	$55 to $195

Snowspeeder (store exclusive)

Ref. No.:	2537
Retail Price:	$14.99
Loose Price:	$25
MISB:	$60 to $80

X-Wing Fighter Vehicle

Ref. No.:	2538
Retail Price:	$8.99
Loose Price:	$10
MISB:	$15 to $155

no background

Ref. No.:	2538

Special Offer with background

Ref. No.:	2539

Super Sonic Power Vans

STAR WARS

Darth Vader Van

Ref. No.:	2559
Retail Price:	$9.99
Loose Price:	$10
MISB:	$90 to $250

Star Wars Heroes

Ref. No.:	42435
Retail Price:	$9.99
Loose Price:	$10
MISB:	$80 to $250

Van Set: Darth Vader vs. Star Wars Heroes with Both Vans, T-Rip Cords, Cones, and Pylons

Ref. No.:	2561
Retail Price:	$29.99
Loose Price:	$20
MISB:	$100 to $300

Weapons

A NEW HOPE

3 Position Laser Rifle

Ref. No.:	4382
Retail Price:	N/A

Loose Price: $40
MISB: $80 to $300

Laser Pistol Han Solo's Blaster

Ref. No.:   4390
Retail Price: $4.99
Loose Price: $25
MISB: $50 to $180

THE EMPIRE STRIKES BACK

Electronic Laser Rifle

Ref. No.:   4385
Retail Price: N/A
Loose Price: $20
MISB: $65 to $105

Laser Pistol

Ref. No.:   4391
Retail Price: $6.99
Loose Price: $20
MISB: $65 to $90

RETURN OF THE JEDI

Biker Scout Laser Pistol

Ref. No.:   4383
Retail Price: $9.99
Loose Price: $20
MISB: $70 to $95

Electronic Laser Rifle Stormtrooper Blaster

Ref. No.:   4386
Retail Price: N/A
Loose Price: $20
MISB: $65 to $105

Laser Pistol Han Solo's Blaster

Ref. No.:   4392
Retail Price: N/A
Loose Price: $20
MISB: $40 to $100

Board Games

A NEW HOPE

Adventures of R2-D2

Ref. No.:   20476
Retail Price: N/A
Loose Price: N/A
MISB: $5 to $8

Escape from the Death Star

Ref. No.:   20494
Retail Price: N/A

Loose Price: N/A
MISB: $6 to $9

THE EMPIRE STRIKES BACK

Hoth Ice Planet Adventure

Ref. No.:   20479
Retail Price: N/A
Loose Price: N/A
MISB: $5 to $8

Yoda, the Jedi Master

Ref. No.:   20480
Retail Price: N/A
Loose Price: N/A
MISB: $6 to $8

RETURN OF THE JEDI

Battle at Sarlacc's Pit

Ref. No.:   20583
Retail Price: N/A
Loose Price: N/A
MISB: $4 to $10

The Ewoks Save the Trees

Ref. No.:   20487
Retail Price: N/A
Loose Price: N/A
MISB: $6 to $9

Wicket the Ewok

Ref. No.:   20488
Retail Price: N/A
Loose Price: N/A
MISB: $5 to $9

Coloring Books

THE EMPIRE STRIKES BACK

Darth Vader cover

Ref. No.:   16569
Retail Price: N/A
Loose Price: N/A
MISB: $3 to $4

Han, Lando, Leia and Chewbacca cover

Ref. No.:   17410
Retail Price: N/A
Loose Price: N/A
MISB: $3 to $4

Leia, C-3PO and Chewbacca cover

Ref. No.:   14231
Retail Price: N/A

| Loose Price: | N/A |
| MISB: | $3 to $4 |

Luke Skywalker Bespin cover

Ref. No.:	N/A
Retail Price:	N/A
Loose Price:	N/A
MISB:	$3 to $4

R2-D2 cover

Ref. No.:	N/A
Retail Price:	N/A
Loose Price:	N/A
MISB:	$3 to $4

Yoda cover

Ref. No.:	14231
Retail Price:	N/A
Loose Price:	N/A
MISB:	$3 to $4

RETURN OF THE JEDI

Luke on Sail Barge cover

Ref. No.:	N/A
Retail Price:	N/A
Loose Price:	N/A
MISB:	$3 to $4

Lando on Skiff cover

Ref. No.:	N/A
Retail Price:	N/A
Loose Price:	N/A
MISB:	$3 to $4

Max Rebo cover

Ref. No.:	N/A
Retail Price:	N/A
Loose Price:	N/A
MISB:	$3 to $4

Wicket the Ewok cover

Ref. No.:	N/A
Retail Price:	N/A
Loose Price:	N/A
MISB:	$3 to $4

Wicket's World cover

Ref. No.:	N/A
Retail Price:	N/A
Loose Price:	N/A
MISB:	$3 to $4

Figurine Paint Sets

THE EMPIRE STRIKES BACK

Boba Fett

Ref. No.:	12184
Retail Price:	N/A
Loose Price:	N/A
MISB:	$5 to $12

Han Solo

Ref. No.:	12183
Retail Price:	N/A
Loose Price:	N/A
MISB:	$5 to $12

Luke Skywalker

Ref. No.:	12181
Retail Price:	N/A
Loose Price:	N/A
MISB:	$5 to $12

Princess Leia

Ref. No.:	12180
Retail Price:	N/A
Loose Price:	N/A
MISB:	$5 to $12

Yoda

Ref. No.:	12182
Retail Price:	N/A
Loose Price:	N/A
MISB:	$5 to $12

RETURN OF THE JEDI

Admiral Ackbar

Ref. No.:	12185
Retail Price:	N/A
Loose Price:	N/A
MISB:	$5 to $12

R2-D2 and C-3PO

Ref. No.:	12187
Retail Price:	N/A
Loose Price:	N/A
MISB:	$5 to $12

Wicket the Ewok

Ref. No.:	12186
Retail Price:	N/A
Loose Price:	N/A
MISB:	$5 to $12

Model Kits

STAR WARS

Artoo-Detoo Snap-Together Van
Ref. No.: 38838
Retail Price: N/A
Loose Price: N/A
MISB: $20 to $35

C-3PO (Authentic)
Ref. No.: 35829
Retail Price: N/A
Loose Price: N/A
MISB: $30 to $40

Darth Vader (Authentic)
Ref. No.: 35831
Retail Price: N/A
Loose Price: N/A
MISB: $30 to $40

Darth Vader Action Model
Ref. No.: 35832
Retail Price: N/A
Loose Price: N/A
MISB: $25 to $45

Darth Vader Snap-Together Van
Ref. No.: 35837
Retail Price: N/A
Loose Price: N/A
MISB: $20 to $35

Darth Vader's TIE Fighter
Ref. No.: 35834
Retail Price: N/A
Loose Price: N/A
MISB: $10 to $20

Han Solo's Millennium Falcon
Ref. No.: 35835
Retail Price: N/A
Loose Price: N/A
MISB: $25 to $50

Luke Skywalker Snap-Together Van
Ref. No.: 35836
Retail Price: N/A
Loose Price: N/A
MISB: $20 to $35

Luke Skywalker's X-Wing Fighter
Ref. No.: 35833
Retail Price: N/A
Loose Price: N/A
MISB: $10 to $20

R2-D2 (Authentic)
Ref. No.: 35830
Retail Price: N/A
Loose Price: N/A
MISB: $30 to $40

THE EMPIRE STRIKES BACK

AT-AT
Ref. No.: 35840
Retail Price: N/A
Loose Price: N/A
MISB: $15 to $20

Battle on Ice Planet Hoth Diorama
Ref. No.: 35843
Retail Price: N/A
Loose Price: N/A
MISB: $15 to $25

Boba Fett's Slave I
Ref. No.: 35841
Retail Price: N/A
Loose Price: N/A
MISB: $15 to $20

Encounter with Yoda on Dagobah Diorama
Ref. No.: 35845
Retail Price: N/A
Loose Price: N/A
MISB: $15 to $25

Han Solo's Millennium Falcon
Ref. No.: 35847
Retail Price: N/A
Loose Price: N/A
MISB: $15 to $20

Luke Skywalker's Snowspeeder
Ref. No.: 35839
Retail Price: N/A
Loose Price: N/A
MISB: $15 to $20

Luke Skywalker's X-Wing Fighter
Ref. No.: 35846
Retail Price: N/A
Loose Price: N/A
MISB: $15 to $20

Rebel Base Diorama
Ref. No.: 35844
Retail Price: N/A
Loose Price: N/A
MISB: $15 to $25

Star Destroyer

Ref. No.:	35842
Retail Price:	N/A
Loose Price:	N/A
MISB:	$15 to $20

RETURN OF THE JEDI

AT-AT

Ref. No.:	35848
Retail Price:	N/A
Loose Price:	N/A
MISB:	$15 to $20

AT-AT Structors Wind-up

Ref. No.:	35857
Retail Price:	N/A
Loose Price:	N/A
MISB:	$5 to $10

AT-ST Mirr-A-Kit

Ref. No.:	35860
Retail Price:	N/A
Loose Price:	N/A
MISB:	$5 to $10

C-3PO

Ref. No.:	35850
Retail Price:	N/A
Loose Price:	N/A
MISB:	$15 to $20

C-3PO Structors Wind-up

Ref. No.:	35859
Retail Price:	N/A
Loose Price:	N/A
MISB:	$5 to $10

Han Solo's Millennium Falcon

Ref. No.:	35856
Retail Price:	N/A
Loose Price:	N/A
MISB:	$15 to $20

It's A Snap AT-ST

Ref. No.:	N/A
Retail Price:	N/A
MISB:	$5 to $10

It's A Snap A-Wing Fighter

Ref. No.:	N/A
Retail Price:	N/A
MISB:	$5 to $10

It's A Snap B-Wing Fighter

Ref. No.:	N/A
Retail Price:	N/A
MISB:	$5 to $10

It's A Snap TIE Interceptor

Ref. No.:	N/A
Retail Price:	N/A
Loose Price:	N/A
MISB:	$5 to $10

It's A Snap X-Wing Fighter

Ref. No.:	N/A
Retail Price:	N/A
Loose Price:	N/A
MISB:	$5 to $10

It's A Snap Y-Wing Fighter

Ref. No.:	N/A
Retail Price:	N/A
Loose Price:	N/A
MISB:	$5 to $10

Jabba the Hutt's Throne Room Diorama

Ref. No.:	17111
Retail Price:	N/A
Loose Price:	N/A
MISB:	$15 to $25

R2-D2

Ref. No.:	35849
Retail Price:	N/A
Loose Price:	N/A
MISB:	$15 to $20

Shuttle Tydirium

Ref. No.:	35854
Retail Price:	N/A
Loose Price:	N/A
MISB:	$15 to $20

Shuttle Tydirium Mirr-A-Kit

Ref. No.:	35861
Retail Price:	N/A
Loose Price:	N/A
MISB:	$5 to $10

Speeder Bike

Ref. No.:	35855
Retail Price:	N/A
Loose Price:	N/A
MISB:	$15 to $20

Speeder Bike Mirr-A-Kit

Ref. No.:	35862
Retail Price:	N/A
Loose Price:	N/A
MISB:	$5 to $10

TIE Interceptor Mirr-A-Kit

Ref. No.:	35863
Retail Price:	N/A

Loose Price: N/A
MISB: $5 to $10

X-Wing Mirr-A-Kit
Ref. No.: 35864
Retail Price: N/A
Loose Price: N/A
MISB: $5 to $10

Y-Wing Mirr-A-Kit
Ref. No.: 85865
Retail Price: N/A
Loose Price: N/A
MISB: $5 to $10

Paint By Numbers

THE EMPIRE STRIKES BACK

Asteroid Chase
Ref. No.: N/A
Retail Price: N/A
Loose Price: N/A
MISB: $4 to $7

Boba Fett
Ref. No.: N/A
Retail Price: N/A
Loose Price: N/A
MISB: $4 to $7

Darth Vader Bespin Freezing Chamber
Ref. No.: 12190
Retail Price: N/A
Loose Price: N/A
MISB: $4 to $7

Hoth AT-AT Attack
Ref. No.: 12188
Retail Price: N/A
Loose Price: N/A
MISB: $4 to $7

Leia and Han Hoth Rebel Base
Ref. No.: 12192
Retail Price: N/A
Loose Price: N/A
MISB: $4 to $7

Luke Bespin Control Room
Ref. No.: 12191
Retail Price: N/A
Loose Price: N/A
MISB: $4 to $7

Yoda
Ref. No.: 12193
Retail Price: N/A
Loose Price: N/A
MISB: $4 to $7

RETURN OF THE JEDI

Boushh and Lando Calrissian Jabba's Palace
Ref. No.: 12195
Retail Price: N/A
Loose Price: N/A
MISB: $4 to $7

Ewoks: Hang Gliding
Ref. No.: 12200
Retail Price: N/A
Loose Price: N/A
MISB: $4 to $7

Ewoks: Hanging On Vine
Ref. No.: 12201
Retail Price: N/A
Loose Price: N/A
MISB: $4 to $7

Ewoks: Wicket and Baga
Ref. No.: 12199
Retail Price: N/A
Loose Price: N/A
MISB: $4 to $7

Jabba the Hutt
Ref. No.: 12196
Retail Price: N/A
Loose Price: N/A
MISB: $4 to $7

R2-D2 and C-3PO Ewok Village
Ref. No.: 12198
Retail Price: N/A
Loose Price: N/A
MISB: $4 to $7

Sy Snootles and the Max Rebo Band
Ref. No.: 12197
Retail Price: N/A
Loose Price: N/A
MISB: $4 to $7

Puzzles

A NEW HOPE

Aboard the Millennium Falcon (1000 pieces)
Ref. No.:   N/A
Retail Price: N/A
Loose Price: N/A
MISB: $3 to $7

Attack of the Sandpeople (140 pieces)
Ref. No.:   N/A
Retail Price: N/A
Loose Price: N/A
MISB: $1 to $3

Brothers Hildebrandt Painting (1000 pieces)
Ref. No.:   N/A
Retail Price: N/A
Loose Price: N/A
MISB: $5 to $10

Corridor of Lights (1500 pieces)
Ref. No.:   N/A
Retail Price: N/A
Loose Price: N/A
MISB: $6 to $12

Darth Vader and Ben Kenobi Duel with Lightsabers! (500 pieces)
Ref. No.:   N/A
Retail Price: N/A
Loose Price: N/A
MISB: $2 to $4

Darth Vader and Obi-Wan (500 pieces)
Ref. No.:   N/A
Retail Price: N/A
Loose Price: N/A
MISB: $2 to $4

Falcon Cockpit (1000 pieces)
Ref. No.:   N/A
Retail Price: N/A
Loose Price: N/A
MISB: $3 to $7

Jawas Capture R2-D2 (140 Pieces)
Ref. No.:   N/A
Retail Price: N/A
Loose Price: N/A
MISB: $1 to $3

Luke and Leia (500 pieces)
Ref. No.:   N/A
Retail Price: N/A
Loose Price: N/A
MISB: $2 to $4

Luke and R5-D4 (140 pieces)
Ref. No.:   N/A
Retail Price: N/A
Loose Price: N/A
MISB: $1 to $3

Luke Skywalker and Princess Leia Leap for Their Lives! (500 pieces)
Ref. No.:   N/A
Retail Price: N/A
Loose Price: N/A
MISB: $2 to $4

Luke Skywalker Meets R2-D2 (140 pieces)
Ref. No.:   N/A
Retail Price: N/A
Loose Price: N/A
MISB: $1 to $3

Millennium Falcon in Hyper-Space (1500 pieces)
Ref. No.:   N/A
Retail Price: N/A
Loose Price: N/A
MISB: $6 to $12

Star Wars Adventure (1000 pieces)
Ref. No.:   N/A
Retail Price: N/A
Loose Price: N/A
MISB: $3 to $7

Stormtroopers Stop the Landspeeder! (140 pieces)
Ref. No.:   N/A
Retail Price: N/A
Loose Price: N/A
MISB: $1 to $3

The Cantina Band (500 pieces)
Ref. No.:   N/A
Retail Price: N/A
Loose Price: N/A
MISB: $2 to $4

The Selling of the Droids (500 pieces)
Ref. No.:   N/A
Retail Price: N/A
Loose Price: N/A
MISB: $2 to $4

Trapped in the Trash Compactor (140 pieces)
Ref. No.:   N/A
Retail Price: N/A
Loose Price: N/A
MISB: $1 to $3

Trash Compactor (140 pieces)
Ref. No.: N/A
Retail Price: N/A
Loose Price: N/A
MISB: $1 to $3

X-Wing Fighters Prepare to Attack (500 pieces)
Ref. No.: N/A
Retail Price: N/A
Loose Price: N/A
MISB: $2 to $4

RETURN OF THE JEDI

Battle on Endor (170 pieces)
Ref. No.: N/A
Retail Price: N/A
Loose Price: N/A
MISB: $1 to $3

Darth Vader (15 pieces)
Ref. No.: N/A
Retail Price: N/A
Loose Price: N/A
MISB: $1 to $3

Death Star Scene (70 pieces)
Ref. No.: N/A
Retail Price: N/A
Loose Price: N/A
MISB: $1 to $3

Ewok Leaders (170 pieces)
Ref. No.: N/A
Retail Price: N/A
Loose Price: N/A
MISB: $1 to $3

Friends of Jabba (70 pieces)
Ref. No.: N/A
Retail Price: N/A
Loose Price: N/A
MISB: $1 to $3

Gamorrean Guard (15 pieces)
Ref. No.: N/A
Retail Price: N/A
Loose Price: N/A
MISB: $1 to $3

Jabba's Throne Room (70 pieces)
Ref. No.: N/A
Retail Price: N/A
Loose Price: N/A
MISB: $1 to $3

Leia and Wicket (15 pieces)
Ref. No.: N/A
Retail Price: N/A
Loose Price: N/A
MISB: $1 to $3

Match Box Puzzle
Ref. No.: N/A
Retail Price: N/A
Loose Price: N/A
MISB: $1 to $3

Wicket (15 pieces)
Ref. No.: N/A
Retail Price: N/A
Loose Price: N/A
MISB: $1 to $3

Wicket and Friends: Fishing (35 pieces)
Ref. No.: N/A
Retail Price: N/A
Loose Price: N/A
MISB: $1 to $3

Wicket and Friends: Nature Lesson (35 pieces)
Ref. No.: N/A
Retail Price: N/A
Loose Price: N/A
MISB: $1 to $3

Wicket and Friends: Swimming Hole (35 pieces)
Ref. No.: N/A
Retail Price: N/A
Loose Price: N/A
MISB: $1 to $3

Wicket the Ewok: Ewok Village (15 pieces)
Ref. No.: N/A
Retail Price: N/A
Loose Price: N/A
MISB: $1 to $3

Wicket the Ewok: Kneesa And Baga (15 pieces)
Ref. No.: N/A
Retail Price: N/A
Loose Price: N/A
MISB: $1 to $3

Wicket the Ewok: Match Box Puzzle
Ref. No.: N/A
Retail Price: N/A
Loose Price: N/A
MISB: $1 to $3

Wicket the Ewok: Wicket And Kneesa On Gliders (15 pieces)

Ref. No.:　　　N/A
Retail Price:　　N/A
Loose Price:　　N/A
MISB:　　　　$1 to $3

Wicket the Ewok: Wicket And R2-D2 (25 pieces)

Ref. No.:　　　N/A
Retail Price:　　N/A
Loose Price:　　N/A
MISB:　　　　$1 to $3

Trading Cards

STAR WARS SERIES 1 (BLUE)

BOXES

36 Pack

Ref. No.:　　　10086
Retail Price:　　N/A
Loose Price:　　N/A
MISB:　　　　$250

CARD PACKS WAX WRAPPER

Wax Wrapper (C-3PO)

Ref. No.:　　　10068
Retail Price:　　N/A
Loose Price:　　N/A
MISB:　　　　$5

TRADING CARD SETS

Card Set 1–66

Ref. No.:　　　42410
Retail Price:　　N/A
Loose Price:　　$25
MISB:　　　　N/A

Sticker Set 1–11

Ref. No.:　　　42411
Retail Price:　　N/A
Loose Price:　　$15
MISB:　　　　N/A

UNCUT SHEETS

Uncut Sheet Cards/Stickers

Ref. No.:　　　10070
Retail Price:　　N/A

Loose Price:　　$50
MISB:　　　　N/A

STAR WARS SERIES 2 (RED)

BOXES

36 Pack

Ref. No.:　　　10000
Retail Price:　　N/A
Loose Price:　　N/A
MISB:　　　　$200

CARD PACKS WAX WRAPPER

Wax Wrapper (Darth Vader)

Ref. No.:　　　9985
Retail Price:　　$0.15
Loose Price:　　N/A
MISB:　　　　$5

TRADING CARD SETS

Card Set 67–132

Ref. No.:　　　42409
Retail Price:　　N/A
Loose Price:　　$25
MISB:　　　　N/A

Sticker Set 12–22

Ref. No.:　　　42412
Retail Price:　　N/A
Loose Price:　　$15
MISB:　　　　N/A

UNCUT SHEETS

Uncut Sheet Cards/Stickers

Ref. No.:　　　9986
Retail Price:　　N/A
Loose Price:　　$40
MISB:　　　　N/A

STAR WARS SERIES 3 (YELLOW)

BOXES

36 Pack

Ref. No.:　　　9916
Retail Price:　　N/A
Loose Price:　　N/A
MISB:　　　　$175

CARD PACKS WAX WRAPPER

Wax Wrapper (R2-D2)
Ref. No.: 9900
Retail Price: $0.15
Loose Price: N/A
MISB: $5

TRADING CARD SETS

Card Set 133–198
Ref. No.: 42408
Retail Price: N/A
Loose Price: $25
MISB: N/A

Sticker Set 23–33
Ref. No.: 42413
Retail Price: N/A
Loose Price: $15
MISB: N/A

UNCUT SHEETS

Uncut Sheet Cards/Stickers
Ref. No.: 9902
Retail Price: N/A
Loose Price: $40
MISB: N/A

STAR WARS SERIES 4 (GREEN)

BOXES

36 Pack
Ref. No.: 9831
Retail Price: N/A
Loose Price: N/A
MISB: $100

CARD PACKS WAX WRAPPER

Wax Wrapper (Ben & Luke)
Ref. No.: 9815
Retail Price: $0.15
Loose Price: N/A
MISB: $5

TRADING CARD SETS

Card Set 199–264
Ref. No.: 42407
Retail Price: N/A
Loose Price: $25
MISB: N/A

Sticker Set 34–44
Ref. No.: 42414
Retail Price: N/A
Loose Price: $15
MISB: N/A

TRADING CARDS

207, C-3PO (Anthony Daniels)
Ref. No.: 9891
Retail Price: N/A
Loose Price: $1
MISB: N/A

Retouched Version
Ref. No.: 9891
Retail Price: N/A
Loose Price: $1
MISB: N/A

X-rated Version
Ref. No.: 9890
Retail Price: N/A
Loose Price: $15
MISB: N/A

UNCUT SHEETS

Uncut Sheet Cards/Stickers
Ref. No.: 9902
Retail Price: N/A
Loose Price: $40
MISB: N/A

STAR WARS SERIES 5 (ORANGE)

BOXES

36 Pack
Ref. No.: 9747
Retail Price: N/A
Loose Price: N/A
MISB: $100

CARD PACKS WAX WRAPPER

Wax Wrapper (X-Wing)
Ref. No.: 9730
Retail Price: N/A
Loose Price: N/A
MISB: $5

With Kenner Ad
Ref. No.: 9730
Retail Price: N/A
Loose Price: N/A
MISB: $5

With Press Sheet Ad

Ref. No.:	9731
Retail Price:	N/A
Loose Price:	N/A
MISB:	$5

TRADING CARD SETS

Card Set 265–330

Ref. No.:	42406
Retail Price:	N/A
Loose Price:	$25
MISB:	N/A

Sticker Set 45–55

Ref. No.:	42415
Retail Price:	N/A
Loose Price:	$15
MISB:	N/A

UNCUT SHEETS

Uncut Sheet Cards/Stickers

Ref. No.:	9733
Retail Price:	N/A
Loose Price:	$40
MISB:	N/A

STAR WARS SUGAR-FREE BUBBLE GUM

BOXES

Full Box with Foil Box Wrapper

Ref. No.:	9046
Retail Price:	N/A
Loose Price:	N/A
MISB:	$250

MOVIE PHOTO PIN UP SETS

Photo Set 1–56

Ref. No.:	42405
Retail Price:	N/A
Loose Price:	$60
MISB:	N/A

WRAPPERS

Darth Vader

Ref. No.:	19797
Retail Price:	N/A
Loose Price:	N/A
MISB:	$5

Han Solo

Ref. No.:	9044
Retail Price:	N/A
Loose Price:	N/A
MISB:	$5

Luke Skywalker

Ref. No.:	19798
Retail Price:	N/A
Loose Price:	N/A
MISB:	$5

Princess Leia

Ref. No.:	19799
Retail Price:	N/A
Loose Price:	N/A
MISB:	$5

THE EMPIRE STRIKES BACK SERIES 1

BOXES

36 Pack

Ref. No.:	8850
Retail Price:	N/A
Loose Price:	N/A
MISB:	$50

CARD PACKS WAX WRAPPER

Wax Wrapper (Red)

Ref. No.:	8806
Retail Price:	N/A
Loose Price:	N/A
MISB:	$4

With Candy Ad

Ref. No.:	8806
Retail Price:	N/A
Loose Price:	N/A
MISB:	$4

With Fan Club Ad

Ref. No.:	8805
Retail Price:	N/A
Loose Price:	N/A
MISB:	$4

With Press Sheet Ad

Ref. No.:	8804
Retail Price:	N/A
Loose Price:	N/A
MISB:	$4

TRADING CARD SETS

Card Set 1–132
Ref. No.:	42404
Retail Price:	N/A
Loose Price:	$20
MISB:	N/A

Sticker Set 1–33
Ref. No.:	42416
Retail Price:	N/A
Loose Price:	$15
MISB:	N/A

UNCUT SHEETS

22″ × 27″ Uncut Press Sheet
Ref. No.:	8811
Retail Price:	N/A
Loose Price:	$30
MISB:	N/A

THE EMPIRE STRIKES BACK SERIES 2

BOXES

36 Packs/12 Cards, 1 Sticker & 1 Gum Per Pack
Ref. No.:	8665
Retail Price:	N/A
Loose Price:	N/A
MISB:	$50

CARD PACKS WAX WRAPPER

Darth Vader
Ref. No.:	8625
Retail Price:	$0.25
Loose Price:	N/A
MISB:	$4

blue wax wrapper w/ Candy Ad
Ref. No.:	8625
Retail Price:	N/A
Loose Price:	N/A
MISB:	$4

blue wax wrapper w/ Collecting Box Ad
Ref. No.:	8624
Retail Price:	N/A
Loose Price:	N/A
MISB:	$4

blue wax wrapper w/ Fan Club Ad
Ref. No.:	8623
Retail Price:	N/A
Loose Price:	N/A
MISB:	$4

blue wax wrapper w/ Press Sheet Ad
Ref. No.:	8622
Loose Price:	N/A
MISB:	$4

TRADING CARD SETS

Card Set 133–264
Ref. No.:	42403
Retail Price:	N/A
Loose Price:	$20
MISB:	N/A

Sticker Set 34–66
Ref. No.:	42417
Retail Price:	N/A
Loose Price:	$15
MISB:	N/A

UNCUT SHEETS

22″ × 27″ Uncut Press Sheet
Ref. No.:	8629
Retail Price:	$2.50
Loose Price:	$30
MISB:	N/A

THE EMPIRE STRIKES BACK SERIES 3

BOXES

36 Pack
Ref. No.:	8532
Retail Price:	N/A
Loose Price:	N/A
MISB:	$40

CARD PACKS WAX WRAPPER

Wax Wrapper (Yellow)
Ref. No.:	8502
Retail Price:	$0.25
Loose Price:	N/A
MISB:	$4

with Candy Ad
Ref. No.:	8502
Retail Price:	N/A
Loose Price:	N/A
MISB:	$4

with Collecting Box Ad
Ref. No.:	8501
Retail Price:	N/A
Loose Price:	N/A
MISB:	$4

with Fan Club Ad
Ref. No.:	8500

Retail Price: N/A
Loose Price: N/A
MISB: $4

with Press Sheet Ad
Ref. No.:   8499
Retail Price: N/A
Loose Price: N/A
MISB: $4

TRADING CARD SETS

Card Set 265–352
Ref. No.:   42402
Retail Price: N/A
Loose Price: $20
MISB: N/A

Sticker Set 67–88
Ref. No.:   42418
Retail Price: N/A
Loose Price: $15
MISB: N/A

UNCUT SHEETS

22″ × 27″ Uncut Press Sheet
Ref. No.:   8506
Retail Price: N/A
Loose Price: $30
MISB: N/A

THE EMPIRE STRIKES BACK PHOTO

TRADING CARD SETS

Card Set 1–30
Ref. No.:   42401
Retail Price: N/A
Loose Price: $30
MISB: N/A

THE EMPIRE STRIKES BACK
PHOTO CARDS

BOXES

36 Pack
Ref. No.:   399
Retail Price: N/A
Loose Price: N/A
MISB: $50

  production series
Ref. No.:   399
Retail Price: N/A

Loose Price: N/A
MISB: $50

Test series
Ref. No.:   398
Retail Price: N/A
Loose Price: N/A
MISB: $100

CARD PACKS PAPER WRAPPER

Giant Full Color Photocards (Darth Vader)
Ref. No.:   397
Retail Price: N/A
Loose Price: N/A
MISB: $3

  paper wrapper, crimped
Ref. No.:   397
Retail Price: N/A
Loose Price: N/A
MISB: $3

  paper wrapper, Test Series—Sealed with Tape
Ref. No.:   396
Retail Price: N/A
Loose Price: N/A
MISB: $3

RETURN OF THE JEDI SERIES 1 (RED)

BOXES

36 Packs/12 Cards, 1 Sticker & 1 Gum Per Pack
Ref. No.:   12837
Retail Price: N/A
Loose Price: N/A
MISB: $25

CARD PACKS WAX WRAPPER

Darth Vader
Ref. No.:   8110
Retail Price: N/A
Loose Price: N/A
MISB: $3

Jabba the Hutt
Ref. No.:   8112
Retail Price: N/A
Loose Price: N/A
MISB: $3

Luke Skywalker
Ref. No.:   8111
Retail Price: N/A
Loose Price: N/A
MISB: $3

Warrick W. Wicket
Ref. No.:   8109
Retail Price: N/A
Loose Price: N/A
MISB: $3

TRADING CARD SETS

Card Set 1–132
Ref. No.:   42400
Retail Price: N/A
Loose Price: $15
MISB: N/A

Sticker Set 1–33
Ref. No.:   42419
Retail Price: N/A
Loose Price: $7
MISB: N/A

UNCUT SHEETS

Uncut Sheet Cards/Stickers
Ref. No.:   8119
Retail Price: N/A
Loose Price: $20
MISB: N/A

RETURN OF THE JEDI SERIES 2 (BLUE)

BOXES

36 Pack
Ref. No.:   12839
Retail Price: N/A
Loose Price: N/A
MISB: $25

CARD PACKS WAX WRAPPER

C-3PO
Ref. No.:   7990
Retail Price: N/A
Loose Price: N/A
MISB: $3

Lando Calrissian
Ref. No.:   7991
Retail Price: N/A
Loose Price: N/A
MISB: $3

Princess Leia
Ref. No.:   7989
Retail Price: N/A

Loose Price: N/A
MISB: $3

Wokling
Ref. No.:   7988
Retail Price: N/A
Loose Price: N/A
MISB: $3

TRADING CARD SETS

Card Set 133–220
Ref. No.:   42399
Retail Price: N/A
Loose Price: $15
MISB: N/A

Sticker Set 34–55
Ref. No.:   42420
Retail Price: N/A
Loose Price: $7
MISB: N/A

UNCUT SHEETS

Uncut Sheet Cards/Stickers
Ref. No.:   7669
Retail Price: N/A
Loose Price: $20
MISB: N/A

STAR WARS GALAXY SERIES 1

BINDERS

3-Ring Binder with #SWB1 Card (Tarkin & Vader)
Ref. No.:   10744
Retail Price: N/A
Loose Price: $15
MISB: N/A

BOXES

36 Packs/8 Cards Per Pack
Ref. No.:   10727
Retail Price: N/A
Loose Price: N/A
MISB: $15

Falcon Factory Set
Ref. No.:   42491
Retail Price: N/A

CARD PACK

8 Premium Cards Series One
Ref. No.:   10728
Retail Price: N/A
Loose Price: N/A
MISB: $2

CHASE CARDS HOLOGRAM

Falcon Factory Set Limited Edition Hologram, Darth Vader
Ref. No.:   10724
Retail Price: N/A
Loose Price: $5
MISB: N/A

PROMOTIONAL CARDS

0, Vader (Box Art)
Ref. No.:   10720
Retail Price: N/A
Loose Price: $1
MISB: N/A

(101) Boba Fett/Dengar
Ref. No.:   10712
Retail Price: N/A
Loose Price: $1
MISB: N/A

(104) Jabba and Crumb
Ref. No.:   10711
Retail Price: N/A
Loose Price: $1
MISB: N/A

(126) Leia
Ref. No.:   10710
Retail Price: N/A
Loose Price: $1
MISB: N/A

(136) Stormtrooper on Dewback
Ref. No.:   10709
Retail Price: N/A
Loose Price: $1
MISB: N/A

Boba Fett and Dengar
Ref. No.:   10743
Retail Price: N/A
Loose Price: $1
MISB: N/A

DH1, Droid Battle
Ref. No.:   9481
Retail Price: N/A

Loose Price: $2
MISB: N/A

DH2, Boba Fett
Ref. No.:   9480
Retail Price: N/A
Loose Price: $2
MISB: N/A

DH3, Falcon, and Star Destroyer
Ref. No.:   9479
Retail Price: N/A
Loose Price: $2
MISB: N/A

Leia/Stormtrooper Double Card, "Special Guest Artist Subset"
Ref. No.:   10708
Retail Price: N/A
Loose Price: $1
MISB: N/A

SWB1 Card (Tarkin and Vader)
Ref. No.:   10719
Retail Price: N/A
Loose Price: $1
MISB: N/A

SWB1 Card (Tarkin and Vader)
Ref. No.:   9478
Retail Price: N/A
Loose Price: $1
MISB: N/A

REDEMPTION CARDS

Autographed Card
Ref. No.:   10745
Retail Price: N/A
Loose Price: $5
MISB: N/A

TRADING CARD SETS

Card Set 1–140
Ref. No.:   42421
Retail Price: N/A
Loose Price: $20
MISB: N/A

Foil Stamped from Falcon Factory Set
Ref. No.:   42421
Retail Price: N/A
Loose Price: $20
MISB: N/A

standard version
Ref. No.:   42398
Retail Price: N/A

| Loose Price: | $15 |
| MISB: | N/A |

Etched Foil Chase Card Set 1–6

Ref. No.:	42422
Retail Price:	N/A
Loose Price:	$10
MISB:	N/A

Falcon Factory Set Prism Chase Card 1–6

Ref. No.:	42423
Retail Price:	N/A
Loose Price:	$10
MISB:	N/A

Millenium Falcon Factory Set

Ref. No.:	10723
Retail Price:	N/A
Loose Price:	N/A
MISB:	$30

no sticker

Ref. No.:	10723
Retail Price:	N/A
Loose Price:	N/A
MISB:	$30

with Publisher's Proof Sticker on Box

Ref. No.:	10722
Retail Price:	N/A
Loose Price:	N/A
MISB:	$40

UNCUT SHEETS

QVC Act of Star Wars Galaxy 9-up Sheet

Ref. No.:	10718
Retail Price:	N/A
Loose Price:	$7
MISB:	N/A

San Diego 1994 Comicon 9-up Sheet

Ref. No.:	10716
Retail Price:	N/A
Loose Price:	$7
MISB:	N/A

San Diego 1995 Comicon 9-up Sheet

Ref. No.:	10715
Retail Price:	N/A
Loose Price:	$7
MISB:	N/A

Set of 2 Uncut Sheets

Ref. No.:	10714
Retail Price:	N/A
Loose Price:	$10
MISB:	N/A

Uncut Sheet of 6 Etched Foil Cards

Ref. No.:	10713
Retail Price:	N/A
Loose Price:	$7
MISB:	N/A

STAR WARS GALAXY SERIES 2

BOXES

36 Packs

Ref. No.:	10387
Retail Price:	N/A
Loose Price:	N/A
MISB:	$15

Deluxe Factory Set

Ref. No.:	42492
Retail Price:	N/A
Loose Price:	N/A
MISB:	N/A

CARD PACKS

Foil Trading Card Pack

Ref. No.:	10390
Retail Price:	N/A
Loose Price:	N/A
MISB:	$2

foil wrapper, with Album Offer

Ref. No.:	10390
Retail Price:	N/A
Loose Price:	N/A
MISB:	$2

foil wrapper, with Book Offer

Ref. No.:	10389
Retail Price:	N/A
Loose Price:	N/A
MISB:	$2

foil wrapper, with Sheet Contest

Ref. No.:	10388
Retail Price:	N/A
Loose Price:	N/A
MISB:	$2

CHASE CARDS HOLOGRAM

Hologram 2, Droids

Ref. No.:	10384
Retail Price:	N/A
Loose Price:	$3
MISB:	N/A

PROMOTIONAL CARDS

00, Darth Vader on Bridge

Ref. No.:	10382
Retail Price:	N/A
Loose Price:	$1
MISB:	N/A

Evil Ewoks

Ref. No.:	10381
Retail Price:	N/A
Loose Price:	$1
MISB:	N/A

P3, Yoda Praying

Ref. No.:	10378
Retail Price:	N/A
Loose Price:	$500
MISB:	N/A

pulled from production

Ref. No.:	10378
Retail Price:	N/A
Loose Price:	$500
MISB:	N/A

Sandpeople (271)

Ref. No.:	10374
Retail Price:	N/A
Loose Price:	$1
MISB:	N/A

TRADING CARD SETS

Card Set 141–275

Ref. No.:	42485
Retail Price:	N/A
Loose Price:	$20
MISB:	N/A

Foil Stamped from Factory Set

Ref. No.:	42485
Retail Price:	N/A
Loose Price:	$20
MISB:	N/A

Standard version

Ref. No.:	42397
Retail Price:	N/A
Loose Price:	$15
MISB:	N/A

Etched Foil Chase Card Set 7–12

Ref. No.:	42425
Retail Price:	N/A
Loose Price:	$10
MISB:	N/A

Factory Set Prism Chase Card Set 7–12

Ref. No.:	42426
Retail Price:	N/A
Loose Price:	$10
MISB:	N/A

Promo Card Set P1–P6

Ref. No.:	42424
Retail Price:	N/A
Loose Price:	$6
MISB:	N/A

UNCUT SHEETS

Set of 2 Uncut Sheets from Contest Giveaway

Ref. No.:	10373
Retail Price:	N/A
Loose Price:	$10
MISB:	N/A

Uncut Sheet Foil Cards

Ref. No.:	10372
Retail Price:	N/A
Loose Price:	$7
MISB:	N/A

Uncut Sheet of 6 Etched Foil Cards from Contest Giveaway

Ref. No.:	10371
Retail Price:	N/A
Loose Price:	$7
MISB:	N/A

STAR WARS GALAXY SERIES 3

BOXES

36 Pack

Ref. No.:	12848
Retail Price:	N/A
Loose Price:	N/A
MISB:	$10

CARD PACKS

Foil Trading Card Pack

Ref. No.:	12844
Retail Price:	N/A
Loose Price:	N/A
MISB:	$2

PROMOTIONAL CARDS

000, Drew Stuzan

Ref. No.:	10162
Retail Price:	N/A

Loose Price: $1
MISB: N/A

(258) Boba Fett

Ref. No.: 10161
Retail Price: N/A
Loose Price: $1
MISB: N/A

TRADING CARD SETS

Card Set 276–365

Ref. No.: 42486
Retail Price: N/A
Loose Price: $20
MISB: N/A

1:1 packs, 1st Day Issue
Ref. No.: 42486
Retail Price: N/A
Loose Price: $20
MISB: N/A

standard version
Ref. No.: 42396
Retail Price: N/A
Loose Price: $15
MISB: N/A

Clear Zone Chase Card Set E1–E6

Ref. No.: 42430
Retail Price: N/A
Loose Price: $15
MISB: N/A

Etched Foil Chase Card Set 13–18

Ref. No.: 42429
Retail Price: N/A
Loose Price: $10
MISB: N/A

LucasArts Foil Chase Card Set L1–L12

Ref. No.: 42428
Retail Price: N/A
Loose Price: $17
MISB: N/A

Promo Card Set P2–P8

Ref. No.: 42427
Retail Price: N/A
Loose Price: $15
MISB: N/A

UNCUT SHEETS

Uncut Sheet of 6 Foil Cards from Contest Giveaway

Ref. No.: 10151
Retail Price: N/A

Loose Price: $7
MISB: N/A

MASTERVISIONS

TRADING CARD SETS

Card Set 1–36

Ref. No.: 43295
Retail Price: N/A
Loose Price: $25
MISB: N/A

STAR WARS MASTER VISIONS

BOXES

Star Wars Master Visions Collector Cards Premiere Edition, One Complete Set Box

Ref. No.: 2161
Retail Price: N/A
Loose Price: N/A
MISB: $15

STAR WARS WIDEVISION

BOXES

36 Packs/10 Cards Per Pack

Ref. No.: 9598
Retail Price: N/A
Loose Price: N/A
MISB: $20

CARD PACKS

10 Super Premium Trading Cards (X-Wing Fighters)

Ref. No.: 9599
Retail Price: N/A
Loose Price: N/A
MISB: $2

foil wrapper, with Album Cover
Ref. No.: 9599
Retail Price: N/A
Loose Price: N/A
MISB: $2

foil wrapper, with Book Offer
Ref. No.: 9596
Retail Price: N/A
Loose Price: N/A
MISB: $2

foil wrapper, with Magazine Ad

Ref. No.:	9595
Retail Price:	N/A
Loose Price:	N/A
MISB:	$2

PROMOTIONAL CARDS

00, Luke by X-Wing

Ref. No.:	9592
Retail Price:	N/A
Loose Price:	$1
MISB:	N/A

79, Han in Gunport

Ref. No.:	9591
Retail Price:	N/A
Loose Price:	$1
MISB:	N/A

K-01, Darth Choking Rebel

Ref. No.:	9590
Retail Price:	N/A
Loose Price:	$1
MISB:	N/A

K-02, Luke in Falcon Gun Port

Ref. No.:	9589
Retail Price:	N/A
Loose Price:	$1
MISB:	N/A

K-03, Interior Falcon Cockpit

Ref. No.:	9588
Retail Price:	N/A
Loose Price:	$1
MISB:	N/A

SWP2, Interior Falcon Cockpit

Ref. No.:	9587
Retail Price:	N/A
Loose Price:	$1
MISB:	N/A

TRADING CARD SETS

Card Set 1–120

Ref. No.:	42394
Retail Price:	N/A
Loose Price:	$20
MISB:	N/A

Chase Card Set C1–C9

Ref. No.:	42432
Retail Price:	N/A
Loose Price:	$15
MISB:	N/A

Chromium Promo Card Set SWP0–SWP6

Ref. No.:	42431
Retail Price:	N/A
Loose Price:	$40
MISB:	N/A

STAR WARS CAPS

BOXES

48 Pack

Ref. No.:	9436
Retail Price:	N/A
Loose Price:	N/A
MISB:	$50

CARD PACKS

Pack

Ref. No.:	9434
Retail Price:	N/A
Loose Price:	N/A
MISB:	$3

CHASE CAPS

Ben (Obi-Wan) Kenobi

Ref. No.:	30867
Retail Price:	N/A
Loose Price:	$2
MISB:	N/A

black slammer

Ref. No.:	30867
Retail Price:	N/A
Loose Price:	$2
MISB:	N/A

gold slammer

Ref. No.:	30859
Retail Price:	N/A
Loose Price:	$2
MISB:	N/A

silver slammer

Ref. No.:	9446
Retail Price:	N/A
Loose Price:	$2
MISB:	N/A

Boba Fett

Ref. No.:	30860
Retail Price:	N/A
Loose Price:	$2
MISB:	N/A

black slammer

Ref. No.:	30860
Retail Price:	N/A

Loose Price: $2
MISB: N/A

gold slammer
Ref. No.:   30868
Retail Price: N/A
Loose Price: $2
MISB: N/A

silver slammer
Ref. No.:   9441
Retail Price: N/A
Loose Price: $2
MISB: N/A

Darth Vader
Ref. No.:   30861
Retail Price: N/A
Loose Price: $2
MISB: N/A

black slammer
Ref. No.:   30861
Retail Price: N/A
Loose Price: $2
MISB: N/A

gold slammer
Ref. No.:   30869
Retail Price: N/A
Loose Price: $2
MISB: N/A

silver slammer
Ref. No.:   9447
Retail Price: N/A
Loose Price: $2
MISB: N/A

Han Solo
Ref. No.:   30862
Retail Price: N/A
Loose Price: $2
MISB: N/A

black slammer
Ref. No.:   30862
Retail Price: N/A
Loose Price: $2
MISB: N/A

gold slammer
Ref. No.:   30870
Retail Price: N/A
Loose Price: $2
MISB: N/A

silver slammer
Ref. No.:   9442
Retail Price: N/A
Loose Price: $2
MISB: N/A

Luke Skywalker
Ref. No.:   30864
Retail Price: N/A
Loose Price: $2
MISB: N/A

black slammer
Ref. No.:   30864
Retail Price: N/A
Loose Price: $2
MISB: N/A

gold slammer
Ref. No.:   30872
Retail Price: N/A
Loose Price: $2
MISB: N/A

silver slammer
Ref. No.:   9444
Retail Price: N/A
Loose Price: $2
MISB: N/A

Princess Leia
Ref. No.:   30863
Retail Price: N/A
Loose Price: $2
MISB: N/A

black slammer
Ref. No.:   30863
Retail Price: N/A
Loose Price: $2
MISB: N/A

gold slammer
Ref. No.:   30871
Retail Price: N/A
Loose Price: $2
MISB: N/A

silver slammer
Ref. No.:   9443
Retail Price: N/A
Loose Price: $2
MISB: N/A

Stormtrooper
Ref. No.:   30865
Retail Price: N/A
Loose Price: $2
MISB: N/A

black slammer
Ref. No.:   30865
Retail Price: N/A
Loose Price: $2
MISB: N/A

gold slammer
Ref. No.:   30873

Retail Price: N/A
Loose Price: $2
MISB: N/A

silver slammer
Ref. No.:   9445
Retail Price: N/A
Loose Price: $2
MISB: N/A

The Emperor
Ref. No.:   30866
Retail Price: N/A
Loose Price: $2
MISB: N/A

black slammer
Ref. No.:   30866
Retail Price: N/A
Loose Price: $2
MISB: N/A

gold slammer
Ref. No.:   30874
Retail Price: N/A
Loose Price: $2
MISB: N/A

silver slammer
Ref. No.:   9448
Retail Price: N/A
Loose Price: $2
MISB: N/A

PROMOTIONAL CARDS

Cap 0-A, C-3PO & R2-D2
Ref. No.:   9439
Retail Price: N/A
Loose Price: $2
MISB: N/A

Cap 0-B, Darth Vader
Ref. No.:   9438
Retail Price: N/A
Loose Price: $2
MISB: N/A

TRADING CARD SETS

Cap Set 1–70
Ref. No.:   42393
Retail Price: N/A
Loose Price: $50
MISB: N/A

Star Wars Galaxy Foil Cap Set 1–10
Ref. No.:   42433
Retail Price: N/A
Loose Price: $20
MISB: N/A

THE EMPIRE STRIKES BACK WIDEVISION

BOXES

24 Pack
Ref. No.:   8338
Retail Price: N/A
Loose Price: N/A
MISB: $30

CARD PACKS

AT-ATs
Ref. No.:   8343
Retail Price: N/A
Loose Price: N/A
MISB: $2

Falcon/Star Destroyer
Ref. No.:   8342
Retail Price: N/A
Loose Price: N/A
MISB: $2

Luke & Yoda
Ref. No.:   8341
Retail Price: N/A
Loose Price: N/A
MISB: $2

Vader in Freeze Chamber
Ref. No.:   8339
Retail Price: N/A
Loose Price: N/A
MISB: $2

PROMOTIONAL CARDS

0, Vader in Meditation Chamber
Ref. No.:   8330
Retail Price: N/A
Loose Price: $1
MISB: N/A

TRADING CARD SETS

Card Set 1–144
Ref. No.:   42392
Retail Price: N/A
Loose Price: $20
MISB: N/A

Chromium Chase Card Set C1–C10
Ref. No.:   42436
Retail Price: N/A
Loose Price: $50
MISB: N/A

Mini Poster Chase Card Set 1–6

Ref. No.: 42435
Retail Price: N/A
Loose Price: $15
MISB: N/A

Promo Card Set P1–P6

Ref. No.: 42434
Retail Price: N/A
Loose Price: $6
MISB: N/A

UNCUT SHEET

Set of 2 Uncut Sheets (QVC)

Ref. No.: 8323
Retail Price: N/A
Loose Price: $10
MISB: N/A

RETURN OF THE JEDI WIDEVISION

BOXES

24 Pack

Ref. No.: 12840
Retail Price: N/A
Loose Price: N/A
MISB: $35

CARD PACKS

B-Wings

Ref. No.: 7812
Retail Price: N/A
Loose Price: N/A
MISB: $2

Han Solo

Ref. No.: 7811
Retail Price: N/A
Loose Price: N/A
MISB: $2

Jabba the Hutt

Ref. No.: 7810
Retail Price: N/A
Loose Price: N/A
MISB: $2

Luke/Biker Scout

Ref. No.: 7809
Retail Price: N/A
Loose Price: N/A
MISB: $2

CHASE CARDS

DIII 0, Admiral Ackbar

Ref. No.: 7833
Retail Price: N/A
Loose Price: $2
MISB: N/A

PROMOTIONAL CARDS

0, Anakin, Yoda & Ben

Ref. No.: 7821
Retail Price: N/A
Loose Price: $1
MISB: N/A

0, in Stars (Previews)

Ref. No.: 7820
Retail Price: N/A
Loose Price: $1
MISB: N/A

TRADING CARD SETS

Card Set 1–144

Ref. No.: 42391
Retail Price: N/A
Loose Price: $20
MISB: N/A

Chromium Chase Card Set C1–C10

Ref. No.: 42439
Retail Price: N/A
Loose Price: $50
MISB: N/A

Mini Poster Chase Card Set 1–6

Ref. No.: 42438
Retail Price: N/A
Loose Price: $15
MISB: N/A

Promo Trading Card Set P1–P6

Ref. No.: 42437
Retail Price: N/A
Loose Price: $6
MISB: N/A

STAR WARS TRILOGY WIDEVISION

BOXES

36 Packs/6 Cards Per Pack

Ref. No.: 9051
Retail Price: N/A

Loose Price: N/A
MISB: $10

CARD PACKS

6 Super Wide Movie Cards (Yoda)
Ref. No.:   9053
Retail Price: N/A
Loose Price: N/A
MISB: $2

TRADING CARD SETS

Card Set 1–72
Ref. No.:   42390
Retail Price: N/A
Loose Price: $20
MISB: N/A

Laser Cut Chase Card Set 1–6
Ref. No.:   42440
Retail Price: N/A
Loose Price: $15
MISB: N/A

UNCUT SHEETS

Uncut Sheet 6 Laser Cut Chase Card
Ref. No.:   12616
Retail Price: N/A
Loose Price: $10
MISB: N/A

SHADOWS OF THE EMPIRE

BOXES

36 Pack
Ref. No.:   11313
Retail Price: N/A
Loose Price: N/A
MISB: $10

CARD PACKS

Boba Fett
Ref. No.:   11309
Retail Price: N/A
Loose Price: N/A
MISB: $1

Darth Vader
Ref. No.:   11311
Retail Price: N/A
Loose Price: N/A
MISB: $1

Luke Skywalker
Ref. No.:   11310
Retail Price: N/A
Loose Price: N/A
MISB: $1

Prince Xizor
Ref. No.:   11312
Retail Price: N/A
Loose Price: N/A
MISB: $1

CASE TOPPER CARDS

Master Visions Hildebrandt
Ref. No.:   11307
Retail Price: N/A
Loose Price: $5
MISB: N/A

1:8 boxes, autographed
Ref. No.:   11307
Retail Price: N/A
Loose Price: $5
MISB: N/A

1:8 boxes, non-autographed
Ref. No.:   11315
Retail Price: N/A
Loose Price: $5
MISB: N/A

TRADING CARD SETS

Card Set 1–100
Ref. No.:   42389
Retail Price: N/A
Loose Price: $10
MISB: N/A

Promo Card Set SOTE1–SOTE7
Ref. No.:   42441
Retail Price: N/A
Loose Price: $20
MISB: N/A

UNCUT SHEETS

Uncut Sheet Cards
Ref. No.:   11326
Retail Price: N/A
Loose Price: $10
MISB: N/A

STAR WARS 3D WIDEVISION

BOXES

36 Packs/3 Cards Per Pack

Ref. No.:	9356
Retail Price:	N/A
Loose Price:	N/A
MISB:	$50

CARD PACKS

Three Deluxe 3-D Widescreen Cards

Ref. No.:	9349
Retail Price:	N/A
Loose Price:	N/A
MISB:	$3

CHASE CARDS

Multi-Motion M1, Death Star Explodes Motion Card

Ref. No.:	9358
Retail Price:	N/A
Loose Price:	$5
MISB:	N/A

PROMOTIONAL CARDS

3D P1, AT-AT

Ref. No.:	9350
Retail Price:	N/A
Loose Price:	$1
MISB:	N/A

3Di/1, Vader on Death Star

Ref. No.:	9353
Retail Price:	N/A
Loose Price:	$5
MISB:	N/A

3Di/2, Luke and Vader by McQuarrie

Ref. No.:	9352
Retail Price:	N/A
Loose Price:	$5
MISB:	N/A

Multi-Motion M2, Ronto, and Jawa Motion Card

Ref. No.:	9351
Retail Price:	N/A
Loose Price:	$1
MISB:	N/A

TRADING CARD SETS

Card Set 1–63

Ref. No.:	42388
Retail Price:	N/A

Loose Price:	$60
MISB:	N/A

STAR WARS FINEST

BINDERS

3-Ring Binder w/ Han Solo and Chewbacca Card

Ref. No.:	11053
Retail Price:	N/A
Loose Price:	$15
MISB:	N/A

BOXES

36 Packs/5 Cards Per Pack

Ref. No.:	11044
Retail Price:	N/A
Loose Price:	N/A
MISB:	$40

CARD PACKS

5 All-Chromium Cards

Ref. No.:	11043
Retail Price:	N/A
Loose Price:	N/A
MISB:	$3

blue foil wrapper w/ binder offer

Ref. No.:	11043
Retail Price:	N/A
Loose Price:	N/A
MISB:	$3

blue foil wrapper w/ magazine ad

Ref. No.:	11041
Retail Price:	N/A
Loose Price:	N/A
MISB:	$3

red foil wrapper w/ book ad

Ref. No.:	11042
Retail Price:	N/A
Loose Price:	N/A
MISB:	$3

red foil wrapper w/ SOTE ad

Ref. No.:	11040
Retail Price:	N/A
Loose Price:	N/A
MISB:	$3

PROMOTIONAL CARDS

Han Solo and Chewbacca

Ref. No.:	11036
Retail Price:	N/A

Loose Price: $3
MISB: N/A

CHROMIUM

Bib Fortuna, Han Solo, and Chewbacca

Ref. No.:   11052
Retail Price: N/A
Loose Price: $3
MISB: N/A

Chromium, Silver Back

Ref. No.:   11052
Retail Price: N/A
Loose Price: $3
MISB: N/A

REFRACTOR

Bib Fortuna, Han Solo, and Chewbacca

Ref. No.:   11051
Retail Price: N/A
Loose Price: $3
MISB: N/A

Refractor, Gold Back

Ref. No.:   11051
Retail Price: N/A
Loose Price: $3
MISB: N/A

TRADING CARD SETS

Card Set 1–90

Ref. No.:   42387
Retail Price: N/A
Loose Price: $50
MISB: N/A

Chromium, Silver Back

Ref. No.:   42387
Retail Price: N/A
Loose Price: $50
MISB: N/A

Refractor, Gold Back

Ref. No.:   42442
Retail Price: N/A
Loose Price: $60
MISB: N/A

Embossed Foil Chase Card Set F1–F6

Ref. No.:   42443
Retail Price: N/A
Loose Price: $15
MISB: N/A

Matrix Chase Card Set 1–4

Ref. No.:   42444
Retail Price: N/A

Loose Price: $10
MISB: N/A

Promo Card Set SWF1–SWF3

Ref. No.:   42445
Retail Price: N/A
Loose Price: $5
MISB: N/A

STAR WARS VEHICLES

BOXES

36 Packs/5 Cards Per Pack

Ref. No.:   9495
Retail Price: N/A
Loose Price: N/A
MISB: $50

CARD PACKS

5 Cards (Shuttle Tyderium)

Ref. No.:   9486
Retail Price: N/A
Loose Price: N/A
MISB: $3

ENVELOPES

Retailer Envelope for Uncut Luke/Leia 3D Card

Ref. No.:   9488
Retail Price: N/A
Loose Price: N/A
MISB: N/A

REDEMPTION CARDS

Redemption Card for Uncut Luke/Leia 3D Card

Ref. No.:   9489
Retail Price: N/A
Loose Price: N/A
MISB: N/A

TRADING CARD SETS

3D Chase Card Set 3Di1–3Di2

Ref. No.:   42449
Retail Price: N/A
Loose Price: $5
MISB: N/A

Card Set 1–72

Ref. No.:   42386
Retail Price: N/A

Loose Price: $30
MISB: N/A

Chromium Promo Card Set P1–P2

Ref. No.:   42448
Retail Price: N/A
Loose Price: $5
MISB: N/A

Cut-Away Chase Card Set C1–C4

Ref. No.:   42447
Retail Price: N/A
Loose Price: $20
MISB: N/A

Refractor Promo Card Set P1–P2

Ref. No.:   42446
Retail Price: N/A
Loose Price: $7
MISB: N/A

UNCUT SHEETS

Uncut Luke/Leia 3D Card

Ref. No.:   9487
Retail Price: N/A
Loose Price: $10
MISB: N/A

JUST TOYS BEND-EM

TRADING CARD SETS

Card Set A–Z

Ref. No.:   42385
Retail Price: N/A
Loose Price: $26
MISB: N/A

STAR WARS CHROME ARCHIVES

BOXES

36 Pack

Ref. No.:   9244
Retail Price: N/A
Loose Price: N/A
MISB: $40

CARD PACKS

Foil Trading Card Pack

Ref. No.:   9240
Retail Price: N/A
Loose Price: N/A
MISB: $3

TRADING CARD SETS

Card Set 1–90

Ref. No.:   42384
Retail Price: N/A
Loose Price: $30
MISB: N/A

Clearzone Chase Card Set C1–C4

Ref. No.:   42450
Retail Price: N/A
Loose Price: $15
MISB: N/A

Double-Sided Chase Card Set D1–D9

Ref. No.:   42451
Retail Price: N/A
Loose Price: $20
MISB: N/A

Promo Trading Card Set P1–P2

Ref. No.:   42452
Retail Price: N/A
Loose Price: $5
MISB: N/A

STAR WARS FINEST TRADING CARD SETS

CHROMIUM

Card Set SWGM1–SWGM4

Ref. No.:   42455
Retail Price: N/A
Loose Price: $7
MISB: N/A

STAR WARS GALAXY MAGAZINE

TRADING CARD SETS

Card Set C1–C4

Ref. No.:   42454
Retail Price: N/A
Loose Price: $10
MISB: N/A

Card Set SW1–SW9

Ref. No.:   42383
Retail Price: N/A
Loose Price: $15
MISB: N/A

STAR WARS SPECIAL EDITION
WIDEVISION

BOXES

36 Packs/9 Cards Per Pack

Ref. No.:	9162
Retail Price:	N/A
Loose Price:	N/A
MISB:	$20

CARD PACKS

9 Super Premium Trading Cards (Stormtrooper on Dewback)

Ref. No.:	9161
Retail Price:	N/A
Loose Price:	N/A
MISB:	$2

PROMOTIONAL CARDS

3D Rebel Fleet

Ref. No.:	9156
Retail Price:	N/A
Loose Price:	$1
MISB:	N/A

TRADING CARD SETS

Card Set 1–72

Ref. No.:	42382
Retail Price:	N/A
Loose Price:	$10
MISB:	N/A

Hologram Chase Card Set 1–2

Ref. No.:	42460
Retail Price:	N/A
Loose Price:	$10
MISB:	N/A

Laser Cut Chase Card Set 0–6

Ref. No.:	42459
Retail Price:	N/A
Loose Price:	$10
MISB:	N/A

Promo Trading Card Set G1–G5

Ref. No.:	42458
Retail Price:	N/A
Loose Price:	$10
MISB:	N/A

Promo Trading Card Set H1–H4

Ref. No.:	42457
Retail Price:	N/A
Loose Price:	$10
MISB:	N/A

Promo Trading Card Set P1–P8

Ref. No.:	42456
Retail Price:	N/A
Loose Price:	$10
MISB:	N/A

EPISODE I WIDEVISION
SERIES 1 (RED)

BOXES

36 Packs/8 Cards Per Pack Retail Box

Ref. No.:	11485
Retail Price:	N/A
Loose Price:	N/A
MISB:	$15

36 Packs/8 Cards Per Pack Special Collector's Edition

Ref. No.:	11483
Retail Price:	N/A
Loose Price:	N/A
MISB:	$10

CARD PACKS

8 Widevision Trading Cards (Anakin Skywalker) Retail Pack

Ref. No.:	12776
Retail Price:	$1.99
Loose Price:	N/A
MISB:	$1

8 Widevision Trading Cards (Anakin Skywalker) Special Collector's Edition

Ref. No.:	13656
Retail Price:	N/A
Loose Price:	N/A
MISB:	$1

8 Widevision Trading Cards (Darth Maul) Retail Pack

Ref. No.:	15643
Retail Price:	$1.97
Loose Price:	N/A
MISB:	$1

8 Widevision Trading Cards (Darth Maul) Special Collector's Edition

Ref. No.:	15644
Retail Price:	N/A
Loose Price:	N/A
MISB:	$1

8 Widevision Trading Cards (Obi-Wan Kenobi) Retail Pack

Ref. No.:   11484
Retail Price: $1.99
Loose Price: N/A
MISB: $1

Foil wrapper, no tab
Ref. No.:   11484
Retail Price: N/A
Loose Price: N/A
MISB: $1

Foil wrapper, with hanging tab
Ref. No.:   13661
Retail Price: N/A
Loose Price: N/A
MISB: $1

8 Widevision Trading Cards (Obi-Wan Kenobi) Special Collector's Edition

Ref. No.:   13658
Retail Price: N/A
Loose Price: N/A
MISB: $1

8 Widevision Trading Cards (Queen Amidala) Retail Pack

Ref. No.:   12777
Retail Price: $1.97
Loose Price: N/A
MISB: $1

8 Widevision Trading Cards (Queen Amidala) Special Collector's Edition

Ref. No.:   13659
Retail Price: N/A
Loose Price: N/A
MISB: $1

8 Widevision Trading Cards (Qui-Gon Jinn) Retail Pack

Ref. No.:   12775
Retail Price: $1.99
Loose Price: N/A
MISB: $1

8 Widevision Trading Cards (Qui-Gon Jinn) Special Collector's Edition

Ref. No.:   13660
Retail Price: N/A
Loose Price: N/A
MISB: $1

COLLECTOR TINS

Anakin Skywalker
Ref. No.:   386
Retail Price: $19.99

Loose Price: N/A
MISB: $7

Darth Maul
Ref. No.:   382
Retail Price: $19.99
Loose Price: N/A
MISB: $7

Obi-Wan Kenobi
Ref. No.:   384
Retail Price: $19.99
Loose Price: N/A
MISB: $7

Queen Amidala
Ref. No.:   383
Retail Price: $19.99
Loose Price: N/A
MISB: $7

Qui-Gon Jinn
Ref. No.:   385
Retail Price: $19.99
Loose Price: N/A
MISB: $7

PROMOTIONAL CARDS

0, Strength in Numbers
Ref. No.:   14945
Retail Price: N/A
Loose Price: $1
MISB: N/A

00, All Bow to the Boss
Ref. No.:   14946
Retail Price: N/A
Loose Price: $1
MISB: N/A

000, The Battle Droids
Ref. No.:   14947
Retail Price: N/A
Loose Price: $1
MISB: N/A

TRADING CARD SETS

Card Set 1–80
Ref. No.:   42381
Retail Price: N/A
Loose Price: $15
MISB: N/A

Chrome Chase Card Set 1–5
Ref. No.:   42466
Retail Price: N/A

Loose Price: $5
MISB: N/A

Foil Chase Card Set F1–F10

Ref. No.:   42465
Retail Price: N/A
Loose Price: $10
MISB: N/A

Hobby Edition Chrome Chase Card Set C1–C8

Ref. No.:   42463
Retail Price: N/A
Loose Price: $15
MISB: N/A

Hobby Edition Subset Trading Card Set X1–X40

Ref. No.:   42462
Retail Price: N/A
Loose Price: $50
MISB: N/A

Promo Trading Card Set H1–H3

Ref. No.:   42464
Retail Price: N/A
Loose Price: $5
MISB: N/A

Sticker Set S1–S16

Ref. No.:   42467
Retail Price: N/A
Loose Price: $10
MISB: N/A

EPISODE I WIDEVISION SERIES 2 (BLUE)

BOXES

36 Packs/8 Cards Per Pack Hobby Edition

Ref. No.:   11639
Retail Price: N/A
Loose Price: N/A
MISB: $15

36 Packs/8 Cards Per Pack Retail Edition

Ref. No.:   13655
Retail Price: N/A
Loose Price: N/A
MISB: $10

CARD PACKS

8 Widevision Trading Cards Hobby Edition (Darth Maul and Battle Droid)

Ref. No.:   12779

Retail Price: N/A
Loose Price: N/A
MISB: $1

8 Widevision Trading Cards Hobby Edition (Qui-Gon and Obi-Wan)

Ref. No.:   11640
Retail Price: N/A
Loose Price: N/A
MISB: $1

8 Widevision Trading Cards Retail Edition (Darth Maul and Battle Droid)

Ref. No.:   15646
Retail Price: $1.99
Loose Price: N/A
MISB: $1

8 Widevision Trading Cards Retail Edition (Qui-Gon and Obi-Wan)

Ref. No.:   15647
Retail Price: $1.99
Loose Price: N/A
MISB: $1

CHASE CARDS

4″ × 8″, # 1

Ref. No.:   14976
Retail Price: N/A
Loose Price: $5
MISB: N/A

4″ × 8″, # 2, Cutting Down Battle Droids

Ref. No.:   14974
Retail Price: N/A
Loose Price: $5
MISB: N/A

4″ × 8″, # 3

Ref. No.:   14977
Retail Price: N/A
Loose Price: $5
MISB: N/A

4″ × 8″, # OS-1, Duelling with Darth Maul

Ref. No.:   14975
Retail Price: N/A
Loose Price: $5
MISB: N/A

4″ × 8″, # OS-2, A Time to Rejoice

Ref. No.:   14973
Retail Price: N/A
Loose Price: $5
MISB: N/A

TRADING CARD SETS

Card Set 1–80

Ref. No.:	42380
Retail Price:	N/A
Loose Price:	$15
MISB:	N/A

Chrome Chase Card Set C1–C4

Ref. No.:	42471
Retail Price:	N/A
Loose Price:	$5
MISB:	N/A

Chrome Chase Card Set HC1–HC4

Ref. No.:	42470
Retail Price:	N/A
Loose Price:	$10
MISB:	N/A

Embossed Foil Chase Card Set E1–E6

Ref. No.:	42469
Retail Price:	N/A
Loose Price:	$6
MISB:	N/A

Embossed Foil Chase Card Set HE1–HE6

Ref. No.:	42468
Retail Price:	N/A
Loose Price:	$12
MISB:	N/A

EPISODE I 3D WIDEVISION

BOXES

36 Packs/2 Cards Per Pack

Ref. No.:	11379
Retail Price:	N/A
Loose Price:	N/A
MISB:	$25

36 Packs/2 Cards Per Pack Hobby Edition

Ref. No.:	11381
Retail Price:	N/A
Loose Price:	N/A
MISB:	$30

CARD PACKS

2 Cards Per Pack (Darth Maul)

Ref. No.:	11380
Retail Price:	N/A
Loose Price:	N/A
MISB:	$3

CHASE CARDS

Multi-Motion 1, Destroyer Droids

Ref. No.:	11377
Retail Price:	N/A
Loose Price:	$5
MISB:	N/A

Multi-Motion 2, The Final Duel

Ref. No.:	11378
Retail Price:	N/A
Loose Price:	$5
MISB:	N/A

PROMOTIONAL CARDS

P1, Qui-Gon Jinn, and Obi-Wan Kenobi

Ref. No.:	11383
Retail Price:	N/A
Loose Price:	$3
MISB:	N/A

TRADING CARD SETS

Card Set 1–46

Ref. No.:	42379
Retail Price:	N/A
Loose Price:	$50
MISB:	N/A

EVOLUTION

BOXES

36 Packs/8 Cards Per Pack

Ref. No.:	14509
Retail Price:	N/A
Loose Price:	N/A
MISB:	$15

CARD PACKS

8 Foil Trading Cards

Ref. No.:	14510
Retail Price:	N/A
Loose Price:	N/A
MISB:	$2

CHASE CARDS

Andrew Secombe as Watto

Ref. No.:	18784
Retail Price:	N/A
Loose Price:	$10
MISB:	N/A

Anthony Daniels as C-3PO

Ref. No.:   18766
Retail Price: N/A
Loose Price: $1000
MISB: N/A

Billy Dee Williams as Lando Calrissian

Ref. No.:   18772
Retail Price: N/A
Loose Price: $500
MISB: N/A

Caroline Blakiston as Mon Mothma

Ref. No.:   18775
Retail Price: N/A
Loose Price: $10
MISB: N/A

Carrie Fisher as Princess Leia Organa

Ref. No.:   18779
Retail Price: N/A
Loose Price: $1000
MISB: N/A

Dalyn Chew as Lyn Me

Ref. No.:   18773
Retail Price: N/A
Loose Price: $10
MISB: N/A

Dermot Crowley as General Crix Madine

Ref. No.:   18770
Retail Price: N/A
Loose Price: $10
MISB: N/A

Femi Taylor as Oola

Ref. No.:   18777
Retail Price: N/A
Loose Price: $10
MISB: N/A

Ian McDiarmid as Senator Palpatine

Ref. No.:   18782
Retail Price: N/A
Loose Price: $100
MISB: N/A

James Earl Jones as Darth Vader

Ref. No.:   18769
Retail Price: N/A
Loose Price: $10
MISB: N/A

Jeremy Bullock as Boba Fett

Ref. No.:   18765
Retail Price: N/A

Loose Price: $10
MISB: N/A

Kenneth Colley as Admiral Piett

Ref. No.:   18763
Retail Price: N/A
Loose Price: $10
MISB: N/A

Kenny Baker as R2-D2

Ref. No.:   18780
Retail Price: N/A
Loose Price: $10
MISB: N/A

Lewis Macleod as Sebulba

Ref. No.:   18783
Retail Price: N/A
Loose Price: $10
MISB: N/A

Mercedes Ngoh as Rystall

Ref. No.:   18781
Retail Price: N/A
Loose Price: $10
MISB: N/A

Michael Culver as Captain Needa

Ref. No.:   18767
Retail Price: N/A
Loose Price: $10
MISB: N/A

Michael Pennington as Moff Jerjerrod

Ref. No.:   18774
Retail Price: N/A
Loose Price: $10
MISB: N/A

Michael Sheard as Admiral Ozzel

Ref. No.:   18762
Retail Price: N/A
Loose Price: $10
MISB: N/A

Michonne Bourriague as Aurra Sing

Ref. No.:   18764
Retail Price: N/A
Loose Price: $10
MISB: N/A

Mike Quinn as Nien Nunb

Ref. No.:   18776
Retail Price: N/A
Loose Price: $10
MISB: N/A

Paul Blake as Greedo

Ref. No.:	18771
Retail Price:	N/A
Loose Price:	$10
MISB:	N/A

Peter Mayhew as Chewbacca

Ref. No.:	18768
Retail Price:	N/A
Loose Price:	$100
MISB:	N/A

Phil Brown as Owen Lars

Ref. No.:	18778
Retail Price:	N/A
Loose Price:	$10
MISB:	N/A

Tim Rose as Admiral Ackbar

Ref. No.:	18761
Retail Price:	N/A
Loose Price:	$10
MISB:	N/A

Warwick Davis as Wicket W. Warrick

Ref. No.:	18785
Retail Price:	N/A
Loose Price:	$10
MISB:	N/A

TRADING CARD SETS

Card Set 1–90

Ref. No.:	42378
Retail Price:	N/A
Loose Price:	$15
MISB:	N/A

Chase Card Set 1A–12A

Ref. No.:	42474
Retail Price:	N/A
Loose Price:	$20
MISB:	N/A

Chase Card Set 1B–8B

Ref. No.:	42475
Retail Price:	N/A
Loose Price:	$15
MISB:	N/A

Chase Card Set C1–C3

Ref. No.:	42473
Retail Price:	N/A
Loose Price:	$5
MISB:	N/A

Promo Trading Card Set P1–P4

Ref. No.:	42472
Retail Price:	N/A
Loose Price:	$5
MISB:	N/A

ATTACK OF THE CLONES

BOXES

24 Packs/7 Cards Per Pack

Ref. No.:	1825
Retail Price:	$47.76
Loose Price:	N/A
MISB:	$10

36 Packs/7 Cards Per Pack

Ref. No.:	1826
Retail Price:	$60.00
Loose Price:	N/A
MISB:	$15

CARD PACKS

7 Movie Cards (Anakin Skywalker)

Ref. No.:	13902
Retail Price:	$1.99
Loose Price:	N/A
MISB:	$2

7 Movie Cards (Jango Fett)

Ref. No.:	13901
Retail Price:	$1.99
Loose Price:	N/A
MISB:	$2

7 Movie Cards (Obi-Wan Kenobi)

Ref. No.:	13903
Retail Price:	$1.99
Loose Price:	N/A
MISB:	$2

COLLECTOR TINS

Anakin Skywalker

Ref. No.:	558
Retail Price:	$19.99
Loose Price:	N/A
MISB:	$7

Count Dooku

Ref. No.:	561
Retail Price:	$19.99
Loose Price:	N/A
MISB:	$7

Jango Fett

Ref. No.:	562
Retail Price:	$19.99
Loose Price:	N/A
MISB:	$7

Mace Windu

Ref. No.:	560
Retail Price:	$19.99
Loose Price:	N/A
MISB:	$7

Obi-Wan Kenobi

Ref. No.:	559
Retail Price:	$19.99
Loose Price:	N/A
MISB:	$7

TRADING CARD SETS

Card Set 1–100

Ref. No.:	42377
Retail Price:	N/A
Loose Price:	$20
MISB:	N/A

Mega-size Foil Chase Card Set 1–5

Ref. No.:	42480
Retail Price:	N/A
Loose Price:	$10
MISB:	N/A

Panoramic Fold-Out Chase Card Set 1–5

Ref. No.:	42479
Retail Price:	N/A
Loose Price:	$10
MISB:	N/A

Priasmatic Foil Chase Card Set 1–8

Ref. No.:	42478
Retail Price:	N/A
Loose Price:	$10
MISB:	N/A

Promo Trading Card Set P1–P6

Ref. No.:	42477
Retail Price:	N/A
Loose Price:	$6
MISB:	N/A

Silver Foil Chase Card Set 1–10

Ref. No.:	42476
Retail Price:	N/A
Loose Price:	$5
MISB:	N/A

ATTACK OF THE CLONES WIDEVISION

CHASE CARDS AUTHENTIC AUTOGRAPH

Ahmed Best as Jar Jar Binks

Ref. No.:	16375
Retail Price:	N/A
Loose Price:	$30
MISB:	N/A

Alethea McGrath as Jocasta Nu

Ref. No.:	16389
Retail Price:	N/A
Loose Price:	$30
MISB:	N/A

Amy Allen as Aayla Secura

Ref. No.:	16373
Retail Price:	N/A
Loose Price:	$15
MISB:	N/A

Andrew Secombe as Watto

Ref. No.:	16394
Retail Price:	N/A
Loose Price:	$20
MISB:	N/A

Ayesha Dharker as Queen Jamillia

Ref. No.:	16379
Retail Price:	N/A
Loose Price:	$25
MISB:	N/A

Bodi Taylor as Clone Trooper

Ref. No.:	26933
Retail Price:	N/A
Loose Price:	$15
MISB:	N/A

Bonnie Piesse as Beru Whitesun

Ref. No.:	16393
Retail Price:	N/A
Loose Price:	$60
MISB:	N/A

Daniel Loganas Boba Fett

Ref. No.:	16388
Retail Price:	N/A
Loose Price:	$15
MISB:	N/A

David Bowers as Mas Amedda

Ref. No.:	16376
Retail Price:	N/A

Loose Price: $20
MISB: N/A

Frank Oz as Yoda

Ref. No.: 16392
Retail Price: N/A
Loose Price: $200
MISB: N/A

Jay Laga'aia as Captain Typho

Ref. No.: 16387
Retail Price: N/A
Loose Price: $20
MISB: N/A

Jesse Jensen as Saesee Tiin

Ref. No.: 16383
Retail Price: N/A
Loose Price: $15
MISB: N/A

Joel Edgerton as Owen Lars

Ref. No.: 16381
Retail Price: N/A
Loose Price: $20
MISB: N/A

Kenny Baker as R2-D2

Ref. No.: 16374
Retail Price: N/A
Loose Price: $10
MISB: N/A

Leeanna Walsman as Zam Wesell

Ref. No.: 16384
Retail Price: N/A
Loose Price: $25
MISB: N/A

Mary Oyaya as Luminara Unduli

Ref. No.: 16391
Retail Price: N/A
Loose Price: $15
MISB: N/A

Matt Doran as Elan Sleazebaggano

Ref. No.: 16380
Retail Price: N/A
Loose Price: $15
MISB: N/A

Matt Sloan as Plo Koon

Ref. No.: 16395
Retail Price: N/A
Loose Price: $30
MISB: N/A

Nalini Krishan as Barriss Offee

Ref. No.: 16386
Retail Price: N/A
Loose Price: $30
MISB: N/A

Rena Owen as Taun We

Ref. No.: 16390
Retail Price: N/A
Loose Price: $20
MISB: N/A

Ronald Falk as Dexter Jettster

Ref. No.: 16382
Retail Price: N/A
Loose Price: $20
MISB: N/A

Silas Carson as Ki-Adi-Mundi

Ref. No.: 16377
Retail Price: N/A
Loose Price: $20
MISB: N/A

Silas Carson as Nute Gunray

Ref. No.: 16378
Retail Price: N/A
Loose Price: $20
MISB: N/A

Zachariah Jenson as Kit Fisto

Ref. No.: 16385
Retail Price: N/A
Loose Price: $15
MISB: N/A

PROMOTIONAL CARDS

P1

Ref. No.: 15362
Retail Price: N/A
Loose Price: $1
MISB: N/A

TRADING CARDS

Card Set 1–80

Ref. No.: 42376
Retail Price: N/A
Loose Price: $20
MISB: N/A

Wal-Mart Promo Set W1–W5

Ref. No.: 42481
Retail Price: N/A
Loose Price: $10
MISB: N/A

CLONE WARS ANIMATED SERIES

BOXES

36 Packs/7 Cards Per Pack Hobby Edition

Ref. No.:   40224
Retail Price: $72.00
Loose Price: N/A
MISB: $65

36 Packs/7 Cards Per Pack Retail Edition

Ref. No.:   40223
Retail Price: $72.00
Loose Price: N/A
MISB: $55

CARD PACKS

7 Trading Cards (Yoda) Hobby Edition

Ref. No.:   41298
Retail Price: N/A
Loose Price: N/A
MISB: $2

7 Trading Cards (Yoda) Retail Edition

Ref. No.:   41419
Retail Price: $1.99
Loose Price: N/A
MISB: $2

CHASE CARDS ARTIST SKETCH CARDS

Dave Dorman

Ref. No.:   40769
Retail Price: N/A
Loose Price: $150
MISB: N/A

Davide Fabbri

Ref. No.:   40759
Retail Price: N/A
Loose Price: $30
MISB: N/A

Doug Wheatley

Ref. No.:   40760
Retail Price: N/A
Loose Price: $20
MISB: N/A

Genndy Tartakovsky

Ref. No.:   40756
Retail Price: N/A
Loose Price: $150
MISB: N/A

Joe Corroney

Ref. No.:   40765
Retail Price: N/A
Loose Price: $20
MISB: N/A

John McCrea

Ref. No.:   40764
Retail Price: N/A
Loose Price: $20
MISB: N/A

Kilian Plunkett

Ref. No.:   40761
Retail Price: N/A
Loose Price: $100
MISB: N/A

Paul Rudish

Ref. No.:   40757
Retail Price: N/A
Loose Price: $100
MISB: N/A

Pop Mhan

Ref. No.:   40766
Retail Price: N/A
Loose Price: $10
MISB: N/A

Rafael Kayanan

Ref. No.:   40768
Retail Price: N/A
Loose Price: $150
MISB: N/A

Robert Teranishi

Ref. No.:   40767
Retail Price: N/A
Loose Price: $20
MISB: N/A

Rudolph Migliari

Ref. No.:   40762
Retail Price: N/A
Loose Price: $200
MISB: N/A

Tomas Giorello

Ref. No.:   40763
Retail Price: N/A
Loose Price: $50
MISB: N/A

WIDEVISION AUTOGRAPH CARDS

Anthony Phelan as Lama Su

Ref. No.:   40222
Retail Price: N/A
Loose Price: $20
MISB: N/A

Jack Thompson as Cliegg Lars

Ref. No.: 40221
Retail Price: N/A
Loose Price: $20
MISB: N/A

TRADING CARD SETS

Battle Motion Card Set B1–B10

Ref. No.: 42483
Retail Price: N/A
Loose Price: $20
MISB: N/A

Card Set 1–90

Ref. No.: 42375
Retail Price: N/A
Loose Price: $20
MISB: N/A

Die-Cut Sticker Set 1–10

Ref. No.: 42482
Retail Price: N/A
Loose Price: $20
MISB: N/A

Promo Card Set P1–P3

Ref. No.: 42484
Retail Price: N/A
Loose Price: $20
MISB: N/A

STAR WARS HERITAGE

BOXES

36 Pack Hobby Edition

Ref. No.: 42490
Retail Price: $60
Loose Price: N/A
MISB: $60

36 Pack Retail Edition

Ref. No.: 42489
Retail Price: $60
Loose Price: N/A
MISB: $60

CARD PACKS WAX WRAPPER

Wax Pack w/ Gum

Ref. No.: 42488
Retail Price: N/A
Loose Price: $2
MISB: N/A

CHASE CARDS ARTIST SKETCH CARDS

Brandon McKinney

Ref. No.: 42258
Retail Price: N/A
Loose Price: N/A
MISB: N/A

Brian Ching

Ref. No.: 42251
Retail Price: N/A
Loose Price: N/A
MISB: N/A

Chris Eliopoulos

Ref. No.: 42259
Retail Price: N/A
Loose Price: N/A
MISB: N/A

Chris Trevas

Ref. No.: 42254
Retail Price: N/A
Loose Price: N/A
MISB: N/A

Dan Parsons

Ref. No.: 42253
Retail Price: N/A
Loose Price: N/A
MISB: N/A

Dave Dorman

Ref. No.: 42247
Retail Price: N/A
Loose Price: N/A
MISB: N/A

Davide Fabbri

Ref. No.: 42242
Retail Price: N/A
Loose Price: N/A
MISB: N/A

Jan Duursema

Ref. No.: 42248
Retail Price: N/A
Loose Price: N/A
MISB: N/A

Joe Corroney

Ref. No.: 42244
Retail Price: N/A
Loose Price: N/A
MISB: N/A

John McCrea

Ref. No.: 42243
Retail Price: N/A

Loose Price: N/A
MISB: N/A

Killian Plunkett

Ref. No.:   42261
Retail Price: N/A
Loose Price: N/A
MISB: N/A

Matt Busch

Ref. No.:   42255
Retail Price: N/A
Loose Price: N/A
MISB: N/A

Mike Lemos

Ref. No.:   42257
Retail Price: N/A
Loose Price: N/A
MISB: N/A

Paul Rudish

Ref. No.:   42260
Retail Price: N/A
Loose Price: N/A
MISB: N/A

Rafael Kayanan

Ref. No.:   42246
Retail Price: N/A
Loose Price: N/A
MISB: N/A

Randy Martinez

Ref. No.:   42256
Retail Price: N/A
Loose Price: N/A
MISB: N/A

Ray Logo

Ref. No.:   42252
Retail Price: N/A
Loose Price: N/A
MISB: N/A

Robert Teranishi

Ref. No.:   42245
Retail Price: N/A
Loose Price: N/A
MISB: N/A

Ryan Benjamin

Ref. No.:   42249
Retail Price: N/A
Loose Price: N/A
MISB: N/A

Seab Philips

Ref. No.:   42250
Retail Price: N/A
Loose Price: N/A
MISB: N/A

Thomas Hodges

Ref. No.:   42262
Retail Price: N/A
Loose Price: N/A
MISB: N/A

TRADING CARD SETS

Card Set 1–120

Ref. No.:   42374
Retail Price: N/A
Loose Price: $10
MISB: N/A

Promo Card Set P1–P6

Ref. No.:   42487
Retail Price: N/A
Loose Price: $12
MISB: N/A

Comic Books

COMIC BOOKS

3-D

1

Ref. No.:   33605
Retail Price: $2.50
MISB: $6.25

2

Ref. No.:   33606
Retail Price: $2.50
MISB: $4.50

3

Ref. No.:   33607
Retail Price: $2.50
MISB: $4.50

ATTACK OF THE CLONES

1: graphic cover

Ref. No.:   26518
Retail Price: $3.99
MISB: N/A

 # 1: photo cover

Ref. No.:	26519
Retail Price:	$3.99
MISB:	N/A

 # 2: graphic cover

Ref. No.:	26520
Retail Price:	$3.99
MISB:	N/A

 # 2: photo cover

Ref. No.:	26521
Retail Price:	$3.99
MISB:	N/A

 # 3: graphic cover

Ref. No.:	26522
Retail Price:	$3.99
MISB:	N/A

 # 3: photo cover

Ref. No.:	26523
Retail Price:	$3.99
MISB:	N/A

 # 4: graphic cover

Ref. No.:	26524
Retail Price:	$3.99
MISB:	N/A

 # 4: photo cover

Ref. No.:	26525
Retail Price:	$3.99
MISB:	N/A

BOBA FETT

 # 1/2

Ref. No.:	39020
Retail Price:	$3.00
MISB:	$6.00

Agent of Doom

Ref. No.:	16950
Retail Price:	$2.99
MISB:	$3.00

Bounty on Bar-Kooda

Ref. No.:	6415
Retail Price:	$3.95
MISB:	$5.00

Enemy of the Empire # 1

Ref. No.:	6773
Retail Price:	$2.95
MISB:	N/A

Enemy of the Empire # 2

Ref. No.:	6774
Retail Price:	$2.95
MISB:	N/A

Enemy of the Empire # 3

Ref. No.:	6775
Retail Price:	$2.95
MISB:	N/A

Enemy of the Empire # 4

Ref. No.:	6776
Retail Price:	$2.95
MISB:	N/A

Murder Most Foul

Ref. No.:	6417
Retail Price:	$3.95
MISB:	$6.00

Twin Engines of Destruction

Ref. No.:	26482
Retail Price:	$2.95
MISB:	$5.00

When the Fat Lady Swings

Ref. No.:	6416
Retail Price:	$3.95
MISB:	$5.00

BOUNTY HUNTERS

Aurra Sing: gold logo

Ref. No.:	41313
Retail Price:	$2.95
MISB:	N/A

Aurra Sing: standard cover

Ref. No.:	6777
Retail Price:	$2.95
MISB:	N/A

Kenix Kil

Ref. No.:	6778
Retail Price:	$2.95
MISB:	N/A

Scoundrel's Wages

Ref. No.:	6780
Retail Price:	$2.95
MISB:	N/A

CHEWBACCA

 # 1: special edition

Ref. No.:	41325
Retail Price:	$2.95
MISB:	N/A

 # 1: standard cover

Ref. No.:	6769
Retail Price:	$2.95
MISB:	N/A

 # 2

Ref. No.:	6770
Retail Price:	$2.95
MISB:	N/A

 # 3

Ref. No.:	26481
Retail Price:	$2.95
MISB:	N/A

 # 4

Ref. No.:	6772
Retail Price:	$2.95
MISB:	N/A

CLASSIC STAR WARS

 # 1

Ref. No.:	6357
Retail Price:	$2.50
MISB:	$6.00

 # 2

Ref. No.:	6358
Retail Price:	$2.50
MISB:	$4.00

 # 3

Ref. No.:	6359
Retail Price:	$2.50
MISB:	$4.00

 # 4

Ref. No.:	6360
Retail Price:	$2.50
MISB:	$4.00

 # 5

Ref. No.:	6361
Retail Price:	$2.50
MISB:	$4.00

 # 6

Ref. No.:	6362
Retail Price:	$2.50
MISB:	$4.00

 # 7

Ref. No.:	6363
Retail Price:	$2.50
MISB:	$4.00

 # 8

Ref. No.:	6376
Retail Price:	$2.50
MISB:	$4.00

 # 9

Ref. No.:	6364
Retail Price:	$2.50
MISB:	$4.00

 # 10

Ref. No.:	6365
Retail Price:	$2.50
MISB:	$4.00

 # 11

Ref. No.:	6366
Retail Price:	$2.50
MISB:	$3.00

 # 12

Ref. No.:	6367
Retail Price:	$2.50
MISB:	$3.00

 # 13

Ref. No.:	6368
Retail Price:	$2.50
MISB:	$3.00

 # 14

Ref. No.:	6369
Retail Price:	$2.50
MISB:	$3.00

 # 15

Ref. No.:	6370
Retail Price:	$2.50
MISB:	$3.00

 # 16

Ref. No.:	6371
Retail Price:	$2.50
MISB:	$3.00

 # 17

Ref. No.:	6372
Retail Price:	$2.50
MISB:	$3.00

 # 18

Ref. No.:	6373
Retail Price:	$2.50
MISB:	$3.00

19

Ref. No.: 6374
Retail Price: $2.50
MISB: $3.00

20

Ref. No.: 6375
Retail Price: $2.50
MISB: $3.50

A New Hope # 1

Ref. No.: 6387
Retail Price: $3.95
MISB: $5.50

A New Hope # 2

Ref. No.: 6388
Retail Price: $3.95
MISB: $5.50

Devilworlds # 1

Ref. No.: 6794
Retail Price: $2.50
MISB: $3.50

Devilworlds # 2

Ref. No.: 6795
Retail Price: $2.50
MISB: $3.50

Han Solo at Stars' End # 1

Ref. No.: 16974
Retail Price: $2.95
MISB: $3.50

Han Solo at Stars' End # 2

Ref. No.: 16975
Retail Price: $2.95
MISB: $3.50

Han Solo at Stars' End # 3

Ref. No.: 16976
Retail Price: $2.95
MISB: $3.50

Return of the Jedi # 1

Ref. No.: 6390
Retail Price: $3.50
MISB: $3.50

Return of the Jedi # 2

Ref. No.: 6391
Retail Price: $3.50
MISB: $3.50

The Early Adventures # 1

Ref. No.: 6377
Retail Price: $2.50
MISB: $3.50

The Early Adventures # 2

Ref. No.: 6378
Retail Price: $2.50
MISB: $3.50

The Early Adventures # 3

Ref. No.: 6385
Retail Price: $2.50
MISB: $3.50

The Early Adventures # 4

Ref. No.: 6379
Retail Price: $2.50
MISB: $3.50

The Early Adventures # 5

Ref. No.: 6380
Retail Price: $2.50
MISB: $3.50

The Early Adventures # 6

Ref. No.: 6381
Retail Price: $2.50
MISB: $3.50

The Early Adventures # 7

Ref. No.: 6382
Retail Price: $2.50
MISB: $3.50

The Early Adventures # 8

Ref. No.: 6383
Retail Price: $2.50
MISB: $3.50

The Early Adventures # 9

Ref. No.: 6384
Retail Price: $2.50
MISB: $3.50

The Empire Strikes Back # 1

Ref. No.: 26517
Retail Price: $3.95
MISB: $3.50

The Empire Strikes Back # 2

Ref. No.: 6389
Retail Price: $3.95
MISB: $3.50

The Vandelheim Mission

Ref. No.:   6386
Retail Price: $2.50
MISB: $3.50

CLONE WARS OBSESSION

1

Ref. No.:   42263
Retail Price: $6.95
MISB: N/A

2

Ref. No.:   42264
Retail Price: $6.95
MISB: N/A

3

Ref. No.:   42265
Retail Price: $6.95
MISB: N/A

4

Ref. No.:   42266
Retail Price: $6.95
MISB: N/A

5

Ref. No.:   42267
Retail Price: $6.95
MISB: N/A

CLONE WARS ANIMATED ADVENTURES

Comic Digest Volume 1

Ref. No.:   42280
Retail Price: $6.95

Comic Digest Volume 2

Ref. No.:   42881
Retail Price: $6.95

Free Comic Book Day 2004

Ref. No.:   17947
Retail Price: N/A
MISB: $2.00

CRIMSON EMPIRE

1

Ref. No.:   6477
Retail Price: $2.95
MISB: $7.00

2

Ref. No.:   6478
Retail Price: $2.95
MISB: $5.00

3

Ref. No.:   6479
Retail Price: $2.95
MISB: $5.00

4

Ref. No.:   6480
Retail Price: $2.95
MISB: $5.00

5

Ref. No.:   6481
Retail Price: $2.95
MISB: $5.00

6

Ref. No.:   6482
Retail Price: $2.95
MISB: $5.00

CRIMSON EMPIRE II

Council of Blood # 1

Ref. No.:   6763
Retail Price: $2.95
MISB: $4.00

Council of Blood # 2

Ref. No.:   6764
Retail Price: $2.95
MISB: $4.00

Council of Blood # 3

Ref. No.:   6765
Retail Price: $2.95
MISB: $4.00

Council of Blood # 4

Ref. No.:   6766
Retail Price: $2.95
MISB: $4.00

Council of Blood # 5

Ref. No.:   6767
Retail Price: $2.95
MISB: $4.00

Council of Blood # 6

Ref. No.:   6768
Retail Price: $2.95
MISB: $4.00

DARK EMPIRE

1
Ref. No.:	6335
Retail Price:	$2.95
MISB:	$9.00

2
Ref. No.:	6336
Retail Price:	$2.95
MISB:	$12.00

3
Ref. No.:	6327
Retail Price:	$2.95
MISB:	$6.00

4
Ref. No.:	6328
Retail Price:	$2.95
MISB:	$6.00

5
Ref. No.:	6329
Retail Price:	$2.95
MISB:	$4.00

6
Ref. No.:	6330
Retail Price:	$2.95
MISB:	$6.00

Empire's End # 1
Ref. No.:	6355
Retail Price:	$2.95
MISB:	$4.00

Empire's End # 2
Ref. No.:	6356
Retail Price:	$2.95
MISB:	$4.00

Gold Edition Cover Boxed Set
Ref. No.:	6341
Retail Price:	$90.00
MISB:	N/A

Preview Copy (Special Price)
Ref. No.:	6346
Retail Price:	$120.00
MISB:	N/A

Wizard # 67 Ace Edition
Ref. No.:	6343
Retail Price:	N/A
MISB:	N/A

DARK EMPIRE II

1
Ref. No.:	6697
Retail Price:	$2.95
MISB:	$5.00

2
Ref. No.:	6699
Retail Price:	$2.95
MISB:	$4.00

3
Ref. No.:	6701
Retail Price:	$2.95
MISB:	$4.00

4
Ref. No.:	6703
Retail Price:	$2.95
MISB:	$4.00

5
Ref. No.:	6705
Retail Price:	$2.95
MISB:	$4.00

6
Ref. No.:	6707
Retail Price:	$2.95
MISB:	$4.00

Gold Edition Cover Boxed Set
Ref. No.:	6353
Retail Price:	$35.00
MISB:	N/A

Hero Special
Ref. No.:	6354
Retail Price:	N/A
MISB:	N/A

DARTH MAUL

1: graphic cover
Ref. No.:	6650
Retail Price:	$2.95
MISB:	$3.50

1: photo cover
Ref. No.:	6656
Retail Price:	$2.95
MISB:	$3.50

2: graphic cover
Ref. No.:	6657
Retail Price:	$2.99
MISB:	$3.50

 # 2: photo cover

Ref. No.:	6658
Retail Price:	$2.99
MISB:	$3.50

 # 3: graphic cover

Ref. No.:	26466
Retail Price:	$2.99
MISB:	$3.50

 # 3: photo cover

Ref. No.:	26475
Retail Price:	$2.99
MISB:	$3.50

 # 4: graphic cover

Ref. No.:	26476
Retail Price:	$2.99
MISB:	$3.50

 # 4: photo cover

Ref. No.:	26477
Retail Price:	$2.99
MISB:	$3.50

DROIDS

 # 1

Ref. No.:	5996
Retail Price:	$0.75
MISB:	$3.50

 # 2

Ref. No.:	5997
Retail Price:	$0.75
MISB:	$3.50

 # 3

Ref. No.:	5998
Retail Price:	$0.75
MISB:	$3.50

 # 4

Ref. No.:	5999
Retail Price:	$0.75
MISB:	$3.50

 # 5

Ref. No.:	6000
Retail Price:	$0.75
MISB:	$3.50

 # 6

Ref. No.:	6001
Retail Price:	$0.75
MISB:	$3.50

 # 7

Ref. No.:	6002
Retail Price:	$0.75
MISB:	$3.50

 # 8

Ref. No.:	6003
Retail Price:	$1.00
MISB:	$3.50

 # 1

Ref. No.:	6250
Retail Price:	$2.95
MISB:	$3.50

 # 2

Ref. No.:	6252
Retail Price:	$2.50
MISB:	$3.50

 # 3

Ref. No.:	6253
Retail Price:	$2.50
MISB:	$3.50

 # 4

Ref. No.:	6255
Retail Price:	$2.50
MISB:	$3.50

 # 5

Ref. No.:	6257
Retail Price:	$2.50
MISB:	$3.50

 # 6

Ref. No.:	6259
Retail Price:	$2.50
MISB:	$3.50

Special One-shot Issue

Ref. No.:	6263
Retail Price:	$2.50
MISB:	$3.50

The Mixed-Up Droid

Ref. No.:	6293
Retail Price:	$2.50
MISB:	$3.50

The Protocol Offensive

Ref. No.:	6294
Retail Price:	$4.95
MISB:	$5.50

EMPIRE

1 Betrayal # 1

Ref. No.:	6205
Retail Price:	$2.99
MISB:	N/A

2 Betrayal # 2

Ref. No.:	6214
Retail Price:	$2.99
MISB:	N/A

3 Betrayal # 3

Ref. No.:	6292
Retail Price:	$2.99
MISB:	N/A

4 Betrayal # 4

Ref. No.:	6771
Retail Price:	$2.99
MISB:	N/A

5 Princess Warrior # 1

Ref. No.:	6779
Retail Price:	$2.99
MISB:	N/A

6 Surrender or Die!

Ref. No.:	6786
Retail Price:	$2.99
MISB:	N/A

7 Sacrifice!

Ref. No.:	26516
Retail Price:	$2.99
MISB:	N/A

8 Darklighter # 1

Ref. No.:	26526
Retail Price:	$2.99
MISB:	N/A

9 Darklighter # 2

Ref. No.:	26527
Retail Price:	$2.99
MISB:	N/A

10 The Short, Happy Life of Roons Sewell # 1

Ref. No.:	26528
Retail Price:	$2.99
MISB:	N/A

11 The Short, Happy Life of Roons Sewell # 2

Ref. No.:	26529
Retail Price:	$2.99
MISB:	N/A

12 Darklighter # 3

Ref. No.:	26530
Retail Price:	$2.99
MISB:	N/A

13 A Stormtrooper's Dilemma—Treason on the Death Star!

Ref. No.:	26531
Retail Price:	$2.99
MISB:	N/A

14 The Savage Heart

Ref. No.:	35805
Retail Price:	$2.99
MISB:	N/A

15 Darklighter # 4

Ref. No.:	35806
Retail Price:	$2.99
MISB:	N/A

16 To the Last Man # 1

Ref. No.:	35807
Retail Price:	$2.99
MISB:	N/A

17 To the Last Man # 2

Ref. No.:	35808
Retail Price:	$2.99
MISB:	N/A

18 To the Last Man # 3

Ref. No.:	35809
Retail Price:	$2.99
MISB:	N/A

19 Target Vader

Ref. No.:	40247
Retail Price:	$2.99
MISB:	N/A

20 A Little Piece of Home # 1

Ref. No.:	40248
Retail Price:	$2.99
MISB:	N/A

21 A Little Piece of Home # 2

Ref. No.:	39779
Retail Price:	$2.99
MISB:	N/A

22 Alone Together

Ref. No.:	42313
Retail Price:	$2.99
MISB:	N/A

23

Ref. No.:	42329
Retail Price:	$2.99
MISB:	N/A

EWOKS

1

Ref. No.:	6004
Retail Price:	$0.65
MISB:	$3.50

2

Ref. No.:	6005
Retail Price:	$0.65
MISB:	$3.50

3

Ref. No.:	6006
Retail Price:	$0.65
MISB:	$3.50

4

Ref. No.:	6007
Retail Price:	$0.65
MISB:	$3.50

5

Ref. No.:	6008
Retail Price:	$0.65
MISB:	$3.50

6

Ref. No.:	6009
Retail Price:	$0.65
MISB:	$3.50

7

Ref. No.:	6010
Retail Price:	$0.75
MISB:	$3.50

8

Ref. No.:	6011
Retail Price:	$0.75
MISB:	$3.50

9

Ref. No.:	6012
Retail Price:	$0.75
MISB:	$3.50

10

Ref. No.:	6013
Retail Price:	$0.75
MISB:	$3.50

11

Ref. No.:	6014
Retail Price:	$0.75
MISB:	$3.50

12

Ref. No.:	6015
Retail Price:	$0.75
MISB:	$3.50

13

Ref. No.:	6016
Retail Price:	$0.75
MISB:	$3.50

14

Ref. No.:	6017
Retail Price:	$1.00
MISB:	$3.50

Star Comics Magazine # 1

Ref. No.:	6018
Retail Price:	$0.75
MISB:	$3.50

Star Comics Magazine # 2

Ref. No.:	6019
Retail Price:	$0.75
MISB:	$3.50

Star Comics Magazine # 3

Ref. No.:	6020
Retail Price:	$0.75
MISB:	$3.50

Star Comics Magazine # 4

Ref. No.:	12367
Retail Price:	$0.75
MISB:	$3.50

Star Comics Magazine # 5

Ref. No.:	6021
Retail Price:	$0.75
MISB:	$3.50

INFINITIES

A New Hope # 1: gold foil reprint

Ref. No.:	38992
Retail Price:	$2.99
MISB:	N/A

A New Hope # 1: standard cover

Ref. No.:	16940
Retail Price:	$2.99
MISB:	N/A

A New Hope # 2

Ref. No.:	16941
Retail Price:	$2.95
MISB:	N/A

A New Hope # 3

Ref. No.:	16942
Retail Price:	$2.95
MISB:	N/A

A New Hope # 4

Ref. No.:	16943
Retail Price:	$2.95
MISB:	N/A

Return of the Jedi # 1

Ref. No.:	35811
Retail Price:	$2.99
MISB:	N/A

Return of the Jedi # 2

Ref. No.:	35812
Retail Price:	$2.99
MISB:	N/A

Return of the Jedi # 3

Ref. No.:	35813
Retail Price:	$2.99
MISB:	N/A

Return of the Jedi # 4

Ref. No.:	35814
Retail Price:	$2.99
MISB:	N/A

The Empire Strikes Back # 1

Ref. No.:	6414
Retail Price:	$2.99
MISB:	N/A

The Empire Strikes Back # 2

Ref. No.:	6418
Retail Price:	$2.99
MISB:	N/A

The Empire Strikes Back # 3

Ref. No.:	6648
Retail Price:	$2.99
MISB:	N/A

The Empire Strikes Back # 4

Ref. No.:	6649
Retail Price:	$2.99
MISB:	N/A

JABBA THE HUTT

Betrayal

Ref. No.:	6298
Retail Price:	$2.50
MISB:	$4.00

The Dynasty Trap

Ref. No.:	6297
Retail Price:	$2.50
MISB:	$4.00

The Garr Suppoon Hit

Ref. No.:	6295
Retail Price:	$2.50
MISB:	$4.00

The Hunger of Princess Nampi

Ref. No.:	6296
Retail Price:	$2.50
MISB:	$4.00

The Jabba Tape

Ref. No.:	6805
Retail Price:	$2.95
MISB:	$4.50

JANGO FETT OPEN SEASONS

1

Ref. No.:	26565
Retail Price:	$2.99
MISB:	N/A

2

Ref. No.:	26566
Retail Price:	$2.99
MISB:	N/A

3

Ref. No.:	26567
Retail Price:	$2.99
MISB:	N/A

4

Ref. No.:	26568
Retail Price:	$2.99
MISB:	N/A

Preview

Ref. No.:	39750

JEDI

Aayla Secura

Ref. No.:	26569
Retail Price:	$4.99
MISB:	N/A

Count Dooku

Ref. No.: 35803
Retail Price: $4.99
MISB: N/A

Mace Windu

Ref. No.: 26570
Retail Price: $4.99
MISB: N/A

Shaak Ti

Ref. No.: 16973
Retail Price: $4.99
MISB: N/A

Yoda

Ref. No.: 42279
Retail Price: $4.99
MISB: N/A

JEDI ACADEMY LEVIATHAN

 # 1

Ref. No.: 6759
Retail Price: $2.95
MISB: N/A

 # 2

Ref. No.: 6760
Retail Price: $2.95
MISB: N/A

 # 3

Ref. No.: 6761
Retail Price: $2.95
MISB: N/A

 # 4

Ref. No.: 6762
Retail Price: $2.95
MISB: N/A

JEDI COUNCIL: ACTS OF WAR

 # 1

Ref. No.: 16959
Retail Price: $2.95
MISB: N/A

 # 2

Ref. No.: 16960
Retail Price: $2.95
MISB: N/A

 # 3

Ref. No.: 16961
Retail Price: $2.95
MISB: N/A

 # 4

Ref. No.: 16962
Retail Price: $2.95
MISB: N/A

JEDI QUEST

 # 1: foil cover

Ref. No.: 39751
Retail Price: $2.99
MISB: N/A

 # 1: standard cover

Ref. No.: 26543
Retail Price: $2.99
MISB: N/A

 # 2

Ref. No.: 26544
Retail Price: $2.99
MISB: N/A

 # 3

Ref. No.: 26545
Retail Price: $2.99
MISB: N/A

 # 4

Ref. No.: 26546
Retail Price: $2.99
MISB: N/A

JEDI VS. SITH

 # 1: Dynamic Forces special foil cover

Ref. No.: 39751
Retail Price: $2.99
MISB: N/A

 # 1: standard cover

Ref. No.: 16948
Retail Price: $2.99
MISB: N/A

 # 2

Ref. No.: 16949
Retail Price: $2.99
MISB: N/A

 # 3

Ref. No.: 16944
Retail Price: $2.99
MISB: N/A

 # 4

Ref. No.: 16945
Retail Price: $2.99
MISB: N/A

5

Ref. No.:	16946
Retail Price:	$2.99
MISB:	N/A

6

Ref. No.:	16947
Retail Price:	$2.99
MISB:	N/A

MARA JADE

By the Emperor's Hand # 1

Ref. No.:	6753
Retail Price:	$2.95
MISB:	N/A

By the Emperor's Hand # 2

Ref. No.:	6754
Retail Price:	$2.95
MISB:	N/A

By the Emperor's Hand # 3

Ref. No.:	6755
Retail Price:	$2.95
MISB:	N/A

By the Emperor's Hand # 4

Ref. No.:	6756
Retail Price:	$2.95
MISB:	N/A

By the Emperor's Hand # 5

Ref. No.:	6757
Retail Price:	$2.95
MISB:	N/A

By the Emperor's Hand # 6

Ref. No.:	6758
Retail Price:	$2.95
MISB:	N/A

MARVEL STAR WARS

1: 30 cents (price in a square or diamond)

Ref. No.:	5899
Retail Price:	$0.30
MISB:	$17.00

1: 35 cents

Ref. No.:	5902
Retail Price:	$0.35
MISB:	$229.00

1: Reprint $1.25 1982

Ref. No.:	14240
Retail Price:	$1.25
MISB:	$5.00

1: Reprint 30 cents

Ref. No.:	5927
Retail Price:	$0.30
MISB:	$17.00

1: Reprint 35 cents

Ref. No.:	5929
Retail Price:	$0.35
MISB:	$21.00

2

Ref. No.:	33272
Retail Price:	$0.30
MISB:	$9.00

2: 30 cents (price in a square or diamond)

Ref. No.:	5903
Retail Price:	$0.30
MISB:	$9.00

2: 35 cents

Ref. No.:	5906
Retail Price:	$0.35
MISB:	$21.00

2: Reprint 30 cents

Ref. No.:	5931
Retail Price:	$0.30
MISB:	$9.00

2: Reprint 35 cents

Ref. No.:	5933
Retail Price:	$0.35
MISB:	$21.00

3: 30 cents (price in a square or diamond)

Ref. No.:	5909
Retail Price:	$0.30
MISB:	$9.00

3: 35 cents

Ref. No.:	5911
Retail Price:	$0.35
MISB:	$21.00

3: Reprint 30 cents

Ref. No.:	5935
Retail Price:	$0.30
MISB:	$9.00

3: Reprint 35 cents

Ref. No.:	5937
Retail Price:	$0.35
MISB:	$21.00

4: 30 cents (price in a square or diamond)

Ref. No.:	5914
Retail Price:	$0.30
MISB:	$9.00

4: 35 cents

Ref. No.:	5918
Retail Price:	$0.35
MISB:	$21.00

4: Reprint 30 cents

Ref. No.:	5939
Retail Price:	$0.30
MISB:	$9.00

4: Reprint 35 cents

Ref. No.:	5941
Retail Price:	$0.35
MISB:	$21.00

5: 30 cents (price in a square or diamond)

Ref. No.:	5913
Retail Price:	$0.30
MISB:	$6.00

5: 35 cents

Ref. No.:	5918
Retail Price:	$0.35
MISB:	$6.00

5: Reprint 30 cents

Ref. No.:	5943
Retail Price:	$0.30
MISB:	$6.00

5: Reprint 35 cents

Ref. No.:	5945
Retail Price:	$0.35
MISB:	$6.00

6: 30 cents (price in a square or diamond)

Ref. No.:	5907
Retail Price:	$0.30
MISB:	$6.00

6: 35 cents

Ref. No.:	5921
Retail Price:	$0.35
MISB:	$6.00

6: Reprint 30 cents

Ref. No.:	5947
Retail Price:	$0.30
MISB:	$6.00

6: Reprint 35 cents

Ref. No.:	5949
Retail Price:	$0.35
MISB:	$6.00

7

Ref. No.:	5923
Retail Price:	$0.35
MISB:	$3.00

8

Ref. No.:	5924
Retail Price:	$0.35
MISB:	$3.00

9

Ref. No.:	5925
Retail Price:	$0.35
MISB:	$3.00

10

Ref. No.:	6066
Retail Price:	$0.35
MISB:	$3.00

11

Ref. No.:	6067
Retail Price:	$0.35
MISB:	$3.00

12

Ref. No.:	6068
Retail Price:	$0.35
MISB:	$3.00

13

Ref. No.:	6069
Retail Price:	$0.35
MISB:	$3.00

14

Ref. No.:	6070
Retail Price:	$0.35
MISB:	$3.00

15

Ref. No.:	6071
Retail Price:	$0.35
MISB:	$3.00

16

Ref. No.:	6072
Retail Price:	$0.35
MISB:	$3.00

17
Ref. No.: 6073
Retail Price: $0.35
MISB: $3.00

18
Ref. No.: 6074
Retail Price: $0.35
MISB: $3.00

19
Ref. No.: 6075
Retail Price: $0.35
MISB: $3.00

20
Ref. No.: 6076
Retail Price: $0.35
MISB: $3.00

21
Ref. No.: 6077
Retail Price: $0.35
MISB: $2.50

22
Ref. No.: 6078
Retail Price: $0.35
MISB: $3.00

23
Ref. No.: 6079
Retail Price: $0.35
MISB: $3.00

24
Ref. No.: 6080
Retail Price: $0.40
MISB: $2.50

25
Ref. No.: 6081
Retail Price: $0.40
MISB: $2.50

26
Ref. No.: 6082
Retail Price: $0.40
MISB: $2.50

27
Ref. No.: 6083
Retail Price: $0.40
MISB: $2.50

28
Ref. No.: 6084
Retail Price: $0.40
MISB: $2.50

29
Ref. No.: 6085
Retail Price: $0.40
MISB: $2.50

30
Ref. No.: 6086
Retail Price: $0.40
MISB: $2.50

31
Ref. No.: 6087
Retail Price: $0.40
MISB: $2.50

32
Ref. No.: 6088
Retail Price: $0.40
MISB: $2.50

33
Ref. No.: 6089
Retail Price: $0.40
MISB: $2.50

34
Ref. No.: 6090
Retail Price: $0.40
MISB: $2.50

35
Ref. No.: 6091
Retail Price: $0.40
MISB: $2.50

36
Ref. No.: 6092
Retail Price: $0.40
MISB: $2.50

37
Ref. No.: 6093
Retail Price: $0.40
MISB: $2.50

38
Ref. No.: 6094
Retail Price: $0.40
MISB: $2.50

39

Ref. No.:	6095
Retail Price:	$0.50
MISB:	$2.50

40

Ref. No.:	6096
Retail Price:	$0.50
MISB:	$2.50

41

Ref. No.:	6097
Retail Price:	$0.50
MISB:	$2.50

42

Ref. No.:	6098
Retail Price:	$0.50
MISB:	$2.50

43

Ref. No.:	6099
Retail Price:	$0.50
MISB:	$2.50

44

Ref. No.:	6100
Retail Price:	$0.50
MISB:	$2.50

45

Ref. No.:	6101
Retail Price:	$0.50
MISB:	$2.50

46

Ref. No.:	6102
Retail Price:	$0.50
MISB:	$2.50

47

Ref. No.:	6103
Retail Price:	$0.50
MISB:	$2.50

48

Ref. No.:	6104
Retail Price:	$0.50
MISB:	$2.50

49

Ref. No.:	6105
Retail Price:	$0.50
MISB:	$2.50

50

Ref. No.:	6106
Retail Price:	$0.75
MISB:	$2.50

51

Ref. No.:	6107
Retail Price:	$0.50
MISB:	$2.50

52

Ref. No.:	6108
Retail Price:	$0.50
MISB:	$2.50

53

Ref. No.:	6109
Retail Price:	$0.50
MISB:	$2.50

54

Ref. No.:	6110
Retail Price:	$0.50
MISB:	$2.50

55

Ref. No.:	6111
Retail Price:	$0.60
MISB:	$2.50

56

Ref. No.:	6112
Retail Price:	$0.60
MISB:	$2.50

57

Ref. No.:	6113
Retail Price:	$0.60
MISB:	$2.50

58

Ref. No.:	6114
Retail Price:	$0.60
MISB:	$2.50

59

Ref. No.:	6115
Retail Price:	$0.60
MISB:	$2.50

60

Ref. No.:	6116
Retail Price:	$0.60
MISB:	$2.50

61

Ref. No.:   6117
Retail Price: $0.60
MISB: $2.50

62

Ref. No.:   6118
Retail Price: $0.60
MISB: $2.50

63

Ref. No.:   6119
Retail Price: $0.60
MISB: $2.50

64

Ref. No.:   6120
Retail Price: $0.60
MISB: $2.50

65

Ref. No.:   6121
Retail Price: $0.60
MISB: $2.50

66

Ref. No.:   6122
Retail Price: $0.60
MISB: $2.50

67

Ref. No.:   6123
Retail Price: $0.60
MISB: $2.50

68

Ref. No.:   6065
Retail Price: $0.60
MISB: $2.50

69

Ref. No.:   6125
Retail Price: $0.60
MISB: $2.50

70

Ref. No.:   6126
Retail Price: $0.60
MISB: $2.50

71

Ref. No.:   6128
Retail Price: $0.60
MISB: $2.75

72

Ref. No.:   6129
Retail Price: $0.60
MISB: $2.75

73

Ref. No.:   6130
Retail Price: $0.60
MISB: $2.75

74

Ref. No.:   6132
Retail Price: $0.60
MISB: $2.75

75

Ref. No.:   6132
Retail Price: $0.60
MISB: $2.75

76

Ref. No.:   6133
Retail Price: $0.60
MISB: $2.75

77

Ref. No.:   6134
Retail Price: $0.60
MISB: $2.75

78

Ref. No.:   6135
Retail Price: $0.60
MISB: $2.75

79

Ref. No.:   6136
Retail Price: $0.60
MISB: $2.75

80

Ref. No.:   6137
Retail Price: $0.60
MISB: $2.75

81

Ref. No.:   6138
Retail Price: $0.60
MISB: $3.00

82

Ref. No.:   6139
Retail Price: $0.60
MISB: $3.00

83

Ref. No.:	6140
Retail Price:	$0.60
MISB:	$3.00

84

Ref. No.:	6141
Retail Price:	$0.60
MISB:	$3.00

85

Ref. No.:	6142
Retail Price:	$0.60
MISB:	$3.00

86

Ref. No.:	6143
Retail Price:	$0.60
MISB:	$3.00

87

Ref. No.:	6144
Retail Price:	$0.60
MISB:	$3.00

88

Ref. No.:	6145
Retail Price:	$0.60
MISB:	$3.00

89

Ref. No.:	6146
Retail Price:	$0.60
MISB:	$3.00

90

Ref. No.:	6147
Retail Price:	$0.60
MISB:	$3.00

91

Ref. No.:	6148
Retail Price:	$0.60
MISB:	$4.00

92

Ref. No.:	6149
Retail Price:	$0.60
MISB:	$4.00

93

Ref. No.:	6150
Retail Price:	$0.60
MISB:	$4.00

94

Ref. No.:	6151
Retail Price:	$0.65
MISB:	$4.00

95

Ref. No.:	6152
Retail Price:	$0.65
MISB:	$4.00

96

Ref. No.:	6153
Retail Price:	$0.65
MISB:	$4.00

97

Ref. No.:	6154
Retail Price:	$0.65
MISB:	$4.00

98

Ref. No.:	6155
Retail Price:	$0.65
MISB:	$4.00

99

Ref. No.:	6156
Retail Price:	$0.65
MISB:	$4.00

100

Ref. No.:	6157
Retail Price:	$1.25
MISB:	$5.00

101

Ref. No.:	6158
Retail Price:	$0.65
MISB:	$5.00

102

Ref. No.:	6159
Retail Price:	$0.65
MISB:	$5.00

103

Ref. No.:	6160
Retail Price:	$0.65
MISB:	$5.00

104

Ref. No.:	6161
Retail Price:	$0.75
MISB:	$5.00

105
Ref. No.: 6162
Retail Price: $0.75
MISB: $5.00

106
Ref. No.: 6163
Retail Price: $0.75
MISB: $5.00

107
Ref. No.: 6064
Retail Price: $0.75
MISB: $19.00

Annual # 1
Ref. No.: 5990
Retail Price: $0.75
MISB: $3.50

Annual # 2
Ref. No.: 5991
Retail Price: $1.00
MISB: $3.50

Annual # 3
Ref. No.: 5992
Retail Price: $1.00
MISB: $3.50

Marvel Age # 4
Ref. No.: 5993
Retail Price: $0.25
MISB: $3.00

Marvel Age # 10
Ref. No.: 5994
Retail Price: $0.25
MISB: $3.00

Marvel Age # 18
Ref. No.: 5995
Retail Price: $0.25
MISB: $3.00

Marvel Movie Showcase # 1
Ref. No.: 6031
Retail Price: $1.25
MISB: $2.50

Marvel Movie Showcase # 2
Ref. No.: 41302
Retail Price: $1.25
MISB: $2.50

Marvel Special Edition # 1
Ref. No.: 14241
Retail Price: $1.00
MISB: $4.50

Marvel Special Edition # 2
Ref. No.: 14242
Retail Price: $1.00
MISB: $4.50

Marvel Special Edition # 3
Ref. No.: 6025
Retail Price: $2.50
MISB: $6.50

Star Wars Treasury Size # 1
Ref. No.: 6028
Retail Price: $1.00
MISB: $3.00

Star Wars Treasury Size # 2
Ref. No.: 6029
Retail Price: $1.00
MISB: $3.00

Star Wars Treasury Size # 3
Ref. No.: 6030
Retail Price: $2.50
MISB: $3.00

MISCELLANEOUS

Dark Horse Comics # 7
Ref. No.: N/A
Retail Price: $2.50
MISB: $5.00

Dark Horse Comics # 8
Ref. No.: N/A
Retail Price: $2.50
MISB: $5.00

Dark Horse Comics # 9
Ref. No.: N/A
Retail Price: $2.50
MISB: $5.00

Dark Horse Comics # 17
Ref. No.: N/A
Retail Price: $2.50
MISB: $2.50

Dark Horse Comics # 18
Ref. No.: N/A
Retail Price: $2.50
MISB: $2.50

Dark Horse Comics # 19

Ref. No.:   N/A
Retail Price: $2.50
MISB: $2.50

Dark Horse Extra # 21 "Hard Currency" part 1

Ref. No.:   N/A
Retail Price: $0.25
MISB: $5.00

Dark Horse Extra # 22 "Hard Currency" part 2

Ref. No.:   N/A
Retail Price: $0.25
MISB: $5.00

Dark Horse Extra # 23 "Hard Currency" part 3

Ref. No.:   N/A
Retail Price: $0.25
MISB: $5.00

Dark Horse Extra # 24 "Hard Currency" part 4

Ref. No.:   N/A
Retail Price: $0.25
MISB: $5.00

Dark Horse Extra # 35 "Heart of Fire" part 1

Ref. No.:   N/A
Retail Price: $0.25
MISB: $5.00

Dark Horse Extra # 36 "Heart of Fire" part 2

Ref. No.:   N/A
Retail Price: $0.25
MISB: $5.00

Dark Horse Extra # 37 "Heart of Fire" part 3

Ref. No.:   N/A
Retail Price: $0.25
MISB: $5.00

Dark Horse Extra # 44 "Poison Moon" part 1

Ref. No.:   N/A
Retail Price: $0.25
MISB: $5.00

Dark Horse Extra # 45 "Poison Moon" part 2

Ref. No.:   N/A
Retail Price: $0.25
MISB: $5.00

Dark Horse Extra # 46 "Poison Moon" part 3

Ref. No.:   N/A
Retail Price: $0.25
MISB: $5.00

Dark Horse Extra # 47 "Poison Moon" part 4

Ref. No.:   N/A
Retail Price: $0.25
MISB: $5.00

Dark Horse Insider # 15

Ref. No.:   N/A
Retail Price: N/A
MISB: $5.00

Dark Horse Insider # 16

Ref. No.:   N/A
Retail Price: N/A
MISB: $5.00

Dark Horse Insider # 17

Ref. No.:   N/A
Retail Price: N/A
MISB: $5.00

Dark Horse Insider # 18

Ref. No.:   N/A
Retail Price: N/A
MISB: $5.00

Dark Horse Insider # 19

Ref. No.:   N/A
Retail Price: N/A
MISB: $5.00

Dark Horse Insider # 20

Ref. No.:   N/A
Retail Price: N/A
MISB: $5.00

Sergio Aragones Stomps Star Wars

Ref. No.:   26538
Retail Price: $2.95
MISB: $4.00

Shadow Stalker

Ref. No.:   6472
Retail Price: $2.95
MISB: $4.00

Star Wars # 0 American Entertainment Special Issue

Ref. No.:   26539
Retail Price: $10.00
MISB: N/A

Star Wars, a Valentine Story

Ref. No.:   16559
Retail Price: $3.50
MISB: N/A

Star Wars Hasbro/Toys "R" Us Exclusive # 1: Full of Surprises

Ref. No.: 15358
Retail Price: N/A
MISB: $5.00

Star Wars Hasbro/Toys "R" Us Exclusive # 2: Most Precious Weapon

Ref. No.: 35327
Retail Price: N/A
MISB: $5.00

Star Wars Hasbro/Toys "R" Us Exclusive # 3: Practice Makes Perfect

Ref. No.: 35328
Retail Price: N/A
MISB: $5.00

Star Wars Hasbro/Toys "R" Us Exclusive # 4: Machines of War

Ref. No.: 35329
Retail Price: N/A
MISB: $5.00

Starfighter Crossbones # 1

Ref. No.: 26551
Retail Price: $2.99
MISB: N/A

Starfighter Crossbones # 2

Ref. No.: 26552
Retail Price: $2.99
MISB: N/A

Starfighter Crossbones # 3

Ref. No.: 26553
Retail Price: $2.99
MISB: N/A

Tag and Bink Are Dead # 1

Ref. No.: 26559
Retail Price: $2.99
MISB: N/A

Tag and Bink Are Dead # 2

Ref. No.: 26560
Retail Price: $2.99
MISB: N/A

Tales from Mos Eisley

Ref. No.: 6470
Retail Price: $2.95
MISB: N/A

QUI-GON & OBI-WAN

Last Stand on Ord Mantell # 1: cover by Tony Daniel

Ref. No.: 26573
Retail Price: $2.99
MISB: N/A

Last Stand on Ord Mantell # 1: graphic cover

Ref. No.: 26571
Retail Price: $2.99
MISB: N/A

Last Stand on Ord Mantell # 1: photo cover

Ref. No.: 26572
Retail Price: $2.99
MISB: N/A

Last Stand on Ord Mantell # 2: graphic cover

Ref. No.: 26574
Retail Price: $2.99
MISB: N/A

Last Stand on Ord Mantell # 2: photo cover

Ref. No.: 26575
Retail Price: $2.99
MISB: N/A

Last Stand on Ord Mantell # 3: graphic cover

Ref. No.: 26576
Retail Price: $2.99
MISB: N/A

Last Stand on Ord Mantell # 3: photo cover

Ref. No.: 26577
Retail Price: $2.99
MISB: N/A

The Aurorient Express # 1

Ref. No.: 26578
Retail Price: $2.99
MISB: N/A

The Aurorient Express # 2

Ref. No.: 26579
Retail Price: $2.99
MISB: N/A

RETURN OF THE JEDI

1984 Hardcover (movie)

Ref. No.: 6037
Retail Price: N/A
MISB: N/A

1985 Hardcover

Ref. No.:   6038
Retail Price: N/A
MISB: N/A

Limited Series # 1

Ref. No.:   6042
Retail Price: $0.60
MISB: N/A

Limited Series # 2

Ref. No.:   6043
Retail Price: $0.60
MISB: N/A

Limited Series # 3

Ref. No.:   6044
Retail Price: $0.60
MISB: N/A

Limited Series # 4

Ref. No.:   6045
Retail Price: $0.60
MISB: N/A

Magazine Sized Edition

Ref. No.:   6046
Retail Price: N/A
MISB: N/A

The Official Comics Version

Ref. No.:   15287
Retail Price: $2.50
MISB: N/A

RIVER OF CHAOS

1

Ref. No.:   6299
Retail Price: $2.50
MISB: $4.00

2

Ref. No.:   6300
Retail Price: $2.50
MISB: $4.00

3

Ref. No.:   6301
Retail Price: $2.50
MISB: $4.00

4

Ref. No.:   6302
Retail Price: $2.50
MISB: $4.00

SHADOWS OF THE EMPIRE

1

Ref. No.:   6422
Retail Price: $2.95
MISB: $3.50

2

Ref. No.:   6423
Retail Price: $2.95
MISB: $3.50

3

Ref. No.:   6424
Retail Price: $2.95
MISB: $3.50

4

Ref. No.:   6425
Retail Price: $2.95
MISB: $3.50

5

Ref. No.:   6426
Retail Price: $2.95
MISB: $3.50

6

Ref. No.:   6427
Retail Price: $2.95
MISB: $3.50

Evolution # 1

Ref. No.:   6712
Retail Price: $2.95
MISB: N/A

Evolution # 2

Ref. No.:   6713
Retail Price: $2.95
MISB: N/A

Evolution # 3

Ref. No.:   6714
Retail Price: $2.95
MISB: N/A

Evolution # 4

Ref. No.:   6715
Retail Price: $2.95
MISB: N/A

Evolution # 5

Ref. No.:   3019
Retail Price: $2.95
MISB: N/A

Kenner Shadows of the Empire Comic (Boba Fett/IG-88)

Ref. No.:   6428
Retail Price: N/A
MISB: $3.00

Kenner Shadows of the Empire Comic (Vader/Xizor)

Ref. No.:   6429
Retail Price: N/A
MISB: $3.00

Mini-Comic w/ AMT models kits

Ref. No.:   6430
Retail Price: N/A
MISB: $3.00

SPLINTER OF THE MIND'S EYE

1

Ref. No.:   6410
Retail Price: $2.50
MISB: N/A

2

Ref. No.:   6411
Retail Price: $2.50
MISB: N/A

3

Ref. No.:   6412
Retail Price: $2.95
MISB: N/A

4

Ref. No.:   6413
Retail Price: $2.95
MISB: N/A

STAR WARS

1 Prelude to Rebellion # 1: foil cover

Ref. No.:   41319
Retail Price: $2.50
MISB: N/A

1 Prelude to Rebellion # 1: standard cover

Ref. No.:   14232
Retail Price: $2.50
MISB: N/A

2 Prelude to Rebellion # 2: foil cover

Ref. No.:   41320
Retail Price: $2.95
MISB: N/A

2 Prelude to Rebellion # 2: standard cover

Ref. No.:   14234
Retail Price: $2.95
MISB: N/A

3 Prelude to Rebellion # 3: foil cover

Ref. No.:   41321
Retail Price: $2.50
MISB: N/A

3 Prelude to Rebellion # 3: standard cover

Ref. No.:   14235
Retail Price: $2.50
MISB: N/A

4 Prelude to Rebellion # 4: foil cover

Ref. No.:   41322
Retail Price: $2.50
MISB: N/A

4 Prelude to Rebellion # 4: standard cover

Ref. No.:   14236
Retail Price: $2.50
MISB: N/A

5 Prelude to Rebellion # 5: foil cover

Ref. No.:   41323
Retail Price: $2.50
MISB: N/A

5 Prelude to Rebellion # 5: standard cover

Ref. No.:   14237
Retail Price: $2.50
MISB: N/A

6 Prelude to Rebellion # 6: foil cover

Ref. No.:   41324
Retail Price: $2.50
MISB: N/A

6 Prelude to Rebellion # 6: standard cover

Ref. No.:   14238
Retail Price: $2.50
MISB: N/A

7 Outlander # 1

Ref. No.:   26511
Retail Price: $2.50
MISB: N/A

8 Outlander # 2

Ref. No.:   26512
Retail Price: $2.50
MISB: N/A

9 Outlander # 3

Ref. No.:   26513
Retail Price: $2.50
MISB: N/A

10 Outlander # 4

Ref. No.:   26514
Retail Price: $2.50
MISB: N/A

11 Outlander # 5

Ref. No.:   26515
Retail Price: $2.50
MISB: N/A

12 Outlander # 6

Ref. No.:   16964
Retail Price: $2.50
MISB: N/A

13 Emissaries to Malastare # 1

Ref. No.:   6485
Retail Price: $2.95
MISB: N/A

14 Emissaries to Malastare # 2

Ref. No.:   6486
Retail Price: $2.50
MISB: N/A

15 Emissaries to Malastare # 3

Ref. No.:   6489
Retail Price: $2.50
MISB: N/A

16 Emissaries to Malastare # 4

Ref. No.:   6487
Retail Price: $2.50
MISB: N/A

17 Emissaries to Malastare # 5

Ref. No.:   6488
Retail Price: $2.95
MISB: N/A

18 Emissaries to Malastare # 6

Ref. No.:   6484
Retail Price: $2.95
MISB: N/A

19 Twilight # 1

Ref. No.:   16977
Retail Price: $2.95
MISB: N/A

20 Twilight # 2

Ref. No.:   16978
Retail Price: $2.95
MISB: N/A

21 Twilight # 3

Ref. No.:   16963
Retail Price: $2.95
MISB: N/A

22 Twilight # 4

Ref. No.:   16979
Retail Price: $2.95
MISB: N/A

23 Infinity's End # 1

Ref. No.:   16955
Retail Price: $2.99
MISB: N/A

24 Infinity's End # 2

Ref. No.:   16956
Retail Price: $2.99
MISB: N/A

25 Infinity's End # 3

Ref. No.:   16957
Retail Price: $2.99
MISB: N/A

26 Infinity's End # 4

Ref. No.:   16958
Retail Price: $2.99
MISB: N/A

27 Star Crash

Ref. No.:   16980
Retail Price: $2.99
MISB: N/A

28 The Hunt for Aura Sing # 1

Ref. No.:   16951
Retail Price: $2.99
MISB: N/A

29 The Hunt for Aura Sing # 2

Ref. No.:   16952
Retail Price: $2.99
MISB: N/A

30 The Hunt for Aura Sing # 3

Ref. No.:   16953
Retail Price: $2.99
MISB: N/A

31 The Hunt for Aura Sing # 4

Ref. No.:	16954
Retail Price:	$2.99
MISB:	N/A

32 Darkness # 1

Ref. No.:	16966
Retail Price:	$2.99
MISB:	N/A

33 Darkness # 2

Ref. No.:	16967
Retail Price:	$2.99
MISB:	N/A

34 Darkness # 3

Ref. No.:	16968
Retail Price:	$2.99
MISB:	N/A

35 Darkness # 4

Ref. No.:	16969
Retail Price:	$2.99
MISB:	N/A

36 The Stark Hyperspace War # 1

Ref. No.:	26554
Retail Price:	$2.99
MISB:	N/A

37 The Stark Hyperspace War # 2

Ref. No.:	26555
Retail Price:	$2.99
MISB:	N/A

38 The Stark Hyperspace War # 3

Ref. No.:	26556
Retail Price:	$2.99
MISB:	N/A

39 The Stark Hyperspace War # 4

Ref. No.:	26557
Retail Price:	$2.99
MISB:	N/A

40 The Devaronian Version # 1

Ref. No.:	26540
Retail Price:	$2.99
MISB:	N/A

41 The Devaronian Version # 2

Ref. No.:	26541
Retail Price:	$2.99
MISB:	N/A

42 Rite of Passage # 1

Ref. No.:	26547
Retail Price:	$2.99
MISB:	N/A

43 Rite of Passage # 2

Ref. No.:	26548
Retail Price:	$2.99
MISB:	N/A

44 Rite of Passage # 3

Ref. No.:	26549
Retail Price:	$2.99
MISB:	N/A

45 Rite of Passage # 4

Ref. No.:	26550
Retail Price:	$2.99
MISB:	N/A

REPUBLIC

46 Republic Honour and Duty # 1

Ref. No.:	26581
Retail Price:	$2.99
MISB:	N/A

47 Republic Honour and Duty # 2

Ref. No.:	26582
Retail Price:	$2.99
MISB:	N/A

48 Republic Honour and Duty # 3

Ref. No.:	26583
Retail Price:	$2.99
MISB:	N/A

49 Republic

Ref. No.:	26584
Retail Price:	$2.99
MISB:	N/A

50 Republic Sacrifice

Ref. No.:	26585
Retail Price:	$2.99
MISB:	N/A

51 Republic Graveyard Moon

Ref. No.:	16970
Retail Price:	$2.99
MISB:	N/A

52 Republic The New Face of War

Ref. No.:	16971
Retail Price:	$2.99
MISB:	N/A

53 Republic Jedi Knight . . . Jedi Dark!

Ref. No.:	16972
Retail Price:	$2.99
MISB:	N/A

54 Republic Jedi Fugitive

Ref. No.:	26586
Retail Price:	$2.99
MISB:	N/A

55 Republic The Battle of Jablim # 1

Ref. No.:	26587
Retail Price:	$2.99
MISB:	N/A

56 Republic The Battle of Jablim # 2

Ref. No.:	26588
Retail Price:	$2.99
MISB:	N/A

57 Republic The Padawans Stand Alone!

Ref. No.:	26589
Retail Price:	$2.99
MISB:	N/A

58 Republic The Battle of Jablim # 3

Ref. No.:	26590
Retail Price:	$2.99
MISB:	N/A

59 Enemy Lines

Ref. No.:	35810
Retail Price:	$2.99
MISB:	N/A

60 The Origin of Asajj Ventress

Ref. No.:	35800
Retail Price:	$2.99
MISB:	N/A

61 Bail Organa Fights for his Life!

Ref. No.:	21031
Retail Price:	$2.99
MISB:	N/A

62

Ref. No.:	38995
Retail Price:	$2.99
MISB:	N/A

63

Ref. No.:	40249
Retail Price:	$2.99
MISB:	N/A

64 Bloodlines

Ref. No.:	40250
Retail Price:	$2.99
MISB:	N/A

65 Show of Force # 1

Ref. No.:	42277
Retail Price:	$2.99
MISB:	N/A

66 Show of Force # 2

Ref. No.:	42278
Retail Price:	$2.99
MISB:	N/A

67 Great Power, Great Restraint . . .

Ref. No.:	42503
Retail Price:	$2.99
MISB:	N/A

#68

Ref. No.:	42504
Retail Price:	$2.99
MISB:	N/A

STAR WARS PIZZAZZ

1

Ref. No.:	6048
Retail Price:	$0.75
MISB:	$8.00

2

Ref. No.:	6049
Retail Price:	$0.75
MISB:	$4.50

3

Ref. No.:	6050
Retail Price:	$0.75
MISB:	$4.50

4

Ref. No.:	6051
Retail Price:	$0.75
MISB:	$4.50

5

Ref. No.:	6052
Retail Price:	$0.75
MISB:	$4.50

6

Ref. No.:	6053
Retail Price:	$0.75
MISB:	$4.50

7

Ref. No.:	6054
Retail Price:	$0.75
MISB:	$4.50

8

Ref. No.:	6055
Retail Price:	$0.75
MISB:	$4.50

9

Ref. No.:	6056
Retail Price:	$0.75
MISB:	$4.00

10

Ref. No.:	6057
Retail Price:	$0.75
MISB:	$4.00

11

Ref. No.:	6058
Retail Price:	$0.75
MISB:	$8.00

12

Ref. No.:	6059
Retail Price:	$0.75
MISB:	$4.00

13

Ref. No.:	6060
Retail Price:	$0.75
MISB:	$4.00

14

Ref. No.:	6061
Retail Price:	$0.75
MISB:	$4.00

15

Ref. No.:	6062
Retail Price:	$0.75
MISB:	$4.50

16

Ref. No.:	6063
Retail Price:	$0.75
MISB:	$4.50

STAR WARS TALES

1

Ref. No.:	41281
Retail Price:	$4.95
MISB:	N/A

2

Ref. No.:	26483
Retail Price:	$4.95
MISB:	N/A

3

Ref. No.:	26484
Retail Price:	$4.95
MISB:	N/A

4

Ref. No.:	26485
Retail Price:	$4.95
MISB:	N/A

5: graphic cover

Ref. No.:	26486
Retail Price:	$5.95
MISB:	N/A

5: photo cover

Ref. No.:	26499
Retail Price:	$5.95
MISB:	N/A

6: graphic cover

Ref. No.:	26487
Retail Price:	$5.95
MISB:	N/A

6: photo cover

Ref. No.:	26500
Retail Price:	$5.95
MISB:	N/A

7: graphic cover

Ref. No.:	26488
Retail Price:	$5.99
MISB:	N/A

7: photo cover

Ref. No.:	26501
Retail Price:	$5.99
MISB:	N/A

8: graphic cover

Ref. No.:	26489
Retail Price:	$5.99
MISB:	N/A

8: photo cover

Ref. No.:	26502
Retail Price:	$5.99
MISB:	N/A

 # 9: graphic cover

Ref. No.:	26490
Retail Price:	$5.99
MISB:	N/A

 # 9: photo cover

Ref. No.:	26503
Retail Price:	$5.99
MISB:	N/A

 # 10: graphic cover

Ref. No.:	26491
Retail Price:	$5.99
MISB:	N/A

 # 10: photo cover

Ref. No.:	26504
Retail Price:	$5.99
MISB:	N/A

 # 11: graphic cover

Ref. No.:	26492
Retail Price:	$5.99
MISB:	N/A

 # 11: photo cover

Ref. No.:	26505
Retail Price:	$5.99
MISB:	N/A

 # 12: graphic cover

Ref. No.:	26493
Retail Price:	$5.99
MISB:	N/A

 # 12: photo cover

Ref. No.:	26506
Retail Price:	$5.99
MISB:	N/A

 # 13: graphic cover

Ref. No.:	26494
Retail Price:	$5.99
MISB:	N/A

 # 13: photo cover

Ref. No.:	26507
Retail Price:	$5.99
MISB:	N/A

 # 14: graphic cover

Ref. No.:	26495
Retail Price:	$5.99
MISB:	N/A

 # 14: photo cover

Ref. No.:	26508
Retail Price:	$5.99
MISB:	N/A

 # 15: graphic cover

Ref. No.:	26496
Retail Price:	$5.99
MISB:	N/A

 # 15: photo cover

Ref. No.:	26509
Retail Price:	$5.99
MISB:	N/A

 # 16: graphic cover

Ref. No.:	26497
Retail Price:	$5.99
MISB:	N/A

 # 16: photo cover

Ref. No.:	26510
Retail Price:	$5.99
MISB:	N/A

 # 17: graphic cover

Ref. No.:	26498
Retail Price:	$5.99
MISB:	N/A

 # 17: photo cover

Ref. No.:	38994
Retail Price:	$5.99
MISB:	N/A

 # 18: graphic cover

Ref. No.:	35815
Retail Price:	$5.99
MISB:	N/A

 # 18: photo cover

Ref. No.:	35816
Retail Price:	$5.99
MISB:	N/A

 # 19: graphic cover

Ref. No.:	19901
Retail Price:	$5.99
MISB:	N/A

 # 19: photo cover

Ref. No.:	41280
Retail Price:	$5.99
MISB:	N/A

 # 20: graphic cover
Ref. No.:   39776
Retail Price: $5.99
MISB: N/A

 # 20: photo cover
Ref. No.:   39775
Retail Price: $5.99
MISB: N/A

A Jedi's Weapon Free Comic Book Day
Ref. No.:   16965
Retail Price: N/A
MISB: $2.00

TALES OF THE JEDI

1
Ref. No.:   6200
Retail Price: $2.50
MISB: N/A

2
Ref. No.:   6201
Retail Price: $2.50
MISB: N/A

3
Ref. No.:   6202
Retail Price: $2.50
MISB: N/A

4
Ref. No.:   6203
Retail Price: $2.50
MISB: N/A

5
Ref. No.:   6204
Retail Price: $2.50
MISB: N/A

Dark Lords of the Sith # 1
Ref. No.:   6208
Retail Price: $2.50
MISB: N/A

Dark Lords of the Sith # 2
Ref. No.:   6209
Retail Price: $2.50
MISB: N/A

Dark Lords of the Sith # 3
Ref. No.:   6210
Retail Price: $2.50
MISB: N/A

Dark Lords of the Sith # 4
Ref. No.:   6211
Retail Price: $2.50
MISB: N/A

Dark Lords of the Sith # 5
Ref. No.:   6212
Retail Price: $2.50
MISB: N/A

Dark Lords of the Sith # 6
Ref. No.:   6213
Retail Price: $2.50
MISB: N/A

Redemption # 1
Ref. No.:   6799
Retail Price: $2.95
MISB: N/A

Redemption # 2
Ref. No.:   6800
Retail Price: $2.95
MISB: N/A

Redemption # 3
Ref. No.:   6801
Retail Price: $2.95
MISB: N/A

Redemption # 4
Ref. No.:   6802
Retail Price: $2.95
MISB: N/A

Redemption # 5
Ref. No.:   6803
Retail Price: $2.95
MISB: N/A

The Fall of the Sith Empire # 1
Ref. No.:   6243
Retail Price: $2.95
MISB: N/A

The Fall of the Sith Empire # 2
Ref. No.:   6231
Retail Price: $2.95
MISB: N/A

The Fall of the Sith Empire # 3
Ref. No.:   6234
Retail Price: $2.95
MISB: N/A

The Fall of the Sith Empire # 4

Ref. No.:	6236
Retail Price:	$2.95
MISB:	N/A

The Fall of the Sith Empire # 5

Ref. No.:	6237
Retail Price:	$2.95
MISB:	N/A

The Freedon Nadd Uprising # 1

Ref. No.:	6206
Retail Price:	$2.50
MISB:	N/A

The Freedon Nadd Uprising # 2

Ref. No.:	6207
Retail Price:	$2.50
MISB:	N/A

The Golden Age of the Sith # 0

Ref. No.:	6221
Retail Price:	$0.99
MISB:	N/A

The Golden Age of the Sith # 1

Ref. No.:	6222
Retail Price:	$2.95
MISB:	N/A

The Golden Age of the Sith # 2

Ref. No.:	6223
Retail Price:	$2.95
MISB:	N/A

The Golden Age of the Sith # 3

Ref. No.:	6224
Retail Price:	$2.95
MISB:	N/A

The Golden Age of the Sith # 4

Ref. No.:	6225
Retail Price:	$2.95
MISB:	N/A

The Golden Age of the Sith # 5

Ref. No.:	6226
Retail Price:	$2.95
MISB:	N/A

The Sith War # 1

Ref. No.:	6215
Retail Price:	$2.50
MISB:	N/A

The Sith War # 2

Ref. No.:	6216
Retail Price:	$2.50
MISB:	N/A

The Sith War # 3

Ref. No.:	6217
Retail Price:	$2.50
MISB:	N/A

The Sith War # 4

Ref. No.:	6218
Retail Price:	$2.50
MISB:	N/A

The Sith War # 5

Ref. No.:	6219
Retail Price:	$2.50
MISB:	N/A

The Sith War # 6

Ref. No.:	6220
Retail Price:	$2.50
MISB:	N/A

THE EMPIRE STRIKES BACK

Comics Version

Ref. No.:	41304
Retail Price:	$2.50
MISB:	N/A

Hardcover # 2 (1982)

Ref. No.:	6036
Retail Price:	N/A
MISB:	N/A

Hardcover Comic 1981

Ref. No.:	6035
Retail Price:	N/A
MISB:	N/A

Marvel Special Edition Vol 2

Ref. No.:	41303
Retail Price:	$2.00
MISB:	$6.50

Treasury Sized # 2

Ref. No.:	6033
Retail Price:	N/A
MISB:	N/A

THE PHANTOM MENACE

1: graphic cover

Ref. No.:	3022
Retail Price:	$2.95
MISB:	N/A

1: photo cover
Ref. No.:   6716
Retail Price: $2.95
MISB: N/A

1/2: graphic cover
Ref. No.:   41310
Retail Price: $3.00
MISB: $6.00

1/2: special edition
Ref. No.:   6453
Retail Price: $3.00
MISB: $6.00

2: graphic cover
Ref. No.:   6717
Retail Price: $2.95
MISB: N/A

2: photo cover
Ref. No.:   6718
Retail Price: $2.95
MISB: N/A

3: graphic cover
Ref. No.:   6719
Retail Price: $2.95
MISB: N/A

3: photo cover
Ref. No.:   6720
Retail Price: $2.95
MISB: N/A

4: graphic cover
Ref. No.:   6721
Retail Price: $2.95
MISB: N/A

4: photo cover
Ref. No.:   6722
Retail Price: $2.95
MISB: N/A

Anakin Skywalker: foil cover
Ref. No.:   6730
Retail Price: $2.95
MISB: N/A

Anakin Skywalker: glow-in-the-dark cover
Ref. No.:   41308
Retail Price: $2.95
MISB: N/A

Anakin Skywalker: graphic cover
Ref. No.:   6727
Retail Price: $2.95
MISB: N/A

Anakin Skywalker: photo cover
Ref. No.:   6729
Retail Price: $2.95
MISB: N/A

Obi-Wan Kenobi: foil cover
Ref. No.:   6733
Retail Price: $2.95
MISB: N/A

Obi-Wan Kenobi: glow-in-the-dark cover
Ref. No.:   41306
Retail Price: $2.95
MISB: N/A

Obi-Wan Kenobi: graphic cover
Ref. No.:   6731
Retail Price: $2.95
MISB: N/A

Obi-Wan Kenobi: photo cover
Ref. No.:   6732
Retail Price: $2.95
MISB: N/A

Pack
Ref. No.:   26542
Retail Price: $9.95
MISB: N/A

Queen Amidala: foil cover
Ref. No.:   6739
Retail Price: $2.95
MISB: N/A

Queen Amidala: glow-in-the-dark cover
Ref. No.:   41309
Retail Price: $2.95
MISB: N/A

Queen Amidala: graphic cover
Ref. No.:   6735
Retail Price: $2.95
MISB: N/A

Queen Amidala: photo cover
Ref. No.:   6737
Retail Price: $2.95
MISB: N/A

Qui-Gon Jinn: foil cover

Ref. No.:	6740
Retail Price:	$2.95
MISB:	N/A

Qui-Gon Jinn: glow-in-the-dark cover

Ref. No.:	41307
Retail Price:	$2.95
MISB:	N/A

Qui-Gon Jinn: graphic cover

Ref. No.:	6738
Retail Price:	$2.95
MISB:	N/A

Qui-Gon Jinn: photo cover

Ref. No.:	6738
Retail Price:	$2.95
MISB:	N/A

THE STAR WARS TRILOGY SPECIAL EDITION

A New Hope # 1

Ref. No.:	6473
Retail Price:	$2.95
MISB:	N/A

A New Hope # 2

Ref. No.:	6474
Retail Price:	$2.95
MISB:	N/A

A New Hope # 3

Ref. No.:	6475
Retail Price:	$2.95
MISB:	N/A

A New Hope # 4

Ref. No.:	6476
Retail Price:	$2.95
MISB:	N/A

THRAWN TRIOLOGY

Dark Force Rising # 1

Ref. No.:	6398
Retail Price:	$2.95
MISB:	N/A

Dark Force Rising # 2

Ref. No.:	6399
Retail Price:	$2.95
MISB:	N/A

Dark Force Rising # 3

Ref. No.:	6400
Retail Price:	$2.95
MISB:	N/A

Dark Force Rising # 4

Ref. No.:	6401
Retail Price:	$2.95
MISB:	N/A

Dark Force Rising # 5

Ref. No.:	6402
Retail Price:	$2.95
MISB:	N/A

Dark Force Rising # 6

Ref. No.:	6403
Retail Price:	$2.95
MISB:	N/A

Heir to the Empire # 1

Ref. No.:	6392
Retail Price:	$2.95
MISB:	N/A

Heir to the Empire # 2

Ref. No.:	6393
Retail Price:	$2.95
MISB:	N/A

Heir to the Empire # 3

Ref. No.:	6394
Retail Price:	$2.95
MISB:	N/A

Heir to the Empire # 4

Ref. No.:	6395
Retail Price:	$2.95
MISB:	N/A

Heir to the Empire # 5

Ref. No.:	6396
Retail Price:	$2.95
MISB:	N/A

Heir to the Empire # 6

Ref. No.:	6397
Retail Price:	$2.95
MISB:	N/A

The Last Command # 1

Ref. No.:	6404
Retail Price:	$2.95
MISB:	N/A

The Last Command # 2

Ref. No.:	6405
Retail Price:	$2.95
MISB:	N/A

The Last Command # 3

Ref. No.:	6406
Retail Price:	$2.95
MISB:	N/A

The Last Command # 4

Ref. No.:	6407
Retail Price:	$2.95
MISB:	N/A

The Last Command # 5

Ref. No.:	6408
Retail Price:	$2.95
MISB:	N/A

The Last Command # 6

Ref. No.:	6409
Retail Price:	$2.95
MISB:	N/A

UNDERWORLD

1: graphic cover

Ref. No.:	6227
Retail Price:	$2.99
MISB:	N/A

1: photo cover

Ref. No.:	6307
Retail Price:	$2.99
MISB:	N/A

2: graphic cover

Ref. No.:	6308
Retail Price:	$2.99
MISB:	N/A

2: photo cover

Ref. No.:	6309
Retail Price:	$2.99
MISB:	N/A

3: graphic cover

Ref. No.:	6310
Retail Price:	$2.99
MISB:	N/A

3: photo cover

Ref. No.:	6315
Retail Price:	$2.99
MISB:	N/A

4: graphic cover

Ref. No.:	6316
Retail Price:	$2.99
MISB:	N/A

4: photo cover

Ref. No.:	6317
Retail Price:	$2.99
MISB:	N/A

5: graphic cover

Ref. No.:	6318
Retail Price:	$2.99
MISB:	N/A

5: photo cover

Ref. No.:	6647
Retail Price:	$2.99
MISB:	N/A

UNION

1: gold edition

Ref. No.:	6750
Retail Price:	$2.95
MISB:	N/A

1: standard cover

Ref. No.:	6747
Retail Price:	$2.95
MISB:	N/A

2

Ref. No.:	6748
Retail Price:	$2.95
MISB:	N/A

3

Ref. No.:	6749
Retail Price:	$2.95
MISB:	N/A

4: foil cover

Ref. No.:	6807
Retail Price:	$2.95
MISB:	N/A

4: standard cover

Ref. No.:	6751
Retail Price:	$2.95
MISB:	N/A

VADER'S QUEST

1: foil cover

Ref. No.:	6743
Retail Price:	$2.95
MISB:	N/A

1: standard cover

Ref. No.:   6742
Retail Price: $2.95
MISB: N/A

2

Ref. No.:   6744
Retail Price: $2.95
MISB: N/A

3

Ref. No.:   6745
Retail Price: $2.95
MISB: N/A

4

Ref. No.:   6746
Retail Price: $2.95
MISB: N/A

X-WING ROGUE SQUADRON

1 The Rebel Opposition # 1

Ref. No.:   6303
Retail Price: $2.95
MISB: N/A

2 The Rebel Opposition # 2

Ref. No.:   6304
Retail Price: $2.95
MISB: N/A

3 The Rebel Opposition # 3

Ref. No.:   6305
Retail Price: N/A

4 The Rebel Opposition # 4

Ref. No.:   6306
Retail Price: $2.95
MISB: N/A

5 The Phantom Affair # 1

Ref. No.:   6651
Retail Price: $2.95
MISB: N/A

6 The Phantom Affair # 2

Ref. No.:   6652
Retail Price: $2.95
MISB: N/A

7 The Phantom Affair # 3

Ref. No.:   6653
Retail Price: $2.95
MISB: N/A

8 The Phantom Affair # 4

Ref. No.:   6654
Retail Price: $2.95
MISB: N/A

9 Battle Ground Tatooine # 1

Ref. No.:   6311
Retail Price: $2.95
MISB: N/A

1/2

Ref. No.:   6311
Retail Price: $25.00
MISB: $8.00

10 Battle Ground Tatooine # 2

Ref. No.:   6311
Retail Price: $2.95
MISB: N/A

11 Battle Ground Tatooine # 3

Ref. No.:   6311
Retail Price: $2.95
MISB: N/A

12 Battle Ground Tatooine # 4

Ref. No.:   6311
Retail Price: $2.95
MISB: N/A

13 The Warrior Princess # 1

Ref. No.:   6659
Retail Price: $2.95
MISB: N/A

14 The Warrior Princess # 2

Ref. No.:   6660
Retail Price: $2.95
MISB: N/A

15 The Warrior Princess # 3

Ref. No.:   6661
Retail Price: $2.95
MISB: N/A

16 The Warrior Princess # 4

Ref. No.:   6665
Retail Price: $2.95
MISB: N/A

17 Requiem for a Rogue # 1

Ref. No.:   6662
Retail Price: $2.95
MISB: N/A

18 Requiem for a Rogue # 2

Ref. No.:	6663
Retail Price:	$2.95
MISB:	N/A

19 Requiem for a Rogue # 3

Ref. No.:	6664
Retail Price:	$2.95
MISB:	N/A

20 Requiem for a Rogue # 4

Ref. No.:	6667
Retail Price:	$2.95
MISB:	N/A

21 In the Empire's Service # 1

Ref. No.:	6668
Retail Price:	$2.95
MISB:	N/A

22 In the Empire's Service # 2

Ref. No.:	6669
Retail Price:	$2.95
MISB:	N/A

23 In the Empire's Service # 3

Ref. No.:	6670
Retail Price:	$2.95
MISB:	N/A

24 In the Empire's Service # 4

Ref. No.:	6671
Retail Price:	$2.95
MISB:	N/A

25 The Making of Baron Fel

Ref. No.:	6672
Retail Price:	$2.95
MISB:	N/A

26 Family Ties # 1

Ref. No.:	6673
Retail Price:	$2.95
MISB:	N/A

27 Family Ties # 2

Ref. No.:	6674
Retail Price:	$2.95
MISB:	N/A

28 Masquerade # 1

Ref. No.:	6675
Retail Price:	$2.95
MISB:	N/A

29 Masquerade # 2

Ref. No.:	6676
Retail Price:	$2.95
MISB:	N/A

30 Masquerade # 3

Ref. No.:	6677
Retail Price:	$2.95
MISB:	N/A

31 Masquerade # 4

Ref. No.:	6678
Retail Price:	$2.95
MISB:	N/A

32 Mandatory Retirement # 1

Ref. No.:	6679
Retail Price:	$2.95
MISB:	N/A

33 Mandatory Retirement # 2

Ref. No.:	6680
Retail Price:	$2.95
MISB:	N/A

34 Mandatory Retirement # 3

Ref. No.:	6681
Retail Price:	$2.95
MISB:	N/A

35 Mandatory Retirement # 4

Ref. No.:	6682
Retail Price:	$2.95
MISB:	N/A

GRAPHIC NOVELS

A Long Time Ago . . . # 1

Ref. No.:	26532
Retail Price:	$12.95
MISB:	N/A

A Long Time Ago . . . # 2

Ref. No.:	26533
Retail Price:	$12.95
MISB:	N/A

A Long Time Ago . . . # 3

Ref. No.:	26534
Retail Price:	$12.95
MISB:	N/A

A Long Time Ago . . . # 4

Ref. No.:	26535
Retail Price:	$12.95
MISB:	N/A

A Long Time Ago . . . # 5

Ref. No.:   26536
Retail Price: $12.95
MISB: N/A

A Long Time Ago . . . # 6

Ref. No.:   26537
Retail Price: $12.95
MISB: N/A

Attack of the Clones: Jango Fett

Ref. No.:   21017
Retail Price: $5.95
MISB: N/A

Attack of the Clones: Zam Wesell

Ref. No.:   20888
Retail Price: $5.95
MISB: N/A

Dark Forces: Jedi Knight

Ref. No.:   20929
Retail Price: $24.95
MISB: N/A

Dark Forces: Rebel Agent

Ref. No.:   20876
Retail Price: $24.95
MISB: N/A

Dark Forces: Soldier for the Empire

Ref. No.:   20891
Retail Price: $24.95
MISB: N/A

COMIC HANDBOOK

EXPANDED UNIVERSE

Star Wars Comic Handbook Volume 1
X-Wing Rogue Squadron

Ref. No.:   6324
Retail Price: $2.95
MISB: N/A

Star Wars Comic Handbook Volume 2
Crimson Empire

Ref. No.:   14239
Retail Price: $2.95
MISB: N/A

Star Wars Comic Handbook Volume 3
Dark Empire

Ref. No.:   26558
Retail Price: $2.95
MISB: N/A

COMIC MAGAZINE

RETURN OF THE JEDI

A Marvel Super Special Magazine # 27

Ref. No.:   6041
Retail Price: $1.50
MISB: $2.50

THE EMPIRE STRIKES BACK

A Marvel Super Special Magazine # 16

Ref. No.:   6034
Retail Price: $1.50
MISB: $2.75

Comic Trade Paperback

Signed, foil-stamped deluxe hardcover with slipcase

Ref. No.:   20681
Retail Price: $79.95
MISB: $60.00

signed leather-bound hardcover

Ref. No.:   21040
Retail Price: $99.95
MISB: $50.00

paperback, 3rd edition

Ref. No.:   21041
Retail Price: $16.95
MISB: N/A

paperback, 2nd edition

Ref. No.:   6455
Retail Price: $17.95
MISB: $8.50

signed leather-bound hardcover

Ref. No.:   6459
Retail Price: $99.95
MISB: $50.00

A Long Time Ago . . . Dark Encounters

Ref. No.:   20663
Retail Price: $29.95
MISB: N/A

A Long Time Ago . . . Doomworld

Ref. No.:   20661
Retail Price: $29.95
MISB: N/A

A Long Time Ago . . . Far, Far Away

Ref. No.:   20695
Retail Price: $29.95
MISB: N/A

A Long Time Ago . . . Fool's Beauty
Ref. No.: 21034
Retail Price: $29.95
MISB: N/A

A Long Time Ago . . . Resurrection of Evil
Ref. No.: 20696
Retail Price: $29.95
MISB: N/A

A Long Time Ago . . . Screams in the Void
Ref. No.: 20757
Retail Price: $29.95
MISB: N/A

A Long Time Ago . . . Wookie World
Ref. No.: 21020
Retail Price: $29.95
MISB: N/A

Attack of the Clones
Ref. No.: 20820
Retail Price: $17.95
MISB: N/A

Boba Fett: Death, Lies and Treachery
Ref. No.: 20825
Retail Price: $12.95
MISB: N/A

Boba Fett: Enemy of the Empire Collection
Ref. No.: 6812
Retail Price: $12.95
MISB: N/A

Bounty Hunters
Ref. No.: 20724
Retail Price: $12.95
MISB: N/A

Chewbacca
Ref. No.: 20824
Retail Price: $12.95
MISB: N/A

Classic Star Wars Boxed Set: ANH, TESB & ROTJ
Ref. No.: 20863
Retail Price: $29.95
MISB: N/A

Classic Star Wars: A New Hope
Ref. No.: 6793
Retail Price: $9.95
MISB: N/A

Classic Star Wars: Han Solo at Stars' End
Ref. No.: 6419
Retail Price: $6.95
MISB: N/A

Classic Star Wars: Return of the Jedi
Ref. No.: 6792
Retail Price: $9.95
MISB: N/A

Classic Star Wars: The Early Adventures
Ref. No.: 6787
Retail Price: $19.95
MISB: N/A

Classic Star Wars: The Empire Strikes Back Collection
Ref. No.: 21035
Retail Price: $9.95
MISB: N/A

Classic Star Wars: Volume 1 In Deadly Pursuit
Ref. No.: 20890
Retail Price: $16.95
MISB: N/A

Classic Star Wars: Volume 2 The Rebel
Ref. No.: 6467
Retail Price: $16.95
MISB: N/A

Classic Star Wars: Volume 3 Escape to Hoth
Ref. No.: 6468
Retail Price: $16.95
MISB: N/A

Clone Wars: Volume 1 Defense of Kamino
Ref. No.: 20813
Retail Price: $14.95
MISB: N/A

Clone Wars: Volume 2 Victories and Sacrifices
Ref. No.: 6788
Retail Price: $14.95
MISB: N/A

Clone Wars: Volume 3 Last Stand on Jabiim
Ref. No.: 40251
Retail Price: $14.95
MISB: N/A

Clone Wars: Volume 4 Light and Dark
Ref. No.: 40252
Retail Price: $12.95
MISB: N/A

Crimson Empire

Ref. No.:	6421
Retail Price:	$17.95
MISB:	N/A

Crimson Empire II: Council of Blood

Ref. No.:	6811
Retail Price:	$17.95
MISB:	N/A

Dark Empire

Ref. No.:	6457
Retail Price:	$17.95
MISB:	N/A

Dark Empire II

Ref. No.:	6810
Retail Price:	$17.95
MISB:	$9.50

Dark Forces: Jedi Knight

Ref. No.:	20928
Retail Price:	$14.95
MISB:	$12.50

Dark Forces: Rebel Agent

Ref. No.:	20877
Retail Price:	$14.95
MISB:	$12.50

Dark Forces: Soldier for the Empire

Ref. No.:	20892
Retail Price:	$14.95
MISB:	$12.50

Darkness

Ref. No.:	20740
Retail Price:	$12.95
MISB:	N/A

Darth Maul

Ref. No.:	20748
Retail Price:	$12.95
MISB:	N/A

Droids Special Collection

Ref. No.:	39015
Retail Price:	$2.50
MISB:	N/A

Droids: Rebellion

Ref. No.:	20895
Retail Price:	$2.50
MISB:	N/A

Droids: The Kalarba Adventures

Ref. No.:	6451
Retail Price:	$17.95
MISB:	$7.65

Droids: The Kalarba Adventures Limited Edition

Ref. No.:	6454
Retail Price:	$99.95
MISB:	$35.00

Emissaries to Malastare

Ref. No.:	20821
Retail Price:	$15.95
MISB:	N/A

Empire: Volume 1 Betrayal

Ref. No.:	21044
Retail Price:	$12.95
MISB:	N/A

Empire: Volume 2 Darklighter

Ref. No.:	16836
Retail Price:	$17.95
MISB:	N/A

Empire's End

Ref. No.:	6810
Retail Price:	$5.95
MISB:	N/A

Infinities: A New Hope

Ref. No.:	6438
Retail Price:	$12.95
MISB:	N/A

Infinities: Return of the Jedi Collection

Ref. No.:	38993
Retail Price:	$12.95
MISB:	N/A

Infinities: The Empire Strikes Back

Ref. No.:	20749
Retail Price:	$12.95
MISB:	N/A

Jabba the Hutt: The Art of the Deal

Ref. No.:	20673
Retail Price:	$9.95
MISB:	N/A

Jango Fett: Open Seasons

Ref. No.:	21015
Retail Price:	$12.95
MISB:	N/A

Jedi Academy: Leviathan
Ref. No.: 20797
Retail Price: $11.95
MISB: N/A

Jedi Council: Acts of War
Ref. No.: 20881
Retail Price: $12.95
MISB: N/A

Jedi Vs Sith
Ref. No.: 20893
Retail Price: $17.95
MISB: N/A

Mara Jade: By the Emperor's Hand
Ref. No.: 6809
Retail Price: $15.95
MISB: N/A

Outlander
Ref. No.: 20912
Retail Price: $14.95
MISB: N/A

Prelude to Rebellion
Ref. No.: 21038
Retail Price: $14.95
MISB: N/A

Rite of Passage
Ref. No.: 38991
Retail Price: $14.95
MISB: N/A

Shadows of the Empire
Ref. No.: 6434
Retail Price: $17.95
MISB: N/A

Shadows of the Empire
Ref. No.: 20982

SOTE: Evolution
Ref. No.: 6808
Retail Price: $14.95
MISB: N/A

SOTE: Limited Edition Signed Leather-Bound Hardcover
Ref. No.: 6435
Retail Price: $79.95
MISB: N/A

Special Edition: A New Hope
Ref. No.: 6790
Retail Price: $9.95
MISB: N/A

Special Edition: Return of the Jedi
Ref. No.: 21036
Retail Price: $9.95
MISB: N/A

Special Edition: The Empire Strikes Back
Ref. No.: 6789
Retail Price: $9.95
MISB: N/A

Splinter of the Mind's Eye
Ref. No.: 20938
Retail Price: $17.95
MISB: N/A

Star Wars The Special Edition Boxed Set
Ref. No.: 21037
Retail Price: $29.95
MISB: N/A

Tales of the Jedi: Dark Lords of the Sith
Ref. No.: 6461
Retail Price: $17.95
MISB: N/A

Tales of the Jedi: Knights of the Old Republic Collection
Ref. No.: 20885
Retail Price: $14.95
MISB: N/A

Tales of the Jedi: Redemption
Ref. No.: 20915
Retail Price: $14.95
MISB: N/A

Tales of the Jedi: The Fall of the Sith Empire
Ref. No.: 6464
Retail Price: $15.95
MISB: N/A

Tales of the Jedi: The Freedon Nadd Uprising
Ref. No.: 6804
Retail Price: $5.95
MISB: N/A

Tales of the Jedi: The Sith War
Ref. No.: 6462
Retail Price: $17.95
MISB: N/A

Tales of the Jedi: The Golden Age of the Sith Collection
Ref. No.: 6463
Retail Price: $16.95
MISB: N/A

Tales: Volume 1
Ref. No.: 20735
Retail Price: $19.95
MISB: N/A

Tales: Volume 2
Ref. No.: 20736
Retail Price: $19.95
MISB: N/A

Tales: Volume 3
Ref. No.: 20734
Retail Price: $19.95
MISB: N/A

Tales: Volume 4
Ref. No.: 35817
Retail Price: $19.95
MISB: N/A

The Hunt for Aurra Sing
Ref. No.: 21016
Retail Price: $12.95
MISB: N/A

The Marvel Comics Illustrated Version of Star Wars
Ref. No.: 2129
Retail Price: $1.50
MISB: N/A

The Phantom Menace
Ref. No.: 2458
Retail Price: $12.95
MISB: N/A

The Phantom Menace Limited Edition
Ref. No.: 26473
Retail Price: $79.95
MISB: N/A

The Phantom Menace: Adventures
Ref. No.: 21039
Retail Price: $12.95
MISB: N/A

The Stark Hyperspace War
Ref. No.: 35804
Retail Price: $12.95
MISB: N/A

Thrawn Trilogy: Dark Force Rising
Ref. No.: 6439
Retail Price: $17.95
MISB: N/A

Thrawn Trilogy: Heir to the Empire
Ref. No.: 6437
Retail Price: $17.95
MISB: N/A

Thrawn Trilogy: The Last Command
Ref. No.: 6440
Retail Price: $17.95
MISB: N/A

Twilight
Ref. No.: 20826
Retail Price: $12.95
MISB: N/A

Underworld: The Yavin Vassilika
Ref. No.: 20882
Retail Price: $15.95
MISB: N/A

Union
Ref. No.: 20674
Retail Price: $12.95
MISB: N/A

Vader's Quest
Ref. No.: 6806
Retail Price: $11.95
MISB: N/A

X-wing Rogue Squadron: Battle Ground Tatooine
Ref. No.: 26474
Retail Price: $12.95
MISB: N/A

X-wing Rogue Squadron: Blood and Honor
Ref. No.: 20662
Retail Price: $12.95
MISB: N/A

X-wing Rogue Squadron: Mandatory Retirement
Ref. No.: 20804
Retail Price: $12.95
MISB: N/A

X-wing Rogue Squadron: Requiem for a Rogue
Ref. No.: 6655
Retail Price: $12.95
MISB: N/A

X-wing Rogue Squadron: The Phantom Affair
Ref. No.: 6465
Retail Price: $12.95
MISB: N/A

X-wing Rogue Squadron: The Warrior Princess

Ref. No.: 20770
Retail Price: $12.95
MISB: N/A

X-wing Rogue Squadron: In the Empire's Service

Ref. No.: 29759
Retail Price: $12.95
MISB: N/A

X-wing Rogue Squadron: Masquerade

Ref. No.: 20763
Retail Price: $12.95
MISB: N/A

MANGA

A NEW HOPE

1
Ref. No.: 20859
Retail Price: $9.95
MISB: N/A

2
Ref. No.: 20798
Retail Price: $9.95
MISB: N/A

3
Ref. No.: 20776
Retail Price: $9.95
MISB: N/A

4
Ref. No.: 20847
Retail Price: $9.95
MISB: N/A

RETURN OF THE JEDI

1
Ref. No.: 20750
Retail Price: $9.95
MISB: N/A

2
Ref. No.: 26591
Retail Price: $9.95
MISB: N/A

3
Ref. No.: 26592
Retail Price: $9.95
MISB: N/A

4
Ref. No.: 20795
Retail Price: $9.95
MISB: N/A

THE EMPIRE STRIKES BACK

1
Ref. No.: 20679
Retail Price: $9.95
MISB: N/A

2
Ref. No.: 26561
Retail Price: $9.95
MISB: N/A

3
Ref. No.: 20678
Retail Price: $9.95
MISB: N/A

4
Ref. No.: 26562
Retail Price: $9.95
MISB: N/A

THE PHANTOM MENACE

1
Ref. No.: 20816
Retail Price: $9.95
MISB: N/A

2
Ref. No.: 20817
Retail Price: $9.95
MISB: N/A

Appendices

GLOSSARY OF TERMS

There are a vast and bewildering number of hobby-specific terms and acronyms used in *Star Wars* collecting. Knowing not only what they mean but what they stand for is an important step to becoming a good collector not only for you, but also for the rest of the community. With the growing number of online auction sales, it is vital that the buyer understands what he or she is looking at, and the seller knows exactly how he or she is describing the item for sale. As such, this section includes a number of examples to better illustrate those terms that are often clouded or confused.

4-up	When Kenner developed the Micro Collection, it sculpted its models four times larger than they were intended to be produced at. The resulting hardcopies were therefore also four times the normal size and they are often referred to as 4-ups. They should not be confused with the original sculpt, which is never called a 4-up.
Action stands	A type of plastic display base used to mount 3³/₄-inch action figures.
AFA	Action Figure Authority: A company that provides a grading and certification service on many *Star Wars* collectibles.
ALS	Autograph Letter Signed: A letter written in a celebrity's own handwriting and signed.
ANH	*A New Hope*: The first movie of the original *Star Wars* trilogy.
ANS	Autograph Note Signed: A note written in a celebrity's own handwriting but not signed.
AOTC	*Attack of the Clones*: The second movie of the prequel *Star Wars* trilogy.

AQS Autograph Quotation, Signed: A handwritten quotation such as "May the Force be with you," written in a celebrity's own handwriting and signed.

Assortment A selection of items from a wave shipped to retailers.

Autopen A mechanical device that prints a signature on an item, rather than an actual person.

Backboards Cardstock boards used to stiffen and support polybags.

Baggies Action figures sealed in bags, typically from mail-away promotions.

Big box store A large consumer retailer like Toys "R" Us, Wal-Mart, or Target because it resembles a large packing carton.

Bin A point-of-purchase display that consists of a cardboard box to hold the merchandise using a plastic tray, with an attractive header card to catch the attention of the consumer.

Blister The plastic bubble that holds the toy to the cardback (also known as bubble).

Blue harvest The term used for many fake prototype *Star Wars* items that appeared in the mid-1990s.

Bootleg An unlicensed version of a preexisting, licensed product. Usually, a bootleg is a direct copy (albeit typically much shoddier in appearance) of its licensed counterpart. Unlike fakes or customs, bootlegs are made in factory environments to be sold in stores as *toys* and are not made specifically to mimic preexisting collectibles. Action figure toys are the most frequently bootlegged items.

Canon Works that are part of the *Star Wars* story line that come directly from George Lucas, such as the movies, screenplays, and scripts. Does not include any licensed material created by any other author (i.e., the Expanded Universe). The definition is such that Lucas can rewrite any part of the Expanded Universe to fit in with his vision of the *Star Wars* saga.

Card surface tear Noticeable rip or tear of the paper, cardboard, print, or ink of the card surface. May occur on either the card front or back. Most commonly caused by the removal of a price tag or sticker. Other causes include removal of store stickers, antitheft devices, or special offer stickers.

Cardback The cardboard packaging onto which a plastic blister containing the toy would be attached. Most often, these are action figures, but a few Mini Rigs were produced on cardbacks instead of boxes.

Carded sample An action figure placed on a cardback to represent a finished example. Many times, the action figure did not match the art of the cardback.

Casting   The solid object made using a mold.

CCG   Collectible Card Game: A turn-based card game where players have their own personal customized decks instead of playing from a common deck (*see also* Trading Card Game).

Chase card   These are bonus cards that are not considered to be part of the basic set, and because they are produced in smaller quantities than regular cards they are more valuable. (Also known as insert cards.)

Clamshell   A hinged plastic case used for protecting carded 3³/₄-inch action figures.

Collection   A manufacturer's expression used to create an umbrella term for ordering waves or product ranges, for example, the Hall of Fame collection.

Complete   The item includes everything that it originally came with. Note that a complete loose item and a complete packaged item are vastly different.

Concept model   A hand-built mock-up generally made from preexisting toys or model kits to demonstrate the notion of the item.

Condition   The particular state of repair or ability to function of a collectible.

Copy   The textual product or character description that is suitable material to print on packaging.

Corner curl   One of the most frequent flaws found with modern carded action figures. Since most of the cards are square or rectangular or have angular edges, corners can be easily curled up because of poor shipping, shelf wear, poor storage, or improper handling. Corners generally curl at approximately a 45-degree angle.

Crack (blister) In terms of a blister, a crack is a noticeable fracture, crevice, split, or chiplike flaw in the plastic covering of the action figure but does not include the separation of the bubble from the card itself (though cracks may be present along the boundary of the separation).

Crack (card)   In terms of the card, a crack occurs when part of the print or ink is removed or damaged. Usually occurs because of a crease or fold, but may also occur spontaneously because of improper exposure to light or heat.

Crease   A severe curl or bend that leaves a permanent mark or crinkle on the print or ink. A crease can occur without completely cracking or removing the print or ink. Severe creases may allow portions of the underlying cardboard to show through.

Cromalin   A color proof sheet of packaging is created using special colored powders on sensitized paper so that the copy and the balance of colors from the color separations can be studied and corrected, if necessary, before the actual press run.

CS

Card Signed: An index card signed by a celebrity. Also known as an SC.

CSW

Canadian Skin Wrapped: The term used for a number of Sears Canada-exclusive figures that were vacuum wrapped instead of placed in blisters.

Curl

A bend in the cardboard that doesn't damage the print or the ink.

Custom

Refers to a homemade toy and is commonly an action figure, vehicle, or play set. Custom toys are made for the enjoyment of the individual and are not usually produced in larger quantities than one.

CW

Clone Wars: The toy line produced by Hasbro in 2003 and 2004 to span the gap between *Attack of the Clones* and Episode 3, and to tie in with the Expanded Universe Clone Wars spin-off series of books, computer games, comics, and television cartoons.

Decal

An adhesive paper or plastic sticker used to decorate an item.

Dent

An indentation or concave section of the clear plastic bubble not originally intended by the manufacturer. May or may not be accompanied by a whitening of the clear plastic.

Ding

Similar to a dent, but on a smaller scale. May or may not be accompanied by a whitening of the clear plastic.

DS

Document Signed: Any document such as a contract, bill, check, or official letter signed by a celebrity.

DT

Double-Telescoping Lightsaber: An early version of the $3^3/4$-inch lightsaber accessory that had a double action of telescoping, meaning that there are two stages of extension. Not to be confused with the common single-telescoping lightsaber.

eBay

The largest online auction Web site in the world.

eBayer

Someone who buys/sells on eBay (also eBuyer—someone who buys on eBay).

EIC

El Imperio Contraataca: The first Lili Ledy line of *Star Wars* action figures based on Kenner's *The Empire Strikes Back* collections.

Ep1

Episode 1: The packaging line produced by Hasbro in 1999 and 2000 to tie in with *The Phantom Menace*.

ERegDJ

El Regreso del Jedi: The third Lili Ledy line of *Star Wars* action figures based on Kenner's *Return of the Jedi* collections.

ERetDJ

El Retorno de Jedi: The second Lili Ledy line of *Star Wars* action figures based on Kenner's *Return of the Jedi* collections.

E-tailer   A retailer with an online store front.

EU   Expanded Universe: The licensed extension of the *Star Wars* story beyond the movies, in comics, novels, children's books, video games, television series, toys, and so on.

Ex-lib   A former library copy. Ex-libs are generally considered not collectible,
especially if the library markings are prominent and pervasive and if
there is the usual pocket glued in the back.

FB   Flashback: The packaging toy line produced by Hasbro to bridge the
gap between the Power of the Force 2 toy line and Ep1/*The Phantom
Menace* toy line.

Fake   An item that is as near to a perfect copy of an original item and is made
to deceive the buyer. Not to be confused with a reproduction item.

First shot   A preliminary piece made as part of the production process in an effort
to determine the accuracy of the mold being used. They are typically
made of different colors of plastic and lack details.

Flash lines   A thin trim that surrounds a plastic item resulting from a gap between
the pieces of a mold.

Forgery   Any unauthorized copy of a signature, passed off as the real thing.

Fraying   When cardboard fiber is pulled apart or stretched, individual fibers
begin to show, giving a fuzzy impression to the cardboard (at the edges
especially). Nonfrayed cardboard is usually tightly packed and firm.

GMFG   General Mills Fun Group: The parent group that owned Kenner,
Model Products Corporation, and a number of other subsidiaries that
had *Star Wars* licenses.

GN   Graphic Novel: A self-contained comic that is not an installment of a
series, generally between sixty-four and ninety-five pages in length.

Grade   A mark to indicate a level, step, or stage in a collectibles condition.

Hall of Fame   The rehashed Saga collection released by Hasbro in 2004.

Hanger   A double-sided display card intended to be hung from the ceiling over
a display area.

Hardcopy   A hand-cast, -painted, and -assembled copy of the original wax sculpts
made of polyurethane to demonstrate the functionality of the toy.

HC   Hardcover: A book bound in cloth, cardboard, or leather rather than
paper.

Header card   Part of an in-store display system that could be hung from the ceiling
or attached to the top of a shelf or to the back of a bin.

Hobby edition	A set of trading cards sold to specialist hobby retailers (such as comic book stores), and usually contains a series of regular cards as well as extended cards such as chasers.
Hole	Any complete piercing or perforation of the card or bubble. Occasionally, some older items did not come with a hook or hole to hang the item on a peg or rack.
HTF	Hard to Find: An item that is elusive is considered hard to find. Not to be confused with rare.
I	Inscribed: A personalized message, such as "Good luck," "Best wishes," "To Dave," and so on to the recipient.
IN	Illustrated Novel: A novel that includes large graphics to illustrate the story line.
Inserts	The cardboard (typically corrugated) inside a box that holds the toy in place. Can also include sticker sheets, instructions, and any catalogs or brochures placed inside the packaging.
ISP	Inscribed Signed Photo: A personalized message, such as "Good luck," "Best wishes," "To Dave," and so on to the recipient on a photograph of a celebrity. Also known as SPI or IPS.
IT	Irwin Toys: A Canadian company that merged with Kenner to create Kenner Products (Canada) Ltd.
KC	Kenner Canada: The abbreviated name for Kenner's Canadian counterpart. Its full name was Kenner Products (Canada) Ltd.
Kit-bash	A model maker's term used to denote an item that has been constructed of parts taken from other toys. These are often used in the early stages of product development for designers to illustrate the basic concept of the toy.
Knock-off	Almost the same as a bootleg, but the major difference is that knock-offs are items that bear resemblance to a licensed property but are not exact in their appearance.
Laid-in	Something is lying loose in the front of the book such as book plate, postcard, or other premium.
Last 17	Refers to the final release of figures in Europe, all of which only appeared on the Tri-logo cardback. The term is often confused with Power of the Force, which, in the United States only included fourteen figures. Though counted as a POTF figure, the American assortment never included Yak Face.
Lenticular	A trading card printed on special plastic, which displays a short animation when tilted from top to bottom.

LFL	Lucasfilm Limited: Owned by George Lucas, this movie and television production company also has divisions for visual effects (Industrial Lights & Magic), sound (Skywalker Sound), video games (LucasArts) and licensing and online activities (Lucas Online).
LGDE	*La Guerre des Étoiles*: French translation of *Star Wars*, and commonly used on Kenner Canada products.
LGDLA	*La Guerra de las Galaxias*: Spanish translation of *Star Wars*, and commonly used on Lili Ledy products.
LL	Lili Ledy: The toy manufacturer that held the *Star Wars* action toy (and accessories) license in Mexico.
Loose	An item that is no longer contained in any packaging.
LS	Letter Signed: A letter written by a third party but signed by a celebrity.
Mail-away	Items offered by companies as premiums through sending in redeemable proof of purchases.
MIB	Mint in Box: A packaged item that can be described as in brand new condition. Often, it also denotes that all cardboard inserts used to hold the item in place are included. By inference, this acronym is only describing the item and not the packaging itself, so an MIB toy could contain a perfect toy that comes in a damaged box.
Micro Collection	The packaging toy line of 1-inch-scale miniatures produced by Kenner between 1982 and 1983.
Milkcap	A small disc, usually made of cardboard, that features an image on one side and is blank or numbered on the other.
MIMB	Mint in Mint Box: An expanded description of an MIB, where the packaging is being described as brand new.
Mint	In perfect condition as when first made.
MIP	Mint in Packaging: An alternative to Mint in Box and Mint on Card. This term is not commonly used because it is purposefully vague about the cardback or packaging.
MOC	Mint on Card: An item that is carded can be described thus if the packaged toy is in brand new condition. By inference, it is only describing the item and not the cardback.
Mock-up	A full-sized model of an item, built to scale and with working parts, used especially for testing or research.

MOMC Mint on Mint Card: An expanded description of MOC, where both the item within the blister and the card itself are being defined as in brand new condition.

Mold A container that gives a shape to a molten or liquid substance poured into it to harden.

MPC Model Products Corporation: The plastic modeling arm of the General Mills Fun Group.

Mylar A polythene plastic made by DuPont that is commonly used in film processing and that is known for its antidegradation properties.

NRFB Never Removed from Box: An item that has been opened but kept in its packaging. It should not be taken as a literal example of the toy's condition because most items that have been opened have been removed from their packaging.

One-shot A self-contained comic that is not an installment of a series, generally no more than sixty-four pages in length.

OSWCC Ohio *Star Wars* Collecting Club: A fan-run collecting group organized to aid collectors in Ohio. It is one of many such clubs throughout North America.

OSWFC Official *Star Wars* Fan Club: The *Star Wars* fan club officially licensed by Lucasfilm.

OT Original Trilogy: The first trilogy of *Star Wars* movies comprising *A New Hope*, *The Empire Strikes Back*, and *Return of the Jedi*.

OTC Original Trilogy Collection: The packaging toy line produced by Hasbro in 2004 to coincide with the release of the Original Trilogy on DVD format.

P Punched: An action figure blister card that has not had the card from the hanging hole removed. Conversely, UP (unpunched) indicates a blister card that has not had its hole opened, but because punched cards are far more common than unpunched, this reference is never used.

Packaging The wrapping or container in which an item is presented for sale.

Paint master A casting whose purpose is to illustrate the correct paint colors to be used for production and is accompanied by the swatches painted in the appropriate colors and annotated.

PB Paperback: A book having a flexible paper binding.

Pegwarmer An item that sits on the hanging pegs or shelves for a long duration of time because it is unpopular or overstocked.

PF
Prestige Format: Similar in length and style to a one-shot but printed on higher quality paper and bound using glue instead of staples.

Photo card
Large-sized trading cards, which are manufactured to look like standard photographs.

Photoart
The master image used on packaging for a toy.

Planogram
The suggested display layout plans sent from manufacturers to retailers in catalogs and display kits.

Plastic master
A casting whose purpose is to illustrate the correct plastic colors to be used for production and is accompanied by swatches of the correct plastic.

Plastic swatch
A sample piece of square plastic of the correct type/color to be used on each part of the figure.

Polybag
A sealable pouch typically made of polythene.

POP
Point of Purchase: In-store displays that are intended to be positioned next to the product. Hangers, shelf talkers, and headers are all point-of-purchase displays.

POTF
Power of the Force: The packaging toy line produced by Kenner in 1985 that encompassed characters and vehicles from the original *Star Wars* trilogy.

POTF2
Power of the Force 2: The packaging toy line produced by Kenner/Hasbro between 1995 and 2000.

POTJ
Power of the Jedi: The packaging toy line produced by Hasbro between 2000 and 2002.

Preprinted
A celebrity's signature that is printed on an image negative and then printed as part of the photo.

Price clipped
The price—usually on the top right of the front inside flap of the dust jacket—has been cut off.

Production error
An item that has been incorrectly painted, manufactured, assembled, or packaged because of a mistake during the mass-production process. Not to be considered a variation.

Promo card
A limited-edition card that is designed to advertise a new trading card series and is often given away as a free gift at collector's exhibitions and in trading card and movie magazines.

Proof card
An early master of a card of packaging example, printed on thin card in matt inks. Typically, they are single sided and hand cut.

Proof of purchase A blue-and-white disc printed on vintage Kenner cardbacks that was used as part of mail-away offers. (Also known as POP but not to be confused with point of purchase.)

Proof sheet An entire sheet that is printed with several individual proof cards with both front and back images.

Prototype Any item resulting from preproduction processes. Not to be confused with first shots, which are part of the production process.

PT Prequel Trilogy: The second trilogy of *Star Wars* movies comprising *The Phantom Menace*, *Attack of the Clones*, and *Revenge of the Sith*.

Rare An item that is in short supply and difficult to get hold of is considered rare. This term can be subjective because one person's idea of rare may not match that of another person.

Reformed Some blister defects can be at least superficially corrected by gently reshaping the bubble by hand. This includes popping out small dents or reshaping dings. Many times, this reformation is evident in a whitening of the clear plastic.

Regular card A standard trading card that forms part of a basic set.

Rehash An item that has been reissued with a minor modification to the item or packaging.

Reproduction Items that are meant to look identical to one that has been produced under license. Typically, these are weapons and accessories (Double-Telescoping Lightsabers and blasters), blisters, dioramas, and cardbacks. Initially, they were meant to act as temporary replacements for missing parts, but nowadays they are used dishonestly to replace vintage parts and accessories. Also known as repro.

Rerelease An item that has been reissued without any changes to it or its packaging.

Retail edition A set of trading cards sold to general retailers, and usually only contains a series of regular cards.

Retro Retrospective: Looking back at a certain style or collection of thoughts. In the case of *Star Wars* collecting, the retro period is considered to be the Original Trilogy years (1977-1985).

ROTJ *Return of the Jedi*: The third movie in the original *Star Wars* trilogy. Also the packaging toy line made by Kenner between 1983 and 1984.

RRP Recommended Retail Price: The maximum price at retail as recommended by the manufacturer.

Rubber stamp   A signature that is applied to an item with a rubber stamp.

Saga   The collector-coined term for the unified packaging toy line produced by Hasbro between 2002 and 2004.

Scalping   The action of buying toys at retail prices to resell at a profit.

SDCC   San Diego Comic Convention: The largest comic book event in the world, held annually in San Diego, California.

SE   Special Editions: The 1997 rereleased and remastered version of the original *Star Wars* trilogy depicting George Lucas's final composition of the story.

Sealed   The box is still sealed with original tape if applicable. If the box was not originally sealed with tape, this term signifies that the box does not appear to have ever been opened or tampered with.

Secretarial   An authorized copy of a celebrity's signature but signed by a third party.

Separation   Since blisters are affixed to card in some manner, there is a chance that they can become detached. Some blisters are detached (at least partially) from the card to remove the figure inside. Conversely, these figures can also be replaced at a later time.

Set   A collection of all the regular cards manufactured for a particular series. A basic set never includes chase cards. (Also known as series.)

Shelf talker   A strip of paper or plastic that would be fixed to the front lip of a display shelf to advertise and promote the product in question.

Sig   Signature: A signature on a piece of paper.

Sniping   Placing a bid in the closing seconds of an auction to prevent counter-bids.

SOTE   Shadows of the Empire: An Expanded Universe story line that bridged *The Empire Strikes Back* and *Return of the Jedi*. It was accompanied by a number of books, computer games, comics, and toy lines.

SP   Signed Photograph: A signature on a photograph. Also known as PS.

ST   Star Tours: An interactive Expanded Universe simulator ride based on aspects of the original *Star Wars* trilogy; found at several Disney parks worldwide. Also a packaging line produced by a number of manufacturers between 1987 and 2004.

Staining   A permanent discoloration of the card or bubble because of contact with some foreign substance. Usually caused by a liquid of some type but may also be the result of contact with other materials (e.g., plastic, rubber, etc.). Separate from bubble or card yellowing, which may occur without contact with any foreign substances.

Star Case A type of plastic clamshell case used to protect carded 3³/₄-inch action figures.

Sticker sheet The sheet of adhesive paper on which decorative decals are printed.

Strip A sequence of drawings telling a story in a newspaper or comic book.

Sunning The term used to describe the fading or browning of the spine, both of the book and jacket.

SW *Star Wars*: The original and alternate title used to refer to *A New Hope*. Also the packaging toy line made by Kenner between 1978 and 1979.

Takara The toy manufacturer that held the *Star Wars* action toy (and accessories) license in Japan.

Tape repair Occasionally, scotch tape (or other type of tape adhesive) is used to repair a card or reseal a bubble. Some types of tape may be removed without further damage. Some tapes themselves can damage the surface of the card or bubble, even if not removed.

TCG Trading Card Game: A turn-based card game where players have their own personal customized decks instead of playing from a common deck (*see also* Collectible Card Game).

TCS Trading Card Signed: A trading card signed by a celebrity.

TESB *The Empire Strikes Back*: The second movie in the original *Star Wars* trilogy. Also the packaging toy line produced by Kenner between 1980 and 1982.

TLS Typed Letter Signed: A letter that is typed and signed by the celebrity.

Tooling master An upsized casting of a play set or vehicle that is used to form a production mold.

Toy run A shopping trip solely dedicated to finding new *Star Wars* collectibles.

TPB Trade Paperback: A book that is typically of better production quality, larger size, and higher price than a mass-market edition and is intended for sale in bookstores. Specifically, it is a bound collection of comic books to encompass all or part of a story line.

TPM *The Phantom Menace*: The first movie of the prequel *Star Wars* trilogy.

Ultra-PRO A manufacturer of high-grade Mylar storage sleeves.

Variation A running change to packaging or an item that makes it different to previously released versions of the same piece of merchandise.

VOTC

Vintage Original Trilogy Collection: The retro vintage packaging toy line produced by Hasbro in 2004 to coincide with the release of the Original Trilogy on DVD format.

WAF

Wicket and Friends: A collection of children's books, puzzles, and toys marketed alongside the animated *Ewoks* cartoon.

Warping

A curving of packaging material caused by moisture.

Wave

A group of items, such as Hasbro *Star Wars* figures, released to retailers at the same.

Widevision

A card that is printed wider than a regular card's dimensions to portray widescreen (usually 16:9) aspect ratios.

WTE

Wicket the Ewok: A collection of children's book, puzzles, and toys marketed alongside the animated *Ewoks* cartoon.

xback

The term used to define the cardback type based on the number of $3^{3}/_{4}$-inch action figures displayed on the rear of the card.

YB

Yellow Bubble: A descriptive term for the condition of a blister bubble that is no longer clear. Also used is Slightly Yellow Bubble (SYB), but since this is subjective it is uncommon.

INDEX